LEGACY

LEGACY

CECIL RHODES, THE RHODES TRUST AND RHODES SCHOLARSHIPS

PHILIP ZIEGLER

YALE UNIVERSITY PRESS
NEW HAVEN AND LONDON

For information about this and other Yale University Press publications, please contact:
U.S. Office: sales.press@yale.edu   www.yalebooks.com
Europe Office: sales @yaleup.co.uk   www.yaleup.co.uk

Set in Minion by J&L Composition, Filey, North Yorkshire
Printed in Great Britain by Biddles Ltd, King's Lynn, Norfolk

Library of Congress Cataloguing-in-Publication Data

Ziegler, Philip,
    Legacy: Cecil Rhodes, the Rhodes Trust and the Rhodes Scholarships/Philip Ziegler.
    p. cm.
    Includes bibliographical references and index.
    ISBN 978–0–300–11835–3 (alk. paper)
    1. Rhodes scholarships. 2. University of Oxford—Funds and scholarships. 3. Rhodes Trust (Oxford, England) I. Title.
    LF503.F8Z54 2008
    378.425'74–dc22
                                                                                2007036428
A catalogue record for this book is available from the British Library.
10 9 8 7 6 5 4 3 2 1

CONTENTS

ILLUSTRATIONS

Unless otherwise indicated, the provenance is the Rhodes Trust.

ACKNOWLEDGEMENTS

Lord Fellowes, a Trustee of the Rhodes Trust, suggested to me that I should write this book; he and Dr John Rowett, then Warden of Rhodes House, persuaded me that the task was feasible; John Rowett, during the first two years of my work, was unstinting in his help and encouragement. To them, therefore, must go the first acknowledgements. John Rowett's successor, Sir Colin Lucas, has been no less helpful. Without his support, and the constant help of Catherine King, Sheila Partridge, Mary Eaton, Bob Wyllie and many others at Rhodes House, it would probably have been impossible to write this book – certainly the task would have been far less pleasant.

Lord Waldegrave was Chairman of the Trustees throughout the period that I was at work; he and all the other Trustees, past and present, with whom I have had dealings, have gone out of their way to help me along the path. Lord Waldegrave, the present Warden Sir Colin Lucas, and Lord Fellowes were kind enough to read the typescript and to make many helpful suggestions. So, with even less cause to do so, did Sir Anthony Kenny, whose sometimes remorseless and invariably cogent commentary on my text showed that he would have been as skilful in publishing as he has proved himself in every other facet of his extraordinary career.

In the last four years, I have spoken to several hundred people whose information and opinions have to some extent contributed to this book. To list them all would seem ridiculous and somewhat pretentious; to pick out those who have been especially helpful would be invidious. I hope that I have made evident along my way how immensely grateful I am for the kindness so many people have shown in putting themselves to considerable inconvenience to talk to me, and for the generosity and hospitality which I have encountered. Sir Edgar Williams said, after one of his many tours, how struck he always was by the extraordinary niceness of Rhodes Scholars. I heartily endorse his words: I have met hardly a single Rhodes Scholar whom I disliked and I have met many whom I would be proud to consider as friends. I could hardly have failed to find this book a fascinating one to write; it is above all thanks to the Rhodes Scholars that the experience has been thoroughly enjoyable as well.

My wife in the past has stoically endured the psychological isolation which writers habitually impose upon themselves; in this case she has had to put up with long physical absences as well, as I toured the various outposts of the Trust's empire. I am, as ever, profoundly grateful for her understanding, her tolerance and her sense of humour – I am the luckiest of men to be married to her.

PROLOGUE

To compress into a single, accessible volume a history of the Rhodes Trust and its Scholarships, with its labyrinth of plots and sub-plots, its multitude of significant and colourful players, is a task that is, to say the least, challenging. Should the approach be chronological? Country by country? Thematic? All are impracticable, all are essential. A compound of the three seems the only possibility, accepting that the results will sometimes be untidy and that, as in some literary game of Snakes and Ladders, readers who have congratulated themselves on having reached the new millennium, will find themselves back at 1945 again. I have sought to put signposts along the way and hope that I have ended up with a narrative that, without invariably being consecutive, is at least comprehensible.

Judith Brown, Beit Professor of Commonwealth History, cogently argued that my book must have an over-arching theme. I agree fully with her but would state the proposition rather differently. There are two questions which above all have preoccupied me during the four years or so that I have worked on this book. The first is relatively straightforward: what happens to a system inspired by a passionate imperialist and run for its first fifty years by men almost equally dedicated to the idea of Empire, when that Empire to all intents and purposes ceases to exist? The second question, or rather group of questions, is: has it worked? Has anything been achieved by bringing to Oxford this group of talented young men and, later, women which would not have happened if the scholarships had never been created? Has the fact that that they got to Oxford by means of a Rhodes Scholarship in any significant way distinguished them from those who found their way there by other means? As a corollary of this, have the Rhodes Scholars worked together in later life in a way which has made their contribution to society more effective than it would have been if they had acted only as individuals? Are the Rhodes Scholars now, have they been, will they ever be what Cecil Rhodes believed they should be – a force that would change the world? Through all the beguiling vagaries of my narrative I have had these questions in my mind. To claim that I have answered them would be vainglorious; but if the questions have not to some extent been defined and illuminated, then this book has failed.

PART I

The Founder

CHAPTER ONE

BUILDING A FORTUNE

The evil that men do lives after them,
The good is oft interred with their bones.

Cecil John Rhodes would have relished the comparison with Julius Caesar, though thinking it no more than his due. Rhodes, however, disproved Mark Antony's adage. In his life he did, if not evil, then at least much which redounded to his discredit. Today, a little over a century after his death, the memories of such misdeeds are largely interred with his bones in the Matopos hills. What lives after him is the renown of the most famous scholarships in the world.

This is not to say that Rhodes's reputation has survived unassailed. Even in his finest hours he had many critics; after the debacle of the Jameson Raid he was ferociously abused.[1] By the time of his death he had been substantially rehabilitated, but even in the honeymoon period that usually follows the death of any great personality people tended to view him in extremes of black or white. To Earl Grey, at the opening of the Rhodes Memorial in 1912, Rhodes was the supreme visionary and idealist – 'no man born during the nineteenth century had exercised a greater influence for good on the character of the present'.[2] Yet in the same year G. K. Chesterton proclaimed that Rhodes had no principles, 'he had only a hasty but elaborate machinery for spreading the principles that he hadn't got. What he called his ideals were the dregs of a Darwinism which had already grown not only stagnant, but poisonous . . . it was exactly because he had no ideas to spread that he invoked slaughter, violated justice, and ruined republics to spread them.'[3] As the pendulum of history has swung, imperialism has become a dirty word and the unacceptable face of capitalism is ritually denounced by the polemicist. The Chestertonian view of Rhodes is in the ascendant. But for the great majority of those who recognise the name today the merits or demerits of Cecil Rhodes are insignificant compared with his momentous legacy. In the United States and Canada;

in Australia, New Zealand and South Africa; still more in Oxford; the name of
Rhodes does not stand for capitalism or for imperialism, even less for bribery,
chicanery and ruthless bullying. It is with the academic excellence and the
unabashed elitism of the Rhodes Scholarships that it is above all associated.

The world into which Cecil Rhodes was born on 5 July 1853 was one in which
his own country was unequivocally predominant. The British Empire, though
territorially it was to expand greatly in the next half-century – notably in
Africa through the agency of Rhodes himself – was politically and economically nearing its zenith. Vast tracts of the global map were already shaded pink,
the Royal Navy was incomparably the most powerful fighting force at sea.
Successive governments might have blown hot and cold on imperial expansion and sceptically weighed the possible benefits against the risks and the
expense, but to the man in the street the Empire was a source of pride and
something for which sacrifices should legitimately be made. That the British
were not only the master race, but that it was thoroughly desirable for the rest
of humanity that they should remain so, became the tacit assumption of the
great majority of men and women in the imperial homeland.

No one visiting the vicarage in Bishop's Stortford ten years or so after
Cecil's birth would have guessed that the Rev. Francis Rhodes's fourth
surviving son was likely to make any significant contribution to the furtherance of this end. He was consigned to the local school, either because the
funds were not available to send him to board at a public school or because
his father did not think him worth the additional expense, and though he
performed respectably both in examinations and on the cricket field, he
showed no extraordinary abilities. His father seems to have felt that he might
be suitable for holy orders; Cecil preferred the idea of a career at the bar;
in either case a university education would be necessary. That could wait,
however. In the meantime, though he was still only sixteen, he took boat to
join his brother Herbert who was cotton-farming in Natal.

The process of growing up was now dramatically accelerated. The lure
of the diamond fields at Kimberley five hundred miles away on the Vaal river
had proved too much for the restless Herbert, and Cecil found himself, with
no experience and severely limited resources, responsible for managing a
plantation of twenty acres with the possibility of trebling its area in the forthcoming season. He undertook the task with energy, resolution and considerable common sense. If he had dreams of greater things, either at the bar in
London or with his brother at the diamond fields, he kept them to himself. To
his mother he wrote that it was enough to have 'land of your own, horses of
your own, and shooting when you like and a lot of black niggers to do what
you like with, apart from the fact of making money'.[4] Such modest ambitions

did not long satisfy him, however. For one thing the future of cotton growing in South Africa became increasingly unpromising, for another the prospects of acquiring real wealth on the Vaal seemed ever more attainable. In October 1871 he set out to join Herbert at the diamond fields.

Between the end of 1871 and February 1888, when Barney Barnato finally agreed to merge his interests with De Beers, Rhodes transformed himself from a callow, almost penniless youth into one of the most powerful figures in the worlds of finance and of mining. It was, by any standard, an incredible achievement. To bring it about he had to ally extreme boldness with exemplary prudence; ruthless intimidation with a sensitive awareness of other people's failings; a capacity to exploit human weaknesses with an uncanny ability to identify and build upon human strengths. He saw that, if the mining of diamonds was to develop in an orderly and profitable manner, then something close to a monopoly of production must be created. He was resolved that, if such a monopoly did exist, he and nobody else should be its master. First he built up De Beers Mining into one of the more powerful players in the game; then he expanded it until only Barney Barnato's Kimberley Central blocked his way; finally he outmanoeuvred Barnato and induced him to accept a merger which put Rhodes in overall control. In the course of these operations he showed high courage, some unscrupulousness, a readiness to bribe and bargain, a capacity to make important allies and use them to the full. Above all, he knew how to persuade. In another context, Barnato paid tribute to his overwhelming powers of advocacy. 'When you have been with him half an hour,' he said, 'you not only agree with him, but come to believe you have always held his opinion. No one else in the world could have induced me to go into this partnership. But Rhodes had an extraordinary ascendancy over men: he tied me up, as he ties up everybody. It is his way. You can't resist him; you must be with him.'[5]

In the course of these years Rhodes made friends who were not merely to play an important part in his life but to help shape his legacy after his death. Alfred Beit, a German-Jewish diamond broker, began with resources almost as limited as those of Rhodes but with better connections and a subtle understanding of business relationships which can rarely have been matched. He was Rhodes's equal, lacking the grandiosity and political vision but wiser in financial matters and at least as capable of taking the broad view. Rudd and Jameson, Rhodes's two closest associates in South Africa, were striking personalities in their own right but compared with the Colossus were mere camp-followers. Charles Rudd was a shrewd and energetic entrepreneur who played a crucial role in Rhodes's battle to establish himself as a major player in the diamond industry, but his ambitions were limited and he neither emulated nor understood the vision that drove his partner on to greater

things. Dr Leander Starr Jameson was one of the few men with whom Rhodes
was truly intimate; he had considerable charm, was bold to the point of reck-
lessness and an opportunist of unusual ability, but he preferred to live for the
day rather than dream dreams for posterity and his judgment was often faulty,
once at least with catastrophic consequences. Finally, the banker Nathan, Lord
Rothschild, provided the essential financial backing when Rhodes's plans for
aggrandisement were on the brink of collapse. Rothschild admired Rhodes
fervently. 'A very great man,' he pronounced him, 'he saw things as no one else
saw them and he foresaw things which no one else dreamt of.'[6] It was to
Rothschild that Rhodes originally entrusted the implementation of his vision
for the reshaping of the world; he was not nominated as a Trustee of the Will
but his spirit brooded benignly over all the deliberations that followed
Rhodes's death.

Somehow, into these crowded years, Rhodes contrived to fit nine terms as
an undergraduate at Oxford. There will always be a touch of mystery about
why he thought it desirable to jeopardise all that he was building up in Africa
by absenting himself for several months, at one point for more than a year at
a time. He was not particularly respectful of learning for the sake of learning,
viewing most professional academics with amicable contempt. Perhaps he
hoped to broaden his acquaintance and get to know those whose co-operation
would be essential if his still inchoate but gradually forming visions were ever
to become reality. Perhaps he felt a degree at Oxford would be an essential
qualification if he decided after all to make his career in England. Perhaps he
hankered for a level of polish and sophistication which he knew would never
be acquired in the rough-and-tumble world of Kimberley. At all events, he
applied to University College, was rejected, and turned to Oriel. 'All colleges
send me their failures,' the Provost of Oriel is supposed to have complained.[7]
Rhodes was accepted all the same, and in October 1873 he began the erratic
progress that was to lead to his gaining his degree some eight years later.

It is tempting to say that Rhodes wasted his time at Oxford. He joined a few
clubs, but only those associated with alcohol or horses; he did no more work
than was necessary to obtain a respectable degree; he made no friends who
were of importance to him in later life; he never attended the Union; he played
no games: he conducted himself, in fact, in a way almost entirely contrary to
what would be expected of the Rhodes Scholars who were to enjoy his bounty
in later years. The spirit of Ruskin brooded over Oxford in those years and
only a short time before he had delivered his famous inaugural lecture in
which he appealed to the youth of England to make their country again 'a
royal throne of kings, a sceptred isle'. It was the duty of England (the concept
of Britain was not one that concerned either Rhodes or Ruskin) 'to found
colonies as fast and as far as she is able . . . seizing every piece of fruitful waste

ground she can set her foot on'. The first aim of any Englishman worthy of the name must be 'to advance the power of England by land and sea'.[8] Such words should have been not only music to Rhodes's ears but an anthem to impel him to glorious action. The pity is that there is no evidence to show that Rhodes heeded or even heard Ruskin's message. Colin Newbury convincingly argues that Rhodes's enthusiasm for the expansion of the British Empire in Africa owed little if anything to his time at Oxford and that 'the drivel of that idiot Ruskin', as Milner disparagingly described the celebrated trumpet call, had died away before the future empire-builder took up residence.[9] It is still the case, however, that it presaged accurately Rhodes's future thinking. Even if Ruskin was not himself a formative element in Rhodes's philosophy, the principles that he preached to the youth of Oxford were those on which Rhodes based the conduct of his life once he had accumulated the funds that enabled him to act decisively.

CHAPTER TWO

THE IMPERIAL DREAM

However undeveloped Rhodes's imperialist dreams may have been when he went up to Oxford or even when he finally graduated, he always considered great wealth to be a means to an end rather than an end in itself. Except when he was trying to impress for a specific purpose he saw no point in conspicuous expenditure; he liked to eat and drink well but took no pleasure from fine clothes, luxurious houses, yachts, liveried servants or any of the other fripperies of the rich. Money meant power; without it little if anything could be accomplished. 'Don't despise money,' he told the editor of the *Pall Mall Gazette*, William Stead. 'Your ideas are all right, but without money you can do nothing.'[1] By the time he had completed the conquest of the diamond mines his own ideas had taken shape. The grand global sweep of his design was still to be revealed – to others certainly, perhaps also to himself – but so far as Africa was concerned he knew now what he wanted and, in broad terms, how his ends were to be achieved.

He based all his calculations on the assumption that the British were divinely selected as the master race. He told Stead that God was 'manifestly fashioning the English-speaking race as the chosen instrument by which He will bring in a state of society based upon Justice, Liberty and Peace'. It was the duty of every God-fearing man to do what he could to bring about this happy conclusion and he, Rhodes, believed that he was uniquely qualified to make a signal contribution. What he was called upon to do was 'to paint as much of the map of Africa British red as possible, and to do what I can elsewhere to promote the unity and extend the influence of the English-speaking race'.[2] For the moment the future of the English-speaking race in the rest of the world must be left to others; Rhodes was in Africa and the spread of British power in that continent became his prime consideration.

Money alone would not be enough. Even before he had taken his degree at Oxford Rhodes had become a member of the Cape Parliament. With Gladstone back in power in London imperialism was viewed with some disfavour by the British government. The consequences in South Africa, in Rhodes's eyes, had been disastrous. The Transvaal and the Orange Free State were suffered to make their own way to independence; in the Cape the Afrikaner party, the Bond, though not in control, was the most cohesive and resolute of the political groupings. Rhodes had no doubt that the Cape would be the better for a British government; for the rest of his life one of his prime concerns was to build up the British population in Southern Africa so that the English-speakers would be in a majority over the Dutch. But the Afrikaners were a fact of life and Rhodes was far too convinced a pragmatist to ignore a fact just because it was inconvenient. They must be conciliated and, so far as possible, assimilated. When it was proposed that certain areas bordering the Transvaal should be reserved for English settlers, Rhodes protested that 'the introduction of race distinctions must result in bringing calamity on this country, and if such a policy is pursued it will endanger the whole of our social relationships with colonists of Dutch descent'.[3] He forged an alliance with Jan Hofmeyr, the moderate Afrikaner leader, in which each implicitly accepted that, though in an ideal world the control of the Cape would rest exclusively with their own racial group, a compromise was far better than outright warfare.

A problem was that the attitude of the Dutch towards the black African population was markedly different to the policy that had been hitherto followed by the British. The 'race distinctions' which Rhodes had deplored were those between Dutch and English; he accepted that different considerations applied when the relationship was between black and white. Rhodes's own instincts were not notably more illiberal than those of most of his fellow Britons. He was accustomed to refer to the black Africans as 'children', who, like children, must be cherished, protected, yet also disciplined.[4] But children grow up and Rhodes believed that once they had become mature they must be allowed the rights of adults. Three years before he died he stated his belief as being 'Equal rights for every civilised man south of the Zambezi. What is a civilised man? A man, whether white or black, who has sufficient education to write his name, has some property or works, in fact is not a loafer.'[5] Such principles, if conscientiously applied, would within a few decades have led to a situation where black voters were in the majority. It seems unlikely that Rhodes gave much thought to such a possibility. If he had done, he would no doubt have seen it as an extra reason for encouraging the immigration of white settlers. What is clear, however, is that, whatever his original conception, in the interests of cementing his relationship with the Afrikaner group in Parliament, he redefined the term 'civilised' so as to exclude many blacks who would once have been eligible to vote. Still worse, he sponsored legislation which made it more difficult for the blacks to obtain an education equivalent to that available to the whites. It was Rhodes who in 1894 forced through the notorious Glen Grey bill, which imposed restrictions on and denied rights to the blacks in a way that would have been inconceivable a decade before. There is no reason to believe that Rhodes was malign in his intentions or that he would have condoned the enormities that were to come. It is hard, however, to dispute the measured conclusion of his leading biographer, Robert Rotberg: 'Rhodes's disregard of (antagonism towards is too strong) the human and political value of Africans foreshadowed, indeed prepared the path for the segregationist attitudes and legislation that were so prevalent during the decades of actual union.'[6]

By this time Rhodes had already been Prime Minister of the Cape for several years; politically as well as economically he had secured the base from which he could launch his crusade to extend the frontiers of the British Empire towards the north. His task was lent urgency by the expansionist policies of President Kruger in the Transvaal and the imperial ambitions of the Germans, who were firmly entrenched in what is now Namibia and building up their position in Tanganyika. He feared that if Britain did not move fast to assert its suzerainty in Bechuanaland and over the Matabele territories of King Lobengula to the north, then the Transvaalers and the Germans would join forces to block British expansion and for ever destroy his dream of an Africa that would be entirely, or at least predominantly, red on the map. To achieve his ends he used means that were ingenious, unscrupulous and spectacularly bold. The chicanery by which his emissary, Rudd, tricked Lobengula into granting a concession to prospect in his territory, which the King thought conferred only limited mining rights but in fact exposed the whole of his country to imperialist incursions, was one of the less attractive episodes in the creation of the British Empire. The charter conferred on the British South Africa Company, which gave Rhodes almost limitless freedom of action over immense areas of as yet unconquered lands, was obtained by means which were discreditable if not actually corrupt. The destruction of the Matabele armies in a brutal if brilliantly executed campaign was the result of a war forced on a reluctant enemy by an aggressive and acquisitive power whose superiority in weaponry more than made up for its inferiority in numbers. At the end of the day 'a mass of land the size of Spain, France and the Low Countries, and containing nearly a hundred separate, hardly consulted, peoples speaking seventy languages' would be added to the Empire.[7] When Southern and Northern Rhodesia were called into existence Rhodes achieved the rare, perhaps unique distinction of having two countries called after him. If he had been given any encouragement by the British government, indeed if he had not been actively restrained, he might well have added Portuguese Mozambique and Belgian Katanga to his booty. One may question the end and deplore the methods, but one can only wonder at the immensity of the achievement.

And then, when Rhodes's power seemed irresistible and his ambitions reached out to new horizons, it all went dramatically wrong. The discovery of seemingly limitless gold reserves in the Transvaal had transformed Kruger's republic into a wealthy state. Prospectors and businessmen poured in and were soon complaining about the restrictions and unreasonable taxes imposed on them. The existence of an independent Boer Transvaal was anyway an affront to Rhodes; what he saw as the persecution of the immigrant *uitlanders*, many of them his fellow countrymen, was both an additional offence and an excuse for decisive action. With the connivance of elements of the British government, Rhodes sought to organise the invasion of the Transvaal by a private army under the command of his friend Jameson. The expectation was that, once the force was on its way to Johannesburg, the oppressed immigrants, for whom arms had secretly been smuggled in, would rise and overthrow Kruger's administration. The new government of the Transvaal would join with the Cape and the unity of South Africa under British rule would be secured.

It was not wholly impractical as a scheme; with luck and better timing it might even have worked. Jameson, however, jumped the gun. Without Rhodes's approval, indeed in defiance of instructions, he crossed the border with a tiny force and no good reason to believe that his supporters in the Transvaal had either the weapons or the will to intervene effectively. Debacle followed. Outnumbered and outmanoeuvred, Jameson's army of liberation was rounded up and locked in Pretoria's prison. 'Old Jameson has upset my apple cart,' wailed Rhodes. 'Twenty years we have been friends, and now he goes and ruins me.'[8]

Ruin was, indeed, almost absolute. Even though he had not actually authorised the incursion, Rhodes's complicity was undeniable and, to compound his humiliation, his brother Frank was in prison with Jameson. Rhodes resigned as Prime Minister and was forced to quit the board of the British South Africa Company. But he did not give up and, astonishingly, in time regained much of his reputation. Only a few months after the raid a new war broke out with the Ndebele. Initially all went well, but soon it seemed likely to degenerate into a bloody and protracted stalemate. Unarmed and almost alone, Rhodes rode into the heart of the Ndebele armies, listened patiently to their grievances, promised them that their worst wrongs would be righted and in the end persuaded them to lay down their arms. It was a striking feat of advocacy and a still more impressive display of courage. As remarkable as anything was the way he restrained the leaders of the British force from following their instincts and continuing the war until the Ndebele had been totally destroyed.

By the time that the intransigent Kruger and the equally belligerent British Governor General at the Cape, Alfred Milner, had manoeuvred their two countries into the South African War, Rhodes had almost regained his heroic status. He welcomed the war, as being likely to lead to the integration of the Transvaal and the Orange Free State into the Empire, but does not seem to have played any important part in its genesis. He chose to sit it out in Kimberley, the town which had done so much to enrich him and which he had so conspicuously enriched. Kimberley was soon surrounded and besieged by the Boers and for four months all attempts to relieve the garrison were frustrated. From the point of view of the British commander Rhodes must have been an infernal nuisance, but his presence in the beleaguered town and the attention which he made sure was paid to it in the press did still more to restore his reputation. By the time Kimberley was relieved he had secured a position from which great new adventures could have been launched in pursuit of his cherished goals. By then it was too late, however: his health had been deteriorating for several years and the privations suffered in Kimberley had speeded up the process. A little over two years later he died and was buried in the Matopos hills at the site he had chosen while negotiating with the Ndebele chiefs.

'In my end is my beginning'[9] was the motto of Mary, Queen of Scots. Certainly the potency of her legend has exceeded the somewhat ignoble circumstances of her life. But the words apply with greater force to Cecil Rhodes. With his death ended an extraordinary life, but through the agency of his Will his death also ushered in a still more extraordinary future.

CHAPTER THREE
LIFE AFTER DEATH

Rhodes had told Stead that he saw his destiny as being not only to spread British power in Africa but 'to do what I can elsewhere to promote the unity and extend the influence of the English-speaking race'.[1] This end he pursued with a crusader's fervour, always with an eye to his own aggrandisement but never ruled solely by self-interest. Leo Amery, later to become one of Rhodes's most ardent champions, compared him with the Elizabethan adventurers whose patriotism was tinged with a love of gain and of adventure for adventure's sake and who did not scruple to use base tools in pursuit of their objectives. But those men, Amery goes on, 'were mostly scholars and men of intense religious feeling as well as adventurers . . . . They were passionately excited by the new learning of the classical renaissance as well as by its offshoot, the Reformation. Walter Ralegh – like Rhodes an Oriel man – lived with history and poetry as well as with his dreams of a new English nation across the Atlantic and of an Eldorado in Guiana. So, too, Rhodes.'[2]

Rhodes would have been gratified by the comparison with Ralegh; the combination of swashbuckling adventurer with poet and visionary was much to his taste. Nor would he have been discomfited by the charge that he was a dreamer. 'It is the dreamers that move the world,' he told Lady Warwick. 'Practical men are so busy being practical that they cannot see beyond their own lifetime. Dreamers and visionaries have made civilisations.'[3] His own most cherished reading was *The Meditations of Marcus Aurelius*, a book which he took with him everywhere and constantly referred to. Rotberg has analysed the 101 passages which Rhodes underlined. They illustrate with remarkable clarity the principles by which Rhodes steered his career. A quarter dealt with death, above all the need to 'live each day as if t'were thy last'. A second group of aphorisms championed the ascendancy of reason over passion: moral judgments should never be made until the other person's reasoning about right and wrong has been fully understood. A belief in hard work and the need to follow a grand design made up the third strand in this philosophical patchwork. Finally, the fourth section emphasised that, though self-reliance was essential, if success in life was to be attained it must be through understanding the needs and aspirations of others and working with them towards a common end.[4] To Rhodes dreams were permissible, even essential, but they must never be divorced from practical possibilities; an aim should not be abandoned because it at first seemed unattainable, but every step should carefully be planned and, if one path proved too difficult, another must be found and followed.

Rhodes first attempted to commit his world vision to paper in 1877 when he was still only halfway through his Oxford years.[5] His 'Confession of Faith' was a document of striking naivety, combining the simplism of a contribution to *Boy's Own* with the fervour of an Old Testament prophet. He took as his starting point the assumption that the English, or, to be more expansive, the English-speaking peoples, were 'the finest race in the world and that the more of the world we inhabit the better it is for the human race'. Regrettably the United States of America had slipped away from the imperial fold, but this could and should be reversed. 'The idea gleaming and dancing before one's eyes like a will-of-the-wisp at last frames itself into a plan. Why should we not form a secret society with but one object, the furtherance of the British Empire and the bringing of the whole civilised world under British rule?' The operations of the Jesuits showed how effective such a society might be; what was needed was 'a Church for the extension of the British Empire'. Young men of energy, talents and the right ideals should be identified and fostered, so that they would form the shock troops of imperial expansion. Africa in particular 'is still lying ready for us. It is our duty to take it.' Another object should be the recovery of the United States; it had been weakened by allowing its English blood to be diluted by 'low-class Irish and German immigrants', but the Americans were still preferable to any other lesser breed and should be cajoled or bullied back into the imperial partnership.

This preposterous document was not, in fact, the first evidence of Rhodes's wish to serve the imperial cause. When aged only nineteen, in a moment of characteristic though unjustified anxiety about his health, he had drawn up a Will leaving all he possessed – which at that point was precious little – to the Secretary of State for the Colonies to be devoted to the extension of the British Empire. In the 'Confession', however, he for the first time set out his vision of what should be done to that end, a programme of action no more precise than that outlined in *Mein Kampf* or the *Communist Manifesto* and with some of the alarming single-mindedness of both those documents. The 'Confession' provided the substance of his second Will. In it the Administrator of Bechuanaland, Sir Sidney Sheppard, and the Secretary of State for the Colonies were enjoined to set up a secret society dedicated to the extension of

British rule throughout the world, the encouragement of emigration and 'especially the occupation by British allies of the entire Continent of Africa, the Holy Land, the valley of the Euphrates, the islands of Cyprus and Crete [Candia], the whole of South America, the islands of the Pacific, the whole of the Malay Archipelago, the seaboard of China and Japan'. The United States was to be reintegrated with the Empire and an imperial parliament was to weld together the resultant colossus so that wars, except of the most trivial and local nature, would become impossible.[6]

This was the high point of Rhodes's fantasies. Though he never ceased to think that the course he had originally advocated would have been beneficial for mankind he gradually accepted that it was unrealistic to expect the United States to rally to the Empire and that the colonisation of South America or the coast of China might be beyond the resources of Great Britain. It took him a long time to come to this conclusion, however; his third, fourth and fifth Wills contained few alterations of substance but changed the individuals charged with seeing that his fortune was properly employed. For the fourth and fifth Wills Lord Rothschild was named as Trustee. The model of the Jesuit Order still figured largely in Rhodes's thinking and in the letter to Rothschild which covered the fourth Will the great financier was instructed 'to establish a society of the elect for the good of the Empire'.[7] Rothschild was required to get hold of a copy of the Jesuits' constitution and 'insert English Empire for Roman Catholic Religion'. It seems unlikely that Rhodes had any real understanding of the aims and methods of the Order, but the Jesuits were believed to be powerful, secretive and adept at promoting their message – the very attributes which Rhodes felt should mark the organisation he planned to create.

As Rhodes grew older, however, he began to think not so much of imperial aggrandisement as of the creation of an elite who would make the Empire work and would foster unity between its various elements. In his sixth and seventh Wills education grew more and more central to his thinking. His first preoccupation was the creation of a university in Cape Town, based upon Oxford in that it would be collegiate and residential. Such an institution would bring together Afrikaners and British in an atmosphere where they could work together in harmony and learn to understand each other's preoccupations and ways of thought. It would be funded – in large part at least – out of the profits from the canteens in the compounds at Kimberley. He meant to build the university 'out of the Kaffirs' stomach', he told the architect Herbert Baker – jokingly, Baker insists, though the joke, if it was one, leaves an unpleasant after-taste.[8] The project foundered on the opposition of the largely Afrikaans-speaking university at Stellenbosch, which feared that such a rival institution would rob it of many of its pupils and, still worse, corrupt Afrikaner youth by exposing it to the decadence and ill-considered liberalism of the English settlers.[9]

A South African university, however, was never more than an element of his vision. Rhodes was not the first to conceive the idea of creating scholarships to send young men from the colonies to study at British universities. The proposal seems originally to have been put forward in 1891 by J. Astley Cooper, editor of the London weekly *Greater Britain*. It was taken up by an Australian expatriate working in England, T. Hudson Beare, who put forward a scheme to fund a hundred Scholars from the Empire. But once Rhodes had been alerted to the possibility he grasped it eagerly and, unlike Cooper or Beare, he had the means to put it into practice.

In his sixth Will he earmarked a substantial part of his estate for the education of South African students in Oxford. He had considered the possibility of endowing Scholarships for the University of Edinburgh, he wrote in his final Will, but had concluded that, since it did not have a residential system similar to that of Oxford, it would be unsuitable for his purpose.[10] In 1892 Oxford had awarded Rhodes an honorary degree which he had been too busy to take. By the time he wished to do so, in 1899, the Jameson Raid had sullied his reputation and a substantial number of dons, including such dignitaries as the Master of Balliol and the historian and future Rhodes Trustee H. A. L. Fisher, protested against the award. Fortunately for Rhodes, General Kitchener was due to receive an honorary degree at the same ceremony, and the victor of Omdurman stated bluntly that, if Rhodes was vetoed, he too would refuse to attend. To offend so popular a national hero was more than the Oxford rebels could undertake; opposition crumbled and Rhodes was duly awarded his degree. It is interesting to speculate whether, if he had been roundly snubbed, the disadvantages of Edinburgh might have seemed less compelling. Perhaps even Cambridge would have seemed a possible alternative.

It was not till his seventh and final Will that Rhodes conceived his master scheme for Scholarships at Oxford to be drawn from all over the English-speaking world. The original version of this provided for fifty-two Scholarships a year, a number which he thought his bequest could comfortably support while leaving a bit over for related purposes. The prescribed apportionment of these Scholarships was erratic, even bizarre. Of the twenty allotted to the colonies three went to Rhodesia and five to South Africa – one for Natal and four for designated schools in the Cape. Canada and Newfoundland, then separate colonies, were given three between them, Australia six and New Zealand only one. For reasons that have never been satisfactorily explained, Jamaica and Bermuda were also included. Bermuda, in particular, seemed unsuitable. Its educational structure made it impossible for any black student to qualify, yet the white population was only five thousand strong and the schools were markedly inadequate. The only convincing explanation suggested for its choice, rather than the Bahamas, Barbados or Trinidad, all of which had larger European populations, was that Rhodes's brother Frank had served there as a soldier and had taken a fancy to it. As an argument it hardly seems conclusive, but for all Rhodes's reverence for reason he was capable of acting on impulse and this may have been such an occasion.

Thirty-two Scholarships were assigned to the United States. Since each state was supposed to have its own Scholar and there were at the time forty-eight states (three of which were still territories but on their way to full statehood) it has been uncharitably suggested that Rhodes thought there were still only thirty-two. This legend was convincingly dismissed by the first Oxford Secretary, Francis Wylie,[11] but the balance between states and Scholars was still to cause some awkward mathematical problems. The fact that Rhodes awarded the United States so many more Scholarships than were given to all the colonies put together showed how much importance he still attached to the Anglo-American partnership. He never wholly abandoned the hope that the United States might one day rejoin the Empire. He realised that this would have to be more of a merger than a takeover and was even prepared to accept the possibility that the balance of power might one day shift so far that Washington rather than London would become the seat of government. Personally, he would have felt the sacrifice worth while. But he realised that so extreme a measure of self-abnegation was unlikely ever to be acceptable to the British. All that could be done was to bring the two nations as close as possible together. What could be more likely to lead to this than sending an elite of American young men to imbibe the wisdom and delights of Oxford and then to return to their own country convinced anglophiles and with an appreciation of the wider international scene?

Then came an afterthought. In a codicil to his Will Rhodes granted five annual Scholarships to Germany. The selection of the Scholars was to be left in the hands of the Emperor. The reason Rhodes gave for this was that the Emperor had recently decreed that the teaching of English should be made compulsory in German schools. No doubt this was a factor, reinforcing his belief that, though Germans were not the equals of English or Americans, they were still a meritorious lot who could reasonably be expected to play a part in the imperial crusade: 'The object is that an understanding between the three great powers will render war impossible and educational relations make the strongest tie.' Another explanation may have been that the Kaiser had given Rhodes permission to extend his telegraph line designed to link British possessions in northern and southern Africa through the German colony of Tanganyika.[12] As British relations with Germany deteriorated in the first decade of the twentieth century it is at least possible that Rhodes would have reconsidered this aberrant element in his Will and have annulled the codicil. Little more than a year after its inclusion, however, Rhodes was dead; like it or not, his Trustees had to accommodate five German Scholars in the motley band that was about to descend on Oxford.

In the century since Rhodes's death international scholarships have proliferated. The idea that young men and women of talent would profit by immersion in another culture and that the youth emerging from the economically under-privileged world should be given a chance to pursue its further education in a more promising environment is accepted throughout the world. The reason the Rhodes Scholarships are still exceptional lies in the vision of their creator. He wanted his Scholars not merely to shine academically but to contribute in the struggle to achieve a world where the standards of the British Empire would reign triumphant. They should be leaders, chosen from among boys 'of moral force and character' who were likely in afterlife 'to esteem the performance of public duties' as their highest aim. Of course they must be intelligent – they could hardly hope to make use of their time at Oxford if they were not – but they should not be 'merely bookworms'. In selecting each Scholar, Rhodes decreed, regard should be had to '(1) his literary and scholastic attainments, (2) his fondness of [*sic*] and success in manly outdoor sports such as cricket, football and the like, (3) his qualities of manhood, truth, courage, devotion to duty, sympathy for and protection of the weak, unselfishness and fellowship and (4) his exhibition during his school days of moral force of character and of instincts to lead and to take an interest in his schoolmates'.

Though insisting that this was a 'mere suggestion', Rhodes put forward an estimate of how much importance should be attached to each of these qualifications. Out of a total of ten, three should be allotted to the first, the academic criterion; two to the second, the sporting; three to the third, the qualities of manhood; and two to the fourth, the powers of leadership. He was too sensible to imagine that such proportions could be applied in any way systematically. He himself revised them, since in the original Will four points had been allotted to scholarship and two to each of the other three categories. It was to this division that he was referring when he explained his scheme, with some cynicism, to his solicitor, Bouchier Hawksley and to W. T. Stead. 'You know', he told them, 'I am all against letting the Scholarships [go] merely to people who swot over books, who have spent all their time over Latin and Greek. But you must allow for that element which I call "smug" and which means scholarship. That is to stand for four-tenths. Then there is "brutality", which stands for two-tenths. Then there is tact and leadership, again two-tenths, and then there is "unctuous rectitude", two-tenths. That makes up the whole. You see how it works.'[13] In more idealistic mood, he explained that he was looking for 'the best man for the world's fight'[14] – a phrase which, while almost meaningless, still caught vividly the grandeur and the nobility of his intentions. He wanted his Scholars to transform the world. How such paragons were to be found was perhaps the most perplexing of the many problems he left to his Trustees.

PART II

Foundations

CHAPTER FOUR

SETTING UP THE SCHOLARSHIPS

Three of the men to whom Rhodes entrusted his cherished dream were titans, four were cronies or hangers-on. All shared his view that in the promotion of the British Empire and its values lay the best hope for the world's peace and prosperity. Five of them were intimately associated with South Africa.

Arch-titan and *de facto* if not *de jure* Chairman of the Trustees was Lord Rosebery: a former Prime Minister, arrogant, opinionated, immensely rich. His own career at Oxford had been abruptly ended when he put his racing stud before his studies, but he had wide-ranging intellectual interests and took it for granted that a spell at a great British university could only do good to any callow colonial or American youth. His passionate devotion to the idea of Empire was matched by that of his fellow Trustee Lord Grey, a former Liberal MP who had served on the Board of the British South African Company and as Administrator of Rhodesia, but for much of the time that he was a Trustee was a much liked and admired Governor General of Canada. Grey's devotion to Rhodes was unwavering; whenever he was faced with a difficult problem he would ask himself: 'How would Rhodes have looked at it?'[1] Jameson disrespectfully referred to him as 'a nice old lady but not a genius',[2] but it was for his integrity, his high-mindedness and his ardent championship of the unity of Empire that he is best remembered. Third of the grandees was Lord Milner; unlike the other two he was no patrician but a brilliant administrator, who was High Commissioner for South Africa when Rhodes died and was to play a vital role in Lloyd George's Cabinet in the First World War. Milner had been one of the Oxford undergraduates inspired by Ruskin's imperial visions. Unlike Grey, he had some reservations about Rhodes's ambitions – he wants 'an absolute monarchy with Rhodes as monarch', he told the then High Commissioner, Lord Selborne[3] – but he subscribed whole-heartedly to the beliefs that underlay the Will. Grey felt that while Milner continued to serve as High Commissioner he should not actively participate as a Trustee, especially since the Will envisaged the Trustees playing a significant if covert role in South African politics, but stressed that, once this obstacle was out of the way, he 'would rely on him more than any other Trustee to do what Rhodes would wish'.[4] Milner fully concurred. 'It would be better for me *not* to take part in Rhodes Trust affairs until I can do so regularly and altogether,' he told the first Secretary to the Trust, Charles Boyd, though he would be happy to advise on South African matters if need arose.[5]

Among the other four Trustees, Jameson was the best known and had been closest to Rhodes. He had almost destroyed his friend by the folly of the Raid, but he had been fully forgiven. He was said to have inspired Kipling's 'If'. Keeping his head when all about him were losing theirs was not his forte, but he had all the energy, the courage and the resilience of Kipling's paradigm. Among the Trustees it was generally agreed that he was best qualified to interpret the real intentions of the founder. Alfred Beit knew Rhodes almost as well and was a far more considerable figure in the world of finance, but he lacked Jameson's brash assertiveness and preferred to guide matters unobtrusively from the background. Lewis Michell, Rhodes's obsequious biographer, banker in Cape Town and successor as Chairman of De Beers, was another devotee – 'I loved Rhodes as I have never loved any other man,' he wrote. He became, in effect, the chief executive of the Trustees in South Africa, a role of particular importance in the first twenty years or so of the Trust's existence. Finally, Bouchier Hawksley, Rhodes's solicitor, performed a similar role in London, keeping the ship afloat while the grander figures among the Trustees were conducting the business of the Empire.

There was originally to have been an eighth Trustee. Politically Stead had been as close as anyone to Rhodes; the two men had endlessly thrashed out their common vision of a strong and united British Empire and the restoration of union with the United States. They had fallen out when Stead had virulently opposed the South African War. Rhodes reproached him for not accepting the views of a majority of their associates. This was 'insubordination. How can our Society be worked if each one sets himself up as the sole judge of what ought to be done?'[6] In his Will Rhodes wrote that he had decided not to appoint Stead as executor because of his 'extraordinary eccentricity'. This comment presumably related to Stead's proclaimed enthusiasm for psychical research,[7] but the quarrel over the war must have been at the bottom of Rhodes's decision. Stead did not go altogether quietly. In March 1904 Michell cabled in panic to Hawksley to report that Stead was claiming to be a Trustee: 'His attitude very disturbing'.[8] Legally it seems possible that the claim was justified; Stead might have been held still to be, if not a Trustee, then at least a co-heir under Rhodes's Will. In the event, however, having thoroughly scared Michell and Hawksley, he let the matter drop. He always felt he had been ill-used, and in 1937 his son complained that, in spite of the enormous contribution his father had made to the shaping of Rhodes's ideas, he was in no way commemorated in Rhodes House. The then Secretary agreed that this was unfair and a photograph was duly provided, only to disappear into a store-room. It was not until 1947, when his son revisited Rhodes House and discovered the omission, that the photograph was resurrected and Stead at last allotted a place among the Founder's other associates.

The Trustees met for the first time on 5 May 1902. Charles Boyd and, for three years, Douglas Brodie were appointed Secretaries, but it was clear from the start that they were not going to be allowed to play any significant role. The unfortunate Boyd, in particular, was constantly being slapped down by one Trustee or another. When he failed to send Grey the minutes of a meeting, he was sharply reprimanded: 'I am unable to understand your reason for not troubling me with these "periodic records".'[9] Rosebery refused him a pay rise, at which Boyd protested that the other Trustees were in favour of it: 'The truth seems to be that your colleagues regard you with a respect which makes it difficult for them to "stand up to" you. You must conceive the relation of a form-master to his form.' This roused the wrath of the other Trustees, who were not pleased to be described as schoolboys cowering before their master's lash. 'I regard Boyd's letter as an impertinence,' wrote Hawksley, while Michell expostulated that he was paid quite enough already: 'He is only a correspondence clerk and almost illegible at that.'[10] The wonder is that Boyd survived in his post until 1908.

Only Milner missed the first meeting, but this was the sole occasion for many years in which there was so full an attendance: Michell, Jameson and Beit were often in South Africa while from 1904 Grey was in Canada. Rosebery and Hawksley were left to transact most of the business. If they had wished to they could have diverted the income of the Trust in any direction that suited them, even to their own private purposes, since the Trust was not formally a charity and the Trustees were residuary legatees. This gave them an independence from any sort of official restraint which Rhodes would have felt most desirable but also exposed the Trust to the payment of death duties whenever one of the Trustees died. The disadvantages of this became clear in 1906, when Alfred Beit's death meant that more than £16,000 had to be paid in tax. The Trustees began to consider setting up separate charitable funds which would be free of estate duty, but Hawksley argued that this would be contrary to Rhodes's wishes. It was not until Hawksley died in 1916, by which time the burden of death duties had become far heavier, that the Trustees concluded independence could be too expensive a luxury and set up a Scholarship trust.[11]

Boyd had reason to resent Michell's disparaging description of his duties, but it was clear that he was never going to be the man responsible for making the Rhodes Scholarships work. Who that man should be was one of the first and most urgent problems confronting the Trustees; it would not be exaggerating to say that the success or failure of the operation depended on the right decision being made. The bias of the Trustees seemed against entrusting the task to an academic. Rhodes had shown his doubts about their capabilities when he appended to the part of his Will that left £100,000 to his old college Oriel the derisive comment: 'As the College authorities live secluded from the world and so are like children as to commercial matters I would advise them to consult my Trustees as to the investment of these various funds.' Of the Trustees, Milner had won academic honours at Oxford but had no more respect than Rhodes for the organisational skills of the professors. 'The thing will never work as it ought to work,' he told Michell, 'or provide the effect which Rhodes intended it to produce if you get a lot of crusted old dons to run it.'[12] Rosebery had been sent down; Grey had done well at Cambridge but held no particular brief for the academic world; none of the other Trustees had been to university. If they did decide that a university background was desirable, then it seemed inevitable that they would turn to Oxford. It came as a complete surprise when the Trustees appointed as Organising Secretary the Principal of Upper Canada College in Toronto.

George Parkin might, in fact, have been invented specifically for the role. Born in Canada, he had matriculated from Oxford – oddly enough on the same day as Cecil Rhodes, though there is no reason to believe the two men had by then ever met. Back in Canada he had resigned as headmaster of a grammar school to devote himself to the work of the Imperial Federation League, of which Rosebery was President and Grey a prominent member. After six years of this he returned to Canada and took over Upper Canada College, which he found in a state of dereliction and transformed into Canada's leading school. For him the British Empire was not merely a cause that he was proud to serve but an all-consuming passion. The future astronomer Edwin Hubble sat next to him at a Rhodes dinner in Oxford and told his mother in wonder: 'Parkin is a man of one idea, an idea which permeates his entire life, his actions, his speech. That idea is the British Empire; how it shall be extended, centralised and made to control the whole world.'[13] He was pig-headed, he was verbose, but he was an immensely articulate and passionate proselytiser for the cause in which he so fervently believed. At Oxford he had been Secretary of the Union when Milner was President and had inspired the younger man with his imperial zeal.[14] Grey had planned to bring him together with Rhodes and had convinced Parkin that their visions of the world were essentially the same.[15] With the three great panjandrums of the Trust united in their admiration for the Canadian it was inevitable that he should come to mind as the perfect person to get the Scholarship scheme under way. It was equally inevitable that Parkin, who saw the Scholarships above all as a means of realising Rhodes's imperial dreams, should grasp the opportunity.

At a meeting in July 1902 the Trustees and a contingent of Oxford dons headed by the Vice-Chancellor met to discuss the establishment of the Scholarships. The Oxonians stressed that whoever was put in charge of the scheme should be 'a person of tact who would get on well with the University and College authorities'. The Trustees wanted 'a man of wide sympathy and stimulating character, quite as much as a man of considerable intellect'. On both counts Parkin seemed most suitable. The only argument against him was that the work he was doing in Canada was so important that he should not be removed, but it did not take the Trustees long to conclude that what they had to offer had a stronger claim. In August of the same year Parkin was formally engaged and given fourteen months to submit a viable scheme for turning Rhodes's dream into reality.[16]

First the foundations had to be laid in Oxford. Parkin circularised the colleges, asking whether in principle they would be ready to accept Rhodes Scholars and, if so, how many. On the whole the response was enthusiastic though there were qualifications. John Rhys of Jesus was anxious that the Scholars should be poor: 'It would never do for us in a small college consisting mostly of men who have no income of their own to have among them Scholars to whom £100 more or less is of no consequence.' Walter Lock of Keble insisted that the Scholars must be 'members of Churches in communion with the Church of England', or, in the case of Germans, 'Old Catholics'. There were doubts about the likely behaviour of the new arrivals: George Brodrick of Merton emphasised that they must 'conform to College discipline', the Provost of Queen's more obscurely was insistent that the college would not give rooms to men 'liable to epileptic fits'. Nobody refused to take them and it was clear that, numerically at least, the fifty-seven Scholars envisaged under the Will could easily be accommodated.[17]

Another urgent problem was that, before an undergraduate could be accepted for Oxford, he had to show a reasonable knowledge of Latin and Greek. Latin was not too much of a problem – most colonial and American schoolboys would have had at least a grounding – but especially in the United States Greek was a rarity. If potential Scholars were to be unacceptable because they had never learnt Greek many of the most promising candidates would be eliminated. To mitigate the ill-effects of this Parkin negotiated a compromise under which Scholars with no knowledge of Greek could nevertheless come up to Oxford, learn as much Greek as was needed in the first few months, and only then take the examination. It must still have deterred some potential candidates from applying, but at least it made it possible for the real enthusiasts to make their way to Oxford.[18] Only in 1920 were Scholars from an approved list of universities and colleges allowed to enter Oxford without any sort of qualifying examination.

Parkin's most onerous task, however, was to tour the world, setting up a system by which the best Scholars could be selected. In the next two years he travelled 140,000 miles: discovering the facts of life in each constituency; endlessly explaining, expounding, preaching, persuading, at one moment conciliatory, at another firm, even threatening. It was exhausting and time-consuming. Yet meanwhile in Oxford preparations had to be made for the first Scholars and the arrangements with the colleges worked out in detail. Obviously Parkin could not handle all this as well as act as a roving ambassador for the Trust. Someone had told Rosebery about a young man called Francis Wylie, a fellow of Brasenose currently serving as a proctor, who was said to be sound on the Empire and to be suitable in every other way.[19] At first Wylie was hesitant; could it be wise to hitch his wagon to a star which had hardly yet come within the purview of any reputable astronomer? The enthusiasm of Parkin and the Trustees quickly overbore him, however, and he was formally appointed 'Rhodes Agent at Oxford', a title derived from that used by Lord Cromer in Egypt and thus redolent with imperial implications (misleadingly so, since his relationship with the colleges was very far from gubernatorial). In 1904 he became the 'Oxford Secretary' and this label remained until the opening of Rhodes House in 1929. He could not expect indefinite tenure, Rosebery told him: 'It can hardly be like marriage – for richer for poorer, for better for worse, till death us do part.'[20] In spite of this warning, his term of office lasted more than a quarter of a century. Parkin too had been on a limited contract but when the time came near for his retirement he concluded that it would be a mistake to waste his laboriously accumulated knowledge: 'It occurred to me that it might be wrong to give up my connection with this thing if I was asked to carry it on.'[21] Sure enough, he was asked to carry it on; the partnership with Wylie lasted until Parkin's retirement in 1922.

The relationship had its moments of tension. Wylie was dismayed when he heard that Parkin was considering buying a house in Oxford: 'I rather feel', he protested, 'that the presence in Oxford, during the first year of the scheme, of a much larger person, holding, within the limits of the Trust province, a more important post, would disturb things and confuse people.'[22] Parkin took the point and settled at Goring, some twenty miles away. He liked and respected Wylie, who was outstandingly good at his job, and Wylie fully reciprocated the admiration. He was not being sycophantic when he referred to Parkin as being 'a much larger person'; indeed he viewed his senior partner with something close to reverence. 'He brooded over the beginnings of the Scholarship system,' he wrote when Parkin finally retired; 'it was his thought that brought it form.'[23] Like Jehovah, Parkin gazed into the darkness and brought forth a new world. And the Trustees looked upon his work and saw that it was good.

CHAPTER FIVE
THE CRITERIA

The Rhodes Scholarships could only be as good as the Scholars themselves. It was Parkin's task to set up a system in all the constituencies specified in Rhodes's Will which would ensure that the most promising young men were identified, induced to apply and finally selected. In time it was hoped that the system would be self-perpetuating, that generations of former Scholars would bring forward their successors and guarantee that the highest standards were maintained. Starting from scratch, however, there could be no such recourse. Parkin had to work primarily through the universities: nowhere else would potential Scholars congregate, only there could their abilities be assessed. But this could not provide the whole answer. Selectors would inevitably tend to choose Scholars in their own image; there was a risk that, if the task were left to the universities, Rhodes's 'mere bookworms' would be sent to Oxford by Milner's 'crusty dons' and the main point of the scheme would be lost. To guard against this, Parkin was resolved that the selection committees should be leavened by the inclusion of suitable dignitaries, divines, lawyers and businessmen from outside the academic world.

Deciding who these potentates should be drew Parkin into a minefield of political and sectarian rivalries. In the United States it seemed, for instance, that the Governor would be a safe appointment to his state's selection committee if he could be induced to take it on – a man of dignity and great position, knowing his constituency, surely above the sordid in-fighting that might disfigure the lower levels of national life. President Theodore Roosevelt advised Parkin not to think of it. 'Take my friend here, for instance,' he remarked, pointing to a state governor, 'if he were on the committee he would be thinking all the time how he could use it for the next election.'[1] Each constituency posed its particular problems. In the Canadian province of Prince Edward Island embarrassment escalated to open scandal. The Director of Education wrote to Parkin to complain that the Governor was so anxious to secure Roman Catholic votes at the next election that he was passing over the best candidates for no reason except that they were Protestant. Parkin looked into it and concluded that the complaint was justified. 'Personally,' he told the Trustees, 'I would have no objection to our reserving and occasionally exercising the right to take the final choice out of the hands of Committees of Selection for at least a time.' The Trustees had no objection either and, to the outrage of the Governor, suspended the Prince Edward Island Committee.[2] They rarely resorted to such drastic action, taking the line that they had appointed what seemed to be the best selection committee and must now support it. Most Governors, fortunately, proved notably impartial. In Newfoundland he played a particularly valuable role. The Anglicans, Roman Catholics, Presbyterians, Methodists and Baptists were so much at each other's throats that it seemed there would never be agreement on the choice of Scholar. The only hope seemed to be that the right to nominate would be passed, year by year, from one sect to another. Only the Governor had the stature to veto this ignoble procedure and to insist that the best men must be elected, regardless of religious background.[3] On selection committees academics were notoriously prone to favour candidates from their own discipline, but the clerics were still worse. In Jamaica the Roman Catholic Bishop protested vociferously when the Church of England Archbishop was included in the selection committee while he was not.[4] The results over the next few years suggested that he was only too well justified in suspecting that his flock would suffer if he were not on hand to defend their interests.

From time to time the Trustees found it necessary to remind selection committees what kind of men they were supposed to choose. Every Trustee felt confident he knew, in principle, what was wanted; precise definitions sometimes proved more difficult. Jameson was sure he knew what Rhodes at least would have expected. 'Another Cecil Rhodes,' he told Wylie.[5] In this he was almost certainly wrong: Rhodes was comfortably sure that he was unique and, anyway, had drawn up the criteria in such a way as to ensure that his own application would have been unsuccessful. Frank Tatum, an American Rhodes Scholar, concluded that Abraham Lincoln would have made the ideal candidate: 'significant intellectual capacity, qualities of moral fibre in the sense of selflessness, the ability to effect constructive leadership – and he certainly had physical vigor'[6] – even if it was usually exhibited in rail-splitting rather than organised games. Parkin told a convention in Chicago that provided each state selected the candidate 'most likely to become President of the United States, Chief Justice of the Supreme Court or American Ambassador to Great Britain, then Oxford and the Rhodes Trustees would probably be satisfied'.[7] All these visions argued great worldly success: Rhodes Scholars, in the eyes of the Trustees, were not expected to do good by stealth.

Yet the Trustees also knew that the sense of responsibility, social consciousness, public spirit, decency, which they expected from their Scholars were not
the qualities best calculated to serve those who wished to carve their way
hungrily to the top. William Plomer, in his acerbic biography of Rhodes,
derided the 'ideal' Rhodes Scholar: 'This successful footballer and kind *littéra-
teur*, this dutiful hero and moral exhibitionist, this cricketing paragon of
muscular Christianity, has none of the splendour of some Greek or
Renaissance imagining, but a close relationship to some common types of
upper-middle-class Victorian manhood. . . . If Rhodes meant to produce men
to influence the thought of their age, he should have known better than to
expect that those "all-round" young men, who are to be found in every school
and university, would be able to fulfil his purpose. As a rule, they neither make
history nor do they even make much of their opportunities.'[8] Plomer's attack
was bad-tempered and to some extent unfair, but it contained enough truth
to have made Parkin wince if it had been published in his lifetime.

The surest route to mediocrity would have been to allow selection committees to behave as they had shown some inclination to do in Prince Edward
Island and avoid acrimonious argument by alternating between candidates
from different colleges or racial groups. Such 'inter-institutional courtesy',
Parkin complained, could 'do gross injustice to the individual candidate'.[9] An
example of what he meant came to light when Mrs Whitcomb of Kansas
bemoaned the fact that her phenomenally gifted son was not allowed to apply
because he was not yet nineteen. The boy will have three other chances, Parkin
pointed out. Oh no he won't, retorted Mrs Whitcomb; the Scholarship went
by rotation between a group of colleges. 'It is the system of rotation that must
be changed, not the age rule,' concluded Parkin.[10] In the end he got his way but
it took much time and effort. Young Whitcomb, possibly for different reasons,
never got to Oxford.

Another issue that much preoccupied both the Trustees and the selection
committees was whether potential Rhodes Scholars must have been educated
in the states or countries in which they sought a Scholarship. As a general rule
Parkin felt strongly that they should be; for instance, to allow boys whose
parents had sent them to English public schools to compete in front of a colonial selection committee would 'weaken the educational effort in the colonies
and give a great advantage to the sons of the rich'. But in some cases, Bermuda
being an obvious example, schools of sufficient calibre did not exist, so
candidates would have had to be educated, at least partly, in Britain or the
United States.[11] How far could this principle be extended? In the early years
in Rhodesia two of the selected Scholars had been to school at Eton and
Marlborough respectively. One of them had not set foot in the country before
the meeting of the selection committee.[12] There was even talk of a family who

had emigrated to Rhodesia specifically so as to give their son a chance of a Scholarship. This would 'unduly stretch the spirit of the Will', felt Parkin. The parents of the applicants must have lived in Rhodesia for some years at least.[13] The issue stirred up particularly violent passions in Jamaica. Those in favour of allowing candidates to be educated overseas claimed that their opponents came from 'the parasitical classes of Society . . . not a single land-holder of any importance has supported their attitude'. It would be deplorable if the sons of the gentry were forced into Jamaican schools 'where it is notorious a great many of the pupils are not subjected, in their homes and surroundings, to the influences of those attributes which Mr Rhodes thought highest in a man'.[14] It was even suggested that, when a white Jamaican sent his son to Canada or England for his education, he was 'carrying out the very idea of unification of Empire which seems to have been the dominant note pervading Mr Rhodes's high conception'.[15] This ingenious argument does not seem to have cut much ice with the Trustees but they still saw the force of the white settlers' arguments. Eventually they opted for a compromise by which every third year the Scholarship would be reserved for a boy educated in Jamaica. Like most compromises, it was illogical and satisfied nobody, but at least it saved the Trustees from any accusation of being biased in favour of one side or the other.

Various other points of principle were settled in these early years. Any idea that candidates should sit a special examination was quickly dropped: the selection should be based on the school and/or university record, on the testimonials provided by the candidates' referees and, above all, on the personal interview. The wealth or poverty of the parents was irrelevant. Parkin was dismayed when he found that the selection committee in Western Australia tended to assume that the under-privileged should be given preference: 'It will harm our representation in Oxford, if all men who have enjoyed social advantages should feel themselves excluded.' But when the luckless selectors in Western Australia tried to redress the balance they were assailed from the other flank. The unconscious class bias had been painfully apparent, complained the Perth *Sun*. 'Too often has it been a case of "no poor boy need apply"'.[16] 'Moral force of character' was another phrase from Rhodes's Will which aroused doubts in the minds of selectors. One committee in the United States chose their Scholar on the grounds that he was the only one who did not smoke. Cowed by this ruling, the American Scholars sailing to England on the SS *Ivernia* in 1904 for the first two days abstained from drink, cigarettes or gambling; then their resolution cracked and they relapsed into their usual sinful state.

But the issue which most perplexed Trustees and selectors alike, and indeed remains a matter for debate today, was the issue of brains against brawn. What did Rhodes mean when he included as one of his criteria 'fondness for and success in manly outdoor sports such as cricket, football and the like'? Parkin characteristically concluded that, when Rhodes talked about 'success' in this context, he was thinking not of runs or goals or cups for championships but of the moral qualities inspired by team games: 'the training in fair play, the absence of all trickery, the chivalrous yielding of advantage to an opponent, the acceptance of defeat with cheerfulness'.[17] It would be hard to conceive any set of characteristics more remote from Rhodes's own practices in politics or in business, but since Rhodes did not envisage his Scholars as being moulded in his own image it is possible that some such thought was in his mind. Presumably, anyway, this was what Jan Smuts meant when he told the assembled Scholars in 1933 that the most important thing they had learnt at Oxford 'was the code of a gentleman and sportsman'.[18]

But a few selectors doubted whether losing gracefully was something of which Rhodes would have approved. To them success meant success; if a candidate was likely to be awarded a blue by representing Oxford in one of the major sports, then he had a head start over a rival who was cleverer but inept when it came to games. The pendulum swung according to the predilections of the selectors, the successes or failures of the previous generation of Scholars and the attitude currently taken by the Trustees, but certain national tendencies quickly became obvious. In South Africa, in particular, the Trustees felt undue importance was attached to sporting prowess. This was largely because four out of the five South African Scholarships were assigned to specific schools, and in these schools the votes of the boys were a significant factor in deciding who would be the successful candidate. At St Andrew's, Grahamstown, for instance, Parkin gloomily noted that the votes of the boys practically controlled the election, which was 'decided almost entirely by the result of play on the football ground. Parents with clever boys told me that they had given up all hope of competition with the sporting interest.'[19] The results were deplorable: Wylie told Parkin that the level of scholarship among the South African Scholars was 'very low, much lower than that of any other Scholars'.[20]

Australian selection committees too tended to emphasise the sporting element. At the University of Sydney Rhodes's suggested basis for marking the candidate was taken seriously, twenty points being allotted for manly sports. C. K. Allen, in time to become a lawyer of great distinction as well as Warden of Rhodes House, was awarded full marks for scholarship, a middling mark for character, but only two for sport. The interview was a formality; as a non-performer on the sporting front Allen was not in with a chance. But unlike the South Africans the Australians held their own academically when they got to Oxford; of the seven academic distinctions won by Rhodes Scholars which were reported to the Trustees in 1906–7, four were claimed by the Australians.[21] Indeed, the brawniest Scholars, to the irritation of the athletically disinclined, often proved to be among the brainiest as well. At a reunion in Oxford the South African Brian Bamford described his fellow Scholars nostalgically pointing out 'the colleges they had lived in, less certainly the libraries they had worked in . . . the windows they had climbed in at, and the fields where they had won their Blues'.[22] Bamford qualified for a leading place among the hearties of his generation, yet he became one of South Africa's leading lawyers and liberal politicians and compounded his offences by getting a first in jurisprudence. The United States varied from state to state and from generation to generation. On the whole the American selectors were less inclined than their colonial opposite numbers to give weight to sporting achievements. Woodrow Wilson, then President of Princeton, argued that the quiet Scholar would often turn out to make a more lasting impact than the more flamboyant and athletic types who shone at university. 'I find my colleagues entirely in sympathy with Mr Rhodes's desire to choose men who will be leaders, but the athletic test is not a test of leadership.'[23]

The Trustees on the whole subscribed to the Wilson view. Prowess in athletics, they ruled, should have 'fair consideration', but the lack of it in a man in every other respect well qualified should not be a bar to his being awarded a Scholarship.[24] Other things being exactly equal, then the better athlete should prevail; since, however, other things were rarely if ever exactly equal the point was not of great significance. Yet though great skill might not be necessary, an enthusiasm for and readiness to join in manly sports were deemed essential. The selectors in Dalhousie University, Halifax, consulted Parkin over whether they could elect a student who was eminently qualified academically and could well have proved a leader but who had been crippled by infantile paralysis. He played quoits, sometimes kept goal in games of hockey, but clearly could never indulge extensively in any serious competitive sports. He hesitated to veto such a worthy candidate, said Parkin; 'on the other hand I wonder whether the appearance at Oxford of a Rhodes Scholar on crutches would not cause undue surprise'. The Trustees considered that it would. Their response was brisk and brutal: 'Undesirable elect Dalhousie cripple.'[25]

But the less adequate – physically, intellectually, socially – from time to time crept through. 'It has always seemed a reproach to us that manifestly inadequate men could work their way in through the net of our regulations,' wailed Parkin.[26] One such weakling was Jael Rogers of Alabama, who resigned his Scholarship after a year, having so disgusted his tutor that he refused to teach him any longer. To compound his sins, Rogers shrank from telling his parents what had happened and clung on in Oxford, running up bills with his landlady.

Parkin wrote to President Abercrombie of the University of Alabama, who had been responsible for Rogers's selection: 'Of course we know perfectly well that human judgment is fallible and human nature weak, but we do feel bound to warn Committees of Selection that it is far better that no appointment should be made rather than an unsuitable candidate be sent.'[27] The counsel was more easily given than followed. The runners-up to Rogers could tell themselves that they had been of the calibre of Rhodes Scholars but had been edged out by a still stronger candidate. If no candidate were selected then they had all been deemed unworthy; worse still, the institution which admitted that it had no suitable candidate was by implication condemning its own performance. It took a lot of courage to make such an admission. Many selection committees screwed themselves to the point of doing so; others, especially when the failure occurred not once but several times, took the easy course and chose a man in whom they had privately little confidence. Over the years, as the base widened from which Scholars could be selected, the danger diminished, but in certain constituencies – Bermuda, the South African schools, where the constituency remained confined – it would never wholly disappear.

CHAPTER SIX
SURPLUS FUNDS

Rhodes in his Will had provided Canadian Scholarships only for Ontario and Quebec. Given that their southern neighbour, despite having so discourteously left the Empire more than a century before, had sixteen times as many Scholarships, the Canadians felt that they had been hardly used. Parkin fully agreed and appealed to the Trustees. It is remarkable how, from generation to generation, the Trustees, dependent it would seem largely on their personal predilections, have felt able in one case to improve on Rhodes's Will yet in another to conclude that they were rigidly bound by the Founder's wishes. Rhodes must have had reasons for his harsh treatment of Canada, but the Trustees chose to ignore them and to conclude that he had been guilty of an aberration which he himself would have been anxious to repair. Even before the first selection committee had been set up, Canada had been awarded six more Scholarships, one for each province. The total number of annual Scholarships was thus increased to sixty-three.

Even with this extra provision it was evident from the start that, after all the expenses of the Scholarships had been covered, a substantial part of the annual income from Rhodes's estate would be left free to spend on other things. Theoretically such funds could be spent by the Trustees in any way consonant with what they considered to be Rhodes's wishes. Nobody could have gainsaid them on legal grounds if they had chosen to squander it all on lavish parties. Instead, guided as much by their personal inclinations as by respect for the Founder, they decided that South Africa should be the principal recipient of Rhodes's bounty.

It is difficult to exaggerate how large the affairs of South Africa and Rhodesia bulked in the thinking of the Trustees in those early years. If the recorded minutes are to be trusted, nearly three-quarters of the Trustees' time was devoted to Southern Africa. This was largely because Rhodes had left vast farming estates for which the Trust was now responsible. Rhodes had never expected to make money out of these enterprises; they were intended as

centres for training and experimentation, where new techniques could be
tried out, new crops introduced, local farmers given a chance to hone their
skills in an environment where immediate profits were not essential but the
long view could be taken. The Rhodesian farms at Inyanga and in the Matopos
hills were, indeed, run with a fine indifference to expense which alarmed the
more prudent of the Trustees. Worse still, the Trust was saddled with two
hotels in the Matopos and an obligation to build a railway which would open
up the region to visitors. Neither of these enterprises had even a remote
chance of making a profit; the most the Trust could hope was that the loss
would not be so substantial that the income available for the Scholarships
would be seriously threatened.

In South Africa the chances of profit for the agricultural enterprises seemed
slightly greater but the scale of the commitments was still more alarming.
From the point of view of the South African economy the pioneering fruit
farms that Rhodes had launched were to prove an outstanding success,
contributing signally to the country's exports over the next century, but it was
not till 1909 that they showed even a marginal profit. Biggest problem of all
for the Trust was the Smartt syndicate, which owned vast tracts of land in
Bechuanaland and the Northern Cape and required formidable sums of
money to furnish the necessary investment. 'I feel seriously uneasy at the
immense drain on our resources which this enterprise constitutes,' Milner told
Michell. Unless something drastic was done there was a real risk that the Trust
would be 'drawn further and further into the morass'.[1] Michell replied hope-
fully that he believed the enterprise would one day succeed and thus show the
South African farmers how, with proper use of water, the most apparently arid
regions could be made to support livestock and yield rich crops.[2] In the long
run he was proved at least partly right, but the run proved to be uncon-
scionably long. Milner spoke for the majority of the Trustees when he said he
feared that in the meantime the farms could bankrupt or at least seriously
incommode the Trust which was responsible for them.

The problem could not easily be resolved. Even if buyers were found for the
vast enterprises at a price which would bear some relation to Rhodes's investment, the responsibility was not one which could lightly be discarded. It was
not just with a view to strengthening the South African economy that Rhodes
had devoted so much thought and money to farming projects. In 1904
Rosebery persuaded his fellow Trustees to put on record that 'after the
Scholarships, the strong intention and wish of Mr Rhodes was to further the
settlement of people of British race in South Africa'.[3] Rhodes, even after
the South African War, felt no animosity towards the Boers, but he still considered it of prime importance that British settlers should be in a majority. To
persuade British emigrants to move to South Africa and to settle them on

farms seemed to him the most effective way of building up a stable population. But there would be no point in sending British farmers to South Africa
if there was nowhere for them to work when they got there. If the Trustees
followed their financial instincts and got rid of the farms, would they not be
betraying one of the crusades which Rhodes held most at heart? Jameson and
Michell at least thought that this was so, and they fought a fierce rearguard
action against any systematic disinvestment in South Africa. It was almost the
end of the First World War before the Rhodesian farms were shuffled off,
while the Smartt Syndicate was not finally disposed of till 1939.

A more controllable but still bothersome problem was posed by Groote
Schuur, the stately home that Herbert Baker had built for Rhodes outside
Cape Town. In his Will Rhodes had instructed that, once the various provinces
of South Africa had federated, the house should be put at the disposal of the
new country's Prime Minister. In 1903 this seemed a distant and uncertain
prospect. By good fortune, however, and with some financial assistance from
the Trust, Dr Jameson's Progressive Party won the election in the Cape and the
Trust offered him the use of the house. To make one of the Trustees the recipient of the largesse of the Trust would today provoke some disapproval but in
1904 it seemed unexceptionable. Certainly it would have won the approval of
Rhodes himself. Jameson was charged £800 a year – a sum which, though hardly
nominal, did not begin to meet the cost of keeping up the house and estate.
Boyd, who had been despatched to South Africa on a visit of reconnaissance,
was told to report on whether Groote Schuur really needed the £4,600 which
was spent annually on its upkeep. Before leaving, he consulted Lady Salisbury,
who commented that the Cecil family palace at Hatfield, with thirty regular
inmates and a dozen or more extra at weekends, cost considerably less to run.
Thus emboldened, Boyd suggested various economies; notably the cancellation of an annual charge of £33 (over £1,000 at current prices) for winding the
various clocks scattered around the house.[4] The Trustees thought this insufficient, and eventually managed to extricate themselves from the whole liability.
In 1910 General Botha became the first Prime Minister of the new Union of
South Africa. Since the Union did not include Rhodesia, as Rhodes had envisaged, it could have been argued that it did not meet the terms of the Will, but
the Trustees were not disposed to quibble. With some relief they handed over
the estate to the government, with a grant of £23,000 thrown in to ensure that
they were absolved from any future responsibilities. The only condition they
made was that, in due course, land from the estate should be made available
as a site for the University of Cape Town.

One of the four schools in the Cape which had been designated in the Will
as a recipient of a Scholarship, the Diocesan College in Cape Town more
familiarly known as Bishops, expressed some disappointment that Rhodes

had not left the bulk of his fortune for founding a 'great Teaching University' in the Cape.[5] Rhodes had never doubted that such an institution was desirable, but it was late in the First World War before the University of Cape Town developed to a point where the Trustees felt ready to contribute more than a site for its construction. Meanwhile another university had demanded their attention. The concept of a university in the Eastern Cape, probably based at Grahamstown, had first been mooted in the 1890s but serious planning did not start till 1902. At this point some bright fund-raiser conceived the idea of calling it Rhodes University College and appealing to the Trust for support. Michell was unenthusiastic but Parkin believed that nothing could better assist the realisation of Rhodes's dream, and Jameson, the MP for the Grahamstown constituency, not merely agreed but took it upon himself to pledge that the Trust would make a contribution of £50,000.[6] After some expostulation from Michell the Trustees accepted the *fait accompli*, Alfred Beit offered another £25,000, and the new university was under way.

The Trustees rejoiced at Jameson's victory in the Cape elections, not just because he was one of them and was the champion of their views, but because they had contributed actively to his campaign. After their first meeting they had concluded that Rhodes would have wished his fortune to be used to promote the political causes that he had at heart, that Jameson was his accredited standard-bearer, and that he should therefore be authorised to make payments for political purposes 'in continuance and on the same scale as Mr Rhodes'.[7] Boyd felt that Jameson was being unduly cautious in interpreting this carte blanche. He was meeting from his own pocket many expenses which Beit or Rhodes would have felt could properly be charged to the Trust: 'Our Political Fund is ample and is administered from Cape Town,' Boyd protested.[8] Hawksley was no less prodigal. 'Now that you are in the thick of the General Election,' he told Michell, 'I suppose the political payments are likely to increase. Will £20,000 from 1st January 1903 to the close of the General Election Campaign be sufficient?'[9] The Rhodes–Beit Share Fund, set up by the two magnates in 1898, was the source of most of this largesse. Theoretically this Fund was not under the control of the Rhodes Trustees; in fact it was representatives of the Trustees who, with a little outside support, were responsible for deciding how it was spent. Milner, in particular, after he began to act as a Trustee in 1905, was deeply involved in the management of the Fund. Under his aegis some £10,000 a year was spent on political purposes, almost entirely in South Africa: the English-language press was subsidised, contributions were made to the Progressive Party's election fund and assistance given to imperial projects.[10] Not until 1929, by which time anyone who knew why the Fund had been set up was long dead, did the Trustees decide that the situation must be regularised and even then it was only after a prolonged battle that the whole Fund was absorbed into the Rhodes Trust proper.*[11]

Though Milner was sceptical about how it would work out in practice, the Trustees in principle were decided that a Union of South Africa including the Transvaal and the Orange Free State was essential if stability and prosperity, and therefore immigration from Britain, were to be secured. In 1906, after some hesitation, they put up £1,000 to finance a study by Lionel Curtis, Milner's protégé and pillar of the Kindergarten, on the '*modalités* and advantages of union'.[12] The report was submitted to the High Commissioner, Lord Selborne, who approved it and published it under his own name as the Selborne Memorandum. Milner was particularly anxious that the role of the Trust in this affair should remain secret; it might indeed have had a calamitous effect on public opinion in the Transvaal if it had been known that so questionable a figure as Rhodes, associated as he was with the Jameson Raid, had been linked with a document advancing the case for South African federation.[13]

Though it was inevitable that, in the first decades at least, the main interest of the Trustees outside the Scholarships should be concentrated on Southern Africa, it was neither their wish, nor the intention of Rhodes, that this should be their sole concern. Rhodes had made it clear how he felt the surplus funds, amounting to something close to half the income from the £3.9 million at which his estate was eventually assessed, should be deployed. First, the Trustees should build up a reserve fund: much of his fortune was in De Beers shares and 'the diamond mines cannot last for ever'. This sensible proposal the Trustees duly observed. Second, they should help the more promising of the Scholars in their professions 'especially if they show indications of higher ideas and a desire to undertake public duties – the paramount object instilled into them being the preservation and consolidation of the British Empire'. This was more difficult to implement. An obvious difficulty was that more than half the Rhodes Scholars were Americans, who could hardly be expected to count the preservation and consolidation of the Empire among their dearest aims. Were they, therefore, to be excluded from any continued interest by the Trust in their careers? The Trustees did occasionally assist Scholars after they left Oxford but such cases were rare – no systematic programme was ever evolved. Third, the Trustees should 'if deemed advisable' promote a 'Parliamentary Party who without any desire for office will always give their vote to Imperial purposes'. The suggestion was not deemed advisable, nor

*See p. 101 below.

even seriously discussed. Possibly it was the difficulty of finding enough MPs 'without any desire for office' which deterred the Trustees from embarking on this hazardous enterprise. Fourth, the Trustees should encourage emigration to Africa – 'the most dangerous portion of the Empire. . . we shall never be safe in Africa until we occupy the soil equally with the Dutch'. Egged on by Milner the Trustees did make some grants to such bodies as the South Africa Colonisation Society, but they felt that they were already making a signal contribution to the cause by keeping afloat the vast farming projects which Rhodes had launched and that little more could be expected of them.[14]

In a letter to Hawksley Rhodes had also advocated sending the cream of the Scholars to different parts of the world 'to maintain the Imperial thought'. 'They had better be unmarried,' he continued, 'as the consideration of babies and other domestic agenda generally destroys higher thought. Please under-stand that I am in no sense a woman-hater but this particular business is better untrammelled with maternal thought.' The problem of selecting and maintaining these celibate shock-troops to act as imperial missionaries evidently daunted the Trustees; they do not seem to have considered Rhodes's proposal at any meeting and no steps were taken to put it into practice.[15]

Though the Trustees certainly kept Rhodes's principles in mind and were predisposed to help any institution or project that would serve the cause of the Empire, it is difficult to see any systematic plan behind their spending. Grants by the Trustees reflected the prejudices of the individuals who happened to be present at any given meeting. South Africa was always going to have priority. 'On the whole,' wrote Milner, 'we are inclined to think that Higher School Education in South Africa, especially of the English public school type, has one of the first claims on us after the Scholarships them-selves.'[16] Three of the four schools nominated for Scholarships fell more or less into this category and could count on a friendly hearing whenever they appealed for any specific project. The fourth, Stellenbosch College School, was more controversial since a majority of its pupils were Afrikaans-speaking and, though in theory non-denominational, it was strongly influenced by the Dutch Reformed Church. 'My visit here has made me think,' wrote Rhodes cryptically in the visitors' book after inspecting the school.[17] Evidently his thoughts led him to conclude that bringing Afrikaners and English together was worth the risk of granting a Scholarship to what Michell angrily described as 'a dangerous hotbed of Afrikaner nationalism'.[18] It seemed that Michell had made a valid point when the first Scholar to be selected, Toby Muller, turned down the offer because he disapproved so strongly of Cecil Rhodes, but though there were to be other such difficulties in the future on the whole Stellenbosch produced candidates as good as or better than the other schools.

After South Africa, Oxford had no doubt that the University should be the principal beneficiary. The Trustees were less convinced. Rhodes had left £100,000 to his old college, Oriel, that, surely, was enough. When it was pleaded that Oxford lost money on every undergraduate and so the net result of the influx of Rhodes Scholars would be a serious loss to the University, Rosebery retorted sternly: 'Rhodes has done his share: it is for others now.'[19] But it was Rosebery who, in fact, sold the pass when in November 1904 he agreed that the Trust would help out if it could be shown that the Scholarships were causing problems. It was not too difficult to demonstrate that they were. A majority of the Scholars were happy to take a second BA degree – or in the case of some of the younger students, even a first BA – but some wanted to break new ground and read for the advanced degree of Bachelor of Civil Law. Postgraduate studies were at that time a concept little understood in Oxford: in 1908 of the twenty students reading for a BCL three-quarters were Rhodes Scholars and the others Indian or American.[20] As a *quid pro quo* for the expense and efforts in which this involved the University the Trustees agreed to pay for a lecturer in pathology – recognition, incidentally, of the fact that Rhodes in his Will had expressed the hope that Oxford would one day have a medical school as good as Edinburgh's.[21] Four years later a further step was taken: the Trustees made a contribution to the cost of a readership in English law.[22] These were the first tentative steps down a path that was to grow ever more well trodden and for a period was to absorb almost all the spare funds of which the Rhodes Trust could dispose.

PART III

The Age of Empire

CHAPTER SEVEN

FIRST ARRIVALS

Shortly before the Oxford term began in October 1903 Francis Wylie returned from a morning's golf, muddy and bedraggled, to find three young men standing outside his door. They wore top hats, frock coats and patent-leather boots; as one man they clicked their heels and bowed.[1] The Rhodes Scholars had arrived. It could be argued that these Germans, though the first to present themselves in Oxford, were not the first Rhodes Scholars. In 1901 Rhodes had decided he should make a trial run for his Scholarship scheme and offered the headmaster of Bishops the chance to send a boy to Oxford. The headmaster urged that the selection should be made from the post-matriculation 'college' class, but Rhodes insisted that he should be from the school proper and there-fore at the most seventeen years old. Two boys tied in the school ballot and the headmaster found it impossible to choose between them. Setting a precedent which the Trustees were resolutely to ignore over the next century, Rhodes gave scholarships to them both. Since they were only sixteen, however, they had to wait till 1904 before they could go up to Oxford. By the time they arrived, the first wave of Scholars had been absorbed into the University.

It was, indeed, more a ripple than a wave. Parkin had not managed to set up the machinery for selection in any of the main constituencies in time for the academic year beginning in October 1903. Only twelve Scholars arrived: two from Rhodesia, where they were nominated by the Director of Education; one from Natal, where a selection committee had been set up with electric speed; four from the designated South African schools; and five from Germany, including Wylie's top-hatted visitors. The Germans were able to steal a march on the other constituencies because Rhodes's Will left to the Kaiser the responsibility for picking the chosen Scholars. The Kaiser handed on the task to Friedrich Schmidt-Ott from the Education Ministry who drew up his personal list of suitable candidates. Even with this streamlined process, however, the Germans did not arrive in Oxford until well after the start of term.

Of the five German Scholars one was a marquess – Hélie, Marquis de Talleyrand, who sounded more French than German – and three carried the honorific 'von'. This was to be a feature of the German Scholars up to the First World War; they were picked exclusively from aristocratic or wealthy upper-middle-class families. This led to protests, which grew after two of the more socially distinguished German Rhodes Scholars had to be reported to the Kaiser for persistent idleness. Wylie pondered the question but concluded that it was not for the Trustees to tell the Emperor from what social class he should draw his Scholars. If the Oxford colleges had no complaints – which, in general, was the case – then he certainly would not favour doing more than drop the discreetest of hints. The experience of the early Germans at Oxford was, however, not entirely happy. Balliol, for one, found that their conversational English was inadequate and that they 'generally keep too much together'.[2] Von Müller, one of the original German Scholars, admitted that when he arrived in Oxford his English was 'hastily acquired from a pocket dictionary'. Müller enjoyed himself and did not agree with his fellow Scholar who found everything in England 'unbelievably out of date and ineffectual'; but he still concluded that the University aimed more at turning out gentlemen than scholars.[3] Both the calibre of the Scholars and their opinion of Oxford improved with the years. Karl von Holtzbrinck, who came up in 1906, spoke hardly a word of English but learnt quickly and proved 'a most satisfactory pupil'.[4] When Sir John Marriott in his history of Oxford included a gratuitous attack on the pre-1914 German Scholars for the 'base uses' to which they had perverted Rhodes's bounty, the Trustees rose in rage to defend them. Geoffrey Dawson, future editor of *The Times* and at that time Secretary of the Trust, went so far as to state: 'They seem to me to have been chosen and to have behaved more like the Founder's ideal Scholar than any others.'[5]

The history of the Rhodes Scholars at Oxford does not begin properly until October 1904, when seventy-two arrived: forty-three from the United States, nine from Canada and Newfoundland, six from Australia, five from Germany, five from South Africa and one each from Rhodesia, New Zealand, Bermuda and Jamaica. Even then it was not a full complement: one of the South African schools failed to nominate while Rhodesia could only scrape up a single Scholar. There were quite enough of them, however, to present Wylie with a tricky challenge when it came to fitting them into the college of their choice. That it should be *their* choice had been a principle quickly agreed between Parkin and Wylie. It would theoretically have been possible to create a college reserved solely for Rhodes Scholars but such a monstrosity would have been flatly contradictory to the Founder's intentions. When Rhodes chose Oxford for his Scholars, the collegiate experience was one of the most important elements, if not *the* most important, in the unique compound of glories which he believed Oxonian education offered. Failing such a college, Wylie might arbitrarily have appointed Scholars among the various colleges that were prepared to take them. This would not have been unreasonable, since it was unlikely that many of the new Scholars would have serious knowledge of the merits or demerits of the various colleges and Wylie would have been able to make a more sensible choice based on their needs and aspirations. This, however, was a responsibility he would have undertaken with reluctance: inevitably some of the Scholars were going to fit in badly at their colleges, and Wylie had no wish to be blamed for the resultant contretemps; besides, if a Scholar had chosen his own college, he would be more likely to seek to make a success of it.

The new Scholars, therefore, were on their own. In some of the colonies, or in the Ivy League universities of America, there might be a few Oxonians who could give advice, but who was at hand to counsel the Scholar from Arkansas or Jamaica? Scholars opted for one of the few colleges of which they happened to have heard or chose a name more or less at random. Out of the first 440 Scholars, 146 put Balliol as their first choice; New College came second, far behind; then Trinity, Christ Church, Oriel and Merton. The less fashionable colleges hardly got a look in, even as second, third or fourth choice. In spite of this Wylie managed to get a little under half into the college of their first choice and another quarter into their second choice, only a handful had to be fitted into colleges which they had not even mentioned. These proportions were maintained with some consistency, especially when colleges had enjoyed a good experience with their Rhodes Scholars and wanted to repeat the dose. They did, however, become increasingly sceptical about the glowing references which Scholars provided as part of the dossier furnished with their application. 'I don't know what we are to do,' said A. L. Smith of Balliol as he worked his way through some forty applications. 'Every one of these men is a cross between the Archangel Gabriel and C. B. Fry.'*[6]

The sad case of the Rhodesian, A. M. Bissett, illustrates the trouble Wylie could get into when he failed to secure a Scholar a place in his chosen college. Bissett was rejected by Balliol on the grounds that he had only the remotest chance of getting an Honours degree. Bissett's father, himself a Balliol man, was outraged. 'It is true that he passed third class in his Matric and probably Balliol objects to take what they fear may be a weak – or bad – worker. They may want all Lord Milners but does the student exist for the College or the

---

*Fry was an all-rounder of daunting ability, who represented England at cricket, football and athletics, held the world long-jump record and played a prominent part in the League of Nations.

College for the student?' Wylie offered to reapply, asking the Director of
Education in Rhodesia for more details about Bissett's matriculation: 'Please
give precise details. Generalities, however amiable, will not help with the
Master of Balliol.' He won a cautious and conditional reprieve for the rejected
Scholar, but Bissett *père* indignantly refused: 'I decline to subject my son to a
possible humiliation at the hands of the Balliol authorities. I regret sincerely
that he ever heard of the Scholarship.' He thought of withdrawing his son altogether but reluctantly agreed that he should take up the place offered him by
Wadham. As it turned out Bissett *fils* justified Balliol's doubts: he failed three
times in responsions, once in pass moderations, and went down at the end of
his second year 'because he feels he has got all the good he is likely to get out
of Oxford'.[7]

Even when Scholars had been allotted their college there might still be
problems. Some Scholars had had enough of institutional life by the time they
reached Oxford and found it cheaper and more congenial to live out of the
college. Wylie reported with dismay 'a plan according to which three of the
Americans, *belonging to different colleges*, are to go into lodgings next October
together'.[8] Nothing, he felt, could be more deleterious to the growth of a
college spirit. His own view was that nobody should move out of the college
in their first year and very few in their second, and then only for exceptional
reasons and with explicit permission. He did not meet with much opposition
from the Scholars. Even those who were initially resentful because they had
been fobbed off with what they saw as an inferior college, quickly settled in
and developed an often fierce loyalty towards their new home. Sport, of
course, played a large part in this: games were a matter of great concern in the
Oxford of the early twentieth century and the Rhodes Scholars almost all
entered whole-heartedly into such activities – even when the game was previously unknown to them. Fifty years after their time at Oxford Scholars of this
generation were still following the doings of their college in the bumping races
or deploring the victory of Cambridge in the annual Varsity Match at
Twickenham.

It was not all plain sailing. Henry James protested vehemently against the
desecration of Oxford by an eruption of young barbarians,[9] and was not alone
in his forebodings. Many undergraduates were suspicious if not hostile. 'It has
already been suggested that the whole system of Oxford life be changed to suit
the ideas of the Colonies and of America,' complained a columnist in *Varsity*.
'We are, however, firmly convinced . . . that we do not want reforming.' Oxford
was 'the last refuge of a liberal education', and should remain so.[10] *Isis*
contended that 'the pushful Yanks' were already renowned for their despolia-
tion of Britain and 'it seemed folly to invite still more'.[11] Such splenetic squibs

were written more to make a lively article than from real conviction. When, a few days after the *Isis* article, the Union debated 'That the Rhodes scheme of Scholarships is impracticable, and incompatible with the best interests of Oxford', the motion was defeated by 133 to a mere thirty. But there was genuine apprehension that the Rhodes Scholars might be uncouth, difficult to assimilate and, worst of all, out to change things. L. E. Jones, who was an undergraduate at the time, dismissed such fears. It was rumoured, he recorded, that the Rhodes Scholars 'had come to teach as much as to learn. If this were so, those we were lucky enough to have at Balliol were entirely successful in disguising their mission.' They were a subject of much speculation, however, and constantly surprising expectations. Jones writes of one Rhodes Scholar who was supposed to be a professor of Latin at some university of the Southern United States. The Merton fellows felt that they could hardly ask so eminent a figure to take responsions so suggested he might like to translate a short poem by Browning into some Catullan metre. 'I guess I'd better put you wise right now,' apologised the Scholar. 'I don't know any Latin.' But we were told you were a professor, expostulated a don. 'Why, that's so, but I got my professorship for *puoily po-litical* reasons.' At the other extreme, when coaching a Canadian Scholar on the river Jones tried to expound the science of rowing. The Scholar replied with a rapid speech in Greek. He was disconcerted and mildly contemptuous when Jones asked him to translate. 'I was merely observing', he said, 'that what you are asking me to do is to implement the Aristotelian doctrine of the *mesotes* or mean.'[12]

The Rhodes Scholars had as many doubts about Oxford. In the wake of the South African War Britain was unpopular in the United States, and Germany was anyway considered a more fruitful field for postgraduate studies. This prejudice was less strong in the colonies, but even there Oxford was not invariably regarded as the academic Mecca. Nor would it necessarily be much use for those of baser preoccupations. Andrew Carnegie told Parkin that he would never get the best young men because 'what Oxford has to give is not what they are after'. And what is that? asked Parkin. 'Dollars.'[13] Even if such resistance was overcome, to adapt to the ways of Oxford sometimes proved arduous. Scholars occasionally found their tutor supercilious or contemptuous; when H. G. Merriam from Wyoming used a system of analysis unknown to his tutor to solve a certain problem, the chilling comment came: 'We have been doing that work by a different method for many years. I think that we shall not change for an American Rhodes Scholar.'[14] But Merriam at least fared better than the Scholar who, after a few months at Oxford, was asked what he thought of his tutor. He replied vaguely that he supposed he must be the little man with the brown beard who had talked to him as if he were his father. 'Which he ain't,' concluded the Scholar.[15]

There were endless problems of adjustment. Though hardly living up to the lurid visions of those who expected all Rhodes Scholars to be pistol-packing hoodlums in cowboy hats, some at least of them, particularly among the Americans, enjoyed playing up to the image. Harry Hinds from Dakota wore cowboy clothes and carried a pistol, once pursuing the college aesthete round the quadrangle of Queen's firing shots behind his heels. William Crittenden also boasted a pistol and once fired it from a window of Trinity to attract the attention of his scout, a college servant. The President of Trinity politely asked him to deposit his gun in safe keeping until the end of term. But such extravagance did not necessarily imply any neglect of academic duties: Hinds got a first in geology, Crittenden a respectable second in law.[16] Nor did many Rhodes Scholars seek to appear out of the ordinary. A scout from University College remembered how easy it was to pick them out in the first few weeks but how soon they were indistinguishable from the rest in grey flannel trousers and tweed coats.[17] A conformist to the point of caricature was Ballard Keith from Maine. Keith, according to his obituarist, was 'a vigorous, full-blooded man, heavy enough for the center of the boat, useful in the scrum'. He 'adapted eagerly to undergraduate ways' and was a welcome figure at every 'Fresher Tea or Togger Binge with pipe in hand'. In later life he became a lawyer, was active in church affairs, barely left his home town and sank, loved by all, into merited obscurity.[18]

English manners seemed quite as curious to the new arrivals. The reminiscences of early Scholars abound in examples of the English propensity to talk affably to a foreign student at a party and then to cut him in the quadrangle the following morning. 'It isn't etiquette in St John's for a second year man to recognise a fresher in public,' the first New Zealand Scholar discovered to his cost.[19] The Americans in particular were dismayed by the inadequate plumbing and the cold, damp rooms: a Scholar at St John's earned much derision by insisting on lighting a fire in several rooms to see whether the chimney had a proper draught before making his final choice of accommodation. One colonial Scholar, three years older than most of the British undergraduates, berated Wylie about the silly regulations that forbade him to stay out late or have women in his rooms: 'That's the sort of thing that lost England the American colonies,' was his parting shot. 'And it may happen again!'[20] The inadequacy of the stipend – £250 a year – was another cause for grumbles. A man had to live 'like a mole' during the vacations if he were to survive, one American complained.[21] Most Scholars, however, found it, if not lavish, then at least adequate. Another American stretched it to cover his girlfriend's education in England – 'very chivalrous, but scarcely in accord with the intentions of Mr Rhodes', commented the President of Harvard[22] – while J. H. Hofmeyr contrived to save £240 during his period at Oxford, at the same time paying for himself and his mother to visit South Africa during the long vacation.

Some of the Scholars who had already spent three years at their national universities did not feel inclined to pass another two or three years doing a second undergraduate degree. Wylie thought that the Trustees would not be averse to their doing something more ambitious in the way of research provided only a minority of Scholars went this way. 'The main thing is that the men selected ... should be themselves appropriate men, that is, who are prepared to approach Oxford sympathetically, and not isolate themselves entirely from the general life of the place. ... The proportion of Rhodes Scholars doing post-graduate work is not likely ever to be very large.'[23] In the short term he was certainly right, since at Oxford in the early twentieth century the facilities for such studies hardly existed. Grey wrote in alarm from Canada to report that there had been letters in the local press saying that Oxford must be prepared to organise 'proper equipment for the instruction and research work of Post Graduates'. That might be so, but how much would it cost and who would pay? 'I am personally strongly opposed to the Rhodes Trust making any more grants out of the funds at its disposal towards University requirements.'[24] The capacity to move rapidly in any given direction has never been one of Oxford's characteristics; it was to be many years before either the funds or the will existed to make the University into a serious centre for postgraduate studies. In the meantime, most Rhodes Scholars found themselves constrained to take a second BA. The majority accepted the inevitable with good grace; a few were disgruntled and pursued their courses with something less than total commitment.

The age of the Rhodes Scholars was another problem. If they came straight from school, as Rhodes intended, then they would be the same age as their British contemporaries but in most cases educationally a year or two behind. Michell argued that this did not matter; boys brought up in the colonies were more mature than their British counterparts – 'If eighteen is not too young for an English boy it is certainly not too young for a Colonist.'[25] Most people, however, felt that the strain of being removed from their families, coupled with the extra academic burden, would be too much for many boys. If, however, they had already been to a university in their own countries then they would be three years older than their British counterparts and would find it harder to settle into their colleges. Wylie himself, who was better placed than anyone to judge how the Rhodes Scholars fitted in at Oxford, had no doubt which was the lesser evil. 'I have always been very much on the side of the rather older man,' he told Parkin. 'I am not in the least blind to the advantages from some points of view of having a man who is contemporary with the other ordinary undergraduates, but I believe strongly myself that greater advantages come with the extra 2, or 2½ years which our Scholars may be said to have in advance of the normal English undergraduate.'[26] The clinching argument was that to remove the brightest boys at the age of eighteen would be to weaken the local universities, which were in many cases still at a precarious stage of their development. 'We certainly do not want that to happen,' concluded the Trustees.[27] They were reluctant to impose an absolute ban on schoolboy entrants, especially from South Africa and the smaller constituencies, but by 1913 they had concluded that for the United States and Canada at least two years or more at a national university should be an essential prerequisite before a Scholar could be selected.[28] It was from the start accepted that any candidate, to be eligible, had to be able to go up to Oxford before his twenty-fifth birthday. On this the Trustees were inflexible. At the end of 1904 Boyd submitted to Lord Rosebery the case of a particularly deserving candidate who was a few weeks too old. 'I am under the impression', replied Rosebery, 'that the Trustees have laid down a hard and fast rule about age, and therefore neither you nor I have any power to dispense anybody from it.'[29]

There were, of course, occasional prodigies who made all such rules seem questionable. One such was Jan Hofmeyr. Hofmeyr was awarded his Scholarship when still only fifteen. He himself wanted to go to Cambridge and had already been offered help by the South African millionaire Abe Bailey, but his mother persuaded him to wait for two years and then take up the Rhodes Scholarship.[30] He was still only eighteen when he arrived at Balliol, intellectually the equal of any of his fellow undergraduates, emotionally and physically still a boy. His mother accompanied him. Mrs Hofmeyr told Wylie's wife that her presence was essential, because it was only with her that her son could properly relax. Mrs Wylie refrained from explaining her husband's point of view: that 'her presence at Oxford was preventing her son from preparing himself for an independent life, the life of leadership that Cecil Rhodes had in mind'.[31]

Forced to consort with undergraduates who were for the most part two or three years younger; deprived of an opportunity to pursue advanced studies; operating on the fringes of poverty; cold and uncomfortable; perplexed by the strange rituals of Oxford life; offended by British snobbishness and standoffishness: the lot of a Rhodes Scholar might not have seemed a happy one. Almost all of them, indeed, needed a period in which to adjust. But this was only the beginning. 'The typical American arriving in Oxford is baffled by the crazy system and, for the first year, is highly critical,' wrote Charles Hitch, a Scholar from Wyoming. 'By the time he goes down ... he is reconciled, worshipful, determined that nothing about it should be changed.'[32] For the typical Australian or Canadian the transition was usually less painful but the apotheosis no less satisfying. There were rebels, there were malcontents, but the vast majority of those early Rhodes Scholars enjoyed themselves greatly at Oxford and felt that they had been given a uniquely valuable experience.

Oxford, for its part, in spite of early doubts, felt that it had benefited from the incursion of these outsiders. Sidney Bell, the Senior Tutor at St John's and himself an acquaintance of Rhodes, summed up his judgment of the Scholars shortly before the outbreak of the First World War. They represent, he wrote, 'a marked influence for steadiness and for work . . . temperate, economical, serious-minded, keen, "professional" in work and play'. Academically the general level 'both of attainment and of ability' had been lower than Bell had hoped for; their training had been 'mechanical and superficial', they were 'not very teachable', verbose and poor in literary style. But to make up for this they had contributed 'in a marked degree to that intellectual give-and-take . . . which constitutes perhaps the most valuable part of an Oxford education'. In college they had been generally popular and 'nearly always on the right side'. It was still early days, but Bell concluded that 'the scheme is having the effect on Rhodes Scholars and on Oxford (it would not be too much to say, on the world) that the Founder desired'.[33] The Founder was not easily satisfied and he would almost certainly have hoped for more. It was a start, though, and one with which Parkin, Wylie and the Trustees could justifiably be content.

CHAPTER EIGHT

TRUST AND EMPIRE

Some, writes Anthony Kenny, have seen Rhodes's purpose in his final Will as being 'the creation of an international band of dedicated imperial missionaries'. If this was indeed his aim, concludes Kenny severely, 'then clearly it failed disastrously and deserved to do so'.[1] That it was at least a large part of his aim, avowed and explicit, can hardly be disputed. When he told Hawksley in 1899 that any surplus income once the Scholarships had been paid for should be devoted to 'the maintenance and extension of Imperial thought in England and the Colonies', he took it for granted that, in part at least, the Scholarships were dedicated to the same end. That is why, Hawksley told Wylie, he 'did not regard the Will as an educational one' in any narrow sense of the word. Wylie agreed; the object of the Scholarships was to give their beneficiaries not just an education but 'a particular view of the world's problems'. That view involved the closer integration of all parts of the British Empire, the fostering of strong ties between the Empire and the United States and a common effort by the English-speaking nations to spread their enlightened values to those parts of the world unfortunate enough to be deprived of them.

The fact that more than half the Scholarships were awarded to Americans shows how much importance Rhodes attached to the part to be played by the United States in this imperial crusade. It may have been vainglorious to imagine that a handful of young men, even if Oxford succeeded in indoctrinating them with imperial values, would be able seriously to influence the policy of their homeland when they returned to it. The concept, however, was not so grotesque as it seems today. In a post-imperial age, when the United States can be identified as a principal factor in speeding the disintegration of Europe's empires, it is easy to forget that when Rhodes wrote his Will expansionism was the popular cry and the disintegration of what was left of the Spanish Empire in the New World was impelling the Americans into enterprises in some ways similar to those of the Europeans in Africa, Asia or the

Middle East. It was only three years since Kipling had enjoined American citizens to 'Take up the White Man's burden', to forget their childish days and search their manhood through all the thankless years. With Theodore Roosevelt as their standard-bearer – Kipling's poem, Roosevelt rather grudgingly admitted, 'made good sense from the expansionist standpoint' – the Americans duly took up the burden in Guam, Puerto Rico, Cuba and the Philippines.[2] Rhodes had some reason to believe that his American Scholars would look sympathetically on the activities of the British Empire and would return home predisposed to preach its merits and to advocate the fostering of a partnership based upon common purposes and common values.

Rhodes was a visionary but not notably successful as a prophet. No more than most of his contemporaries did he realise that the British Empire had within it the seeds of its own inevitable decay. He did not foresee that within a few years the Russo-Japanese War would shake the myth of white supremacy and foster a new mood of aggressive nationalism; nor that the replacement of the Liberal Party by the Labour Party in British politics would lead to a change of attitude towards the dependent peoples. He could never have guessed how quickly after the First World War it would be accepted that full self-government must be granted to any country within the Empire which was qualified to enjoy it, nor that after the Second World War the criteria used in assessing such qualifications would be so radically revised. He never suspected that Oxford, old world, high church, Tory by tradition, would in the twentieth century be as likely to produce progressive free-thinkers as champions of the established order. His Will was the product of the times in which he lived and even to those who did not share his principles its aims seemed rational and sustainable.[3] Milner did share Rhodes's principles but he was suspicious of extravagant theorising and conspicuously hard-headed. 'I believe that Rhodes's permanent fame will rest on the Scholarship scheme as embodying the noblest form of Imperial aspirations,' he told Parkin. 'That will live and grow and may be one of the very greatest influences in the future of the Empire, and more than the Empire.'[4]

The Trustees as a whole would have said much the same but were cautious in the furtherance of their ends. They were alive to the risk that they might be treated as a milch-cow by any charlatan keen to exploit them in the name of Empire. When a Mr James King wrote to say that he had heard Rhodes had left considerable sums for the purpose of empire-building and that he was anxious to use some of it for that purpose, the Secretary replied coldly that he had been misinformed: 'There was no capital left by Mr Rhodes for the purpose of empire building.'[5] Nor did they do much to implement some of Rhodes's wilder propositions: they despatched no celibate Scholars to preach the cause of empire, and if they made any attempt to build up an imperial interest in the House of Commons they did so with such discretion that no traces of their efforts remain. When Leo Amery, not himself a Trustee until 1919 but always involved with the implementation of Rhodes's Will, returned from South Africa in 1904 he was shocked to find that there was no provision at Oxford for the teaching of imperial history. He did not appeal to the Trust, however, but took advantage of a dinner party at which he was sitting next to Alfred Beit to explain what he felt was needed. Beit promptly provided it and later offered £50,000 to endow a chair of Imperial History. Their concept of their responsibilities would evolve with time, but in 1904 the Trustees would have hesitated to do as much.[6]

Though they ignored Rhodes's advocacy of imperial missionaries they liked the idea that Scholars should be encouraged to join the Indian Civil Service or similar bodies. This was a particular hobby-horse of Grey's, who strongly supported a suggestion by Richard Jebb, author of *Studies in Colonial Nationalism*, that a fixed number of places in the ICS should be reserved for Rhodes Scholars: 'There is nothing more inspiring in the history of the Empire than the picture of the chariot containing 300 million of mankind drawn by 1,000 white horses.'[7] The trouble was that those responsible for selecting these particular white horses had their own ways of doing so and did not feel disposed to accept an arbitrary number of outsiders; they had nothing against Rhodes Scholars but on the whole preferred the products of English public schools. Things looked rather more promising when the Administrator of Southern Rhodesia professed himself ready to guarantee a limited number of appointments each year in the British South Africa Company's civil service, but this too withered. In the end all that was forthcoming was a promise that 'when any vacancies occur, we shall be most happy to consider favourably any application which may be made by Rhodes Scholars'.[8] Parkin welcomed joyfully the news that two Australian Scholars had been taken on by the ICS and was even more impressed by the fact that Canadian and Australian universities were beginning to 'seek professors among our men, without reference to the particular Colony in which they were born'. Here were the first signs that a wider, more cohesive Empire was developing, without legislation, without trumpet fanfares, but at the working level. 'When I first took charge of its organisation,' he wrote triumphantly, 'I told my Trustees that there would have to be somebody dreaming all the time if the bequest of the great dreamer were to attain the ends he aimed at.'[9] Now the dreams were beginning to attain reality. That reality, in his mind, was confined to those countries where a white settler population might be built up, large enough to furnish an effective ruling class. Milner was still more rigid. Even he had to admit that India was a special case which posed perplexing problems but for the most part he felt that those parts of the Empire where there was little or no chance of building up a substantial white population were alien to the system and should ideally be extruded.[10]

Though the pre-eminence of Empire as a background to the Scholarships was taken for granted by the Trustees there were differences of opinion about how far it should be rammed down the throats of the Scholars. Stead was seriously concerned by what he saw as the benighted ignorance in which they were left to wallow. Here were these eager young minds, open to new impressions, ready to be informed, and yet nothing was being done to shape or direct them. 'It is not any fault of yours,' he told Parkin, 'but I do not feel that Rhodes's ideal is being carried out with regard to the boys at Oxford.'[11] Parkin needed no convincing: he felt like a missionary surrounded by needy pagans but deprived of any means of converting them. Grey was the Trustee most likely to sympathise and to him Parkin poured out his heart. 'These young fellows', he wrote,

> come to us very much like the spirits in Shakespeare's play, called 'from the vasty deep'. They know very little as a rule about why they are there, and what the spirit was that actuated Rhodes. The question is how to get hold of them, and fill them with a little of the divine fire. I myself have been rather full of the idea of always getting together each group of men when they first come and having the ideas which inspired Rhodes put to them clearly and forcibly by one of the Trustees or some other very competent person.

The Trustees may have remembered Hotspur's retort when Owen Glendower boasted of his ability to call spirits from the vasty deep: 'But will they come when you do call for them?' Would the students rally to Parkin's call? Parkin sadly reported that the Trustees were disinclined to follow his advice; believing that young men 'do not like direction or what they call a "jaw"'.[12] The furthest that the Trust was prepared to go was to send each new Scholar extracts from the Will and the text of Lord Rosebery's address at the unveiling of the Rhodes memorial tablet in Oxford in June 1907.[13] Grey, backed by Michell, continued to believe that the Trustees were falling down in their sacred duty. His own particular contribution to the cult of Empire was to arrange to have distributed to schools in the various colonies a copy of Millais' picture *The Boyhood of Ralegh*, each one captioned 'What is my Country? The Empire is my Country. Canada/South Africa/Australia [or whatever was applicable] is my home.' The then London Secretary, Mrs Mavor, told Canon Groser in Southern Australia that Lord Grey felt the picture 'extremely likely to inspire children early with some Imperial thought'.[14]

It was at Grey's behest that the Trustees indulged in one of their few exercises in proselytisation. He persuaded them to send the Canadian humorist and professor of politics Stephen Leacock on a world tour as an imperial missionary: 'He has all Parkin's enthusiasm for the Empire and a refreshing twinkle in his eye.' Grey was convinced that Leacock would make his audiences realise 'what the present position of the Empire is, and how necessary it is that every Briton, in whatever part of the Empire he may be, must be up and doing if we are to hold the hegemony of nations'. The results were calamitous. Leacock travelled at break-neck speed, shirked his lectures, omitted to call on most of the dignitaries who were expecting him, dashed through England without bothering to see Parkin or go as far as Oxford, and finally compounded his sins by failing to report on his mission: 'I do not understand that it is necessary that I should make any formal report of my tour. I have already had the opportunity of discussing in detail with Lord Grey such matters as seemed to me of especial interest.' After this debacle the Trustees viewed with some suspicion any suggestion that they should play a direct role in propagandising for the imperial cause.[15]

Despite what Parkin considered to be this regrettable, even pusillanimous reticence, a group of conspiracy theorists obstinately believed that, even outside South Africa, the Trust was active in operating that secret society which Rhodes had envisaged in the earlier and most naive of his Wills. Arch-exponent of such fantasies was Carroll Quigley, whose *Tragedy and Hope* caused a ripple of excitement when it was published in New York in 1966. According to Quigley, the power of what he describes as the Rhodes–Milner group 'can hardly be exaggerated. We might mention as an example that the group dominated *The Times* from 1890 to 1912 and has controlled it completely since 1912.... From 1884 to about 1915 the members of this group worked valiantly to extend the British Expire and to organise it in a federal system.' Chatham House, the centre for international studies, was their creation and their instrument while, in 1910–13, 'they organised semi-secret groups, known as Round Table groups, in the chief British dependencies and the United States'. At the heart of this conspiracy was the 'Circle of Intimates' comprising Grey, Balfour and Rothschild; the outer circle, known as the 'Association of Helpers', under Milner's aegis was to provide the core of the 'Round Table organisation'.[16]

As with most conspiracy theories, there was just enough truth in this to satisfy those determined to believe it. Rhodes Trustees and their officers did play a role of great importance in *The Times*; they did have a hand in creating Chatham House; they were instrumental in launching the Round Table movement. But their semi-detached relationship with the Round Table and its eponymous journal illustrates the somewhat equivocal nature of the Trust's approach to the cause of Empire. The movement began in the summer of 1909, when members of Milner's South African Kindergarten began to meet at Fred Oliver's country house. Of the regular attenders Milner was a Trustee, and Lord Lovat and H.A.L. Fisher were to follow suit. Edward Grigg and Philip Kerr were future Secretaries. Grigg and Kerr were the first editors of the quarterly review *Round Table* which was launched in the spring of 1910 'to give a reasoned survey of current events and problems from the Empire angle'.[17] The Trust gave financial support to the project and was to continue to do so until the 1970s. The Round Table might have followed a roughly similar course if the Rhodes Trust had never been heard of, but the fact that the Trust was there and that so much of the most influential membership was duplicated in the two organisations was of immeasurable importance to the Round Table throughout its existence. That existence, however, never at any time involved the secret plotting and chicanery postulated by Quigley's fantasy. Serious-minded, upright, conscientious, the members of the Round Table rejoiced in any publicity they could win for their activities and were never more than a ginger group encouraging wider debate about the affairs of Empire.

It is noteworthy that Lionel Curtis, one of the most brilliant members of the Kindergarten and a potent force in the Round Table, never became a Trustee. In 1907 the Trust granted him £1,000 to prepare the paper on South African Union which eventually saw light as the Selborne Memorandum.[18] It was Milner who five years later urged his appointment as Beit Lecturer in Colonial History. But in the last resort the Trustees could not swallow his extreme and clamorously expressed views on imperial federation and found him too strident and opinionated: 'All my life', Curtis ruefully admitted, he had been 'painfully conscious of a faculty for presenting my views in a way that makes it least possible for anyone else to accept them.' He was an inspired teacher who did more than anyone to make Oxford aware of the Empire and the need to foster it. He attracted many Rhodes Scholars among his followers, among them Vincent Massey, a future Governor General of Canada. But he was not entirely to the taste of the Trustees.

They displayed some of the same reticence when it came to Cecil Rhodes himself. They showed a proper reverence for the Founder's reputation, jealously guarding his papers unless they felt sure that nothing to his discredit would emerge, but abstained for many years from themselves commissioning an authorised biography. They refused to have much to do with plans to convert his birthplace in Bishops Stortford into a shrine at which he might be worshipped. Parkin was worried that the Scholars would in the future be drawn from 'remote generations which cannot be expected to know much about Rhodes'. Surely it was necessary for 'the successful development of the foundation' that this gap should be filled?[19] The Trustees were unenthusiastic. Both Rosebery and Milner were 'sceptical about the merits of speeches for Scholars on Rhodes's ideals', Boyd told Wylie. Rosebery in particular had been dismissive: 'There is such a thing as running an idea to death.'[20] Only Grey saw no reason for restraint. It was he who proposed that a vast statue of Rhodes, modelled on the Statue of Liberty, should be erected on Lion's Head where it would greet every visitor by sea to Cape Town, and who was in large part responsible for the imposing memorial which stands today beneath Table Mountain. The other Trustees did not oppose the plans but felt the money could be better spent. They were as much champions of Rhodes as they were ardent imperialists, but they felt it ungentlemanly to force their views on other people; they were crusaders but crusaders in *sub fusc*, who deplored unseemly display and liked to keep their banners discreetly furled.

CHAPTER NINE
LESSER MORTALS

'I am in no sense a woman-hater,' Rhodes had told Hawksley in 1899.[1] Rhodes's sexual proclivities are difficult to establish and are mercifully beyond the scope of this book. He told Stead, however, that it was out of the question that his Scholarships should be extended to cover women.[2] He would have been ahead of his time if he had reached any other conclusion. When he drew up his final Will only a handful of women were at Oxford, and they on sufferance and playing an inferior role. It was not till 1920 that they were permitted to take degrees. It never occurred to the Trustees that they should seek to interfere with Rhodes's wishes. Not everyone was so acquiescent, however. In 1903, Miss Leroy, a high-school mistress in Winchester, maintained that 'the future of our Colonies . . . depends as much on the *women* as the men' and pleaded that they should share in the Scholarships and 'imbibe that love of England and her ways which will help to cement the Empire when they return home'. It seems unlikely that the Trustees debated the question with any seriousness; the minutes merely record that the application was refused.[3] They must have been disconcerted when in 1909 the *New York Times* announced the selection of a female Rhodes Scholar; anxious enquiries revealed that all that had happened was that the Society of American Women had established a fund to send one female student a year to Oxford. In 1912 Miss Saleski of New York State actually contrived to take the preliminary examination under the impression that it was open to women. 'I set her right as quickly and decisively as possible,' reported Parkin.[4] Still the women would not accept their fate and in 1916 Michell forwarded a similar application from Rhodesia, commenting: 'We have never done anything for women students, but that is no reason why we should not begin now.' The other Trustees thought that it was an excellent reason for not doing so. 'The whole of the Scholarships are [*sic*] specifically allotted to male students,' they expostulated, the excitement of the occasion evidently overcoming their grasp of grammar, 'and none are [*sic*] at present available for female students.'[5] Not until 1976 did the walls finally crumble, when the 'qualities of manhood' were struck from the Will and women admitted on equal terms with men.

Race proved more permeable a barrier. In theory, at least, there should have been no barrier at all. Rhodes's Will stated that: 'No student shall be qualified or disqualified for election to a Scholarship on account of his race or religious opinions.' That might seem categoric enough for anyone, but Boyd questioned whether to Rhodes 'race' meant the same as 'colour'. 'Had he not Dutch, English, Jew and the rest in his mind?'[6] Hawksley thought that such quibbling was unworthy of the Founder, but Jameson, who had been closer to Rhodes than anyone else alive, had no doubt that he did not intend to include black men: 'He would turn in his grave to think of it.'[7] The most probable conclusion is that, while Rhodes would not have wished to rule out the possibility of a black Rhodes Scholar being one day elected, at the beginning of the twentieth century it seemed to him that it would be many years before one would be ready. Indeed, in South Africa and Rhodesia in 1903 the education system was such that it would probably have been impossible to find a black student who could have coped with an Oxford education.

In the United States, however, things were different. In the election for 1907 Pennsylvania selected Alain LeRoy Locke, a negro. It was subsequently claimed that the selectors had been so impressed by Locke's written credentials that they decided he must be chosen even before the interview and felt that they could not go back on their conclusion when they discovered that he was black.[8] This seems improbable; it is hard to believe either that no selector was aware of Locke's colour or that they were so irrevocably committed to him in advance that they could not change their minds. Whatever the background, however, the Trustees were now faced with the arrival of a black Rhodes Scholar in Oxford at a time when such racial integration was virtually unknown in Britain and anathema in the Southern states of America from which so many of Locke's future colleagues were drawn.

Their reaction was confused. Parkin had been in favour of black scholars from the start; he had told the Trustees as long ago as 1903 that he thought they should share 'every possible opportunity that the white man has'.[9] The Trustees sought to evade the issue; the matter was one for the selection committees, they concluded. No issue of principle was involved.[10] Privately they had hoped that selection committees would prove prudent and that they would never be confronted by a choice which might stir up violent reactions, in Southern Africa as well as in the United States. Now they could not dodge the issue. Milner, egged on by Michell, was at first in favour of rejecting Locke out of hand, then reconsidered and concluded that the terms of the Will made such a course difficult if not impossible. Boyd suggested that they should play for time: 'I think we might fairly refer the matter back to Pennsylvania and ask them if they are quite sure that their choice represents American feeling.'[11] Rosebery, as so often, provided the decisive voice. The choice was most unfortunate, he felt. It would cause uproar all over the United States: 'The idea that the loathing of black blood is confined to the Southern States is, I believe, entirely fallacious.' But the terms of the Will left them no leg to stand on; the Trustees could not possibly reject the selection or even ask the committee to reconsider. He saw no reason why the other American Scholars should object: 'They need have no contact with the "untutored mind" or the black body of this American citizen, and I do not see how he touches them in any way.'[12]

The other American Scholars did not agree. Three Scholars from Southern states called on Wylie – 'all very sensible people', Wylie considered – and painted a lurid picture of the damage that would be done all over the United States.[13] Locke was boycotted by most of the other American Scholars and excluded from their national gatherings. When the American Rhodes Scholars were invited to their Embassy for a celebratory lunch, they were seated at tables for two. Locke was placed by himself. The Ambassador then entered, 'bowed to his guests, crossed the room and sat down with the black man'. 'As an unspoken rebuke', comments the man who recorded the anecdote, 'it was a masterpiece.' As an effort to make Locke acceptable to his peers it sounds singularly inept.[14]

It would be pleasant to record that Locke survived these travails and became, if not a popular member of the American colony, then at least a success at Oxford. It was not to be. The Principal of Hertford, who had only taken Locke after five other colleges had rejected him, reported that his knowledge of Greek and Latin was so elementary that he could not be entered for any regular Oxford course.[15] Wylie had been against him from the start: 'though clever he is decidedly objectionable. I do not know him personally but he is not at all pleasant to look at.'[16] His conclusion after studying him more carefully was that Locke's standards were superficial 'and his mind, apparently, unscholarly. Moreover, he lacks balance and a sense of responsibility.' Wylie accepted that Locke had confronted 'really great difficulties' but regretted that he had failed to overcome them.[17] 'I like the little fellow myself very well,' he somewhat unconvincingly told the Chairman of the selection committee, but the Principal of Hertford had found him 'too self-satisfied and unwilling to take a really hard grind in work'.[18] Things got still worse as his Oxford career went on; he consistently failed every examination, ran into debt and was finally sent down. His highly distinguished subsequent career as a philosopher and leader of the black cultural movement suggests that it was indeed the difficulties under which he laboured at Oxford rather than his character or his abilities which had led to his disasters. At the time, however, he was counted a failure; liberal America was unnerved by the debacle and it was nearly sixty years before another black American was selected as a Scholar.

It would be interesting to see whether the two coloured Scholars from Jamaica and Queensland would do better, commented Wylie at the end of his report on Locke. There had already been complaints from Jamaica that a black student had been passed over in favour of an obviously inferior white candidate,[19] and whether or not these were justified it came as no surprise when a black man, Frederick Mercier, was selected in 1910. He was a 'most refined and estimable fellow', Wylie found to his relief. His fellow coloured Scholar, G. F. Hall from Queensland, was only half black but had very obviously negroid features. The Chairman of the selectors wrote anxiously to explain that they had worried over the implications of their choice but had concluded that 'he seems such a fine stamp of young fellow that I trust he will soon wear down any prejudice'.[20] Wylie had problems fitting him into a college – mainly, it seems, because many of the obvious choices had Rhodes Scholars from the Southern American states who might have made trouble if confronted by a black colleague. Keble volunteered but was rejected by Hall's headmaster on the grounds that the Scholar was a Methodist and so would be grossly out of place in so high-church a college. In the end Lincoln found a vacancy. Neither Mercier nor Hall met any serious problems: they were both good at games, which helped a lot; they were used to consorting with white contemporaries; above all, in Wylie's words, they had 'more balance and more grit'. The American Rhodes Scholars who had been vociferous in rejecting Locke did not try to make life difficult for the new arrivals, sensibly concluding that they could not very well interfere in the way Jamaica or Australia chose their Scholars.[21] Wylie reflected wryly on the prejudice which had fuelled their earlier protests: 'It is rather amusing that this hostility was first shown by Scholars who came from the land where all men are supposed to be "free and equal".'[22]

At one moment it seemed possible that the Trust might find itself with a still more exotic Scholar. In 1908 Christopher Lobengula, son of the late Ndebele monarch, was eighteen and at school in England. The directors of the British South Africa Company, who had accepted responsibility for his education, asked the Trustees whether he would be eligible for a Rhodes Scholarship. The thought of the son of Cecil Rhodes's old adversary benefiting from his bounty must have seemed appealing to the Trustees. They ruled that, provided he had the blessing of the Rhodesian Government and could pass responsions, there was no reason why he should not put himself forward.[23] What happened next is unclear; it seems that Lobengula suffered from severe depression and had to return to Rhodesia. At all events, he never applied for a Scholarship.[24]

There were other racial groups which found some difficulty in fitting in to the Rhodes community. One was the French Canadians. In his Will Rhodes had specifically allotted a Scholarship to Quebec and the Trustees felt it particularly important that his views about race should be honoured by the election of French- as well as English-speakers from the province. The trouble was that the French were less than enthusiastic. The only way by which one could be sure of a French-speaking Scholar was if the Scholarship alternated between the French university of Laval and the English McGill. Such a solution was unpalatable to the Trustees, who wanted competition within any given area to be entirely unrestricted, but in the circumstances acceptable. When Laval selected its first candidate, however, he cast one dismayed look at Oxford and decided not to take up the offer. His place was taken by Talbot Papineau from McGill, a selection which delighted Parkin, who thought that they had caught a French Canadian after all, only to discover that in spite of his name the new Scholar spoke hardly a word of French.[25] Laval in 1907 did at least find a candidate prepared to go to Oxford but, as Parkin pointed out, Laurent Baudry had as much English blood as French; probably the selectors at Laval had 'simply found someone who was willing to take the Scholarship'.[26] That year the Rector of Laval, O. E. Mathieu, told Parkin frankly what problems he had had convincing the French Canadians 'that Oxford would not wreck the souls of their young men'.[27] It seemed that such inhibitions had been overcome but fresh difficulties arose when it appeared that, while Mathieu's branch of Laval University in Montreal was ready and eager to provide Rhodes Scholars, his more intransigent colleagues from Laval in Quebec City were resolved not to appoint at all. Parkin told them bluntly that, unless they agreed to open competition between both sections of the University, then the Trustees would have to increase the proportion of Scholars given to McGill. 'This will, I think, secure a definite decision on their part,' he reported with some satisfaction.[28] He proved right. It was not till well after the First World War that the problems of the French Canadian Scholars again became apparent.

The Rhodes Scholars selected from Stellenbosch College School, progressively more and more of whom had spent two years at least at Stellenbosch University, were in much the same position: members of a racial group which had forcibly been embedded in a country whose government it disliked and who suspected that a sojourn at Oxford would sap the patriotism and moral fibre of its young men. Though he habitually considered any decision by Rhodes as being the equivalent of the tablets from Mount Sinai, Michell never ceased to deplore the award of a Scholarship to Stellenbosch. But the Trustees as a whole believed that the very fact that many of the students at Stellenbosch were 'opposed to British ideals' made it all the more important to get them to

Oxford where some at least might be converted. Wylie rejoiced when
Gerhardus Hattingh was selected to be the 1908 Scholar from Stellenbosch:
'He is a genuine Afrikander (who fought all through the war on the Boer side)
and three years here will, I believe, have their fruit.'[29] On the whole they did.
Though one Afrikaner former Rhodes Scholar was arrested in 1915 for taking
part in an anti-war rebellion, the majority of his colleagues were either loyal
to the British during the First World War or, at least, discreetly neutral. Not all
Rhodes Scholars, whether American or Australian, French Canadian or
Afrikaner, black or white, made good use of their time at Oxford; many of
them found things to criticise about their education or the British way of life;
but few went home without a warm feeling towards the University that had
nurtured them and an inclination to do what they could to help it and Britain
in the future.

CHAPTER TEN
AMERICANS ARE DIFFERENT

It was one of the paradoxes of the Rhodes Scholarships that while at Oxford the Scholar was urged to pay allegiance to his college or his university, and not to seek out the company of other Americans or colonials, once he was back at home it was hoped that he would bond with others in the same position and form a Rhodes community, dedicated to the Founder's dreams and aspirations. Parkin told Grey that he had been worrying how best to ensure that the 'Rhodesian spirit' was kindled and continued to burn in all the Scholars: 'If we fail to do this, it will be falling short of the great imagination which created the bequest.' A few days before, Rudyard Kipling had cross-examined him on what was being done. 'I told him of plans that I am already working out: first, a complete Register of the career of each individual man . . . second, an annual report to be given out to the press . . . third, a statement to be published every year and sent to every Scholar who has left, giving information about every Rhodes Scholar.' Michell had suggested an annual dinner in every country, preferably on Rhodes's birthday. Kipling himself thought that there should be a magazine with contributions from the Rhodes Scholars of every constituency.[1]

Wylie for his part felt that he had a unique role to play in creating some sense of common purpose among the Scholars. By the time that a Scholar left Oxford, he told the Trustees, 'I do in most cases, at any rate in many cases, know him with some degree of personal intimacy: and if by correspondence I can keep a little of that intimacy alive; that, so far as it goes, will be something that will make for the man's keeping more in touch with Oxford and Oxford associations.'[2] With the encouragement of the Trustees he set to writing a personal letter once a year to every former Rhodes Scholar. At first the task was relatively light, but after the first few years the numbers snowballed. In 1927, by which time there were more than 1,100 living Scholars, he was forced to send out a standardised letter but he still tried to write a few personal lines in almost every case. Even after his retirement he sent Christmas cards to all the Scholars who had been at Oxford during his tenure of office. Though Wylie was occasionally testy and never adventurous in his ideas, he was a warm-hearted and generous man. He deserved and won the affection of many generations of Scholars, providing by his personal efforts the heart of a network which linked them tenuously together.

While there were only a handful of Rhodes Scholars to be found over the vast territories of Canada or Australia it was hardly likely that even the most flimsy organisation would be set up. Even if every Canadian or Australian had hastened back to his homeland there would only have been thirty or so of them by the time the First World War broke out. As it was, many lingered on the way, some got a taste for a life in exile and never went back at all. Only in one country was there a body of Scholars sufficiently large to form any sort of cohesive group. It so happened that that country was also the one where the cult of the old boy was most commonly to be found.

The United States was so distinct from every other constituency within the Rhodes community that sometimes it seemed that there were two Scholarships, the American and the rest. The most obvious difference was that the United States did not form part of the British Empire. In so far as they had thought about it at all, the American Scholars assumed that they would share with the Scholars from the Empire a common resentment of the British claim to be the imperial overlords of so huge an area. They were disconcerted to find that the Australians and Canadians, though keen to assert their national identity, on the whole tended to side with the old colonialists rather than with the brash young republicans from the New World. Lawrence Gipson, in time to become one of America's most eminent historians, found himself required in a debate to propose the motion 'It would be to the best interest of Great Britain if her overseas possessions would secure their independence'. To his surprise he found himself vociferously opposed by undergraduates from Canada, Australia and New Zealand. 'For the first time I was made to realise what intense pride the people living beyond England had in the Empire of 1905.'[3]

The Americans too, partly because of their greater numbers, hung together as a social group more than the Scholars from other countries. The bonding process began on the boat coming over, since they travelled together and knew each other well by the time they arrived in Britain. They were fêted during their journey: Cunard gave them first-class tickets for second-class fares; a Boston sweet-maker presented each Scholar with a huge box of chocolates; the President sent each one a personal telegram of congratulations and a reminder 'that they had an obligation to uphold the best traditions of American scholarship and culture'.[4] Such treatment made them decidedly nervous about what would be expected from them when they got to Oxford but also made them feel secretly that they must be something rather special. If somebody tells you often enough that you are a member of an elite, you begin to believe you are.

Tucker Brooke, himself a veteran of 1902 and one of the most assiduous of American Rhodes Scholars, denied that they had ever laboured under such an illusion. Three out of four, he said, came from 'remote and backward colleges, from institutions that quite clearly knew themselves to be second rate and had never had the idea of putting their students into competition with those of an ancient, famous university. They were, with very few exceptions, simply a scared, serious, diffident group.'5 Socially speaking, the majority came from middle- or working-class families. Nearly all of them had been educated in their own states (the awkward problem of covering forty-eight states with only thirty-two Scholarships had been met by selecting the full forty-eight for two years running and then – as in the rotation of crops – letting the land lie fallow in the third year). The system made it inevitable that they would not represent the best that America had to offer: it was likely that in most years Massachusetts for one would have two or three candidates superior to any to be found in Wyoming or Idaho, with their smaller populations and inferior universities. In some of these weaker constituencies there was no guarantee that the best man would be chosen even from the limited field available: the first Scholar from Arkansas told Wylie that the Governor had made a determined effort to impose his candidate on the selectors, while in Oklahoma political interference became so intolerable that the Trustees suppressed the selection committee and announced that in future they would nominate the Scholar themselves.6 Some states admitted frankly that they could not find candidates of suitable calibre: Montana, for instance, selected only two Scholars in the first ten years. Even where there was a galaxy of talent, the best men had not always come forward. Professor Munro of Wisconsin took advantage of a stay in Oxford in 1907 to see as many as possible of the Rhodes Scholars. He was disappointed: 'I did not feel that they were, on the whole, worthy representatives of our young men.' Many potentially excellent candidates did not apply. 'They want to start their careers, and know very little about Oxford.'7 The Dean of Pomona College in California found the same thing: 'Most of our young men are so keen towards the commercial side of life and so unappreciative towards culture that they look with suspicion on any plan for life which seems to take a year or two from their business career.'8

The early American Rhodes Scholars must therefore have known that they were not necessarily the best students of their year, but at the least they had no serious doubts that they would be able to hold their own. Some of them could, others had a sad disillusionment. 'The English make us mad and rightly so by

the way they treat the colonials and Americans with condescension,' wrote
Paul Hubbell angrily.[9] Too many Oxford dons were determined to put down
these upstarts and dismiss their previous education as worthless. Sometimes
they were given grounds for doing so. John Crowe Ransom, in time to be one
of America's most distinguished poets and critics, told his tutor with some
confidence that he had already studied philosophy for two years, including a
course in deductive logic. 'Whom did you read?' asked the don. 'We had a
book by Noah K. Davis.' The don admitted the name was unknown to him
and asked what other courses Ransom had followed. 'Inductive logic.' 'And
whom did you read?' 'We had a book by Noah K. Davis.' 'A most ubiquitous
man. Did you take any other courses?' Ethics, Ransom said. 'Whom did you
read? Please don't say Noah K. Davis.' 'Noah K. Davis,' admitted Ransom, 'and
then we had a course in psychology.' 'I can't bear it, but I feel you had Noah K.
Davis.' 'Yes.' It finally became clear that Ransom had been encouraged to read
the works of no other philosopher, alive or dead. 'Come to my rooms next
Thursday evening at eight,' concluded the don, 'and bring me an essay entitled
"What is Thought?"'[10] Some, like Ransom, responded to the challenge and
showed that their potential was as great as any of their English peers. Others
floundered. Among the Scholars of 1904 seven got no degree, one a pass, three
took fourths, twelve thirds, eleven seconds and six firsts. It was not disgraceful,
but well below the level of those who had got Scholarships from British
schools. A report commissioned by the Carnegie Foundation listed
complaints from Oxford dons that the American Scholars, except for a
handful of outstanding successes, were pleasant enough but often 'restless and
volatile', suffered from a 'curious superficiality of training' and were sometimes even 'singularly uneducated'.[11] The reaction of some of the Scholars to
such criticism was to opt out. The average American, wrote a jaundiced victim
of the system in 1910, 'accepts the Rhodes Scholarship as giving him a modern
equivalent of the Grand Tour, and looks on his Oxford terms as rather less
important than his successive vacations on the continent.'[12]

Oxonians viewed the new arrivals with some suspicion. At the worst the
suspicion was tinged with spite; a critic in 1912 accused them of being either
'Puritans' or 'rather despicable'.[13] More often attitudes were amicably patronising. Though not delivered so much *de haut en bas*, the opinions of most
undergraduates on the American Rhodes Scholars were not unlike those of
the Duke of Dorset in Max Beerbohm's *Zuleika Dobson*. The Duke went out
of his way to cultivate Rhodes Scholars, though 'more as a favour to Lord
Milner than of his own caprice'. He found them, 'good fellows though they
were, rather oppressive. They had not – how could they have? – the undergraduate's virtue of liking Oxford as a matter of course. The Germans loved it
too little, the Colonials too much. The Americans were . . . the most trouble-

some as being the most troubled of the lot.' The Duke held, 'in his enlightened way, that Americans have a perfect right to exist. But he did often find himself wishing that Mr Rhodes had not enabled them to exercise that right in Oxford. They were so awfully afraid of having their strenuous native characters undermined by their delight in the place.' He condescended so far as to invite Abimeleck V. Oover of Trinity to dine with the exquisitely select dining club over which he presided. It was not a success. American Rhodes Scholars, he reflected, with 'their splendid native gift of oratory, and their modest desire to please, and their not less evident feeling that they ought merely to edify, and their constant delight in all that of Oxford their English brothers don't notice, and their constant fear that they are being corrupted, are a noble, rather than a comfortable, element in the social life of the University'.[14]

Whether spurned or patronised, the American Rhodes Scholar unsurprisingly felt forlorn and far from home. 'I had forgotten how lonely and homesick I was,' said one early arrival, while another tried to resign his Scholarship after only a week.[15] They formed an American Club, with its own rooms, where they could read American papers, exchange American gossip and escape the unsettling atmosphere of Oxford. Wylie deplored the step but did not think that he could do anything to discourage it; the *Daily Mail* more forthrightly complained that, while the English did all they could to make their visitors feel at home, the American 'retired to his shell . . . and might indeed just as well be back in America for all the good he does to himself or Oxford'.[16] John Crowe Ransom criticised the Club on different grounds. The members, he felt, were too boisterous, too ready to make a joke out of what should have been serious programmes: 'This is after the fashion of the English clubs, but I think the American Club ought to be somewhat more serious and dignified.'[17]

This catalogue of woe is far from a complete picture. The great majority of American Scholars quickly adapted and grew to accept, even to value, the vagaries and tribulations of Oxford life. Though the Scholarships had not yet acquired anything like the renown that they won between the two world wars, returning Scholars found that they were regarded with respect and that their reputation opened doors that would otherwise have been closed. Looking for work in Chicago Alfred James 'investigated several openings and in each case the fact that I had been a Rhodes Scholar was of great service in securing the interest of the men at the helm of affairs'.[18] The importance that was attached to their Oxonian experience was shown by the fact that, as early as 1907, an alumni association of American Scholars was set up. A few years later, after a dinner of a dozen or so Rhodes Scholars in New York, one of the first wave in 1904, David Porter, reported to Parkin that there had been much talk of 'the Rhodes ideal and the part that we all ought to have in making it an ideal embodied'. Everyone agreed that the Scholarships were too little known in America and that, when they were mentioned, they got an unfairly bad press. 'It was suggested that it might be wise to have some man in this country who could be free for part or all of his time to become sort of a "clearing house" for the Rhodes Trust.' Michell immediately intervened to oppose the creation of what would 'practically be an American Secretary'. It was up to Parkin to ensure the scheme got better publicity in the United States.[19] For the moment Michell's view prevailed, but Porter had pointed the way towards the future.

Almost at once the new Association tried to publish a magazine, but the potential readership was at first not large enough to support even a modest pamphlet. In 1913 the new Secretary of the Association, Grover Huckaby, decided that the solution must be to think large. He announced the future appearance of a new international magazine to be called *The Colossus*, aimed at the international Rhodes community. Parkin and Wylie were appalled at what they saw as a blatant attempt to take over the whole movement. The Trustees considered the issue and resolved 'not to offer any assistance to the contemplated publication'. The first draft of the conclusions had continued, 'and to discourage the scheme'. Rosebery struck out the words, presumably because he thought they were too harsh towards a project which was tactless but certainly well intentioned.[20] Discouragement was what was administered in any case; Huckaby scuttled his ship without demur and *The Colossus* never appeared.[21]

Before the moon of *The Colossus* had set, Leonard Cronkhite, from the second year of Scholars, appealed eloquently for the development of the alumni Association so as to link it more firmly with the Scholarships; it is 'not yet founded on "the idea" (a favourite and significant expression of Mr Rhodes)'. If the Association were to exercise the influence which Rhodes would have wished for it then there must be 'organisation, a definiteness and certainty of effort'.[22] The hour had come and the man was there. Frank Aydelotte had come up in 1905, resigned his Scholarship on marrying at the end of his second year and, at the beginning of 1913, applied to take up his unused third year so as to complete his work on Elizabethan rogues and vagabonds. Michell had met him on first arrival and found him 'an exceptionally engaging young fellow and likely, I think, to do us credit'.[23] The judgment proved perceptive; when Wylie supported Aydelotte's application to return in 1913 he said that he was 'one of the best Rhodes Scholars that we have had'. There may have been one or two who were better scholars and plenty who were better athletes, 'but there have been few, if any, who came nearer realising the combination of intellect, character and physical vigour which the Rhodes ideal suggests'.[24] Aydelotte had been dismayed that only a handful of Rhodes Scholars were associated with the selection process in the

United States; he was disgusted that Scholarships should be held by states which time and again proved incapable of finding a worthy candidate; he was convinced that the whole system needed drastic overhaul; he believed that he was the man to do it. The Trustees agreed, and when he returned to the United States fully supported his plea to launch a new version of the alumni magazine, the *American Oxonian*, with himself as editor. It was a first stage in a momentous crusade to reshape the system. Parkin had got the Scholarships going, Aydelotte transformed them into something uniquely important, in the United States first, ultimately throughout the English-speaking world.

In 1918 his new journal contained a collection of pieces written by members of the class of 1904 in which they summarised the results of their time at Oxford. All agreed that they had been in no way de-Americanised; all agreed that they had been immeasurably broadened in outlook by their experience: 'Oxford taught me the *livingness* of things'; 'it has meant breadth . . . a certain catholicity of interest and taste'; 'the most valuable treasure is a sense of world citizenship'; it has given me 'independence of thought and judgment'. The comment that would probably have pleased Rhodes most was that 'the way many of the best Englishmen were planning to give their lives to government service in India . . . helped me more than any other single thing to think in world terms'. He might have been less pleased by the fact that thirteen out of the sixteen contributors and twenty out of the forty-three Scholars were holding academic posts, but at least Oxford had taught them the right lessons.[25] Wylie had toured America and found that in almost every case the Scholars retained a genuine affection for Oxford: 'It is difficult to be other than hopeful of the Scholarships scheme when one sees the impression left on Scholars by their three years over here.'[26] There was still a lot to be done to make the American Scholarships work to best advantage, but at least a sound foundation had been laid.

CHAPTER ELEVEN
THE COLONIALS

Though the United States may always to some extent have been distinct from the other Rhodes Scholarship nations, it does not follow that those others were all the same. Parkin had quickly found on his travels that each colony had its own quirks and prejudices; the system had only been in operation for a few years before it became clear that the differences would be no less apparent in the future.

Australia produced the Scholars who seemed to approximate most closely to Rhodes's ideal. Few would have predicted as much at the beginning. For one thing the Australian selectors seemed to take altogether too seriously the 'manly outdoor sports' criterion in the Will. From time to time they tried to make an exception but when they did there was a fearful rumpus. In 1904 in Victoria the undergraduates had strongly supported the selection of a medical student with many athletic triumphs to his credit. The selectors instead opted for J. C. V. Behan, an academically formidable lawyer with the humblest of sporting records. When the undergraduates protested, Behan's professor pointed out that the chosen Scholar had gained first-class honours in three schools at once, which did not leave much time for sport. Exactly, said the sportsmen; this is just what we were complaining about; he is a 'mere bookworm'. The selectors stuck to their guns and the Trustees accepted their assurance that Behan, though not much of a games players, was brimful of manly qualities. He went on to a brilliant academic career and to serve for thirty years as Secretary for the Rhodes Trust in Australia. In that role he was frequently to encounter what proved to be the second of Australia's weaknesses: the ferocious rivalry between the states that for half a century made impossible any national selection process. So entrenched was the instinct for independence that Queensland, which at that time had no university, insisted on sending its Scholar direct from school rather than allow him to be polluted by further education in Sydney or Melbourne.

But in no constituency did the Scholarships more quickly gain popular renown. In Queensland the Minister of Education each year presented a trophy to the school that had produced the winner; the label of 'Rhodes' as a symbol of excellence became so far recognised that even girls' schools presented prizes named after the Founder. 'This great imaginative scheme was on everybody's lips,' wrote C. K. Allen.[1] And the Australian Scholars responded by fully holding their own. In sport they almost all represented their college, some their university; out of seven academic distinctions won by Scholars in 1907, four belonged to Australia.

New Zealand, though on a far smaller scale, emulated its neighbour. As in Australia, each Scholar was treated as a hero. When Allan Thomson won the prize in 1904 there was rejoicing in Dunedin. The Boys' High School had a half-holiday and the City Council passed a resolution congratulating his father.[2] Parkin concluded that New Zealand was 'the most English Colony in the Empire by far', and that any Scholar from there would fit in at Oxford with great ease and drop back naturally into New Zealand when he returned.[3] In Thomson's case Parkin was proved right on the first point but the second went by default. Thomson got a first in geology, only to find there was no job for him at home. Many New Zealanders were to encounter the same problem over the next decades.

The Canadians, too, were judged to reflect well on the selectors: 'a fine set of fellows,' said Parkin, though with one or two exceptions.[4] Among those exceptions was perhaps the Scholar whom a future Trustee, the banker Edward Peacock, reported as having had his head completely turned by Oxford, so that he made himself ridiculous and unpopular when he returned home.[5] Aping English manners seems to have been a vice found mainly among North Americans; Edwin Hubble, the future astronomer, cultivated an Oxford accent and used phrases such as 'Bah Jove' and 'to come a cropper', only drawing a line when it came to carrying a cane.[6] Such pretensions were much resented in Canada, where strenuous efforts were being made to assert a national identity. Perhaps it was partly for this reason that there was so fearful an uproar when an Englishman called Albert Sturley, who had only lived in Canada for three years, was selected as the Scholar for Quebec by a panel which happened to contain four Englishmen. Sturley would have been an unpopular choice, however transcendent his qualities; as it was he was dismissed by one Canadian patriot as being 'a good, plodding student, a recluse, a man of sedentary life'. 'Rhodes Scholarships. No Canadians need apply' was the headline above a letter sent to the editor of the *Standard*. Parkin publicly defended the selectors, pointing out that, of the Canadians currently at Oxford, one was Icelandic by birth and one Norwegian. Privately, he admitted that the decision was injudicious, 'and on the whole opposed to the intention of Mr Rhodes'. On reflection the Trustees concluded that a Scholar should be colonial born or a *bona fide* colonial from childhood, but that the invitation to Sturley could not now be withdrawn. If he voluntarily resigned the Scholarship, the Trustees would be happy to accept a replacement.[7] Sturley showed no wish to fall on his sword, and when Parkin toured the west of Canada a few months later he was disconcerted to find that everyone was in favour of immigrants being free to enter for the Scholarship soon after their arrival. In the end the Trustees decided on a compromise: an immigrant would be eligible only after five years in his country of adoption.

South Africa did not present so satisfactory a picture. Parkin argued that the South African Rhodes Scholars were inadequate not so much because most of them were picked from the restricted field offered by the four schools as because 'the stimulating air of the high veldt and plateau country tends to nervous exhaustion' and because their 'reliance on black people meant that they were ill-prepared for Oxford'.[8] Scholars from Natal, the only Scholarship assigned to South Africa apart from the four schools, proved little better. 'Very nice fellows, gentlemanly, industrious and anxious to do their best,' Parkin found them, 'but poorly prepared and several not of special ability.'[9] Not merely were they poorly prepared but the South Africans found the problems of adjustment harder than did most colonials. Hofmeyr, who in time became a committed devotee of Oxford, at first felt his fellow undergraduates to be 'arrogant, supercilious and extraordinarily self-satisfied', while he was shocked when required to sit next to an Indian at dinner: 'It is rather hard getting used to different ideas about colour just at first.'[10] Michell complained that even when South Africans lasted the course at Oxford they returned ill equipped for any career that might be open to them; 'the majority take to the law as ducks take to water, whereas the Colonial Bar is already over-crowded'.[11] One way by which they could make better use of their time at Oxford, he suggested, would be if they were made to spend two years at a local university before going overseas. It was partly at least so as to make this possible that the Trustees proved so ready to support the creation of Rhodes University at Grahamstown and to look kindly on the birth pangs of the University of Cape Town.

Rhodesia had the same problem in exaggerated form; the disproportion between the number of Scholarships available and the tiny field of eligible candidates was still more grotesque. 'Nothing much to be said of him,' wrote Wylie gloomily of a 1912 Scholar, E. C. Coxwell. 'He does not seem to be a man of any ability: but I do not expect him to give any trouble.'[12] At least the selectors thought Coxwell was worth sending to Oxford: in the first ten years of the Scholarships eleven vacancies were unfilled while another nine Scholars had been educated in Britain or in South African schools.[13] The Trustees thought that education abroad was desirable and might even have to be a prerequisite; those responsible for building up the education system inside Rhodesia were not surprisingly dismayed by such proposals. Gradually things improved; by 1912 Parkin was modestly hopeful. 'I entirely sympathise with you', he told the Director of Education, 'in hoping that men brought up in Rhodesia and thoroughly impregnated with the feeling of the country, will soon fill up the whole list of fellows.'[14] Two years later there were five or six quite strong candidates for the three places: 'We have now evidently reached a point where we are likely to have a good deal of competition,' wrote Parkin with satisfaction.[15]

Bermuda and Jamaica, the odd men out in Rhodes's ramshackle list of beneficiaries, were still less qualified to produce a convincing Scholar. Parkin admitted sorrowfully that the Bahamas, Barbados and Trinidad could all supply candidates as good as those from Jamaica and better than those from Bermuda.[16] The last in particular offended him; of the five thousand whites, nearly a quarter were Portuguese and a tiny in-bred English elite controlled both the colony and the Scholarships. 'There are a good many self-respecting and progressive negroes,' reported Parkin, but since there was 'no admission of social equality', there was no question of them competing for a Scholarship.[17] Nor could the negroes have reached the necessary academic level: there were no schools in Bermuda able to prepare a boy for Oxford, and potential Rhodes Scholars were usually sent to England for two years to bring them up to scratch.

Jamaica posed a different problem. There was no colour bar on the island but the richer of the white settlers tended to send their children to England or Canada to be educated – partly to secure them a better education; partly, no doubt, to ensure that they were not contaminated by association with their black contemporaries. If such migrant pupils were allowed to enter the competition for a Rhodes Scholarship they would obviously be better quali-fied than somebody given inferior schooling at home. No black Scholar would ever be selected. The Trustees decided to compromise: every third year the Scholarship would be reserved for a boy who had been educated in Jamaica. The principle was never formally discarded, but between 1909 and 1914 every Scholarship went to a boy educated in Jamaica. There were no pure blacks among them, but two at least were of mixed blood. One was Norman Manley, a brilliant lawyer, architect of Jamaica's independence and for seven years its Chief Minister. It is ironic that one of the first conspicuous successes among the Rhodes Scholars should have been a man whom Cecil Rhodes would almost certainly have felt an unworthy recipient of his Scholarship.

'The whole matter is an experiment,' Rhodes had told the Archbishop of South Africa, when expounding his master plan for the Scholarships.[18] Given the number of changes he made to his Will in the last few years of his life and his notably pragmatic approach to the detailed application of his great idea, it is at least possible that he would have revised the list of Scholarships when he found some of them were producing better results than others. It was not to be, however; the Trustees were free to add additional Scholarships if the funds were there – as they had quickly done in Canada – but could not try to remove any Scholarship listed in Rhodes's Will without the most fearful legal pother and the probability of eventual defeat. All they could do was hope that the educational systems in the weaker constituencies would be so much improved that the standard of the candidates would rise. It seemed reasonable to expect that, as Rhodes Scholars from Oxford returned to their own countries, some at least of them would put their energies into bringing about this regeneration. Unfortunately, when it came to the point, not all Rhodes Scholars *did* return to their own countries.

In 1909, in an article in the *Fortnightly Review*, a Mr Vaile casually threw in the charge that almost no Rhodes Scholars returned to 'the countries that take advantage of the great South African's munificence'. Wylie roundly contended that this was nonsense. Almost every American and German had returned to his country; of the seventy-eight colonials who had left Oxford, six or seven were still in England, another ten elsewhere, mainly in the Empire.[19] Even on Wylie's figures, however, nearly a quarter of the colonial Scholars had not gone home. When asked whether Rhodes would have viewed this as a dereliction, Wylie would reply that, while the Founder certainly assumed return to the homeland would be the normal course of a Scholar's career, he had not expected that such a return would necessarily be immediate, nor had he ruled out the possibility that a Scholar's duty might keep him away from home. The Trustees did not impose any condition on candidates about where they should make their life after Oxford, nor would they even press them to return home. There were, indeed, often excellent reasons for staying abroad. Allan Thomson was not the only New Zealander to find that his skills were not needed in his homeland; Michell was not the only inhabitant of South Africa to conclude that the education of the Rhodes Scholars had not equipped them for the tasks that needed doing when they returned from abroad.

What, after all, was home? If a Tasmanian, finding no suitable occupation in his own island, took a job in Sydney or Melbourne, was he defeating the intentions of Cecil Rhodes? If an Australian found employment in the Indian Civil Service was he not doing just what the Founder would have wished? The Trustees certainly felt he was. To their mind, the Australian sweltering in the Punjab was serving the ideals of Rhodes far more effectively than the American Scholar who returned to Philadelphia and made a comfortable living as a lawyer without concerning himself too much about the world's fight. In his Will Rhodes had stressed his hope that their education at Oxford would instil in the minds of Scholars 'the advantage to the Colonies as well as to the United Kingdom of the retention of the unity of the Empire'. If the Rhodes Scholar was serving that cause then surely it made no difference where he chose to do it? If not a quarter but half or even three-quarters of the colonial Rhodes Scholars were to make their careers in other countries, it would signify nothing provided the work they were doing served the Founder's ends. The Empire was an entity far greater than the sum of its parts and he who could demonstrate that he was working for that entity was doing all that the Trustees or Rhodes himself could have asked of him.

CHAPTER TWELVE
FIRST IMPRESSIONS

By 1914 enough Rhodes Scholars were or had been at Oxford to allow some tentative conclusions about how the experience had affected them. In 1962 the then Warden of Rhodes House, Edgar Williams, summed up the cycle of the Rhodes Scholar in words that applied as well half a century earlier. When he is first awarded the Scholarship the successful Scholar's reaction is nearly always that there must have been a mistake; he cannot possibly possess the semi-divine attributes which Rhodes demanded in his elect. Next comes the realisation that no mistake had been made: 'Quite a lot of fuss is made of him, particularly locally, and he comes to regard himself as a very remarkable chap, although in most cases he keeps his head about it.' Finally he arrives at Oxford, still conscious of his glory, and finds, 'in some cases to his surprise, that he is of no importance at all, and the one thing Oxford requires of these leaders of tomorrow is that they should not start leading today'.[1] Rhodes Scholars from the first two or three years enjoyed some modest curiosity value: overseas students were in those days rarities and this was a new and interesting species. Soon the novelty wore off: the Scholars were taken for what they were – students a little older than most of their undergraduate contemporaries, but often of no other obvious distinction.

Almost always the Scholars accepted their demotion with good grace, indeed with relief. Their object was to blend in and become accepted: certainly to excel, since an element of competitiveness was almost by definition part of the make-up of any successful candidate, but not to stand out too prominently from the herd. Nearly all of them avoided the trap of undue anglicisation, but they managed too to shed, or at least temper, any national characteristic that would have made them too conspicuous. They took enthusiastically to college life: the sport, the revelry, the anguished debates that continued late into the night.

The real troubles began for the Rhodes Scholars when they finished their time at Oxford and returned home. Sometimes they were ignored, found that they had grown away from their friends and associates, were not offered rewarding work. More often they were greeted as returning heroes and given every opportunity to demonstrate their transcendent merits. In the first case they were lonely and demoralised, in the second borne down by an awful burden of responsibility. They were heroes, so they must behave like heroes – the second best was not admissible. 'When he returns,' explained Parkin, 'much is expected of him, and if he is not a man of inherent strength he causes disappointment and the blame is laid on Oxford for having, as one University President said, "taken the punch out of him". He probably never had it in him.'[2] Worse still, as Rhodes Scholars they had been charged with the duty of putting the world to rights; if they did anything less they would be betraying the trust that had been put in them. It was often said of Rhodes Scholars that they were men 'with a great future behind them'. For the Scholars themselves the joke had a sour taste. Had they indeed experienced their finest hour? Were they to spend the rest of their lives blaming themselves for not living up to standards that were unattainable? In some this showed itself in an exaggerated hankering for an Oxford which in truth had never existed but which seemed more real every year that they spent away from it. Earle Murray, the first editor of the *American Alumni Magazine*, the journal that was later to be reborn as the *American Oxonian*, wrote that his correspondence with former Scholars showed that 'it is above all the "Spirit of Oxford" that is missed. If any fear is to be expressed it is not that Oxford has had no influence and will be too soon forgotten, but that Oxford has had too much influence and will be too long remembered.'[3] 'If such is our apprehension, where can be the harm?' Murray concluded. The answer lay in the peculiar burdens which the Rhodes Scholars laid upon themselves. Like Ernest Dowson's decadent lover they were 'desolate and sick of an old passion', but as well as wallowing luxuriously in nostalgia they felt the bracing trumpet call of duty. It was their destiny to do great things for humanity, yet all too often humanity seemed neither to recognise the need nor to provide the necessary openings.

It is, of course, easy to make too much of this. A large majority of former Scholars, after some initial qualms, settled down to make the best use they could of their abilities and the opportunities offered them by society. A few indulged in agonising heart-searching; most hardly ever thought about it or, if they did, reckoned that they were doing their best and no more could be hoped for. But there was a burden of expectation: the expectation of others and, more urgent, the expectation within themselves. The Rhodes Scholar who was placidly content was to be found, but he was something of a rarity.

In those early years the burden seemed particularly unfair because a large number of Rhodes Scholars were commonplace in their abilities – the extraordinary was being demanded of the ordinary. Wylie's reports abound in mildly disparaging comments. 'Diligent', 'industrious', 'pleasant', 'kindly', are the words of praise most commonly employed; 'he means well and is not without interest in some of the sides of Oxford life' is a typically tepid judgment. Sometimes he was sharper in his criticism. One of the German Scholars had given more time to amusement than to study – 'a pleasant fellow but wanting in character', judged Wylie. The Nevada Scholar of 1908 played rugger for his college but 'has not shown any intellectual ability and his work is poor'; N.E. Ensign of Illinois worked hard but still only got a fourth. 'Not a particularly interesting man,' judged Wylie, 'well-meaning but somewhat limited. How did he get elected?'[4] Of course there were stars in one or other of Oxford's constellations but they were few and far between. In 1910 forty-four of the Scholars taking their finals got seconds or thirds; there were four firsts but also four fourths and three fails. 'We have to recognise', Wylie summed up, 'that we have not yet succeeded everywhere in getting the best men. I feel this especially about the United States: not because the American Scholars are, on the average, weaker than those from our own Colonies, but rather because the supply in the United States, not of scholarship but of *ability*, is such that we might reasonably have hoped to obtain as Rhodes Scholars invariably men of mark, or at least of promise.'[5]

'Promise' was, of course, all important: what mattered was not what a Rhodes Scholar did at Oxford but how he fared in later life. It was not reasonable to expect men who were at the most in their early thirties to have made any great strides in their chosen fields, but by 1914 it was possible to form some tentative impressions about what those fields were going to be. Rhodes would have been disconcerted to see how many Scholars found their way to schools or universities. From the first year alone three Scholars were awarded fellowships at Oxford colleges. The Trustees congratulated themselves but wondered what the Founder would have thought. In fact it would be eleven years before another Scholar won an Oxford fellowship, but the flow into academic life went on.[6] Rhodes would have known that to form the minds of the next generation was a noble and responsible role. He would have accepted too Parkin's argument that in America 'Universities and colleges have a more direct influence upon public opinion than is the case in this country'[7] – a former head of Princeton, Woodrow Wilson, was indeed, when Parkin wrote, President of the United States. But he would still have wished that, in the colonies at least, more of his Scholars had chosen a life in public affairs rather than join the ranks of the 'remote and ineffectual' dons.

Second only to teaching, Rhodes Scholars flocked into the law. Michell had complained that in South Africa too many Scholars joined an already over-crowded bar; the same was as true in Canada and the United States. Rhodes would have comforted himself with the thought that the law was traditionally a jumping-off ground for public work – Norman Manley was far from being the only Rhodes Scholar to progress from the bar to the highest levels of government – but, once again, it was not the sort of work he had imagined his Scholars taking on when he had dreamed his dream. Where were the idealists, the adventurers, the toilers in the imperial field? Instead there was a bunch of, on the whole, intelligent, honourable and diligent young men, doing respectable work in respectable careers but not yet showing many signs of great achievement, still less of building a new Empire.

His judgment on this first decade of Scholars would probably have been a cautious: 'Not bad, but could do better.' They were to do better; the process was both made more easy and yet brutally checked by the watershed of the First World War.

CHAPTER THIRTEEN

THE FIRST WORLD WAR

Those responsible for the activities of the Rhodes Trust can hardly be blamed for sharing the illusion of most of the inhabitants of the British Isles that the war would be over in a few months. Parkin, perhaps, could have been more prescient when, early in 1915, he told Aydelotte that 'Surely things will be normal in October, 1916',[1] but even by then few people had taken in the protracted horror that lay ahead. For the first few months of the war, at least, it was assumed that this was only a brief hiatus in civilised life and that normal service would quickly be resumed. Most of the colonial Rhodes Scholars followed the example of their British counterparts and volunteered to fight against Germany; so far as the eighty or so American Scholars then at Oxford were concerned, however, there seemed no immediate reason why their studies should be interrupted.

Parkin certainly believed that this was so. When Aydelotte asked him, shortly after the outbreak of war, whether 1914's generation of Scholars should come over in the usual way, Parkin, without even consulting the Trustees, replied that he 'couldn't possibly conceive that there would be any objection to their doing so'.[2] Milner was more dubious. If Oxford decided to carry on, he told Wylie, 'a course of the wisdom of which I am doubtful – it would not do for us to work against the decision of the University authorities by gratuitously advising our Scholars not to come'. If asked for advice, however, Milner suggested that it would not be going too far to point out that the ordinary life of the University would inevitably be much interfered with and that the new Scholars might at least consider deferring their arrival for a while.[3] To this Parkin retorted that never could 'acquaintance with England be of more use than when it is in this great struggle for right and the liberty of the nation'.[4] Wylie backed Parkin; in the summer of 1915 he was still maintaining that, so long as Oxford did not shut down altogether, the presence of the surviving Rhodes Scholars would be an important asset: 'It has been a good thing for them and for Oxford that they have been here.'[5]

As the demands of war bit ever deeper into Oxford life this line became harder to maintain. The 3,097 undergraduates in residence in 1914 became 1,087 in 1915 and 550 in 1916, many of the younger dons too had left and some colleges were so depleted that any sort of communal life became impossible. Sadly, Wylie concluded that, though academic life still dragged on in an emaciated form, 'it was impossible for a man to get out of Oxford the things that made the Scholarships valuable. He went away without having known what we generally mean by Oxford.'[6] The Scholars themselves grew discontented. 'The old buoyancy, liveliness and vigor has given way to soberness, and an almost sombre hush,' wrote Brand Blanshard, an American Scholar who had come up in 1913.[7] It was disagreeable to live in a country totally absorbed by a conflict in which you could not take part, especially when feelings grew against those who were deemed to be shirking their responsibilities. One Rhodes Scholar told Parkin that he 'could not stand any more the way in which the girls looked at him in Oxford'.[8] By 1918 only nine Scholars, including two Americans, were in residence, several of them doing work in one way or another connected with the national war effort.

Even from the start some of the American Scholars had contrived to quiet their consciences without defying President Wilson's plea to his countrymen to observe neutrality by working in ambulances or in relief schemes in Belgium; in 1914 more than half of them worked with the YMCA in military camps during the Christmas vacation. A few were not content with a non-belligerent role. Even before America finally entered the war, four Scholars left to join the French artillery. William Fleet, a Scholar from an earlier generation, joined the Grenadier Guards in 1916 and was killed two years later: 'So the Scholarship bears fruit,' wrote Parkin proudly.[9] In the United States the former Rhodes Scholars were almost unanimous in their support for Britain. Frederic Schrader, a propagandist for Germany in the United States, inveighed against the efforts of Scholars to draw America into the war, claiming that 'the virus of high treason under the mask of serving civilisation has penetrated the whole political system of our country'.[10] 'We must frankly plead guilty to the charge,' admitted the American Oxonian with some satisfaction.[11] When America finally entered the war in April 1917, Parkin reported that all the best young men were volunteering for national service. He called for an immediate suspension of elections: 'We cannot afford to have slackers, or men exempted for physical defects, coming over to us. And it would be very unfair to the finer type of man, who at once tried to do his duty.'[12] The Trustees heeded his call; the elections for 1917 were cancelled, with the proviso that everyone who would have been eligible to come forward would still be free to do so once the war was over.[13]

By the time the war ended, 240 Rhodes Scholars from the British Empire had taken part. Eighty-three had gained honours and distinctions. When the final tally was in it was known that seventy had died. 'It is terribly sad to feel that all these splendid young fellows are taken away before they had a chance to prove what they can do in life,' wrote Parkin. 'It must be our consolation that these lives are not "lost" but given to their country.'[14] Such platitudes today are customarily derided; yet a majority of the victims would probably have said something very similar.

At a Rhodes dinner in 1914 Parkin was explaining how the German Scholars, of whom there were fifteen present, fitted into the Founder's vision of the future. A 'rather exhilarated' Scholar from British Columbia shouted out, 'Damned spies – every one of them!' and was carried out by his friends.[15] Not many of his contemporaries would have expressed themselves with such ferocity, but not a few felt that the German Scholarships did not fit in with the system as a whole. The outbreak of war was seen as an excellent opportunity to get rid of them for ever. This was not at all Parkin's view. When a story appeared in the press suggesting that their abolition was inevitable he 'took the earliest opportunity of repudiating this suggestion. I am sure that the Trustees feel as I do that it would seem very petty and unbecoming to do anything of the kind.'[16] To Aydelotte he said that it would be some years before the Germans could be expected to return but 'the Scholarships will be here for them to take when they want them'.[17] The Trustees were somewhat less high-minded than their standard-bearer. Milner agreed with Parkin, but more on grounds of expediency than principle. To abolish the German Scholarships would involve varying the terms of the Trust and this could only be done with the approval of Parliament. 'Once you open that door, goodness knows how many fads you might let in,' he told the historian and ardent imperialist John Marriott. 'You and I would be agreed that any change should take the form of giving more Scholarships to the Empire, but could a majority of the House of Commons be counted on to take the Imperial view?'[18]

By early 1916, however, public opinion had become so incensed against the Germans that Milner concluded further delay would seriously damage the reputation of the Trust. Michell alone stood out, partly, it seems, from pique that he was not being properly consulted. Rhodes 'was very farsighted and liked to plan his work over a long period', he told Parkin. 'In any case, one Trustee is as good as another and I refuse to be "rushed".'[19] Rosebery pleaded with him not to sabotage the bill which was now ready to go before Parliament and which provided for new Scholarships to be distributed around the Empire in place of Germany. 'If the Bill is withdrawn,' he concluded menacingly, 'withdrawal will be attributed to you and great inconvenience caused.'[20]

Eventually Michell gave way, but with bad grace. 'I entirely dislike parliamentary intervention,' he wrote, 'which may lead to our having to take orders from the Charity Commissioners! I equally dislike having to create new Scholarships, especially specified Scholarships.' But for his respect for Rhodes's memory, he concluded, and his reluctance 'to back out of what I have always regarded as a sacred trust, I would resign my Trusteeship and publish my reasons in full'.[21]

Part at least of Michell's cantankerousness stemmed from his belief that the Scholarship reserved for Stellenbosch deserved abolition every bit as much as its German counterparts. Already one former Stellenbosch Scholar had been arrested in the Transvaal for taking part in an Afrikaner anti-war rebellion. The young Stellenbosch students of the future were going to be '*much worse than the Germans*', he told Milner. If the Trustees were logical they would reject 'all disloyal nominations everywhere'. The logical conclusion of the present proceedings was that, if Britain were to quarrel seriously with the United States, the American Scholarships would in their turn have to be abolished. The Trustees' decision 'would destroy the whole spirit and intent of this great and original Will'.[22] Milner was not impressed by this line of argument, very reasonably distinguishing between a country with which one was at war and one with the policies of which one disagreed. The political opinions of Scholars were not the business of the Trustees. In 1918 another Rhodes Scholar from Stellenbosch, A. H. Brocksma, told the Rector of Exeter that he was an ardent Nationalist, opposed to British rule and deeply disapproving of Rhodes and his ideal. Exeter rejected him, but Wylie offered to put his name to another college. The Trustees supported Wylie; it was, they agreed, 'impossible for them to conduct any sort of inquisition into a Scholar's opinions'. Fortunately they were saved further embarrassment by Brocksma's decision to renounce the Scholarship.[23]

Long before the decision to abolish the German Scholarships had been taken, the scramble was on to secure a part of the booty. H. A. L. Fisher argued the case for France: 'the future of Europe depends on the closest possible co-operation between France and England'; various Governors in the West Indies pleaded for the 'ancient and loyal colonies'; Austen Chamberlain spoke for India; Gilbert Murray insisted that 'so far as I understand what was in Mr Rhodes's mind, the Scandinavians would be the right successors to the Germans'.[24] The Trustees' first line of defence was that, since De Beers would be producing little or nothing over the next years, the Trust needed every penny they could save from the German Scholarships.[25] By 1916, however, savings from the other suspended Scholarships were so substantial that this position could no longer be held; some new Scholarships must be created. As Milner had feared, an internationalist lobby led by Lord Hugh Cecil proposed that they should be awarded on a worldwide basis; this attack was beaten off, however, and the Trustees were empowered to allocate the new Scholarships within the Empire.[26] Three went to South Africa – one to the Transvaal, one to the Orange Free State and one to alternate between Kimberley and Port Elizabeth; the fourth was given to the Prairie Provinces of Canada.

Twelve German Rhodes Scholars died in action in the First World War, one at least of them having refused to fight against the English, only to be killed in Russia.[27] A group of Scholars in the German Foreign Office claimed to have opposed the war so far as they were able, though not pushing their opposition to the point of resignation. One of them, the anglophile Count Bernstorff, managed to get a letter to Wylie in July 1915. 'Fate has built up a wall between us,' he lamented, 'and to my mind it seems to be one of the greatest tragedies in history that we should fight against [one] another, where we might give and exchange and work together. . . . Oxford was a great and beautiful experience to me and many others, and we are grateful for it.' In an earlier letter he had asked what the Trustees thought 'of the future of the German Scholarships'.[28] In 1915 the future of the German Scholarships was not a matter to which the Trustees were likely to give much thought. But the knowledge that there was a group of well-disposed Germans eager to do what they could to heal the breach must have been of some comfort to anyone considering how Germany should be handled after the war. An American Rhodes Scholar who served with the Armistice Commission in Berlin in December 1918 told Wylie that 'the entire German Foreign Office was being run by Rhodes Scholars'. They too asked anxiously what the future was for the German Scholarships. They too got no answer.

By the end of the war most of Rhodes's original Trustees had departed the scene; their replacements, however, were very much in the same tradition. Alfred Beit had died in 1906; after that there were no further casualties until Hawksley fell gravely ill at the end of 1915. 'I don't think our business will suffer in the least,' Milner told Rosebery with some brutality, 'rather the contrary.'[29] Hawksley's dilatoriness and idiosyncratic ways of working had made him a liability in recent years; the lesson Milner drew from this was that no future solicitor to the Trust should be himself a Trustee. Hawksley died a few days later, Grey followed in August 1917 and Jameson after another three months. The death of Jameson in particular, because of his close relationship to Rhodes, seemed to the other Trustees disastrous. At their meeting of 13 December they recorded 'their sense of the irreparable loss which they have suffered in the death of Dr Jameson, who in the work and in their hearts stands second only to the Founder'. A few months earlier Rosebery had told Milner he felt he should resign on his seventieth birthday. 'From my want of knowledge of South Africa's affairs, I have never been of much use,' he wrote, adding with some complacency: 'The Scholarships now go of themselves.'[30] Michell hastened to say that he too would go. He was persuaded to hold on for a few more months, but by the beginning of 1918 Milner was the only survivor of the original Trustees. As he was in the War Cabinet at the time his hands were clearly going to be extremely full.

If Michell had had his way, there would not have been much for Milner or any other Trustee to do. At the end of 1915 he had suggested transferring the Scholarship funds to the authorities at Oxford: 'They at any rate would always administer the Bequest on Educational lines, such as Rhodes himself would approve.'[31] Milner was horrified at the thought. 'I am all for converting ourselves into a formal Trust,' he told Michell (something that was duly done in 1916 after Hawksley's death),

> but I am dead against our handing it over to Oxford. . . . I am quite sure we could not render a greater disservice to Oxford itself than by giving up our independent position as regards the Scholarships. The last thing we want is to have them run by Dons with donnish ideas. . . . No body of typically Oxford Dons could possibly have done what Parkin has. . . . [T]he thing will never work as it ought to work, or produce the effect that Rhodes intended it to produce, if you get a lot of crusted old Dons to run it.[32]

New Trustees were urgently needed, but they had to be men who could be relied on to manage affairs in the way which the Founder had laid down. He had discussed the matter with Rosebery, Milner told Michell, and they had agreed that at least three younger men were called for: the first someone in the Rhodes tradition; the second a lawyer; the third – somewhat surprisingly, given Milner's view of the genus – a prominent academic. The first was relatively easy to provide. Alfred Beit's nephew Otto was a man very much in the mould of his uncle and notably sympathetic to Rhodes's ideas; the only drawback to his appointment, in Milner's view, was that 'the present craze against Germans might provoke some opposition'.[33] If it did, it was ignored. Beit was invited to become a Trustee in 1917 and accepted with alacrity. The need for a lawyer and an academic seems quickly to have been forgotten. The second new Trustee was Lord Lovat, one of the founders of the Round Table and an ardent imperialist. Miner told him that up till now little had been done beyond the running of the Scholarships, 'but in future we shall I believe have the opportunity of much more extended usefulness'. There would be a lot of money to be given away, and it was vital that its disposal 'should be in the hands of people who sympathise with the aims of Rhodes and have at least some of his breadth of vision'.[34]

The third recruit was also an ardent admirer of Rhodes. 'No words could give any idea of that great spirit's power or the extent to which the country worshipped him,' Rudyard Kipling had written at the time of the Founder's death.[35] Rhodes was as admiring of Kipling, and had offered him for life the Woolsack, a house in the grounds of Groote Schuur. He accepted without hesitation when invited to become a Trustee: it was, his wife wrote in her diary, 'a bit of work he would like more than any else'.[36] With such allies as these, Milner could feel confident that Rhodes's legacy was in safe hands. The don and the lawyer could come later.

CHAPTER FOURTEEN
PLAY RESUMED

The Oxford which resumed normal life in the autumn of 1919 was bound to be almost intolerably over-crowded. Some at least of the undergraduates who had been up in 1914 and who had survived the war would want to finish their courses; many of those who would have come up in 1914 or over the next five years were similarly anxious to complete their education; finally, the new generation of eighteen- and nineteen-year-olds felt no inclination to stand aside and wait till their seniors had earned their degrees. It would have been difficult for the Oxford Secretary to find places even for the normal annual intake of Rhodes Scholars. As it was he was faced by an almost impossible task. Wylie had concluded that two hundred Scholars was the maximum Oxford could be asked to accommodate at any time; by the beginning of the academic years of 1920–1 the total was already 282; for another year at least it was likely to get still larger. To compound the problem, the number of overseas students from other sources had risen sharply. It would have gone badly for the Rhodes Scholars if their predecessors had not generally made so good an impression that the colleges were prepared to cram still more of them into their already stretched accommodation. But there must be a limit to what was possible. 'We shall less and less be able to rely on the colleges showing our Scholars specialist consideration,' Wylie warned the Trustees. 'This gives increasing importance to the quality of the Scholars elected. Already it is very desirable, and in time it will be essential, that Rhodes Scholars should stand out as unmistakably representative of the best that the Dominions or the United States can offer.'[1]

There were a few preliminaries to be decided. Should Scholars who had refused to fight for their country be allowed to take up their Scholarships? The Trustees probably hoped the point would never arise, but Ordean Rockey, who had been selected in 1917 for Pennsylvania, declared himself a pacifist when the United States entered the war and wrote to ask whether this would affect his Scholarship. Unsurprisingly, given the feeling of the times, he was told that his award had been cancelled. He wrote again and was again rebuffed, then announced he was coming to England to plead his cause. This would be 'a mere waste of time and money', Wylie assured him, but he persisted. 'In America, in school and college, we, as students, were told what the spirit of sportsmanship means and, translated for us by a great American, that spirit commands: "Don't foul, don't shirk, but hit the line hard!" This is the spirit I have been obeying and am glad to obey in my attempt to become a Rhodes Scholar.' He won Wylie's heart, saw Milner and Lovat who were politely non-committal, then confronted Parkin, who felt very doubtful about the whole matter at first, but ended by supporting him: 'I think he has good stuff in him.' Parkin's voice prevailed; Rockey was reinstated. The original cancellation of the Scholarship, reflected Wylie, 'was as understandably human as its subsequent restoration was semi-sublime'. [2]

A more complicated issue concerned those Scholars who would have been at Oxford during the war, found continued celibacy intolerable, married and now wished to start or complete their studies. The problem was first posed when an Australian Scholar who had come up in October 1914, joined up three months later and married in 1916, asked whether he could return to Oxford after the war. Wylie was predictably sympathetic. A married man was not what Rhodes envisaged, he wrote, but 'these fellows have made sacrifices for a national cause. I do not suppose that the number would be great.'[3] The Trustees initially took a harder line, but by the end of the war there were twenty-one such cases. The colleges wanted them back, with or without wives, pleaded Wylie; to refuse them would be to treat them more harshly than the British undergraduates and would leave them with a sense of grievance.[4] Milner and Kipling still hesitated, Kipling in particular. Married Scholars, he argued, would be cut off from their college and spend their stipends on domestic housekeeping: 'Thus they will be handicapped in all matters of sport and fellowship and will make a species apart from all institutional life.'[5] In the end he grudgingly gave way, but only on the strict understanding that the Scholar was already married and not taking unfair advantage of the Trustees' generosity. One Scholar, who had spent several years in the Army, decided that this was a bluff and married early in 1920. He forfeited his Scholarship, though he contrived to stay on at Oxford and eventually was given a grant which compensated him for some of his loss.[6]

Though Rhodes Scholars were generally older than their British contemporaries, the reimposition of celibacy was acceptable to most of them. Oxford in the 1920s was still massively masculine; mixed colleges would have seemed certainly distasteful, probably immoral; women huddled in bleak caravanserais on the fringes of the University. There were occasional revolts, however. In 1931 Carl Spaeth from New Hampshire, in his third year, admitted to having been married for two months. He claimed to have been misled by Aydelotte, who had said that Scholars in their third year might be allowed to marry, but since he had taken trouble to conceal his marriage it did not seem that he had much confidence in this assurance. Aydelotte insisted that he had done no more than say that Scholars whose third years had been deferred *might* be allowed to return to Oxford with a wife (as he himself had done), but there was enough confusion to mean that the Trustees felt justified in allowing Spaeth to stay on, though with his wife exiled from Oxford.[7] When the Canadian David Lewis brought his fiancée to England he was similarly told he must leave her in London, since her presence in Oxford would 'disturb his studies and stop him integrating in university life'. If this rule was not strictly enforced, he was told, there would be a colony of fiancées in Oxford. 'Why this should pose such a menace I never understood,' wrote Lewis.[8] Robert Penn Warren got away with it; marrying in his third year but never admitting the fact. 'He is not exactly the kind of ideal Rhodes Scholar of whom we sometimes think,' wrote Wylie, 'but we may be glad in the future to claim Warren as an old Rhodes Scholar for he is certainly a man of ability and character'[9] – a perceptive judgment, since Warren was to become America's first Poet Laureate and the only person ever to win Pulitzer Prizes for both poetry and fiction.

The level of the stipend was another point that had quickly to be settled. Wartime inflation meant that the £300 a year (roughly speaking £7,500 at current values) which had seemed generous before the war was now barely if at all sufficient. 'Trustees may feel that there's no money, or that it's too early to fix an amount,' suggested Wylie: a possibility might be to award a temporary bonus of £50 a year and review the situation later. As he no doubt anticipated, the Trustees were happy to grasp at a solution which saved them from making any final commitment; as he no doubt also anticipated, a year later it was obvious that the bonus could not be rescinded and the stipend was fixed at £350.[10] But this was still not enough for some. In 1921 Behan argued that the cost of transport from Australia and New Zealand was unfairly high compared with that from any other Rhodes constituency. A special allowance should be made. The Trust could not afford it, was the reply, and even if it had been able to it would be invidious to discriminate in favour of one country or another. Though the Scholarship might not cover total expenses, it was still 'incomparably larger than any other scholarship offered in England and there are obvious objections to accentuating this disproportion'. The best chance for the Australian Scholars lay in persuading the shipping companies to be more generous.[11]

The new Rhodes Scholar was told from the start that he would be well advised to add £100 or so of his own money each year to the stipend if he wanted to get the full benefits from his Scholarship. This caused offence to some egalitarians. The *South African Review* wrote angrily that, if the funds did not exist to increase the stipend to a realistic figure, then the number of Scholarships should be cut. The present situation reflected the attitude of 'certain Trustees of Tory (we almost said snobbish) proclivities who think that young fellows with a private income are likely to be more "classy" than penniless ones. Rhodes must be turning in his grave.'[12] Uneasily, Otto Beit admitted that, though the phraseology was offensive, 'I am afraid there is a certain amount of truth in the statements.'[13] But money really was short. Even if they had wanted to reduce the number of Scholarships the Trustees could not have done so without great pother; there was not much to be done. They managed to increase the stipend by a further £50 in 1925 and then a period of deflation followed. It was another fifteen years, and in a very different world, before the annual stipend was again increased.

CHAPTER FIFTEEN

THE TRUST BETWEEN THE WARS

Apart from the two world wars which so disastrously interrupted the work of the Rhodes Trust there are two years above all in which the operations of the Trust seemed to take on a changed momentum. The second was 1959; the first, manifesting more of a change in the balance of power than of policy, was 1925.

The Trust had, indeed, evolved considerably between the end of the war and that date. Until 1919 the potent figure of Parkin had been privy to every important decision; never a Trustee himself but so much the founding figure that his views were considered with some deference even by men as autocratic as Rosebery or Milner. The day-to-day running of the office was left to a series of superior functionaries, reporting in practice to Hawksley, who were not expected to influence policy and generally got short shrift if they tried to do so. Boyd, Mrs Mavor, Gilmour, were indispensable but insignificant: when Mrs Mavor had the temerity to fall ill, Rosebery wrote indignantly: 'a bedridden female Secretary is really an absurdity, if not a scandal'.[1] Thomas Gilmour, who took over from Mrs Mavor, was neither female nor, generally, bedridden, but he was on a month's notice and was given the job on the understanding that his appointment would end automatically 'within a month of the declaration of peace'.[2] By then Parkin was on the way out; still to remain associated with the Trust for another year or so but no longer expected to exert himself or contribute much to the making of policy. 'My idea', Milner told Beit early in 1919, 'has always been that, at no very distant date, we should pension Parkin liberally, roll his position and that of the Secretary into one, and get a thoroughly able youngish man of progressive ideas to fill it.'[3]

Edward Grigg filled the bill admirably. He was a journalist on *The Times*, whose father had been in the Indian Civil Service and who had shown conspicuous gallantry and ability as a wartime soldier. He was youngish – under forty – and, if not notably progressive, had edited the *Round Table* and

was imbued with the most impeccably imperialist ideas. He was also opinionated, arrogant and unable to understand why other people could not see
things as clearly as he did himself. He was a compulsive reorganiser and rarely
stopped to think whether his proposed reforms would be acceptable to those
involved or compatible with the obligations imposed by Rhodes's Will.

He was a protégé of Milner and moulded in the great proconsul's image.
Milner may sometimes have questioned the younger man's impetuosity, but
with his objectives he whole-heartedly concurred. In the long run two such
assertive and abrasive characters would almost inevitably have clashed. The
run, however, was not to be long enough. Almost before he had settled in
Grigg was abruptly uprooted and despatched to accompany the Prince of
Wales, the future King Edward VIII, on his first Empire tour. In theory he was
supposed to take advantage of this expedition to make contact with Rhodes
Scholars around the world and inspect the workings of the system; in practice
he found himself more than occupied by the activities of his wayward master.
When he did have time to look out for Scholars he found the experience disil-
lusioning. There were, he felt, too many lawyers and doctors preoccupied by
their careers, too few civil servants, journalists, politicians, people striving to
improve the standards of the nation: 'Too many Rhodes Scholars look upon
the Bequest simply as a means to making better livings for themselves.'[4]

While he was thus preoccupied, another protégé of Milner's, Geoffrey
Dawson, was enlisted as caretaker. Dawson was a smoother character than
Grigg, but as a former member of Milner's Kindergarten and a devoted recruit
to the Round Table he was equally attuned to the ideals of Cecil Rhodes. He
had served during the war as editor of *The Times*, but in 1921 was relatively
under-employed and delighted to help out in so worthy a cause. He was to
become temporary Secretary again when Grigg took leave to act as Lloyd
George's private secretary, only to hand back the duties for a second time
when Lloyd George's government fell in 1923. The boxing and coxing was
then over; by the time Grigg left the Trust again to become Governor of Kenya,
Dawson had returned to *The Times* and become a Trustee himself. The consequence of this bewildering series of interchanges was that neither of these two
powerful and intensely active men ever fully settled into the role. In 1925 it
was obvious that another 'thoroughly able youngish man of progressive ideas'
had to be found and that this time it must be someone who would stick rather
longer in the job.

Several of the Trustees with whom such a man would have to work were
newly in place at this time. Leo Amery had become a Trustee in 1919 and was
to remain a central figure for more than thirty-five years. He was himself
almost a caricature of what a Rhodes Scholar should be: a first in greats, fellow
of All Souls, half-blue for athletics, intrepid mountaineer. He had been

enthused by a lecture from Parkin on imperialism while still a schoolboy, had preceded Grigg as colonial editor on *The Times* and in 1919, on Milner's insistence, had served under him as Under-Secretary at the Colonial Office. The encouragement of migration to the Empire – 'overseas settlement' as he preferred it to be known – was his most cherished cause. So long as he served as a Trustee it was certain that the ideals of the Founder would never be forgotten.[5] In 1925 he was joined by Dawson; Edward Peacock, a Canadian who as a schoolboy had had Parkin as his headmaster and who was now a director of that most patrician among merchant banks, Baring Brothers; Douglas Hogg, future Lord Hailsham, the Attorney General; and H. A. L. Fisher, former Minister of Education and newly appointed Warden of New College. At Kipling's suggestion his cousin, the Prime Minister Stanley Baldwin, was also asked to join. Baldwin's membership was more decorative than useful; when, in 1941, it was suggested that his portrait should be hung in Rhodes House, Amery supported the proposal with the cautious judgment: 'He has not done very much as a Trustee, but he has an interesting face.'[6]

The appointment of Fisher, the first Oxford head of house to become a Trustee, followed shortly after the death of Milner. Milner's death, and the subsequent departure of Grigg to Kenya, threw the Trustees into some disarray. It was a great shock, Wylie told Aydelotte, 'and will certainly shake the Rhodes edifice for the time being'. Wylie had been a champion of Grigg – 'keen as mustard – the best they could want to have, I should think', and he was nervous about any possible replacement: 'I rather shudder at the prospect of a new man, ignorant of the history of the last twenty years.'[7] On this point at least he had no reason for concern. The new man, Philip Kerr, knew much about the history of the last twenty years; as a member of Milner's Kindergarten (a role which he said he cherished more than any honour that had ever come his way) and a devotee of the Round Table he seemed, indeed, almost boringly in the mould of his predecessors.[8] But though he was also close to Lionel Curtis, he did not share the latter's *idée fixe*. 'The Empire', he once told his friend, 'is a noble thing, but not fit to be God.'[9] 'I hesitate to profess myself an Imperialist,' he had told H. A. L. Fisher in 1905, and though he went on to say that his service in South Africa had largely converted him, he stressed that it was not the machinery of Empire which attracted him: 'I believe more can be done by making England the centre from which a "liberal education" radiates than all material bonds in the world.'[10] He was above all an internationalist; the fostering of the nation-state must inevitably lead to dissension and then war; the 'federation of mankind' should be the highest aim. What attracted him most about the Rhodes ideal was the call for a close association with the United States, 'and also France (in place of Germany) as a genuinely liberal power'.[11]

In espousing such beliefs Kerr distinguished himself markedly from his predecessor. 'Patriotism is the only sure foundation for a political faith,' Grigg wrote in 1936, while 'internationalism with its misty enthusiasms and perverted sense of duty is a treacherous mirage'.[12] He must, to some extent, have had Kerr in mind when he wrote those words. Kerr would almost have reversed Grigg's judgment: patriotism was the treacherous mirage, internationalism the sure foundation. To Kipling, who did indeed think that Empire, if not quite fit to be God, certainly had elements of the divine about it, Kerr's appointment seemed intolerable. He advanced several reasons for his opposition. Kerr was 'brilliantly clever, but he did not fight in the War'; he was closely associated with the obnoxious Lloyd George (so was Grigg, but that did not seem to have worried Kipling); his mixture of Catholicism and Christian Science was nauseating; so was his smile: all these no doubt contributed, but it was Kerr's internationalist leanings and lukewarm imperial fervour that must have been the decisive factors.[13] The appointment opened the Trust to grave misrepresentation, Mrs Kipling noted in her diary, and as her husband had so vociferously opposed it he felt that he must now retire: 'They try to persuade him to resign for some innocuous reason. He insists on the truth.'[14] If they had had any idea that Kipling felt so strongly about it, wrote Amery, the Trustees might have decided otherwise, but his resignation came as a surprise. 'Poor old Beit has been very much worried and distressed. I cannot say that it has worried me much because Kipling has not contributed anything that really mattered.'[15] Kipling continued to plague the Trustees long after he had ceased to be one of them. Even though he never used it he refused to give up the house on the Groote Schuur estate which Rhodes had offered him. They had tried to turn him out, he told his daughter, so that 'some tired artist, writer or musician could go down there and add to the uplift of South Africa by giving lectures on uplifting subjects or composing sonatas. . . . Translated, this means some sort of soft billet for some pet of the Trustees – possibly a pink Bolshie. . . . I declined with a certain amount of directness.'[16]

Kerr, who as heir to the Marquess of Lothian possessed a worldly consequence denied to Grigg or Dawson, would anyhow have stood a better chance than either of those two of establishing himself as General Secretary with a degree of independence. Beit, who had succeeded Milner as Chairman of the Trustees, and Lovat, who later took over, were both more easygoing and disinclined to be authoritarian. Kerr was able to strengthen his position. When his cousin died in March 1930 and he became Marquess of Lothian, owner of Blickling Hall, one of the finest Elizabethan houses in England, not to mention serving as Chancellor of the Duchy of Lancaster in Ramsay MacDonald's all-party Cabinet, it was obvious that he was as great a figure as any of the Trustees, perhaps greater.*[17] Amery, who succeeded Lovat as Chairman in 1933, must have been piqued when he was excluded from MacDonald's government while the Secretary of the Rhodes Trust found a place there, but he does not seem to have held any grudge against Lothian and the two men worked together amicably enough. Amery was more involved in the running of the Trust than Beit or Lovat had ever been, but the balance of power in the organisation had shifted in favour of the Secretary. Lothian knew that he was the servant of the Trust and he was meticulous in seeking its approval for any new departure of importance. His view, however, counted at least as much as that of any Trustee and he allowed himself a freedom of action which Grigg would have baulked at and Gilmour would not even have contemplated. The impression was generally held that Lothian was doing the Trust something of a honour by agreeing to remain in office; it did little harm but was, perhaps, not the healthiest basis for a relationship between a paid official and his board.

He had plenty to do to earn his pay. The Rhodes Trust Act of 1929 was made necessary by the need to secure approval for a radical reform of the system for allocating the American Scholarships. It will best be considered in later chapters. Fortunately for Kerr he had not yet inherited the marquessate, so he did not find himself required to debate in the House of Lords issues with which he was so intimately involved, but the preparation and passage of the bill involved him in an enormous amount of detailed work. The task was the more onerous because it coincided with a protracted and at times embittered debate between Kerr and the then Chairman, Otto Beit. The Rhodes–Beit Share Fund** had been carrying on quietly for more than twenty years, under no very clear control and accumulating much of its income. What was obvious was that its present uses bore little relationship to the purposes that Rhodes and Alfred Beit had had in mind when they set it up. Everyone agreed that it was high time that the structure was regularised. The tidy-minded Kerr, however, insisted that it must be established exactly why the Fund had been set up and on what the money had been spent. Otto Beit pleaded that sleeping dogs should be let lie: 'Honestly, I think it best not to enquire too deeply into those old matters but to take them for granted to some extent seeing that the past Trustees – Milner, Michell, Jameson, Rosebery and Hawksley – have all been parties to it.'[18] Thwarted in his quest for clarity, Kerr then insisted that, whatever it might have been used for in the past, things should be different in

---

*Lothian professed to loathe his transmogrification: 'A moribund House [of Lords],' he told Aydelotte, 'terrific financial complications and an absurd personal position. However, I shall carry on with the Trust for the present.'
**See p. 41 above.

future: 'It is no doubt reasonable to leave money to be expended on political or analogous purposes for a time. . . . But it is quite a different thing to continue such a Fund . . . when the political conditions are entirely different. . . . It seems to me very doubtful whether the present Rhodes Trustees ought to take any responsibility, direct or indirect, for continuing the application of the Fund for ordinary political purposes.' He felt the Fund should be closed and all the assets transferred to the Trust for use on public purposes.[19]

In his letter to Beit, Kerr wrote in rather pompous terms of the responsibility that rested on him for giving advice to the Trustees on the issue. Beit retorted that Kerr's advice was based on the assumption that what Rhodes thought in 1898, when the Fund had been set up, was not relevant today: 'I cannot help feeling that I am perhaps more correctly and more closely informed as to the political party complications in South Africa which continue to urgently need the support of outside assistance.' He was prepared to agree to a proportion of the Fund being handed over to the Trust, but the bulk of it should be retained in South Africa for ten years at least.[20] The other Trustees supported him; £80,000 came immediately to London, a further £28,000 was transferred in 1935 and only in 1939, by which time Beit was long dead, did the remaining £167,000 accrue to the Trust.

It was a defeat for Kerr – unsurprising since Beit, nephew of one of the two creators of the Fund and fully conversant with the situation in South Africa, was fighting on his home ground. The other Trustees were anyway inclined to share Beit's point of view: the item which had particularly offended Kerr – an annual payment of £3,000 a year to General Smuts's party – seemed to Amery at least a thoroughly proper way to spend the money. Kerr learnt his lesson and used his increasing power with discretion over the next decade. He would probably have liked to continue for ten years more, but, early in 1939, was invited to take up the post of Ambassador to the United States. As his successor he recommended Godfrey Elton, a former don at Queen's who had been ennobled by Ramsay MacDonald. He had met Elton, he told Wylie's successor C. K. Allen, had liked him and had found 'his ideas on the United States and the Empire and the Rhodes Trust generally sensible'.[21] H. A. L. Fisher was less sure. He had consulted the Provost of Queen's and had been given a discouraging report. Elton had been much disliked at Balliol 'for his affected and superior manners' and when he stood for a Labour seat after the war he 'wore a monocle, walked about with a bloodhound and generally affected the airs of a youthful Dizzy'. Unsurprisingly he had not been elected and these affectations had worn off, but he was now unpopular with the left-wing members of Queen's, who regarded him as a rigid Conservative who had used Labour connections to get into the House of Lords. The Provost doubted whether he would go down well with the Australians, he was 'so aristocratic in temper and bearing'. On the other hand, he was admitted to be an excellent speaker and writer and full marks were given to his Norwegian wife.[22] The Trustees concluded that his youthful indiscretions need not be held against him and that his good points far outweighed his bad. On the whole they were proved right: Elton was occasionally criticised for verbosity or indecision, but his generosity and affability were never questioned. If the Australians found him too aristocratic, they certainly failed to say so.

'The administrative work of the Trust, once you have mastered it, will not constitute a full time job,' Lothian assured him. 'They [the Trustees] therefore regard the promotion of the general ideals underlying Mr Rhodes's Will and the Rhodes Scholarship system by writing and speaking and keeping in touch with the United States and the Dominions as an important aspect of your duties.'[23] The instructions could hardly have been more welcome. It is difficult to believe that Elton could have refrained from writing and speaking; to be officially informed these activities were an important part of his duties must have convinced him that he had found a job as near the ideal as was possible.

CHAPTER SIXTEEN
THE OXFORD EXPERIENCE

In spite of the pressure which they were under, the Oxford colleges made prodigious efforts to take the augmented inflow of Rhodes Scholars. Balliol was particularly accommodating: 'They are genuinely interested in them,' wrote Allen gratefully some years later, 'and, what is more important, they really want to have them in the College.'[1] Balliol was no longer such a breeding ground for imperial administrators as it had been at the turn of the century, but it was still the ideal college for those who took the world's problems seriously and planned to do something to help solve them. Eugene Forsey, in time to become a Senator and one of Canada's foremost constitutional experts, found Balliol 'alive with new professors and new courses, all of which aimed to rectify the past wrongs of a world that had led itself into a disastrous world war'.[2] Even Norman Robertson, another Canadian, who was sharply critical of the 'contagion of sleeping sickness' that seemed to him to hang over Oxford, admitted that Balliol had a reputation for being immune to any such affliction. 'But such a reputation is a frightful commentary on the other colleges,' Robertson went on.[3]

The Oxford into which the Rhodes Scholars fitted was itself evolving, in part at least, in response to the needs of the foreign invaders. Increasingly Scholars, particularly those from the United States, were no longer content to take undergraduate degrees – thus, as they saw it, leaving Oxford with no academic credentials more significant than those they had already acquired at home. The President of Harvard told Allen that, unless Oxford could provide more in the way of research facilities, the Trust must expect progressively to recruit Scholars only from the smaller universities.[4] He was ahead of his time even by the time of the 1929 Reunion in Oxford a large majority of those consulted felt that the undergraduate course was the one best suited to almost every Rhodes Scholar: 'The importance of higher degrees and research work as a method of education is largely over-stated.' But the same report admitted that things were changing; facilities for postgraduate work were clearly 'going

to be of great importance in the near future'.[5] It was a process which the traditionalists deplored, yet which even someone as conservative by nature as Wylie
accepted was inevitable, even proper. 'Conceptions of the Rhodes Scholar as a
kind of enlarged, if somewhat cruder, English schoolboy, which may have
served at first, are no longer adequate,' he told the Trustees. 'Some Rhodes
Scholars are not at all like an English schoolboy. And we need not be afraid to
admit that the type can vary without prejudice – even with advantage – to the
purposes which underlie the Scholarship.'[6]

Even before the end of the First World War Oxford had taken some steps to
meet this new demand. The introduction of a new DPhil degree occurred in
1917 and, though the figures shifted from year to year, overall the flow was
towards research work for the Scholars. The new course was not instituted
only in recognition of the needs of the Rhodes Scholars, but their importance
in the process is shown by the fact that, of the two hundred research students
at Oxford in 1935, sixty-four were Rhodes Scholars. Over the same period
there had been a marked shift from the study of law and the humanities to
science and the newly invented course of PPE – politics, philosophy and
economics. 'Stinks, bugs and statistics are what people seem to want from
Oxford nowadays,' wrote Allen gloomily. 'I see many signs that we are rapidly
becoming one vast laboratory.'[7] Allen unabashedly deplored the process; Kerr,
who fancied himself as a progressive, was more restrained but even he
doubted whether the move towards the sciences would be 'an advantage from
the point of view of Mr Rhodes's larger ideals'. Rhodes had picked Oxford as
being the university most likely to produce Scholars dedicated to 'the
discharge of public duties'.[8] Were 'stinks, bugs and statistics' really the best
path towards such an end? But even in the sciences there was still a gulf
between learning for the sake of learning and technical instruction. When a
French Canadian Scholar from Quebec announced that he wanted to study
copyright law, Allen replied firmly: 'You won't find that at Oxford. This
university is for general education, not for specialist professional training.'[9]

The increasing readiness of Oxford to accept degrees from other universities as exempting foreign students from the need to take an entrance examination or first public examination meant that it became easier for Scholars to
finish their courses in two years. Rhodes had assumed that his Scholarships
would normally extend over three years, but Wylie urged that this was a positive deterrent to candidates who wanted to get on with their career and who
often frittered away their third year in aimless study.[10] When Scholars did
want to take a third year there was a growing tendency to apply to do so away
from Oxford: in chambers for a lawyer, in a hospital for a medical student. At
first the Trustees held the line that, except in the most unusual circumstances,
the Scholar must study in Oxford. Even as early as 1920, however, they were

showing some flexibility, giving a Rhodesian Scholar a grant equivalent to a year of the Scholarship to enable him to study in South Africa.[11] By 1930, John Fairbank, an American Scholar, was allowed to spend his third year in China consulting British consular records.[12] The issue of third years produced one of the few disagreements between Lothian and Allen. Lothian thought that most third years were a waste of time and some positively harmful; they should be reserved for Scholars who could 'prove that they propose to use it in a way which will promote Mr Rhodes's ultimate ends in an exceptional way'. Allen felt that this would be unfairly restrictive and that third years should be available whenever the Scholar could use them profitably.[13] The Trustees formally took note of Lothian's doubts but continued in practice to show much the same liberality over the granting of third years as had been their practice in the past. One thing, however, on which Lothian and Allen agreed was that there should be no new Scholarships. Partly this was because the financial crisis of 1929–30 meant that funds were stretched; partly because, as Wylie had already discovered before his retirement, it was increasingly difficult to place all the Scholars in colleges of their choice or, indeed, in any colleges at all. Wylie's first failure had come in 1927 when P.C. Kimball from Utah was rejected by every college. Aydelotte suggested that he should go to Cambridge; Wylie felt that this would be unacceptable to the Trustees and that, anyway, no Cambridge college would be likely to accept an Oxford reject, especially one who was a Mormon. Eventually Kimball was fitted into one of the non-collegiate institutions which existed on the fringes of the University. Wylie told the Trustees that he was the first Rhodes Scholar to suffer this fate – 'It is perhaps too much to hope that he will be last.'[14] It would indeed have been too much, it was not till three years later that he was able again to boast that all that year's scholars had found a college.[15]

The question of the ideal age for a Rhodes Scholar to arrive in Oxford was reopened in 1925 when the Trustees despatched a recently retired headmaster of Winchester, Montague Rendall, to tour the main Rhodes constituencies. Rendall was 'an attractive and inspiring personality', according to Milner; 'very charming, as well as distinguished', wrote Grigg:[16] but to most of those who met him on his wanderings he seemed pompous, pig-headed and startlingly tactless. He assumed from the start that to take Rhodes Scholars who had already graduated in their own countries was a 'perverted and unnatural arrangement'; the ideal must be for them 'to be educated side by side with their strict contemporaries so that they may sharpen their wits on one another'.[17] Wylie was horrified. He had already seen too many cases of callow schoolboys ripped from home, intellectually unable to hold their own and emotionally bereft: 'I am not frightened of an occasional picked schoolboy;

but I should be frightened of any real change of policy tending to substitute schoolboys for more mature Rhodes Scholars.'[18] He took soundings in the Oxford colleges and was able to report that, out of fifty-six replies, forty-four favoured graduates, seven were uncertain, and only five favoured school-boys.[19] The Trustees had by then already grown weary of Rendall, who had stirred up angry controversy in almost every country he visited. They tacitly rejected his recommendations and were no more enthusiastic when he suggested they should buy him a former vicarage some twenty miles from Oxford so that he could entertain Rhodes Scholars at weekends. Any such entertainment, they felt, was the function of the Oxford Secretary.[20]

The entertainment of Scholars, in so far as it contributed to their happiness, was, however, a preoccupation of the Trustees. A handful of Scholars never settled down at all; the majority had problems in the first few months. 'Most Rhodes Scholars would gladly go home at the end of their first term,' wrote Escott Reid, who was later to be one of Canada's most eminent diplomats and economists. 'There seems no possibility of knowing anyone. . . . Many Rhodes Scholars give up the struggle and say the Englishman is not worth knowing and from then on consort only with their own nationals or with other Rhodes Scholars.'[21] The 'most', describing those who hankered for home after their first term, was probably justified; 'many', for those who gave up the struggle, was an exaggeration. Cliques did form, especially among the Americans, but after the first period of sharp disorientation a great majority of Scholars seem to have found that the British were human after all and to have formed close bonds with them. Outside the colleges, there was a group of public-spirited worthies resolved to give the Scholars a taste of the home life which they had forfeited. Wylie himself was indefatigable; the Wylies 'entertain almost contin-ually', John Crowe Ransom told his mother.[22] Before the war Lady Wantage had been wont to entertain grandly at Lockinge Park. Wylie was nervous lest such outings became rather too much like school treats: 'I think our Scholars are for the most part rather too old and too independent for it to be easy to "run" them.'[23] Offence may sometimes have been taken, but most Scholars seem to have been more amused than annoyed and were appreciative of Lady Wantage's efforts.

After the war Lady Wantage's mantle descended on the shoulders of Lady Frances Ryder. Lady Frances was one of those aristocratic English ladies who had time on their hands, infinite energy, and self-confidence so complete as to be simultaneously irritating and awe-inspiring. She decided that it was her role in life to ensure that in their vacations the Rhodes Scholars saw some-thing of the countryside and the British way of life and appealed to the Trust to accord her semi-official status as well as financial aid. The Trustees were sceptical but in the end were borne down by her persistence and obvious goodwill and in 1924 granted her £500 a year to organise visits by Rhodes Scholars to British homes.[24] She proved indefatigable, resourceful and, on the whole, successful. Not all Scholars proved easy to accommodate. Of a Maltese Scholar she reported: 'Owing to his fat damp hands – poor thing! – he was a little difficult to place, but I pleaded with, I think, just the right kind of host-esses' (hostesses with thin, dry hands or even fatter, even damper hands?). Wylie was afraid that the Scholars would find Lady Frances and her hostesses intolerably patronising. One Scholar at least believed that he was being invited into a British home in the hope that he would provide a solution for an other-wise unmarriageable daughter, but to 'Ryderise', as the process became known, was something to which most looked forward and spoke about nostalgically in future years.

Lady Astor, an intimate friend of Lord Lothian, was perhaps Lady Wantage's direct successor, giving sumptuous garden parties for Rhodes Scholars at Cliveden and at least one ball in London, for which thirty of her friends were dragooned into giving dinner parties and at which the Prince of Wales was present. (Her popularity may have taken something of a dip when the Astors' horse, Rhodes Scholar, started favourite for the St Leger. It was unplaced.) Wylie himself lived and entertained in all simplicity, but he saw the value of style when style was called for. For the Rhodes Dinner of 1929 he proposed an excellent sherry, Chablis with the fish, for champagne a Bollinger 1921, for claret a Beychevelle 1920 ('I have some of this claret myself, and personally think it good,' he told Beit) and a youngish but sound vintage port. 'I suppose for this dinner you want pretty good wines,' he suggested. Beit concurred.[25]

Wylie's swan-song came in July 1929 when the opening of Rhodes House coincided with the twenty-five-year jubilee of the Scholarships. Again the Prince of Wales attended and Aydelotte remembered Wylie presenting each Rhodes Scholar in turn, 'mentioning for each man his Oxford College and country of origin, without a note or scrap of paper of any kind'.[26] Already the search was on for his successor. 'The wider his interests, and indeed his affili-ations the better,' recommended Wylie. He should be versed in imperial studies but not seek to become a Director of Studies; his first and all-important role was to get to know the Scholars. Unless there was some over-whelming argument to the contrary he should be a fellow of an Oxford college.[27] This last proviso was not universally accepted. Aydelotte wanted an American and had several strong candidates to offer.[28] Vincent Massey, a Canadian Rhodes Scholar who was by now a senior politician, argued that the new Oxford Secretary should be neither English nor American 'and yet should be capable of understanding the North American point of view. Canada would seem to be the best national background.' His favoured runner was his closest friend, George Smith. Peacock dryly noted: 'Having made a list of

George Smith's virtues he sets them down as the essential qualities of the new secretary and in applying them to George is astonished and delighted to find that they fit.'[29] H.A.L. Fisher wanted a 'high class Englishman', the 'class' presumably referring more to intellectual and moral stature than to lineage; and by mid-1930 Lothian felt able to tell the presumably disappointed George Smith that the Trustees had concluded that an Englishman would be best.[30] They then proceeded to choose an Australian, though admittedly one who had been a fellow of University College since 1920 and had recently become Professor of Jurisprudence.

Carleton Allen – 'C.K.' as he was usually known – was a less approachable figure than his predecessor but his wife Dorothy more than made up for it: 'vivacious, humorous, tirelessly active and always ready with sympathy and understanding', Elton wrote of her.[31] She needed it all, for on her more than on her husband would fall the business of running the newly opened Rhodes House, a substantial mansion with eight servants. Every day during term (except Wednesday, which was reserved for children) there were lunches, dinners, dances, sherry parties, and every Sunday an open tea party for anyone to drop in uninvited; 'huge musical evenings for brows of mingled height' were held regularly; 'at all times there seemed to be somebody staying with us, old Rhodes Scholars, relations of Rhodes Scholars, convalescing Rhodes Scholars, speakers for meetings, or just one's own friends'. At one moment the Allens seemed destined to entertain Gandhi, with his entourage and some goats to provide his daily milk, but in the end he opted for Balliol. The Allens religiously learnt the names of all Rhodes Scholars by assembling photographs and potted biographies and shuffling through them, announcing triumphantly: 'Smith, Tennessee. New College. History.'[32] Dorothy Allen was loved by all; C.K. was generally respected, usually liked, occasionally feared and invariably admitted to be conscientious and hard-working. By disposition he was cautious and conservative, and shunned any kind of publicity. When it was proposed that a Rhodes Scholar should broadcast about his experiences on Canadian radio Allen rejected the idea with distaste. 'You never quite know what these wireless people, who are very much Americanised in Canada, will do,' he warned Lothian. 'Anything in the nature of a description of experiences at Oxford might be undesirable.' When Robert Taylor, then one of America's most prominent film stars, was making *A Yank at Oxford* it was suggested that he and a few of his co-stars should put in an appearance at a dance in Rhodes House. 'I strongly discouraged the idea,' wrote Allen, 'as I felt sure it would be associated with publicity of some kind.'[33]

Allen could justifiably argue that the Rhodes Scholarships did not need publicity. In 1919 they had still been a little-known feature of the Oxford landscape, but by 1939 they were established as a major force. Between the wars the number of overseas students in Oxford veered between 525 and 600; of these a third were Rhodes Scholars. It seems likely, says the historian of the University, 'that the scale, regularity of recruitment and reputation of the Rhodes scheme made a qualitative difference to Oxford's attitude towards foreign students', and also that, 'as the scheme became more known generally, it encouraged applications from a much wider overseas constituency than before 1914, with favourable implications for academic standards'.[34] The internationalisation of the world's leading universities was a feature of the twentieth century; the Rhodes Scholarships played a pioneering role in this development. And, with a few exceptions, some of them conspicuous, the individual Rhodes Scholars contributed greatly to the colleges to which they were assigned. In his report on the academic year of 1937–8 Allen recorded how impressed he had been when the head of a college which, 'in the post-war years, has rapidly advanced in status and reputation', told him that the Rhodes Scholars 'had been more responsible than any other single cause for the strengthened tone of the College'. There were, wrote Allen, only about three colleges which still regarded Rhodes Scholars as being, if not 'undesirable aliens, at least as quaint exotica; and it is unnecessary to say that they are not the most distinguished societies in the university'.[35] Aydelotte believed that the flow of American students to German universities which had been so pronounced a tendency at the beginning of the century and had been checked by the First World War, need never resume. Oxford was destined to become the foremost university of the English-speaking world. 'I am not surprised that there are people in Oxford who do not like that, but I hope they don't represent the majority. Undoubtedly the University will lose something in the change, but it will also acquire a character that no English-speaking university has ever had before.'[36] If Oxford had been changed by the Rhodes Scholars, so it had also affected the Scholars themselves. For Eugene Forsey, Oxford 'opened subjects, ideas, languages, civilisations, some of which might other- wise have remained closed to me. . . . It gave me a deeper devotion to parlia- mentary government, to the rule of law, to the freedom that "slowly broadens down from precedent to precedent", a stronger determination to do what I could to see that Canada also should be "a land where, girt with friends or foes, a man may speak the things he will".'[37] For another Canadian, Michener, Oxford was 'all he had dreamed of or expected: the shining city of culture and civilisation'.[38]

It was also old-fashioned, inefficient, complacent, arrogant, damp and cold. It triumphed in spite of its defects; sometimes, it seemed, because of its defects. Its aloofness, its introverted self-satisfaction, at first repelled and then, as the newcomer slowly penetrated its inner fastnesses, were transformed into charms. 'Its methods are antiquated,' wrote Stephen Leacock in 1922. 'It despises science. It has professors who never teach and students who never learn. It has no order, no arrangement, no system. Its curriculum is unintelligible. It has no president. It has no state legislation to tell it how to teach, and yet – it gets there. . . . It is at present the greatest University in the world.'[39]

CHAPTER SEVENTEEN

RHODES HOUSE

Though Wylie had lived in Rhodes House for two years or so before retiring, it was to C.K. Allen that fell the task of making it work. It was a daunting prospect. Most people, when commissioning a building, decide what they need and instruct the architect accordingly. The Trustees commissioned the building first and only later considered what it was to be used for.

The idea that there should be a building in Oxford which would serve as a monument to Cecil Rhodes and as a headquarters for the Oxford Secretary had been around almost as long as the Scholarships themselves. Various sites were considered and rejected, then Parkin's death in 1922 and the wish to open a memorial library of books on the Empire in his honour led to the subject being revived with increased urgency. At one point it had seemed that a site in Wadham garden might be a possibility, but only one and a quarter acres were available and the project foundered. Subsequently a plot of two acres was offered and accepted. You can assume, Grigg assured Wylie, that the building will be 'in every way worthy both of the importance of the Rhodes Scholarship Trust at Oxford and of the University'.[1]

There was no dispute over the architect. Herbert Baker had been a friend of Rhodes as well as having done much work for him; the Union Buildings in Pretoria and the Secretariat beside Viceroy's House in Delhi were only two of the massive monuments with which he adorned what turned out to be the twilight of the British Empire. His brief was to produce a building in which the Oxford Secretary could live and entertain and which would also house an extensive library and offer various grandiose halls in which the Scholars could from time to time gather and other unspecified functions take place. At Milner's insistence, the original plan had been for a large but basically simple Cotswold manor house, but Baker took advantage of Milner's death to insert, ostensibly in the great imperialist's memory, a massive Ionic portico and a rotunda symbolising Rhodes's ideal of service. The Founder's favourite quotation from Aristotle – 'the good for man consists in the exercise of excellence in a well-rounded life' – encircled the dome; more mundanely a no-smoking sign in Greek reminded Scholars how lucky they were to be spared the travails of that intractable language. 'The building is an oddity, but it has personality enough to rouse affection in some,' was the architectoral historian Pevsner's, guarded judgment.[2] He does not seem to have included himself among their number. The Trustees were delighted, congratulating their architect 'on the successful completion of one of the most notable buildings in Oxford'.[3] Others too were enthusiastic: the *American Oxonian* had published disparaging comments about the mean entrance and the cramped site; now it recanted and concluded that Rhodes House was 'doubtless the most beautiful and impressive modern building in Oxford, and is comparable with the finest architecture of earlier times'.[4] Over the years the building has not won much praise or inspired more than a tepid loyalty. 'Ah, well, back to Lenin's tomb,' was Edgar Williams's gloomy observation as he set off home after his lunch at Balliol.[5]

It was at least clear what Rhodes House was not. It was not intended to serve as a centre for Scholars. Rhodes Scholars 'must continue to mix with other men in their own colleges,' said Otto Beit, and anything that weakened the collegiate tie would be directly contrary to the Founder's intentions.[6] But there was a real risk that it might prove a white elephant, 'of no practical use either in University or College life', Kerr warned the Trustees. Somehow it must be organised so that it would 'help the University to maintain its position'.[7] This was Allen's role. He had a new title to help him on his way. When the rumour spread that Allen was to be styled Warden, the Warden of Wadham wrote to deplore the change and the Warden of All Souls too felt that it would be unfortunate. The solidarity of the league of Wardens was broken by the Warden of New College, H.A.L. Fisher, who also happened to be a Trustee. 'Anything new in Oxford would be objected to by someone,' he wrote. 'The term Warden is certainly more suitable than any other. . . . As the Vice-Chancellor has given his consent, I really do not see why we should recede from our project. There may be a little fuss but it will die down.'[8] Allen professed to find his title faintly ridiculous. He held it, he told the Warden of Merton, 'on the same principle as the directors of prisons and lunatic asylums, and because they couldn't find anything else to call me. . . . I believe your predecessor always referred to me as "the man who calls himself Warden of Rhodes House!"'[9]

It was Fisher who had the clearest ideas about the purpose of Rhodes House. It should be used, he said, for University lectures, societies and the like with the emphasis on imperial studies and still more on Britain's African possessions: it should 'do the same kind of work for the now rapidly growing African Civil Service that the Indian Institute does for the Indian Civil

Service'. The concept that African studies should be at the heart of Rhodes House's activities was given considerable support at the end of 1929, when Smuts pleaded for the creation of an Institute of Government 'with special reference to Pan-African studies'. The Trustees were ready to place their buildings at the disposal of such a body but had no wish to find themselves saddled with the costs of professors, researchers and supporting staff. Somebody else must take the initiative. 'I don't think the Trustees should or would further the scheme at this stage,' Kerr told Fisher. 'Nor do I think that it would help things if they did. Oxford is still pretty suspicious of them.' He asked Smuts whether he would approach the Rockefeller Foundation for £10,000 a year for ten years – 'the more enthusiastic you can make the letter, the better'. Smuts's enthusiasm was genuine, but the Rockefeller Foundation was nervous lest 'the Oxford School might be involved in political and economic controversy'.[10] In the end they refused to help and the African Survey, a by-product of Smuts's vision, was finally published by Chatham House.

Even if the African project had taken off it would not have satisfied Lionel Curtis and Reginald Coupland, the historian of Empire. Coupland wanted to establish Rhodes House as a centre for overseas studies; not necessarily confined to the Empire but certainly concentrating on it. 'Why should not Rhodes House establish a kind of Collegiate individuality?' he asked Curtis. 'It would be a pity if the new RH development were cramped or spoiled by the Middle Ages.' Kerr took up the idea and proposed a School of Government at Oxford which would study how the principle of responsible government was being applied in different parts of the Empire.[11] It was at the conference which grew from this initiative that Smuts hijacked the enterprise in favour of African studies. Perhaps the wider vision might have succeeded better in finding backers; as it was Coupland's hopes of taking over Rhodes House for his imperial purposes perished with the rebuff from the Rockefeller Foundation.

The great rooms did not stand idle, however. In 1933 Allen listed the activities that had taken place there: lectures and seminars; the meetings of fourteen or more University clubs and many charitable and learned societies; a conference of rural librarians; entertainments for boy scouts and Canadian authors. 'It is gratifying to know that as a result of your energy the building plays a really live part in Oxford,' Kerr (by now Lothian) told Allen approvingly.[12] The Raleigh Club, under the guidance of Coupland, met there regularly to discuss aspects of Commonwealth affairs. Such enterprises caused some uncertainty among the more radical of the Rhodes Scholars. 'Was it possible to reconcile membership of an old-fashioned imperial outfit like the Raleigh Club . . . with the generally left-wing current in which I was moving?' asked James Bertram, a New Zealander who was to become an eminent sinologist. On reflection, he decided that it was: 'It was the prestige of old-style liberals like Cecil and Toynbee that for me justified such activity.'[13]

One innovation of Kerr's which lasted for more than a decade and brought some glory to Rhodes House was the Rhodes Memorial Lecture, an annual lecture designed to attract to Oxford figures of world renown. The series got off to an uncertain start when the Canadian Prime Minister, Robert Bordern, attracted only a small audience – deservedly, it would seem, since when he asked Kerr for comments on his draft text he received the somewhat brutal reply that it was 'unnecessarily dull . . . too much history, too little interpretation . . . a not very exciting narrative, almost, I might say, a catalogue of persons and events'.*[14] People who thought that they would have done better thrust themselves forward: Francis Younghusband of Tibet fame applied on the grounds that he had known Rhodes; the Duke of Kolachine on the still more flimsy claim that he had offered the University a cast of a Chinese Nestorian Monument of AD 781, a gift politely declined by Lord Curzon.[15] Instead the Trustees decided to follow Bordern with the American education-alist Abraham Flexner and the French historian Elie Halévy – both worthy figures but not likely to attract the sort of attention Kerr had hoped for. It was Jan Smuts, in whose honour the venue was changed to the Sheldonian, who, both by his renown and by his choice of subject – Africa and the Empire – gave the lectures some of the significance that had been intended. His successor, Albert Einstein, was in his own way still more celebrated and attracted capacity audiences to Rhodes House. His subject was relativity, and since he spoke in German and there could not have been more than a dozen people in Oxford capable of following his reasoning even in English, there was a certain lack of rapport between lecturer and listeners. Had it been a good audience, Wylie asked anxiously. 'Ils ont bien dormi,' Einstein replied, adding charitably: 'Ils avaient le droit.'[16] The Trustees hoped to publish the text of the lectures; Einstein politely refused on the grounds that he had subsequently concluded that all his theories were wrong.[17]

The lectures never again achieved this peak of celebrity. Early in the Second World War Elton made efforts to revive them, suggesting that an eminent Indian, perhaps Nehru, would be welcome. The former Viceroy, Halifax, agreed, provided Nehru was not then engaged in 'a violent anti-British campaign', but his successor, Linlithgow, vetoed the idea on the specious grounds that leading Indian politicians ought not to be 'out of India at so critical a time'.[18] Other suggestions were Marshal Pétain, then French Ambassador in Spain, and the Portuguese dictator, Dr Salazar. The latter 'combined all the statesmanlike and the academic qualifications,' wrote Dawson. 'There is

---

*A charge which weighs heavily upon the present writer.

immense admiration in England for all that he has done for his country.'[19] All these projects foundered and in 1954 Elton administered the last rites to the moribund lectures. They should be revived, he ruled, only 'if there was a very obvious person . . . who would be good for Oxford, who would be unlikely to visit it otherwise, and whose topic would not be completely alien to the Rhodes idea. I cannot think of any such person myself, and the Rhodes Memorial Lectures have probably shot their bolt.'[20]

Rhodes House was proving useful enough to Oxford, but Kerr's grand design of transforming it into a centre for international and imperial studies had come to little. There remained the Library. It had always been intended that this would house the Commonwealth and American history sections of the Bodleian, and would be administered by Bodley while housed and maintained by the Trustees. That seemed a generous suggestion, but librarians are notoriously touchy and when the Trust proposed to appoint a committee to represent its interests suspicions were aroused. 'My Curators agreed to take over control of Rhodes Library as another step in the co-ordination of Oxford libraries,' wrote Dr Cowley. 'They don't expect or desire to gain any advantage for the Bodleian.' The creation of this committee seemed to suggest that the interests of Rhodes House and the Bodleian might be in conflict.[21] Since the committee, in addition to Lionel Curtis and H.A.L. Fisher, included among its members the Beit Professor of Colonial History, the Harmsworth Professor of American History and the Gladstone Professor of Political Theory the chances of any serious clash of interests seemed remote. Kerr hurriedly assured Cowley that the purpose of the committee was only to keep an eye on the preliminary selection of books. 'Rhodes House is not only a library,' he told Fisher, 'but a centre for seminar work and research.' The Bodleian should be in charge of the technical management of the Library but 'they clearly ought not to be deciding the use which is to be made of the Rhodes House Library and of Rhodes House itself'.[22] Cowley had been smoothed over, Fisher replied, 'but his feelings will have to be considered rather delicately'.[23] It was not to be the last time that the affairs of the Library embroiled the Trustees with the Bodleian, nor the last time that what the Trustees believed to be a gift horse was looked sceptically in the mouth by the University.

CHAPTER EIGHTEEN
MONEY AND EMPIRE

The building of Rhodes House was expected to cost the then considerable sum of £84,000. The money for this was intended to come substantially from the savings achieved by the failure to take up Scholarships between 1914 and 1919. But the inrush of Scholars at the end of the First World War quickly eroded this nest-egg. Worse still, though the Scholarship Fund set up in 1917 was exempt from death duties, the rest of the Trust's considerable holdings were not accepted by the Inland Revenue as being destined for charitable purposes only. With the benefit of hindsight it seems extraordinary that this situation was allowed to drift on until 1921. In that year the bulk of the Trust's money not already in the Scholarship Fund was transferred to a newly created Public Purposes Trust, the income to be used on such charitable purposes as the Trustees felt suitable or to bail out the Scholarship Fund if need arose. It was to this Trust that the residue of the Rhodes Beit Share fund eventually accrued.* Even this left a residual £250,000 in the Rhodes Trust, largely to meet the still-outstanding death duties incurred by Grey and Jameson in their capacity as Trustees.

By 1925, when Kerr took over as General Secretary, the Trust was, if not in financial disarray, at least considerably less rich then was supposed by the uninformed. Of the £3.7 million left by Cecil Rhodes only £2.27 million remained, well over half being in the Scholarship Fund. The losses had been incurred principally in realising Rhodes's investments and in endowing Groote Schuur and other estates which had been handed over to the South African Government; £350,000 had been paid in death duties.[1] The situation was not disastrous – if disaster involved an inability to pay for the Scholarships and the Trust's other inescapable commitments – but it was uncomfortably tight; and it was clearly incompatible, Kerr told the Trustees,

*See p. 101 above.

'with a continuance of their generous expenditure either in South Africa or elsewhere on anything like the scale which they have adopted hitherto'.[2] That was the nadir of the Trust's fortunes: though there were storms ahead, the overall growth of its investments continued until the Second World War threw all financial calculations into disorder. This improvement was largely due to the acumen of Edward Peacock who, from his vantage point at Barings, made sure that the Trust's investments were wisely deployed.

One of the storms came with the financial crisis of 1931 and 1932. The Trust's investments lost 12.5 per cent of their value, and Peacock, with the support of a new recruit to the Trustees, Sir Reginald Sothern Holland, urged a more cautious approach, with the emphasis on gilt-edged securities.[3] Lothian would have been more adventurous, favouring a foray into American equities. On this he was defeated, but his other recommendation – that the Trust should invest in property – was more kindly viewed. Some £100,000 was invested in urban property – a policy that in the long run paid off, though it caused much heart-burning along the way. At the end of 1933 Lothian gloomily foresaw a situation in which the slump would be intensified and inflation would force the Trustees to increase the value of the Scholarships. In such a case he favoured cutting back on the Scholarships, particularly on the awards of third years: 'Personally, I think that some of the non-Scholarship expenditure promotes Mr Rhodes's fundamental purposes as well as the Scholarships, and in any case, I think the prestige and utility of the Trust would greatly diminish if they accept in perpetuity that its sole purpose was to finance the Scholarships and that it had no money available for any other purpose.'[4] His reasoning is obscure – why should a cut-back in grants be any more or less perpetual than a cut-back in Scholarships? – but fortunately the Trustees did not have to make any decision in such a stark form. Even as Lothian wrote, the financial clouds were lifting; within a few months it was apparent that the Scholarships could be maintained and yet a substantial amount still be left for other purposes.

One consequence of the Depression was that many Rhodes Scholars found themselves out of a job. The Trust was deluged with letters applying for help. One victim even went public; an entry in the personal column of *The Times* read: 'BSc Oxon, Rhodes Scholar, married, two children, ruined by failure of company, absolutely penniless. Will some good person HELP?' 'We certainly do not want this sort of advertisement to appear,' wrote Allen disapprovingly, but he could neither stop it nor offer any hope to the luckless Scholar.[5] Even when times grew better and there was money to spend again, the Trustees would neither run an employment agency nor hand over subventions to indigent Scholars. What they did do with their surplus income was as good a gauge as any of their preoccupations at the time. In the two periods between the wars in which substantial donations were being made – 1919–29 and 1933–9 – it is possible to detect a significant shift of emphasis.

In the first phase, with Milner in charge till 1925 and Otto Beit succeeding him, South Africa remained at the centre of the Trust's activities. Money was still being poured into Rhodes's experimental farms; until the end of 1920 Rhodes University was almost kept afloat by subventions from the Trust; substantial grants were made to individual boys' and girls' schools. Oxford was not excluded from the Trust's munificence, but by far the most significant donation – £20,000 – was for the establishment of a chair of Roman Dutch Law, a line of study of particular relevance to South Africa. Emigration to Southern Africa remained a first priority: the 1820 Memorial Settlers' Association received large grants in the early 1920s. Emigration was, of course, not just a South African concern; Rhodes's dream that the Empire should be peopled by white settlers of British origin was still very much in the Trust's mind. Kingsley Fairbridge had been a Rhodes Scholar from Rhodesia, but his scheme for child emigration bore fruit more in Australia and Canada than in his native Rhodesia.

Fairbridge is of special interest as being, in Behan's words, 'the one man among us who, by his life-work, pre-eminently justified his tenure of a Rhodes Scholarship.' The Trustees so far endorsed this judgment as to inscribe his name on what was to be a roll of heroes in the rotunda of Rhodes House (they later realised how many hours of acrimonious debate would be involved in selecting Fairbridge's peers and solved the problem by obliterating the inscription). Yet he made an unpromising start: his aunts thought him 'a horrid little boy'; he was, he told his wife, very unpopular as a youth.[7] He made a strong impression on Lord Grey – 'I like these mad enthusiasts,' Grey told Parkin. 'He hopes to be a Rhodes Scholar. I share his hope'[8] – but before being able to compete he failed three times to pass responsions. 'I am very doubtful about Fairbridge even if he passes his examination this time,' wrote the Rhodesian Director of Education. 'He has ability in certain directions (literary) but little ballast.'[9] At Oxford he got a blue for boxing, played every game on offer, joined several wine clubs, played cards endlessly and made innumerable friends: 'Not for the gold of Ophir would I exchange one hour of that life.'[10] He did not seem to be the stuff of heroes, yet Wylie saw the promise in him: 'He is likely to bring more credit to the Trust than some who negotiated Responsions more rapidly.'[11] So it turned out. His ambition was to establish farm schools around the Empire, to which the underprivileged children of Britain's industrial slums could be brought to lead healthier, happier lives, to the benefit both of themselves and of their country of adoption. The British South Africa Company rebuffed him, saying they thought Rhodesia too young a country to be ready for such a scheme, but he won the support of the Colonial Club and founded the first Fairbridge Farm School in Western Australia before the First World War. The Trustees looked fondly on their prodigal's enterprise, made grants to his Child Emigration Society and supported the Balliol Boys' Club, which managed the London operation.[12]

By the time Amery took over from Lord Lovat as Chairman in 1933 none of the Trustees had any close personal involvement with Southern Africa. It did not follow that they had lost interest in the area, nor did they entirely eschew the sort of political involvement which had been so marked a feature of their pre-war activities. They took, for instance, a large holding in the company that published the *Argus* newspaper, the chief mouthpiece for British policy in the Cape. For the first time, too, they began to make substantial contributions to black education in South Africa. Kerr had long been an enthusiastic advocate of this course. Recommending a grant to the Ohlange Institute in Natal in 1925 he had argued that Rhodes had always been active in promoting the progress of the natives: 'Rhodes, who altered his formula of "equal franchise for every *white* man south of the Zambezi" to "every civilised man" when the injustice of the first version was made clear to him, would, I am confident, have admitted the reasonableness of my submission had he been here today.'[13] Whether or not Kerr's confidence was justified, or the Trustees shared it, his case was accepted, as was Bishop Carey's plea for support for the Modderpoort Native Training College which he hoped would train a black elite 'in the public school tradition of leadership' as opposed to the 'communistic type of leader' now being produced all over the country.[14] Modderpoort got £4,000, and other grants were made to mission schools and to the black university, Fort Hare.

But though South Africa continued to be pre-eminent, the Trustees remembered that there was a world elsewhere and that Africa did not end with the Zambezi. Between 1936 and 1938 the anthropologist Louis Leakey was financed for his work among the Kikuyu in Kenya, while Margery Perham was encouraged to study the British treatment of African populations, an opportunity which, she told Lothian, 'changed my life ... and started a rather precarious but enthralling career in the study of Africa'[15] (and, incidentally, earned the outraged disapproval of Edward Grigg, who deplored her socialistic nonsense). Both Leakey and Perham were protégés of Lothian, who used his position to shape the Trust's activities in a way that his predecessors had not attempted. Sometimes he seems to have been actuated by little more than whim. In 1935 he was asked whether there was no way to redress the 'general ignorance in the West about the developing peoples and regions of Asia'. Certainly, said Lothian, 'I shall talk to the Trustees.' His proposal was to create a travelling Scholarship to the East for a suitable Australian or New Zealand

Scholar: 'I am sure Rhodes would have approved,' he stated, with that endearing confidence that he could read the Founder's mind which marked so many of his démarches. James Bertram from New Zealand was appointed and had a thoroughly rewarding tour, though whether Western ignorance of the East was significantly diminished as a result must be uncertain.[16]

One thing that neither Lothian nor the Trustees sought to do was to burnish the Founder's reputation beyond the very conspicuous monument they had created in his name in the shape of Rhodes House. When the South African Government reneged on its obligations to Rhodes University the Trustees refused to come to the rescue; they had already done a great deal and the mere fact that the University bore the name it did was not enough to justify endless handouts. They underwrote a biography of Dr Jameson by Ian Colvin (though somewhat disconcerted by the quality of the final product) but showed no enthusiasm for a proposal that Kipling should write a life of Cecil Rhodes. They evidently shared Allen's views about the untrustworthiness of the cinema and broadcasting, since they refused to put up any money when twice approached with proposals for the making of a film about Rhodes, and turned down with equal alacrity a suggestion that a portrait of Rhodes should be hung in every school in Rhodesia. The Trustees took the line that they should stick to what they knew about, which was education, and keep all other ventures to a minimum. Their support for the *Argus* newspaper was something of a hangover from the past and could only have happened in South Africa. When *The Times* was on the market in 1922 and it seemed as if there was a real threat that it might be bought by Lord Beaverbrook, it was rumoured that the Rhodes Trust might come to the rescue.[17] It is conceivable that Dawson may have hinted at the possibility, but it never seems to have been put to the Trustees and certainly would have been rejected out of hand if it had been.

What was new about the Trust's activities in the ten years before the Second World War – a trend certainly encouraged if not inspired by Lothian – was the emphasis on Oxford. Oriel had, of course, been a conspicuous beneficiary under Rhodes's Will, and the Trust had from time to time made donations to the Oxford Preservation Trust, but the Trustees traditional line had been that Rhodes had done his bit for the University when he set up the Scholarships and that no more could be expected. In 1937, however, an appeal was launched for £500,000 to improve research facilities, half dedicated to the Bodleian, half to science and social studies. Strongly supported by Aydelotte, Lothian pleaded that this was in the interests as much of the Rhodes Trust as of the University.

Unless Oxford can keep its reputation as being one of the first half dozen Universities in the world the Rhodes Scholarship System itself would begin to collapse because the best Scholars overseas would refuse to compete. I do not think there is any doubt that since the war Oxford has begun to lose some of its old reputation. . . . No University can keep in the first rank unless a considerable proportion of its leading figures are actively engaged in extending the limits of human knowledge rather than in imparting to successive generations of students the body of learning which they themselves have inherited.[18]

The acceptance of the fact that the quality of applicants for Rhodes Scholarships would relate directly to the academic standards of Oxford University and that it was therefore the responsibility of the Trustees to do all that they could to ensure that the standards of the University were improved reshaped the activities of the Trust for the rest of the century. The Trustees contributed £100,000 – say £2.5 million at present values – to the Research Fund on the condition that it should be earmarked for 'social studies, with special reference to politics and in particular the political and administrative problems of the British Empire'.[19] These restrictions were little more than a pious nod in the direction of the Founder and the early Trustees. By the end of 1937 it was already apparent that 'the political and administrative problems of the British Empire' were increasingly going to become matter for the historian rather than the active participant in public life. Nobody could have predicted how quickly it would happen; nobody in his senses could have denied that the process was already under way. In 1937 the Trustees – whether they knew it or not – were pinning their standard to the mast of academic excellence. The imperial role was not yet in the past but a future without it had been envisaged.

That is, of course, an over-simplification and one which would have been contested by any of the Trustees of the time. Empire and Commonwealth were to remain prominent in their minds for many years. But a seismic change was in progress, not so much in the Trust itself as in the world about it. The fact that Britain was now no more than *primus inter pares* in a Commonwealth whose form of association was still to be defined was one that had implications for the Trust and the way it conducted its affairs. 'Your job is inevitably, in my opinion, to a certain extent an Imperial job,' J. M. Macdonell, the first Canadian Secretary of the Rhodes Trust, told Allen in 1935. 'I hope you do not dislike the word. If I am correct in that, then you to a certain extent belong to the Dominion of Canada.'[20] Macdonell had married Parkin's sister and was very much part of the movement for closer federal ties within the Commonwealth.

His closest ally among the Trustees was not Amery, who was still imbued by a more traditional concept of empire, but H. A. L. Fisher. Fisher used to hang on his walls a number of maps showing the extent of the British Empire and would draw the attention of the New College Rhodes Scholars to this remarkable phenomenon. Hugh Collis Barry, from New South Wales, remembered that Fisher would encourage the Scholars to mix with the English students as much as possible: 'He seemed to suggest that in this way we might be able to discover why so much of the map was coloured red.'[21] But this was not a one-way relationship in Fisher's eyes; the English undergraduate had quite as much if not more to learn from his Rhodes Scholar contemporary. Each individual citizen of the Empire had an obligation to serve the whole, and in that service they would find, if not perfect freedom, then at least a measure of freedom not enjoyed by other, less privileged communities.

Initially the Trustees viewed this trend with some caution. Close co-operation was clearly desirable, political integration something to be approached tentatively if at all. In 1921 they decided, 'While looking favourably on the suggested federalisation in the Dominions, to reserve the proposal for further consideration.'[22] They approved a suggestion that the Secretary should lobby the Commonwealth Prime Ministers then gathering in London to see whether they would be prepared to reserve places for Rhodes Scholars in their respective civil services but were wary about a suggestion that such Scholars should be truly interchangeable between the various countries: a Canadian serving in Australia, a New Zealander working in the Indian Civil Service. Grigg might have espoused such a prospect but Lothian was less enthusiastic, fearing that closer imperial cohesion might be at the expense of collaboration with the Americans, who still constituted by far the largest element among the Scholars. In 1938 he pronounced that, while participation in the League of Nations and Anglo-American co-operation were both of the highest importance, 'it was the latter which must in no circumstances be sacrificed'.[23] He would have expressed it rather differently if the word 'Commonwealth' had been substituted for 'League of Nations' but his private judgment would probably not have been so very different. When Allen suggested that Leo Amery should be asked to revise the short biography of the Founder in the Rhodes House booklet, Lothian deplored the idea: 'I am afraid that he would put into it some of that Jingoism which is fatal from the point of view of the American Rhodes Scholar and most of our modern Dominion Scholars.'[24]

Lothian's concept of what constituted a 'modern Dominion Scholar' was also less rigid than that of the more traditional Trustees. He was sympathetic to the idea that Scholarships should be given to India. This had first been mooted seriously in the First World War when the German Scholarships were abolished, was put into a pending tray and then revived in the early 1920s.

Wylie was consulted and frankly admitted that 'from the point of view of the easy working of the machine here – or of the ideal of the Rhodes Scholars as a corporate body bound together by interests and traditions on the whole similar – I cannot avoid the feeling that the introduction of the Oriental element will be a somewhat disturbing complication'.[25] Lothian was less inclined to agree that East was East and West was West and when R. A. Butler, as Under Secretary of State for India, returned to the charge, he accepted that the Indians had a strong claim. The Trustees still proved reluctant, and rejected the plea on the – questionable – grounds that Rhodes's Will made no provision for India but was intended for the Dominions and self-governing colonies.[26]

Lothian's determination to move the Rhodes Trust away from the traditional view of Empire to a brave new world where internationalism would be the cry and old loyalties subsumed into a greater union was exemplified by his efforts to cut off support to the Empire Day Movement. Under the leadership of the fossilised Lord Meath it seemed to Lothian that by 1930 the movement had lost all contact with reality: 'Flag-wagging societies of all kinds tend to degenerate after the initial impulse has died away.' The Trustees nevertheless decided to renew their support for another year. By then Lord Meath had been replaced by the slightly less ancient but no less stridently patriotic Lord Jellicoe. The movement was still a waste of money, claimed Lothian: 'I doubt if the modern Empire is much strengthened by circulating messages like Lord Jellicoe's.'[27] The Trustees were still not convinced that Lothian's concept of modernity was compatible with the ideals of Cecil Rhodes; they again renewed their support, while asking Amery to discuss with Jellicoe 'the methods of the movement'. The following year they cut their subvention by half, but it was not till 1933 that Lothian got his way and the Empire Day Movement was left to its own devices. The Second World War put an end to all such philosophising while radically altering the underlying realities. It was only in 1947, when the pink finally began to vanish from what was left of H. A. L. Fisher's maps, that the Trustees began to come to terms with what had by then become a fact: the Empire of Cecil Rhodes was dead or dying and the Trust would have to redefine its role.

CHAPTER NINETEEN

POLITICS AND THE SCHOLARS

Questions of Empire did not greatly preoccupy the Rhodes Scholars at this, indeed perhaps at any, period. They were, in the broadest sense, liberal in their views. Most would have favoured any move towards complete independence on the part of the other members of the Commonwealth and, with some reservations on the part of the South Africans, Rhodesians and perhaps Bermudans, as rapid as possible an advance towards self-government in the less advanced countries of the Empire. Certainly a majority would have felt that progress towards self-rule in India should be speeded up. But they do not seem to have considered such issues with any urgency. Political questions did increasingly loom large in their minds but these were above all related to communism and fascism, the two great creeds that threatened to plunge the world into a second and still more destructive war. Compared with such matters, the sluggish advance of the British Empire towards democracy seemed of parish-pump importance, nothing that called for undue expenditure of energy or emotion.

Within the University the Rhodes Scholars were generally a force for greater tolerance and a more equitable social regime. Kerr, in 1928, remarked that many Scholars disliked the social gradations at Oxford. He cautiously welcomed this – 'the zest for life, the interest in action, the personal and social equality' – while deploring the fact that they were often 'slovenly in their thinking and intellectually uninterested and uninteresting'.[1] On the whole he was inclined to think that the weaknesses outweighed the strengths and that a little less social consciousness and more intellectual ambition would not come amiss. The Bursar of Balliol would have agreed; he was put out when Philip Kaiser, an American Rhodes Scholar and future ambassador, established a precedent by becoming the first American President of the Junior Common Room and then waged a doughty campaign to secure better pay and working hours for the college servants. The Master of Balliol, A.D. Lindsay, himself a political activist, was more impressed. 'It took an American to point out how badly we treated our staff,' he said regretfully.[2] Kaiser was unusual, though, in taking steps to right what he thought was wrong. Most Scholars were content to make the best of the situation as they found it. They deplored the British penchant for social stratification but it did not affect them personally since they were deemed to be outside the system; they found it strange that one group of their friends did not seem ready to mix with another but viewed it as more comic than despicable. Howard Smith – journalist and author of the highly influential *Last Train from Berlin* – had heard a lot about British snobbishness and had expected to find himself cold-shouldered. On the contrary, he found his fellow students friendly though curious, 'watching each of us with the expressions of people at the zoo observing a panda, waiting for something extraordinary to happen'.[3] Some Scholars failed to notice any problem at all. Wilson Lyon came from a small town in Mississippi; his father had been a cotton farmer; his home had no electricity or running water. He found 'the upper class that you meet is usually the essence of good manners'; it was unjust to think them aloof or cold. 'It is true they are not as friendly at first as the people of the South, but when they know you, they are cordial. With those they know, reserve is an unknown thing.'[4]

The General Strike of 1926 provided an interesting snapshot of political views among Rhodes Scholars at the time. The majority took the same line as most of their British counterparts: that the country was under threat and they must therefore do what they could to help, also that to dress up as a special constable or drive a bus was an adventure which made an agreeable change from attending lectures. 'With no compelling ideological basis,' wrote the Canadian, Arnold Heeney, 'I found myself, with other Oxford and Cambridge undergraduates, a "Special" in the Southampton Dock Police.'[5] To be a 'Special' involved taking an oath of allegiance to the Crown, so Americans were debarred. Many of them still wanted to contribute, however. Paul Havens found himself driving a tram in Hull. When an English friend asked him why he had involved himself in a purely British crisis, Havens responded, 'If I were a guest in your house and the house caught fire, wouldn't it be normal for me to help put it out?' His friend considered this proposition, 'That's damned decent!' he finally concluded.[6]

But a substantial minority of Rhodes Scholars felt that strike-breaking was, if not indecent, then at least questionable behaviour for a visitor to Britain. Most of these lay low and said nothing. E.J. Knapton asked for an exeat from Oxford to go to work on a conciliatory news-sheet. The Dean of Queen's denied him permission – though, since the news-sheet in question appeared under the auspices of the Master of Balliol and the Archbishop of Canterbury, the Dean's disapproval cannot have been too severe. Norman Robertson went further. He deplored the strike but felt that he could not be neutral. 'So I did what I could,' which turned out to be working in the offices of the communist *Daily Worker*.[7] Wylie would have thought this conduct misguided – when Scholars from the Empire, though not the Americans, asked his advice he encouraged them to offer their services to the government – but if people like Norman Robertson felt that their sympathies pulled them another way, he made no effort to restrain them. He never threatened to suspend the stipends of Scholars who sided with the strikers; there is no reason to think that he even considered doing so. In this he reflected the firm conviction of the Trustees: provided a Rhodes Scholar did not get into trouble with the civil authorities or breach the regulations of his college or the University, his political views were no more the business of the Trust than his religious beliefs and observances.

If the General Strike had taken place seven or eight years later, many more Rhodes Scholars, indeed many more Oxford undergraduates, would have been inclined to take the other side in what they would have seen as a struggle between the workers and the capitalists. Oxford in the 1930s was as highly politicised as at any other period of its history. The Spanish Civil War and the rise of fascism in Italy and Germany made the average undergraduate aware of international issues; not many of them felt moved to do anything about them, but those who did were vociferous and energetic. The Rhodes Scholars, who had consciously been selected as being concerned about matters outside the immediate range of their domestic preoccupations, were prominent in that minority. The Spanish Civil War, in particular, impelled the more idealistic Rhodes Scholars towards the left, sometimes as far as the Communist Party, which seemed the only organisation doing anything effective to help the legal government. At Merton Richard Schlatter joined a group of fellow Rhodes Scholars who were committed to the cause of the republicans and once actually acted as a courier to the government in Madrid. He joined the communist October Club: 'The membership was supposed to be secret. We talked and talked and talked. . . .' Beyond driving to London to see the proudly left-wing Paul Robeson in *Stevedore* and talk to him after the performance, his political activities were minimal, but he never regretted his period as a communist or tried to conceal it when it became dangerously unfashionable in the United States.[8] Allen was aware of the existence of the group, deplored it, yet saw no need to take any action. Most Rhodes Scholars visited Italy and Germany at least once during their years at Oxford; in the 1930s the majority came back distressed and alarmed by what they had seen; some preached vehemently about the perils fascism represented for the democratic world. Howard Smith, who helped organise the Labour Club, exhausted 'not only the British but some of his best Rhodes Scholar friends . . . as he warned about Hitler'.[9]

There were rebels among the Rhodes Scholars beyond those with a particular political axe to grind. In a speech at a Trustees' Dinner in June 1924, the American William Greene somewhat ungraciously remarked that the best part of his tenure of the Scholarship had been the vacations on the continent, that he returned home 'gladly, eagerly', and that at least his time at Oxford had made him a better American.[10] Greene had neither judgment nor good taste, commented Wylie crossly; his speech was deplorable and had been resented by most of the other Scholars present.[11] He was not alone, however. A few years later Escott Reid berated the Trustees for using the outdated term 'colonial' and urged them to reform their selection procedures.[12] It was hardly surprising that, after an intemperate attack on the character of Cecil Rhodes and the principles of imperialism by the Canadian David Lewis, at another Trustees' Dinner in 1935, Allen proposed that Scholars should no longer be invited to talk on such occasions. 'These speeches have never been a success and on several occasions have been very much the reverse.' If appreciative they became mawkishly sentimental, if jocular they sounded critical and in bad taste: 'It's a burden on them and on their audience.'[13]

Lewis's speech differed from those of Greene and Reid in that it was based upon a coherent socialist philosophy – something which made it no more acceptable to the staunchly conservative Allen. Allen wrote in dismay to Aydelotte about what he saw as the disagreeable tone of the *American Oxonian* under its new editor, Crane Brinton. Brinton, though confessedly left-leaning, claimed to be impartial. 'In my experience, however,' complained Allen, 'the more convinced supporters of the left are quite incapable of being this. . . . they are the most intolerant and suspicious people I know, which is doubtless inevitable since they have a monopoly of righteousness.'[14] In his report to the Trustees for the academic year 1935–6 he remarked with dismay that, where Oxford had once been suspected of turning radical colonials into conservatives, now the contrary was true. Many Rhodes Scholars found Oxford 'a nursery of somewhat revolutionary ideas'. One Scholar from Winnipeg had said that his time at Oxford had made him 'more or less a socialist', and that he was now completely at variance with his friends and family at home.[15] On his visit to Australia, Rendall was dismayed to hear of F.W. Paterson, who had come to Merton as a 'meek theology student' and emerged a 'red-hot socialist' who was eventually tried for sedition. Paterson was always a sincere man, recorded Wylie sadly, 'almost over-earnest. But his communism is regarded as a very unfortunate result of a Rhodes Scholarship.'[16] In Allen's eyes, not the least unfortunate part of Lewis's attack on the Empire at the Rhodes House dinner in 1935 had been that some of the other Scholars present applauded enthusiastically; that the immersion in Oxford which Rhodes had thought would cement the imperial connection should be having the opposite effect was a particularly uncomfortable reflection.

Different groups of Scholars responded in different ways. The Australians and South Africans were relatively inactive politically. The Americans displayed a shift towards internationalism. Isolationism for them was not an acceptable approach to the world of the 1930s; the vast majority 'returned home fervent supporters of the League of Nations'. But this did not preclude political involvement in the left. This was, considered Wylie, 'the natural result of the youthful spirit of scepticism and enquiry. . . . I hope, however, it will not take extreme forms which are likely to attract publicity.'[17] It was north of the 49th parallel that the forms became more extreme. David Lewis was only the most prominent of a generation of radicals. He had nailed his colours firmly to the mast at his selection committee when the Chairman, who happened to be President of the Canadian Pacific Railway, asked him what was the first thing he would do if he became Prime Minister of Canada. 'Nationalise the CPR, sir,' replied Lewis defiantly. Since he was also Jewish and made no pretence of being a sportsman he rated his chance of getting the Scholarship extremely low, but the selectors liked his honesty and enthusiasm and took a risk on him.[18] He repaid them by being the first Rhodes Scholar to become President of the Union. He was not in sympathy with Lewis's views, wrote Allen philosophically, but 'nowadays we must expect this type of opinion. . . . This is specially true of Canada, where I find that most of the intelligent young men lean towards socialism. . . . To my mind, it is most important that Rhodes Scholars should feel that Oxford is a place of tolerance, free thought and free expression, always provided that they are not being merely silly or noisy or insubordinate, none of which terms, I think, can be applied to Lewis.'[19]

David Lewis was a fervent democrat; Bob Rae, another Canadian Rhodes Scholar and future Premier of Ontario, believes that Lewis's influence was considerable in ensuring that Oxford did not move so far towards communism as Cambridge was to do.[20] The same could not be said of P.R. 'Inky' Stephensen from Queensland. Stephensen's selection was even more surprising than Lewis's. He was already an avowed member of the Brisbane branch of the Communist Party and had stated publicly that the 'whole imperial scheme is a capitalist dodge to make more money and profits from the blood and sweat of the toiling masses'. Perhaps the selectors thought that Oxford would moderate his views; on the contrary he joined the local Communist Party at the same time as A.J.P. Taylor and began to recruit Indian students to the cause. He was active during the General Strike and, according to Taylor, 'impressed the railway workers as a potential leader of the working class'.[21] Only a threat from the Vice-Chancellor that he would otherwise be sent down led him to moderate his activities. News of his activities got back to the British Association of Loyalists in Melbourne, who wrote to express their dismay; should not any 'selected candidate be required to sign a declaration of loyalty to the Crown?' Kerr's response was that the provisions in Rhodes's Will were already sufficient and that, anyway, half the Scholars were American and so owed no loyalty to the Crown.[22]

Allen fully concurred. The selection committees knew what was expected of them; if, occasionally, they blundered, that was no reason for the Trustees to overrule them. But he still regretted that the resolve of selection committees to pick young men of independent mind led them habitually to choose left-wingers: 'it seems to me to be a fallacy to suppose that merely because a young man is aggressively on the left he is, therefore, necessarily intelligent'. He cited one noisily self-avowed socialist as being 'a very empty sort of fellow without any real solidity', though grudgingly admitting that this was probably better than 'a roaring, drinking, rowing blood'.[23] Allen considered that the selection committees picked left-wing troublemakers and sent them to Oxford to do their worst. The selectors might have retorted that, in most cases, they picked young men of independent mind but no firm political connections and Oxford transformed them into firebrand left-wingers. Both arguments had some force. What was clear to Allen, to Lothian and to the Trustees was that no radical overhaul of the system was called for. 'We cannot help it if Rhodes Scholars become Communists,' Allen told Lothian, 'and it is perfectly certain in the present state of affairs that an increasing number of them will do so, at all events for some years of their lives. We shall always hear howls about that from the elder generation, and it is not a circumstance which is very palatable to oneself, but clearly we can do nothing and ought to do nothing about it.'[24]

CHAPTER TWENTY

NEW RULES FOR THE NEW WORLD

One matter that the Trust *could* do something about was the working of the Scholarships in the United States. In the years before the First World War the American Rhodes Scholars had been not conspicuously bad but on average not nearly as good as the population and educational resources of the United States should have ensured. Even in the larger states there were too few applicants, while many of the weaker states either failed to appoint Scholars at all or, worse still, produced representatives who were manifestly inadequate. The absurd system by which forty-eight selections were made for two years and none in the third was discarded in 1915 in favour of thirty-two selections every year, but that did little to improve the quality of the applicants. Parkin, who spent much of the war in the United States, was dismayed by what he saw. Accompanied by Aydelotte he visited almost every state and concluded that many of them were incapable of regularly producing acceptable Scholars and must be stripped of the chance: 'The more adequate representation of America at Oxford is a far more important thing ... than sticking to the precise terms of the Will.'[1] This was further than the Trustees were prepared to go, but they were ready to accept Parkin's first recommendation, that in future every selection committee should consist of former Rhodes Scholars under an outside chairman. When the remoter constituencies could not find a caucus of Scholars, volunteers should be drafted in from neighbouring states. This would, Parkin believed, gain greater renown for the Scholarships, ensure better selections and, incidentally, produce a sense of comradeship among the Scholars who sat on the committees.

Even more important, in 1918 the Trustees, now that Michell had resigned, saw their way to appointing Aydelotte as the first American Secretary, charged with administering the Scholarship scheme in the United States. Aydelotte was made responsible for reshaping the selection committees and organising the open Scholarships which, on a provisional basis, the Trustees authorised in the years after the war. These Scholarships were destined for the best runners-up in those states where there had been the strongest competition. In March 1920 Aydelotte reported that he was much better pleased by the quality of the four Scholars-at-large than he had been by several of the men selected for the weaker states; indeed, a few of the rejects from the at-large competition were patently superior to those who would be going to Oxford as Rhodes Scholars: 'The situation brings out very clearly the inherent difficulty which we face in trying to get as many good Scholars from States with a population from 100,000 to 500,000 as from States with a population of from 5 to 10 million.'[2]

In 1924 Aydelotte arrived in London and confronted Milner. He had two plans for reforming the Scholarship scheme, he explained, one legal, the other probably not. 'Doubtless the illegal plan is the better,' guessed Milner.[3] He was right, Aydelotte was proposing a district plan that would amalgamate the states into eight groups of roughly similar size. Each state would continue to select its candidate but the final choice would then be made by the district committee. The Trustees eventually concluded that they liked the idea, that it was certainly at variance with Rhodes's Will, that an Act of Parliament would therefore be necessary, and that assent would not be obtained unless it could be shown that the Americans most concerned were overwhelmingly in favour of the change. Aydelotte was therefore sent back to the United States and told not to return until he had secured the necessary support.

Battle royal was now joined. A small but passionate minority opposed the change, mainly on the grounds that Rhodes himself had wanted each state to have a Scholar and his wishes should be respected. If the states were pooled, it was argued, the smaller states would never see their candidate accepted and would lose interest in the process. And yet it was in these states that the Scholarship would above all have effect. It was in Britain's interest to stop this happening: 'The narrowest and most anti-British views are most likely to be expressed by Senators representing the most remote and smallest populated states. Therefore, the greater desirability for such states to have a Rhodes Scholar and the softening effects of an Englishman's benefaction.'[4] There was obviously some force in such arguments, yet the Trustees believed they were outweighed by the need to get the best possible Scholars from America. After years of bickering, it was established that some 85 per cent of the Rhodes Scholars were in favour of the change; so too were the leading academics and educational bodies. When the Trustees finally authorised Aydelotte's scheme in 1929 they stressed that their decision was not final and that the process would be reviewed after a few years; but nobody seriously believed that the reform would be reversed.[5]

When the results of the first elections under the new system were announced it was seen that the direst prophecies of the critics had been confounded. Among the less populated states Wyoming, Idaho and Alabama won Scholarships and a third of the successful candidates came from small and unfashionable institutions. Arizona, New Mexico and Nevada were among the states that failed to secure a Scholarship, but this, in Aydelotte's view, proved the success of the scheme since Oxford was saved from students who would have been inadequate while securing much stronger Scholars in their stead. The best were no better than in the past, was his conclusion, but the general level was palpably higher.[6] The degree which he was awarded was not the only, indeed arguably was not even the most important, gauge of the use a Rhodes Scholar had made of Oxford, but it was still striking that the change in the selection system led to the proportion of firsts rising from 15 to 21 per cent while the number of Scholars failing to take a degree or obtaining a derisory fourth fell from four or five a year to one or none at all.

Aydelotte was also eventually proved right in his belief that the involvement of Scholars with the selection process would foster a sense of unity among the Rhodes alumni. One of the problems that preoccupied him was how the convictions that Oxford had supposedly inculcated in Rhodes Scholars could be kept alive after their return. Charles Sunderlin, who was to become one of America's leading space scientists and a special assistant to the President, bemoaned the fact that when he returned home 'the ideal which inspired the Scholarships seems to have faded. . . . It should be: I *am* a Rhodes Scholar; not: I *was* a Rhodes Scholar.'[7] Wylie, who visited the United States in 1933, found the Scholars 'no less loyal to the Trust, nor any less concerned for the future of the Scholarships than are the Scholars from the Dominions', but he also noted that they were above all preoccupied by their own careers and had little time for any common enterprise.[8] At a dinner in New York he urged the assembled Scholars to meet regularly: this would be, he urged, 'some expression of the common interest which holds together all those who have at one time or another been Rhodes Scholars at Oxford. It would be very much within the scope of what Rhodes envisaged.'[9] It was presumably as a result of this visit that, at the annual meeting of the Association of American Rhodes Scholars in 1934, it was announced that the Warden of Rhodes House would each year circulate a list of returning Rhodes Scholars who had not yet secured positions at home in the hope that 'older men who are likely to have vacancies to fill will have their attention directed to Rhodes Scholar candidates'.[10] This vision of the Rhodes Trust as a superior employment agency was not as idealistic as Aydelotte would have wished, but it was a function he happily performed himself, indefatigably working to fit former Scholars into suitable academic slots. Dean Rusk, J. F. Kennedy's future Secretary of State, was only one of the many young men whom Aydelotte was responsible for placing in his first job.

It was, indeed, largely a sign of Aydelotte's overwhelming influence that in the first fifty years of the Scholarships twice as many Scholars went into education as any other profession, law being the runner-up at 20 per cent.

Rusk, on his first trip to Britain, was interrogated by an Englishwoman who, hearing that he came from the South, asked: 'Oh, isn't that where you butcher your negroes?' 'Oh, yes,' replied Rusk, 'and we consider them rare delicacies.'[11] He was not the only American to be disconcerted by the – usually, but not always, latent – hostility to Americans to be found among the British. William Fulbright, who as a Senator was to do so much to further the cause of international study, felt thoroughly out of place during his first year at Oxford, making his friends among Rhodes Scholars or other foreigners. After going to a play he complained: 'They never fail to make Americans out as a bunch of rich damn fools.'[12] And yet Fulbright was at Oxford when that home-from-home of lonely American Rhodes Scholars, the American Club, finally foundered. The main factor in its collapse seems to have been its politicisation under a series of left-wing presidents, who invited Fabians, communists and anarchists to address the Club, a strategy which offended, and still worse, bored the less committed members. The climax came when an address by Shapurji Saklatvala, the communist MP for Battersea, led to a riot and the intervention of the police.[13] Attendance fell off, subscriptions remained unpaid, and in 1927 the Club closed. Kerr claimed this showed that the American Rhodes Scholars were entering fully into the life of Oxford; the closing of the Club was 'a clear proof that they are satisfied with the life of their own colleges'.[14] There may have been an element of wishful thinking about that, but if the American Rhodes Scholars had really hankered so much for their own company the Club would surely soon have been reopened under new management.

Kerr was not wholly deceiving himself: most American Rhodes Scholars of this period, after the first few months at least, thoroughly enjoyed their time at Oxford, felt that it had played an important part in their development and went home with kindly feelings towards the United Kingdom. Whether the Scholarships achieved Rhodes's most cherished aim, the drawing together of the most important countries in the English-speaking world, is another matter. In assembling a news-letter for the class of 1921 to appear in the *American Oxonian* the Secretary, Newton Trenham, among other questions, asked his contemporaries what they were doing to promote Anglo-American understanding. Most said that they were doing nothing, one said 'Not a damn thing!', only five claimed to be making any special effort. Was this, wondered Trenham, because 'we are too busy to try, too short-sighted to see the need, too selfish to be concerned, or too modest to admit we try?'[15] Probably it was mainly the first of these; the men of 1921 had been back in

America for little over a decade and were hectically engaged in making homes, fathering families and building a career. In another ten or fifteen years their answer might have been different. Yet the number of former Rhodes Scholars who were actively involved in international affairs, still less who were preoccupied by the future of Anglo-American relations, was always going to be inconsiderable. A benevolent if rather distant interest was usually the most that could be expected. When King George VI and Queen Elizabeth visited the United States in 1939, four Scholars from the class of 1933 thought that it had been a huge success and a real stimulus to better relations between the two countries; five, though, felt that it was part of a subtle plan to entangle America in the war which was clearly coming in Europe, eight believed the visit trivial and four that it was a bore. When Lothian was plucked from the Rhodes Trust to become British Ambassador in Washington, thirteen members of the same class welcomed the appointment but eight objected, 'characterising the appointee in a variety of pungent ways'.[16]

So American Rhodes Scholars could not be relied upon automatically to support the cause of Britain. More often than not they did, however; certainly they were more aware of and sympathetic towards British problems than any other group within the American elite. And they were beginning to occupy positions where they could make a significant difference. In the years before the Second World War, for instance, Stanley Hornbeck, one of the earliest and most loyal of Rhodes Scholars, was a highly influential figure in the State Department. Clarence Streit, from a later generation, was already prominent as a champion of Atlantic Union. It was to be a little time yet before Colonel Robert McCormick would 'expose' the Rhodes Scholars as a bunch of treacherous anglophiles seeking to subvert the best interest of the American people, but already he had some grounds for suspicion. Cecil Rhodes would not have been entirely content with the working of his scheme, but he would have felt that something had been achieved.

CHAPTER TWENTY-ONE
THE OTHER MAIN
CONSTITUENCIES, 1919–1939

Once the United States had got its own Secretary it was inevitable that the other main constituencies would follow suit. Canada and South Africa had their offices up and running in 1921; Australia, where the issues were more complex, delayed until 1922.

Canada, indeed, could almost claim to have had its own Secretary since the earliest days of the Scholarship, since Parkin had always retained a proprietorial interest in all that went on in his native country. He can hardly be said to have lost control with his retirement since the first Secretary was his brother-in-law, the craggily austere Presbyterian businessman J.M. Macdonnell. Aydelotte saw the passing over of the torch in Canada as being an opportunity to make a takeover bid. It might prove 'a convenience and an economy', he suggested, to append the Canadian selection committees to the list of American committees: 'It seems to me important that the regulations of the two countries should be as nearly alike as possible, and I think that everything we can do, even in such a small way, to cultivate relations between the two countries, the better.'[1] An economy, possibly; a convenience, no: Macdonnell was as resolved as any Canadian to keep national affairs distinct from those of his country's overbearing neighbour.

The problem of the French Canadians continued to worry the Trustees. To Grigg, when he went to Canada in 1923, the circumstances seemed analogous to those of the Afrikaners in South Africa; in both cases Rhodes would have been anxious that they should be included and the Scholarships serve as a bridge between the communities. In some ways French Canadians were even more desirable since, as Grigg told the Trustees, French Canadian candidates were more often interested in public life than their English-speaking counterparts 'and the influence on them of Oxford would therefore be more important'.[2] But any attempt at alternating between French and English candidates had broken down; almost always the English-speaker was better qualified both educationally and in sporting prowess. There was a real risk that the French

Canadians would lose all interest in the Scholarships. The only solution seemed to be to provide a second Scholarship for Quebec; but to do this without granting the more populous Ontario a second Scholarship as well would obviously be inequitable. In the end the Trustees decided to allow them both: one being entirely new, the other removed from a furiously indignant Prince Edward Island.[3]

So far so good; but there was still the probability that the best two candidates from Quebec would both be English-speaking. The Trustees were not prepared to make a ruling that one of the two Scholarships should be reserved for a French-speaker, since this would be to infringe Rhodes's sacred rule that nobody should be denied a Scholarship because of his race. Nor were they prepared to apportion the Scholarships between the two leading universities – McGill and Laval – since such an arrangement had been tried in the past and had always 'led to great difficulties ... the Trustees have everywhere abandoned it in favour of the system of open competition'.[4] Instead, they reached a thoroughly mealy-mouthed compromise by which the Quebec selection committee was advised that it should divide the Scholarships between the two races 'provided candidates of adequate quality were forthcoming'.[5] 'Adequate' was a word that allowed much leeway to the discretion of the selectors; they were left in no doubt that it was their duty to err on the side of generosity.

By 1936 it was clear that Macdonnell had been long enough in the job. He was replaced by a successful young lawyer, Roland Michener. Allen had his doubts about him; 'unless I misread him, he lacks just the quality I should have liked to see in the new Secretary – I mean "drive" and imagination'.[6] Allen did misread him: Michener proved an energetic and efficient Secretary and remained in that office even after he had entered politics and become Speaker of the House of Commons.

It was easier to get Afrikaners to Oxford than French Canadians since the existence of the Stellenbosch Boys' High award made it probable that at least one such candidate would be selected. The Scholarship awarded to the Orange Free State during the war had the same result. Its first award, in 1918, went to Peter Dixon who, in spite of his innocuous Anglo-Saxon name, had an Afrikaner mother, had been interned in one of the notorious concentration camps during the South African War and had refused to fight in the war against Germany. Unsurprisingly, Kipling resigned in protest, though on this occasion he was persuaded to recant. Afrikaans-speakers were more likely to miss out on Oxford from disinclination than from lack of opportunity; they were particularly incensed by the fact that, alone among British universities, Oxford refused to accept their language as 'European' for the purposes of student admission.[7] It is notable that, though the Trust made quite substantial grants to institutions concerned with the education of the black or coloured population, the idea that black South African students should be eligible for Rhodes Scholarships was a possibility so remote as not to warrant consideration. They were not specifically ruled out; they were simply not in the frame as potential candidates. During the inter-war period Wylie (twice), Kerr and Allen paid prolonged visits to South Africa and reported extensively to the Trustees. In none of their reports was there a single mention of the possibility that there might one day be black Rhodes Scholars from the region.

The man designated to be the first local Secretary was unlikely to agitate this or any other satisfactorily sleeping dog. Percy Lewis, who was appointed in 1921 with responsibilities for Rhodesia as well as South Africa, had been badly injured during the war and proved as reluctant a correspondent as he was a traveller. Allen conceded his 'slight lack of initiative and energy' yet felt that this was outweighed by his 'character, personality and standing' which were of the greatest value to the Scholarships.[8] Others were more struck by his inertia. He was urged to set up an Association of South Africa Rhodes Scholars but did nothing about it; he was instructed to attend meetings of the regional selection committees but never did so. In 1934 the Trustees tried to change the system by which provincial Administrators were automatically Chairman of the committees in their area. Lewis opposed any such reform. The South Africans were the most conservative people he knew, Allen had to concede, so 'we will come up against this negative attitude whenever any change is proposed'.[9] As early as 1931 Wylie had been told to decide whether Lewis was up to the job and, if not, seek out a successor.[10] Patently he was not up to the job but it was to be another fifteen years before a successor was appointed.

He would have had to be superhuman to bring the South African Scholars up to the level of the other main constituencies. The four schools were the chief culprits. Of the 1924 Scholar from Bishops the Senior Tutor at Worcester said that he was unable to understand how he had ever been given an award 'for his intellectual qualifications seem of the slightest'; a few years later Professor Hogben of the University of Cape Town attacked the Bishops' selectors for picking brawn before brain and making South African Scholars 'a signal for merriment in educated English society'.[11] In 1937 Allen reported that there had been three abrupt resignations by Scholars from Stellenbosch who, 'though entirely estimable in themselves, seemed quite unable to fit into the Oxford system'. Amazingly, St Andrew's was still worse: 'undistinguished by comparison with the other schools', said Allen.[12] Nor was it just the Cape schools which let down the average; in 1932 Lothian had to complain that the last three Scholars from Natal had all been unsatisfactory and that the latest of these had been forced to resign his Scholarship 'under unsatisfactory circumstances'.[13] When he visited South Africa in 1926 Kerr had complained that many of the South Africans were 'not really up to Rhodes Scholar standard. They have not much personality or ability.' He cautiously hoped that things were getting better. Ten years later, it did not seem that his optimism had been justified.

In Canada French-speakers were pitted against English; in South Africa it was Dutch against English; in Australia there were six warring tribes. 'The main thing now is to get a uniform system adopted for the whole country,' Parkin told Grigg in 1920. When he had set up the Scholarship system in Australia he had had to make many concessions to suit the individual states. 'We must try to knock these all away. . . . The question to be decided is whether Australia has yet reached this stage of civilisation or, if you prefer it, nationalisation.'[14]

It had not, as the Trustees discovered when they appointed John Behan as the first Australian Secretary. It was in some ways an ill-judged choice: Behan was a man of great academic distinction and much energy but he was intolerant, tactless and, in Rendall's words, 'inclined to impress his own somewhat pedantic views upon other Committees'.[15] His reference to the 'utterly erroneous notion of the "good all-round man"' caused great offence to those Australians who believed Rhodes's injunctions to avoid 'mere bookworms' should be taken seriously.[16] But anybody appointed Secretary with responsibility for the whole of Australia would have run into trouble. Sir Francis Newdegate, the Governor of Western Australia, was particularly offended by the idea that anyone living in Melbourne – two thousand miles further away from England than was Perth – should in any way interfere with the working of the local selection committee.[17] In fact all that the Trustees were suggesting was that the selection committee's recommendations should be sent to Melbourne to be forwarded to London with those of the other states; they thought that the individual states were being absurdly touchy in resenting such modest proposals for standardisation but had no wish to pick a quarrel on the subject. When Behan asked to be sent on a tour of the various states, the Trustees played for time and told him to delay his visits; when they eventually gave their Secretary the green light, Grigg instructed him to make it clear that he came to see what was going on on the ground, not to impose some central edict. He was sure, Grigg added with more hope than confidence, that Behan would manage to put things right with the selection committee in Perth, 'with the tact which, I know, you possess'.[18]

In 1920 Grigg arranged for a one-off Australia-at-Large Rhodes Scholarship to be awarded on a national basis. The beneficiary was W.K. Hancock, a brilliant historian who was to make a notable contribution to Commonwealth studies. Grigg felt that this should be the pattern for the future; the uneven distribution of population and good universities around the various states meant that the best candidates would not necessarily end up as Scholars. Behan agreed in principle – 'it is time we began to look at these matters more from a federal point of view' – but foresaw furious opposition from the states.[19] He was proved right; when Rendall took soundings on his tour of Australia he found that only in Sydney was there any enthusiasm for the proposed reform.[20] It was fifty-seven years before another Australia-at-Large Scholar was elected.

The Australian selection committees, particularly in the case of New South Wales, had a reputation for attaching too much importance to sport. In Sydney, Allen complained, they had 'always been over-impressed by athletic qualifications or by a certain goody-goodyness'.[21] The two criteria might seem contradictory but the result certainly was that the Rhodes Scholars from New South Wales were conspicuously less successful in their examinations at Oxford than their contemporaries from other Australian states. They were still quite as good, however, as most of those from other countries. Allen told Behan that the record of the Australian Rhodes Scholars at Oxford, whether in terms of academic achievement, sport or contribution to college or university life, had been outstanding: 'In fact, although one does not wish to stress comparisons too much, the Australian constituencies are far ahead of any other, with the possible exception of New Zealand, in the types of men they are sending.'[22]

Australia was surpassed by New Zealand in another, more equivocal respect. About half the Australian Rhodes Scholars settled outside their homeland; for New Zealand the figure was almost two-thirds. The reason in both countries was much the same: lack of opportunity. As early as 1907 the New Zealand geologist Allan Thompson had found that there was no suitable work for him to do at home when he had finished at Oxford.* The same was often equally true in the schools and universities, or in government service. In both countries the civil service tended to recruit its members at the age of eighteen or nineteen; there was, reported Lothian after a visit to Australia, 'widespread "democratic" prejudice against admitting that a man with a superior education has any claim to preferment as a result'.[23] Wylie found the situation quite as bad in New Zealand. No encouragement was given to men who continued their education overseas to return: 'On the contrary; in the government service, administration and education, these men are obliged to start at the bottom alongside men many years their junior.'[24] Inevitably, the frustrated Scholars resolved to try their luck elsewhere, though this did not happen without some soul-searching. Geoffrey Cox, author and architect of

*See p. 77 above.

Independent Television, reproached himself for staying in Europe after his years at Oxford. He comforted himself with the reflection that he had served with the New Zealand Army during the war and that, anyway, New Zealanders of his generation were taught to think of themselves as Commonwealth citizens. To serve the Commonwealth was to serve New Zealand.[25]

The problem had been compounded in 1926 when a second Scholar was awarded to New Zealand. Kerr had championed the proposal: 'It is a real nation in the making,' he urged. 'It has held an extraordinarily high record in the achievements of its Rhodes Scholars, and provided they go back, they can probably exercise more influence on the thought and education of New Zealand than any other Dominion.'[26] The proviso was, of course, significant: if one Scholar could not be found a decent job how much more would this be true of two. Yet, at the moment of their selection, there was no country in which the new Scholar was more lavishly fêted: 'Successful candidates were paraded around the country like shining birds, prize peacocks in a world where glitter is applauded and at the same time deeply mistrusted.'[27] Part of the glamour was owed to the fact that a succession of Governor Generals presided over the selection committees and took a keen interest in the Scholarships. Usually this was unequivocally an asset, sometimes it posed problems. Lord Bledisloe, an autocratic chairman of the committee, emulated his fellow aristocrat Lord Emsworth in his enthusiasm for pigs. On one occasion a candidate is said to have won his Scholarship by mugging up on the Governor General's interests and professing his passion for Large Whites. He wanted to study Agricultural Science: 'It seems odd to send a man all the way from New Zealand to study purely utilitarian subjects,' complained Allen.[28] On another occasion Bledisloe was so outraged when his favoured candidate was not even nominated by the University that he declared none of the others was up to standard. To compound the insult he issued a statement to the effect that 'the average New Zealand Rhodes Scholar coming before him had been pretty dim'.[29] They were not in the least dim, though perhaps less colourful than Lord Bledisloe, but they were thin on the ground. Lothian could not even find a Scholar to act as Secretary and look after the business of selection.[30] It would be twenty years before New Zealand could build up that critical mass of Scholars needed to operate a viable association.

CHAPTER TWENTY-TWO

SMALL FRY AND ASSOCIATIONS

What was true of New Zealand applied *a fortiori* to those lesser constituencies that Rhodes had arbitrarily tacked on to his Will. Bermuda and Jamaica caused the Trustees continual concern. Dawson told the future Lord Halifax that their long-term objective was to add a third Scholarship and then to throw Bermuda and Jamaica into a common West Indian pool. 'I expect they would kick,' he wrote in 1921, 'but clearly the field would be a very much better one.'[1] It was to be another eight years before the Trustees discovered how potent that kick would be, but in the meantime every fresh development seemed to prove how sorely reform was needed.

In Bermuda it was the stranglehold imposed on the Rhodes Scholarships by the Smith family that caused most disquiet. In 1927 a Colonel Gray protested that his much better-qualified son had been passed over in favour of a member of that ubiquitous clan, 'and there are more brothers to come!' Wylie told Kerr that the Smith in question was 'not clever' or 'of much ability', but that he was trying quite hard.[2] The Trustees took no action. Two years later another brother was duly selected even though a stronger candidate was said to be on offer: another protest followed. Again the Trustees took no action.[3] They proposed dropping the words 'success in' from the phrase 'fondness and success in manly outdoor sport', leaving only an enjoyment of sport as a criterion for acceptance; the Bermudan selectors bluntly told them that they proposed still to demand success from *their* candidates.[4] Still the Trustees were acquiescent. But when the American Scholarships were reformed and the weaker constituencies amalgamated with the stronger, they resolved that the time had come to do the same in the Caribbean. The private bill introduced in the House of Commons in July 1928 to permit the trustees to reorganise the American Scholarships omitted Bermuda and Jamaica from the list of Scholarships whose existence was guaranteed.

An explosion of indignation followed; the Bermudans being the more vociferous and energetic in their lobbying. Their Parliament lodged the 'strongest possible protest'; the Trustees were bombarded with letters from people with links with the island. It was soon clear that the American reorganisation would not get smooth passage through the Commons unless Bermuda and Jamaica were reinstated. 'I hate capitulating to those confounded Bermudans,' protested Fisher, but there was no alternative.[5] The best that could be achieved was an assurance on the part of both colonies that they would make serious efforts to improve secondary education, in particular by developing 'public schools on the best English model'.

No noteworthy changes followed immediately. In his report for the academic year 1936–7, Allen was still grumbling that Jamaica and Bermuda were 'a serious incongruity in the whole system'.[6] One Jamaican was 'miles below any conceivable Rhodes standard', another so weak that 'one is at a loss to understand' how any selection committee could have picked him. Lothian protested to the Governor, who took the charges to heart and promised that in future more would be done to prepare the chosen Scholars for Oxford.[7] The next Jamaican to be selected was sent over six months in advance with a grant enabling him to be crammed for Oxford. Allen was asked to fix accommodation, possibly in the centre for foreign students, London House. Allen hesitated, 'because I do not know from the photograph whether Levy is black, white or coffee-coloured. As he is a Jew, I should imagine that he probably has no tar-brush about him, but, of course, it is no use suggesting him for London House unless he is as white as the driven snow. Otherwise, I doubt not there would be trouble with South Africans.' In the event all was well; Levy classified himself as Church of England and proved to be 'a nice, simple sort of lad'.[8]

Certainly the low calibre of the Bermudan and Jamaican Scholars did cause problems at Oxford, but one can feel some sympathy with the Jamaican selection committee which protested that Rhodes Scholars should not be judged solely by their performance at Oxford but also by their activities in later life. Henry Fowler was a case in point. Allen dismissed him as 'an extremely weak man, and definitely below Rhodes Scholarship standards. He is entirely virtuous and well-meaning, but there is simply no quality to him whatever.'[9] And yet Fowler went on to become Chairman of the Jamaican Broadcasting Corporation, twice Visiting Professor at the University of North Carolina, Jamaican Ambassador to UNESCO and author of *Education and Training for Developing Countries*. He may not have made much of a mark on Oxford but it seems that Oxford may have made a mark on him. Reviewing the careers of Jamaican Rhodes Scholars, Allen said they were not 'complete duds' but 'ordinary and undistinguished members of different professions'. The only possible exception he allowed was a man who became British Minister to Bolivia and Norman Manley, who was a KC – 'whatever that may be worth in Jamaica',

Allen added disparagingly.[10] The worth was considerable enough to make
Manley the father of Jamaican independence and the island's first Prime
Minister. The Jamaican selection committee had a point when they pleaded
that the proof of the pudding was not in the cooking but in the eating.

In Rhodesia the disparity between the number of Scholarships and the
number of possible candidates was even more marked. Here the main subject
of debate was the eligibility of students educated abroad. In 1919 the
Rhodesian Teachers' Association urged that, in the interest of building up the
country's secondary education, boys whose parents had chosen to educate
their sons abroad should be excluded. Wylie argued that the Trust was not
administering a charity to help poor Scholars but was bound to favour the
most eligible candidate.[11] Over the next fifteen or twenty years, however, a
steadily growing proportion of Rhodesian Rhodes scholars had their
secondary education at home and the battleground switched to the insistence
of the Trustees that Scholars should spend two years at a South African
university before coming to Oxford. Even though the Beit Trust was in many
cases prepared to pay for this, the more patriotic Rhodesians took offence. 'We
don't appreciate the idea that our boys should have to take a degree in a Union
university,' Godfrey Huggins, shortly to become Prime Minister of Rhodesia,
told Lothian. 'This is not pure racialism but is more because the South African
Universities are so over-run by Dutchmen and Jews' (impure racialism?).[12]

Early in 1936 Allen admitted that, compared to Bermuda and Jamaica, the
standard of Rhodesian Scholars was satisfactorily high – 'It always surprises
me that so small a community can keep up such a decent average.'[13] But then
things went sharply downhill; by 1939 he was 'shocked and perturbed' by the
credentials of the two new Scholars. He blamed it on the selection committee:
'They will never get better selections there until they have on the Committee
more sensible and unpretentious Rhodes Scholars, instead of all these red-
tape officials'. He took it up with the Secretary to the committee who claimed
that the Governor, Sir Herbert Stanley, was responsible. Stanley was said to be
dictatorial in his chairmanship and snobbish by nature, preferring polite
young men of good family to those who might distinguish themselves at
Oxford.[14] Allen pleaded with Lothian to challenge the Governor head-on but
Lothian's disappearance to Washington and the Second World War delayed
any confrontation until long after Stanley had retired.

In spite of the problems posed by the smaller constituencies the Trustees chose
to make their life more difficult by creating more of them. The establishment
of a Scholarship for East Africa was, indeed, so half-hearted as hardly to be
worth mentioning. The plan was that, once every three years, a young man

from Kenya, Uganda or Tanganyika should be sent to Rhodes University in South Africa and then, if considered worthy, continue as a Rhodes Scholar to Oxford. In theory the Rhodes Scholarship proper was open to people of any race and not confined to the man who had been to Rhodes University; in practice the line of succession to Oxford by way of Grahamstown became established and no black man was ever considered. The procedure was so erratic that Allen claimed to have forgotten all about it, and, when the first East African Rhodes Scholar, William McEwen, came on the scene, asked anxiously if he was 'of dusky hue'. In view of his scepticism, the Trustees decided to postpone a decision on whether to continue the Scholarship until after McEwen had graduated. In fact McEwen had a perfectly respectable career, both at Oxford and subsequently in colonial administration, and the scheme limped on till 1950 when Allen, who had always felt it was an undesirable irrelevance to the Rhodes system as a whole, was able to secure its indefinite suspension.

Malta was a more interesting and more enduring experiment. It was granted a Scholarship once every three years on the insistence of Leo Amery, who argued that the Maltese were in the same situation as the French Canadians or the Afrikaners, people of foreign stock who were nevertheless citizens of the British Empire and whose loyalty must therefore be fostered. The first Scholar came up in 1921 on a trial basis; it would be decided when he went down whether to select a successor. He was 'a pleasant little man', judged Wylie, but of no 'particular force or ability'; he had done nothing to lead the Trustees to discontinue the Scholarships, but, equally, nothing to suggest that they should carry on.[15] On the basis of this somewhat tepid recommendation it was decided to continue the experiment. The second Maltese Scholar, E. J. Scicluna, was a success; the third a disaster who had to be removed in his second year. The real difficulty about the Maltese Rhodes Scholars, said the Governor after this debacle, was not so much the shortage of adequate candidates as the fact that there was nothing for them to do when they got back. After two years, Scicluna was still unemployed.[16] In spite of such discouragement the Trustees decided to persist. Their determination was rewarded – or, perhaps, betrayed – when in 1939 the Scholarship was awarded to Dom Mintoff, the man who was eventually to do more to change the face of Malta than any other individual in the twentieth century.

Constituencies like Malta and Bermuda might throw up the occasional Scholar of stature; individually their Scholars might profit by their time at Oxford and make a valuable contribution when they returned home. It would be a long time, however – if, indeed, such a time ever came – before a sufficiently large body of former Scholars would exist to make possible the formation of any national association. Yet the idea that the Rhodes Scholars should have some sort of corporate existence, certainly in their own country, ideally in a wider Rhodes community, had always been in the minds of the Trustees. There was some imprecision about this vision, but the Trustees hoped that former Scholars, sharing certain experiences, holding in common certain ideals and values, should meet from time to time, to reminisce and enjoy a jolly reunion undoubtedly, but also to exchange ideas, to compare notes, with luck to form common projects and carry them through. But, though this was desirable, it was not something to be promoted too energetically. 'Once the thing has been suggested as, in the Trustees' view, worth doing, it should be left to grow of itself,' Wylie told Allen. 'I should be against any thrusting of it down their throats.'[17] Allen fully concurred, and disclaimed any intention of setting up Rhodes House as a central organisation which would keep the different associations in touch with each other. If he knew that a Canadian Rhodes Scholar was about to visit Australia he would, of course, pass on the news, but he would not seek out the information or accept any formal responsibility for its transmission.[18]

In the United States no more was called for, but the Commonwealth countries needed more encouragement. Until the late 1930s New Zealand could legitimately plead lack of potential members. In May 1932 Wylie found that there were only thirteen Scholars in residence and they were widely scattered over the two islands. The spirit was willing, though, and once two Scholars were elected each year the total rose more briskly. In 1938 the New Zealand Rhodes Scholars asked for more power to nominate those of their number who sat on the selection committee. Lothian took advantage of this to suggest they first set up an Association and within two months one had been established.[19] Without the fissiparous tendencies of Australia or the racial divisions of Canada and South Africa, the Association throve and proved one of the most cohesive and constructive within the Commonwealth. Australia too, once it had been satisfactorily determined that no one state was seeking to impose its leadership on the others, was able to establish a worthwhile organisation. Wylie in 1932, indeed, found that there was even more 'corporate sense' to be found there than in any other dominion.[20] The Association took as its objective 'to further the aims of the Founder of the Rhodes Scholarships' – an alarmingly far-reaching ambition which in practice boiled down to taking a commendable interest in the improvement of higher education in Australia.

In Australia and New Zealand, still more in the United States, the Rhodes Scholar was deemed to be a superior being, destined for success in whatever field he chose to adorn. Canada was more sceptical. Many of the most eligible candidates doubted whether it was sensible to spend three years at Oxford when they might be getting on with their careers; if they overcame their doubts they found on their return that there was no apparent feeling 'as there is in the United States, that a Rhodes Scholar is a man worth keeping an eye on'.[21] Wylie, Allen and Lothian in turn, in defiance of the principle that countries should be left to their own devices when it came to the formation of local associations, urged the Canadians to show more corporate spirit. Macdonnell, the Canadian Secretary, in 1932 retorted that he had heard the same thing from Parkin ten years before. Most Canadian Rhodes Scholars, he stated bluntly, did not think that having spent some time at Oxford provided a sufficient bond to bring them together except on gala occasions of a social nature. Any sort of formal association was almost inconceivable: 'Rhodes Scholars are infinitely various, and the thirty or more living in Toronto have their various contacts and move in their various surroundings.' Parkin had seemed to hope that the Rhodes Scholars would form 'a kind of huge imperial federation league . . . capable of being banded together for certain common objectives. I do not think this is likely to happen and I doubt if it is desirable.'[22]

If the Trust's chosen representative took so unaccommodating a line, the Trustees might well have despaired. In fact Lothian had never shared Parkin's vision of an 'imperial federation league', but he still felt that some sort of association of Rhodes Scholars in Canada would serve a useful purpose. He continued his campaign to bring this about and claimed to have been encouraged when he visited the country at the end of 1934. Rhodes Scholars, he found, were no longer sensitive to the charge that they had been corrupted by Oxford and had ceased to be patriotic Canadians; all that was forgotten, today they were 'self-confident, and actively interested in Rhodes affairs'.[23] There was no reason to believe that Canadian opinion had, in fact, evolved so dramatically, but Macdonnell's retirement, to be replaced by the more amenable Michener, did signal an evolution in the thinking of Canadian Rhodes Scholars. By the time the Second World War broke out the way was almost clear for the formation of the association Lothian so much desired.

South Africa proved a still tougher nut to crack. When Wylie visited the country in 1931 he found the absence of corporate spirit 'perhaps more noticeable than in any other Dominion'. He had urged the creation of an association of Rhodes Scholars and had met with polite assent and the suggestion that it would be best to start on a regional basis. Yet within the regions there seemed equally little enthusiasm for the idea; when a dinner was organised for him in Durban the man responsible did not even know that three Rhodes Scholars had been living in his city for the last few years. 'The whole Scholarship business is not as alive as it might be,' he concluded, but the formation of an association could transform the situation.[24] Whether it would in fact have had so salutary an effect was to remain uncertain; when Allen visited South Africa two years later he found that no progress had been made

and a succession of Secretaries and Wardens over the coming decades were to
have the same experience.

Association, of course, could mean many things. At one extreme, Parkin's
vision of a 'huge, imperial federation league' had always been impracticable
and was every year becoming more irrelevant. At the other, a casual system for
the arrangement of occasional social get-togethers was easy to arrange and
almost entirely worthless. In the middle was the American approach, an energetic association with a strong centre that published a quarterly magazine in
which news of members could be transmitted and matters of common
interest discussed, that organised reunions and regional meetings, that
supported charitable or even political causes, that acted as a lobby group and
was prepared to press its views on the American Secretary or the Trustees and
officers of the Trust in England. Such an organisation required leadership,
money and a large and committed membership. By 1939 only in Australia was
anything similar to be found; New Zealand had the inclination but not the
numbers, Canada and South Africa doubted the need for any such operation.
Some at least of the Trustees had a lingering loyalty to the Parkin template. It
must have been slightly galling for them to reflect that the United States, in
which the idea of the Rhodes Scholarships was most clamorously promoted,
was also the country in which Rhodes's imperial ambitions were viewed with
indifference, if not hostility.

CHAPTER TWENTY-THREE

SELECTION, 1919–1939

One of the more useful things that a local association could do was mobilise the Rhodes Scholars so that the most suitable were available to help in the process of selection. It was the conviction of the Trustees that former Rhodes Scholars made the best members of selection committees, both because they had experience of Oxford and thus knew which candidates would make good use of it and because, in principle at least, they understood and enshrined the values of the Scholarships and were qualified to pass them on, like an Olympic torch, to future generations. Whether or not this was true, Rhodes Scholars could at least be trusted to avoid the extremes of weedy scholarship and bovine athleticism and to produce something approximating to that Renaissance figure, Rhodes's all-round man. With luck they would also be free from that allegiance to institutions which had dogged the early selection committees, when college presidents dominated the proceedings and ensured that their own protégés were given a favourable wind.

The United States, when there were enough Scholars to staff the majority of the committees and the indefatigable Aydelotte was there to push the process along, led the way in this reform. Wylie and Aydelotte in 1919 decided to proceed as directly as they could towards a system where, except for a chairman who would usually be a distinguished academic, all the members of the selection committees were former Scholars. If a particular state was short of suitable Scholars, members would be drafted in from better favoured neighbouring states. Within a few months they had achieved a remarkable measure of success. Wyoming alone seemed to have defeated them: 'We only knew for certain of one Rhodes Scholar resident there; it is a singularly inconvenient state to reach and we had exhausted our Pacific Coast material in providing peripatetic committees for Idaho, Montana, Nevada, Arizona and New Mexico.' Even in Wyoming the future was relatively hopeful; it seemed likely that two more Scholars would be returning within a couple of years.[1]

The magic did not always work. In New Jersey in 1921, for instance, the committee was said to have indulged in institutional bias at the expense of merit. 'That is disgusting,' fulminated Aydelotte, 'and I intend to make several changes in the committee next year.'[2] Wylie was duly shocked; he had been sure, he wrote, 'that, as ex-Scholars, our men would vote on the candidates, not on the institution', but the circumstances were exceptional and even in this case the Scholar in question turned out to be both a fine character and a very fast runner. Within a year or two the calibre of the average American Rhodes Scholar had risen markedly, so much so that Wylie felt justified in urging the Trustees to give 'ex-Scholars in the dominions an increasing share in the responsibility for appointing their successors'.[3]

In general, the dominions were happy to fall in with the suggestion, though not all of them were as brisk in pushing through the reform as the Trustees would have liked. Canada was to the forefront – 'possibly owing to the nearby example of the United States', Wylie thought;[4] South Africa and Australia followed; only in New Zealand did the dispossessed selectors put up a fight. The proposed reorganisation, the Chairman of the Professional Board in 1923 told the Governor General, Lord Jellicoe, was '*not acceptable*'. It ignored 'the Colleges who form the living force behind this university'. Jellicoe was outraged, particularly by the underlining of the words '*not acceptable*', and quelled the mutiny with some brutality,[5] but six years later there was still only one Rhodes Scholar on the New Zealand selection committee. Kerr was forced to take the matter up once more. 'Mr Rhodes wished his Scholars to be men interested in public affairs,' he told the local Secretary; 'the assumption of responsibility for the selection of Rhodes Scholars is precisely the sort of duty which properly qualified Rhodes Scholars should undertake.'[6] Though retaining the last word, the Trustees in practice let the selection committees choose their own members. This was even more true of the selection of new Scholars. Though no Scholar could claim to be more than a candidate until his selection had been formally endorsed in England, the Trustees made a point of never second-guessing their committee and, whatever protests were made to them about individual choices, would respond that they had full confidence in the selectors.

If Grigg had had his way the whole system would have been radically over-hauled, and the reform of the American system which substituted selection from groups of states for selection from individual states would have been extended to the other constituencies, so that Australia and Canada would have picked their Scholars from a central list. If something of this kind was not quickly done, he believed, the standard of candidates would fall unacceptably low and the colleges begin to lose their taste for Rhodes Scholars.[7] What he said made good sense but ignored the underlying realities; the Trust was able to get away with the reforms in the United States because they had been supported by the great majority of the Scholars; there was little prospect that Australia and Canada would see the matter in the same light. When in 1928 a story appeared in the *Christian Science Monitor* suggesting that the American plan was about to be extended elsewhere, Kerr quickly denied it: 'The initiative in the whole business has come from America and not from the Trustees, and it is highly improbable that the latter will do anything about the Dominions.'[8] Imperfect though the system might be, the Trustees would have to make the best of it.

Each generation the Trustees re-examined certain basic principles, but usually ended up leaving things much as they were. The ideal age for new Rhodes Scholars to arrive in Oxford was one such issue. Grigg believed that the ideal scholar would come direct from school or after a year or two at most in some centre of higher studies; Wylie remained convinced that any influx of eighteen- or nineteen-year-olds would be a reason for alarm: 'They would not have acquired sufficient stability to stand the transplanting.'[9] The Trustees agreed with Grigg in that they felt 'the normal Rhodes Scholar should be young enough to mingle freely with all the other members of his College, instead of associating, as an advanced student is apt to do, mainly with older men', but saw the force of Wylie's contention that the boy straight from school would find Oxford too much of a problem: the ideal Rhodes Scholar, they concluded, should be twenty or over but less than twenty-three.[10]

Kerr felt that too many Rhodes Scholars still had 'weaknesses on the intellectual side' and that selection committees, though no longer obsessed by sport, were prone 'to stress unduly the moral and social qualifications' at the expense of the academic. So far, he maintained, the Scholars had made little mark in the world; not because they were 'deficient in character and energy, but because they are not deep thinkers. They belong to the upper ranks of the average good citizen rather than to that band of leaders into which no man can enter unless he has some capacity for original thought.'[11] He was dismayed when he found that an Oxford don of some standing was starting a campaign urging the Trust 'to abandon the intellectual qualification and to select good Rugger toughs, as they are the people the Empire really wants'.[12] Allen, though he would never have put it so crudely, had some sympathy for the don's point of view. He regretted that the New Jersey selectors had turned down 'a fine athlete' in favour of 'an extremely dim chemist'. 'We have now got our American selection committees into such a virtuous frame of mind that they seem to me to be afraid of an athlete.'[13] Selection committees, to his mind, particularly in the United States, were trying to 'extract from candidates a type of intellectualism, or highbrowism, which is spurious and "would-be". . . . Instead of trying to get to the core of a man, some members of the selection committees, I suspect, ask rather pompous questions about the books the candidate reads, or the music he likes.'[14]

The charge that the selection system produced not original thinkers or natural leaders but decent mediocrities – honourable men who served society in a humdrum way – was one that was brought against Rhodes Scholars at every period. In a letter to *The Times* of June 1933 the South African novelist and biographer of Cecil Rhodes, Sarah Gertrude Millin, claimed that the Scholars were 'decent fellows' and not 'uncommon spirits'; the qualities demanded of a Rhodes Scholar were 'brains, sportsmanship, fellowship and school-leadership. It seems to me that only the first is an essential and measurable requisite of greatness, and that the last three practically demand the rejection of uncommon spirits.' To this Allen retorted that, if 'decent fellowship' was indeed the main criterion there would be much to criticise, but it was not: 'If every Rhodes Scholar is not a "world leader", that is because world leaders occur extremely rarely, and no system of selection which human ingenuity can devise can ensure infallibly the choice of "world leaders" and "uncommon spirits".' Lothian found rather more force in Mrs Millin's argument. He believed with her that 'distinction of intellect and character' must be the primary consideration for selection committees. 'An undistinguished uniformity of all-round qualities without particular excellence in the more important ones leads inevitably to mediocrity.'[15] The comments curiously illustrate the personalities of the two men. Allen, though himself possessing a powerful intellect, reflected faithfully the values of the 'good fellow'; Lothian, with his many frailties and sometimes notoriously bad judgment, contained something of the 'uncommon spirit'.

Selection committees inevitably consisted of more good fellows than uncommon spirits and made their choices accordingly. Between the two world wars American selection committees rejected George Gallup of the Gallup Poll; Walter Heller, Chairman of J.F. Kennedy's Council of Economic Advisers; Alger Hiss, senior diplomat and, allegedly, communist spy; David Lilienthal, head of the Tennessee Valley Authority and the Atomic Energy Commission; and Robert McNamara, Kennedy's Secretary of Defense.[16] None of these, perhaps, was a world leader but all of them made more of a mark than most Scholars of the same period. Some selection committees were strikingly idiosyncratic, often reflecting the prejudices of an authoritarian chairman. Judge Ferdinand Geiger used to boast that no Liberal or Jew had ever been sent forward from the Wisconsin state committee while he had been in charge of it. When Philip Kaiser was to appear before the committee the judge complained at a dinner party that the University was 'trying to force us to pick a Jewish kike from New York'. Fortunately for the kike in question, the woman sitting next to the judge was a close friend of Kaiser's family and defended him so vehemently that he was given the Scholarship.[17] The committees for Western Australia and for New South Wales were unregenerate in their determination to make sporting distinction the most important single criterion in their selections; of the latter Behan said that 'Nothing short of a revolution will shake them out of their present attitude.'[18] The Victoria selection committee on the other hand, selected a Scholar who listed marbles as his sport.[19]

In his intelligent and often controversial memoirs the radical New Zealand Scholar and journalist James Bertram deplored the fact that 'the highly moral tone of the late Victorian era' had affected both Rhodes's Will and its implementation. If the selection committees had merely been asked to find 'good all-round students who had shown vigour in outdoor sports as well as the examination room', then the scheme might have functioned more modestly and sensibly. But the Will called for the impossible: 'Future leaders and statesmen, those who could somehow combine ambition and the will to win with pure altruism, Christian charity and the compulsive improving instincts of the do-gooder'.[20] The resulting selections were cranky and inconsistent. A more common charge would be Sarah Gertrude Millin's: that the selectors looked only for good all-rounders and ignored the qualities that Bertram mockingly adduced. Millin was more often right: lip-service was paid to the need to look for the uncommon spirit but the good all-rounder usually won the day. The main difficulty for those selectors with wider horizons was that, even if they found a potential leader, they could not necessarily be sure that their favoured candidate would lead in the right direction. What should a South African selection committee have done in 1919 when the candidate who was clearly the most outstanding in every way had spent the previous four years making propaganda against the war while his competitors fought in Europe? Did the fact that a candidate accepted a Scholarship imply any undertaking that he would support, or at least not wilfully subvert, the British Empire? Should the selectors have rejected Dom Mintoff if they had known or even suspected that he would work so effectively to destroy the imperial link with Malta? The short answer obviously is that not even the most prescient selection committee could have determined in what direction Mintoff's radical zeal was going to take him; all they could know was that he was a young man of outstanding energy and persuasive powers who was likely to make an impact in his native land. In 1939, it was not unreasonable for the selectors to have hoped that two or three years at Oxford would make that impact more beneficial both for Malta and for the British Empire.

As set out by James Bertram, the qualities looked for by the selection committees seemed vapid, pretentious and faintly comical. There is an element of truth in all those charges, and yet the selectors who stuck to their, or to Rhodes's, guns were still on the right track. Those who settled for the easy compromise, the second best, could indeed be said to be betraying their trust; those who sought for the stars often failed to find them, sometimes looked foolish, occasionally made awful mistakes, but they were performing their duty as Cecil Rhodes would have wished and as their great charge required of them.

CHAPTER TWENTY-FOUR
SUCCESS?

By 1939 there was still no Rhodes Scholar who had reached what would normally be considered retirement age. Most of them were still in the process of building a career. It was still therefore early days in which to decide whether the Scholars were achieving what the Founder had demanded of them. Did they 'esteem the performance of public duties' as their highest aim? Had they attained what Rhodes or the early Trustees would have considered success? The evidence was still thin; the jury could not even be said to be still out for it had not yet retired; no summing up was possible.

'Success' is notoriously one of the most slippery words in the English language. One man's success is another man's failure. A Rhodes Scholar who amassed a vast fortune in property deals or by speculation on the stock market would deserve no praise in the eyes of those whose job it was to interpret and apply Rhodes's Will; only by conspicuous benevolence in using his fortune could he earn a degree of credit. A Rhodes Scholar who became Prime Minister might be seen as earning glory for the system but could not properly be considered a success unless he used his power to good effect. A Rhodes Scholar who set up as a surgeon in Melbourne or Philadelphia, worked hard, performed his duties well and made a prosperous living might well be respected by his fellows, but unless he taught extensively, made professional innovations, in some way contributed in a wider sphere, then he too was no success in the sense suggested by the Founder. The most unequivocal success in that interpretation of the word was that enjoyed by Kingsley Fairbridge.* Fairbridge won no renown at Oxford, he died in 1924 a poor man, he was awarded no titles or decorations, but by his efforts he contrived significantly to reduce the sum total of human misery. He was unique, but if he is taken as the paradigm of success in the meaning of Rhodes's Will were there others

---

*See p. 119 above.

who, by their activities or example, had significantly improved the lot of their fellow men?

In spite of the thinness of the evidence, Dawson at the end of 1920 began to agitate for an examination of what the Scholarships were actually achieving. The time had come, he told Wylie, to 'take stock of the purposes to which this great endowment has been put when the beneficiaries return to their homes'.[1] Only in the United States was any attempt being made to keep track of returning Scholars. What such figures as were available seemed to suggest was that disappointingly few Scholars were playing a part in public life or had much intention of doing so. Grigg felt that to accept this was to betray the Founder's intentions. Scholars, he wrote, should be 'directed' into public service, prudently adding the words 'so far as possible' to this somewhat authoritarian proposition. Furthermore, the public service should be 'directed' to accommodate them; dominion Prime Ministers, he suggested, should be asked to guarantee a certain number of places for Rhodes Scholars, who would be paid rather more than other civil servants and 'concentrated about the prime minister of their own dominion'. When Grigg put this idea to the Trustees, Lovat cautiously commented that he thought the idea would be extraordinarily difficult to implement and that 'any request on our part for special facilities might be regarded with suspicion'.[2] Like so many of Grigg's bolder ideas it was quickly dropped.

In 1932 John Behan delivered a vehement attack on the Scholars at Oxford and in later life, not confining himself to his own parish of Australia but targeting the wider Rhodes community. At Oxford many of them had been amiable nonentities, but even more disappointing was their performance in later life. The majority were doing exactly what they would have done if they had never been Rhodes Scholars. Should not selection committees be instructed to tell candidates that, if they were given a Scholarship, they would incur 'a debt of honour which they in after life are bound to discharge by service to the public weal?' Should they not be reminded when they left Oxford that 'their lives are not well-lived while they continue to seek their personal profit and success?'[3] The Trustees evidently considered that this high-minded if not sanctimonious diatribe was going too far. Only a few months later they pronounced that, on the contrary, they found the performance of Rhodes Scholars, whether at Oxford or in later life, was generally satisfactory and justified the faith of Cecil Rhodes; in the great majority of cases they were 'making a success of their lives' and were 'beginning to exercise that influence in their own communities for which Mr Rhodes hoped'.[4] Allen told Behan he was being unrealistic in his ambitions: 'I become more and more convinced of the necessity of not expecting too much from average human nature and average human intelligence.' Only a tiny proportion of people possessed 'real influence and distinction'; if even a handful of the Scholars appeared among them it would be a matter for rejoicing. Behan had bemoaned the fact that so few Scholars went into politics; to Allen this was 'much more the fault of democracy than of the individuals themselves'.[5] Behan was perhaps starry-eyed, Allen was certainly complacent. Sarah Gertrude Millin had a point when she complained that the Scholars were 'creditably following their professions'.[6]

Aydelotte mentioned that Rhodes Scholars had done much to transform higher education in the United States. Of the nine hundred former Scholars living in the United States in 1935 over a third were engaged in education: 'They have risen to full professorships and administrative positions on the staffs of practically all the stronger colleges and institutions, and it was inevitable that they should seek to import into our education the best of what they learned at Oxford.'[7] Aydelotte was a zealot; it was largely thanks to him that so many Scholars were involved in education and he studied their doings with an attentive eye. It is doubtful whether the impact of Oxford on American universities was as marked or as enduring as he supposed, but at least nobody could deny that between the wars Rhodes Scholars occupied many positions of great influence in American academic life. So far, so good; yet there was only one Congressman and only a handful of Scholars in state politics. Lothian agreed with Allen that this was the fault of the system rather than the Scholars. 'Intelligent, honest and candid men' stood little chance of being elected, substantial financial backing was essential and 'the atmosphere of politics is repellent to any sensitive person'.[8] This was not just the view of a prejudiced Englishman. R. W. Burgess, Professor of Mathematics at Brown University, concluded that the absence of Rhodes Scholars from politics and diplomacy said more about those worlds than it did about the Scholars.[9] Whatever the reason, however, only a few Scholars were involved in these conspicuous forms of public service.

Early in 1927 a vengeful article in *American Mercury* denounced Rhodes Scholars as being ineffectual, arrogant and conceited. The fact that they were considered worth an article was in itself something of a compliment, but Tucker Brooke, the editor of the *American Oxonian*, was stung into replying. Rhodes Scholars, he claimed, tended to be found in the 'hard-working and less obviously remunerative occupations; preachers and missionaries as well as teachers. Where there was a banker or businessman, it almost always transpired that he was devoting an absurd proportion of his time and strength to public-spirited and unremunerative enterprises.' Whatever he might be doing, the Rhodes Scholar would ordinarily be found 'rather particularly hard at work at something which rather particularly' needed doing.[10] Nor, as the *American Mercury* had suggested, was the Scholarship a short cut to glory, opening every door to profitable advancement. On the contrary, in most professions to have spent two or three years at Oxford meant that one's contemporaries had stolen a march on one and that it would be a struggle to get back into the race. This was especially true in the fields of industry or commerce, where 'a few years of travel and highbrow study abroad' do not seem to have increased the value of the potential recruit. Brooke had a point; a Rhodes Scholarship could be of limited value to the young aspirant and was occasionally even a handicap. But on the whole it smoothed the way to success in almost any field. As David Halberstam puts it in *The Best and the Brightest*, 'all Rhodes Scholars become brilliant, as all ex-Marines are tough. . . . Doors will open more readily, invitations will arrive, the phone will ring.' One young applicant, who must have known these rules, was asked at his selection committee what epitaph he would like written on his tombstone. 'Rhodes Scholar,' he replied. He got his Scholarship.[11]

The argument that a Rhodes Scholarship might be as much a handicap as an advantage was more true in Canada than the United States. Visiting the country in 1926, Kerr found that parents tended actively to persuade their sons not to apply for Rhodes Scholarships on the grounds that they were a waste of time; much better get stuck in at once at a profitable career. Allen in 1937 found the record of Rhodes Scholars in Canada 'creditable if not remarkable'. He found one bishop, two MPs, one member of the government but only two in government service – 'this is not enough, but there are not very many opportunities at present in this sphere'.[12] Within a few years he would be confounded, as the golden age of the Rhodes Scholar in government service dawned over Canada.

Australia was a still slower starter. Grigg visited it when escorting the Prince of Wales on the grand tour of 1920. He had met everyone of importance in public life, he said, yet apart from Behan there had not been a single Rhodes Scholar among them. Since the oldest Scholar at the time would have been well under the age of forty, Grigg was showing characteristic impatience; he had a point, though, when he complained that they were not even involved in the sort of work which would have meant that, twenty years later, he might have been more likely to meet them. Only three were teaching; none was in the civil service, journalism or public life. 'Too many Rhodes Scholars look upon the Bequest as a means of making better livings for themselves.'[13] Unique to Australia was the small proportion of Scholars who went into the academic world. This remained the case for the next two decades. In 1934 it was calculated that half the holders of the three other scholarships which took Australians abroad had taken university appointments on their return; the corresponding figure for Rhodes Scholarships was 4 per cent.[14]

The Australian Rhodes Scholars mouldered peacefully for a few more years, then came an explosion of intemperate criticism. Under the headline 'They do not shine' the *Sydney Labour Daily* accused the Australian Rhodes Scholar of returning home with 'an Oxford accent, a considerable share of that boredom which characterises the idle rich of England, and, generally, contempt for the ideals of his motherland'. The *Adelaide Advertiser* followed with a claim that the scheme had failed: 'How many leaders of the Commonwealth or of the state are ex-Rhodes Scholars?' it asked.[15] Two years later in the *Sydney Sun* the Professor of Philosophy at Sydney University attacked the 'pitiful catalogue of manly virtues' which Rhodes considered requisite for the public man. Not only had the scheme failed to produce any outstanding figures, it had corrupted the student body of Australia with its 'Philistine glorification of sport and nauseous cult of leadership'.[16]

In 1932, not long after the Professor's outburst, Wylie visited Australia. Unsurprisingly, he reached a different conclusion. There was no great achievement to be attributed to the Rhodes Scholars, he admitted, but they were making considerable positions for themselves: 'They are not yet much in public life or the public eye, but by degrees they are getting there.'[17] He did not mention one Australian Rhodes Scholar, then working in Oxford, who was shortly to be prominent in the public eye. Howard Florey had certainly not been tainted by the boredom that characterises the idle rich of England – on the contrary, he was nauseated by 'the aesthetes who wear gilded ties and other odd things', and found even some of those who played games 'insufferable' – but Oxford itself was 'a wonderful place . . . I got very little, intellectually, from the chaps at Adelaide Varsity. Quite the reverse here.'[18] Even by 1939 he was well known in scientific circles for his pioneering work on penicillin, in 1944 he was knighted and the following year he shared the Nobel Prize for medicine. In so far as the Rhodes Scholarships in Australia needed to be put on the map, Florey's success achieved it; one Nobel Prize-winner does not make a revolution but his glory heralded a period in which a newspaper article headed 'They do not shine' would seem not merely unfair but patently ridiculous.

Wylie found the state of affairs in South Africa similar to that in Australia. He felt that complaints that Rhodes Scholars were not making a mark in public life were unfair since, in 1931, they were mostly under forty and establishing themselves in their various careers. But he was still disappointed: 'I do not think as many Rhodes scholars are taking an interest in public affairs as we could have wished. Nor do I think that the spirit of public service, and of responsibility to the Rhodes ideal, is as alive among them as we might perhaps have expected.'[19] With the conspicuous exception of J. H. Hofmeyr, who in 1933 became a minister in Smuts's Cabinet, and perhaps E. H. Cluver, who at the end of the 1930s was appointed Secretary for Public Health, no Rhodes Scholar was well known outside South Africa and very few within it. Hofmeyr himself blamed this on the inadequate selection procedures which had prevailed up to the First World War. Things had improved since 1919, he felt, and the results were beginning to become apparent: 'when once that generation of Rhodes Scholars has been given fifteen or twenty years to establish itself, I am confident that the verdict will be very different.'[20] Hofmeyr wrote that in 1928; he could not know that within twenty years the climate of public life would so have altered that it would offer bleak prospects of advancement for anyone who cherished 'the Rhodes ideal'. Anyone of liberal convictions would be driven into a laager where it would be a struggle to keep a torch burning, let alone to carry it to the uplands of political power.

As they surveyed their empire in 1939 the Trustees may have felt a certain dissatisfaction. No Scholars in any country had achieved as much as they had hoped. Most of them were prospering, but prospering in the furtherance of their own careers, not in service to the community. But this, the Trustees must have hoped, was just a phase through which the Scholars had to pass. Left in peace, given just a little encouragement from time to time, it did not seem unreasonable to expect that the performance of public duties might play the central role in the lives of the Scholars that Rhodes had envisaged in his Will. But they were not to be left in peace.

CHAPTER TWENTY-FIVE

GERMANY

The German Scholarships had been abolished, not suspended, and the Trustees, after the war, held that Rhodes's hopes of perpetual peace had been confounded and that he would be as reluctant as anyone to see the Scholarships revived. In 1922 Wylie found that, when he tried to get information about what had happened to German Rhodes Scholars so as to bring his records up to date, he met with embittered resentment; the surviving German Scholars felt that their own behaviour was tacitly being condemned by the continued refusal to restore the Scholarships. Wylie told Dawson that he accepted the time had not yet come for renewal – Germans would not be comfortable at Oxford, nor would the colleges want them – but if the intention was eventually to restore one or two Scholarships, then it would be a good idea to drop a hint to that effect in Germany.[1] The Trustees at that moment felt no inclination to relent but the pressure grew steadily. By a substantial majority, the Oxford Union in 1923 passed a motion urging the resumption of friendly relations with Germany; an Australian Rhodes Scholar wrote to *The Times* arguing that the renewal of the Scholarships was essential if Bolshevism in Germany was to be checked; even the egregious children's historian Arthur Mee pleaded for their restoration.[2]

A change of heart on the part of the Trustees was precipitated by the announcement of several German Rhodes Scholars that they proposed to attend the reunion in October in 1929. Clearly, if the Scholarships were to be reinstated, this would be the right time and place to do it. At the end of 1928 the Trustees rather grudgingly concluded that, if the money was there, they were 'minded to recreate' two German Scholarships at an early date. Not all of them agreed. Peacock dissented, but did not feel so strongly on the issue as to consider resignation; Lord Hailsham, as Douglas Hogg had become on his appointment as Lord Chancellor, could not reconcile it with his conscience to remain a Trustee, though, as he told Kerr, 'if I profoundly differ from them as to the wisdom and desirability of using the surplus money for the German

Scholarships rather than for the Empire, that is no reason why I should endeavour to mar the success of the scheme'.[3] He therefore gave pressure of work as his reason for resignation – not unreasonably since he had missed several of the Trust's recent meetings. Tipped off in advance as to what was to be announced, eleven German Scholars attended the reunion.

Forty-five Germans applied for the first two Scholarships, as well as the unfortunate Dr Josef Bihl, who had been due to come up in 1914 and now asked whether he might belatedly begin his time at Oxford. Lothian explained that, as the object of these Scholarships was to bring young men to Oxford, Bihl hardly fulfilled the criteria.[4] The first German Scholars arrived in 1930. Within three years the Nazis had taken power. From then until the outbreak of the Second World War the selection committee was striving to retain its independence while at the same time not falling out irreparably with the government. On the whole it succeeded pretty well. As early as April 1933 Konrad Adenauer's nephew, Hans, complained to Lindsay of Balliol that, since his uncle had been dismissed by the new government, he stood no chance of being picked by the selection committee. 'I wonder on what grounds Adenauer's apprehensions are based?' speculated Allen. 'Possibly he is Jewish.' He was not, but one member of the committee, Mendelssohn-Bartholdy, was. So long as he and two or three others members of liberal convictions remained on the committee, Mendelssohn-Bartholdy assured Lindsay: 'I hope I can vouch for an independent selection.'[5]

Suspicions had been aroused, however. That pillar of upper-class English Jewry, Robert Waley-Cohen, wrote to Amery to complain that Rhodes's money was being spent on 'German Scholars selected by the German government'. Lothian replied that the selections were made not by the German government but by an independent committee. He conceded, however, that difficulties might arise the following year: 'If the Nazi government will not allow the Trustees to appoint their own committee and select their own candidates . . . I would recommend suspension of the Scholarships.'[6] The colleges, too, became increasingly reluctant to accept Scholars who, whatever their private convictions, would have to profess allegiance to the Nazi government. People 'tend to think that all Germans are tarred with the same brush', wrote Allen. This was unreasonable, but it was undoubtedly true that German Rhodes Scholars were carefully watched for signs of disloyalty: 'I have even suspected – and I am not alone in the opinion – that there have been German spies in Oxford.'[7] Sometimes the doubts of the colleges led to German Scholars being unfairly treated. New College rejected Alexander Böker in the mistaken belief that he was an ardent Nazi and a relative of Göring. Other colleges followed suit, until the President of Corpus Christi declared: 'If this young man is really a Nazi we'll try to convert him. And if he is not, we should be happy to have him.'[8] That Böker was very far from being an ardent or even lukewarm Nazi is shown by the fact that he spent most of the war in the United States and later rose to become one of Germany's most eminent diplomats.

The presence of a Jewish member on the selection committee gave the Trustees the comfortable conviction that essentially all must still be well; but when Mendelssohn-Bartholdy left the country, Count Schwerin von Krosigk, a Rhodes Scholar who had come to terms with the regime and was serving as Finance Minster, was nominated in his place. Count Bernstorff, a liberal diplomat and himself one of the most dedicated of Rhodes Scholars, reluctantly recommended this on the grounds that there should be one member of the committee who could, if necessary, satisfy the government that they were acting in accordance with Rhodes's Will.[9] The Trustees accepted the proposal: the committee were still 'predominantly, if not entirely, liberal in make-up', Lothian told them soothingly.[10] Then, the previous Secretary having disappeared into a concentration camp, his successor, Georg Fritsch, was given a job in the Ministry of War. Lothian wanted him replaced as Secretary so as to preserve the independence of the committee, but the Trustees were persuaded to let him stay on for another year. Bernstorff was by now seriously alarmed. The committee's independence was waning, he told Lothian, the wrong people were being elected: 'We are rapidly coming to the point where the Trustees must take the matter into their own hands and be a little more dictatorial.'[11]

This was a point at which Lothian was reluctant to arrive. Lothian was not pro-German, considered the future proprietor of the *Observer*, David Astor, but was haunted by his personal involvement in the preparation of what he saw as the punitive clauses of the Treaty of Versailles and thus disposed to make every concession to the susceptibilities of the German government, even if that government was Nazi.[12] 'He is favourably inclined towards Germany,' the German Ambassador reported, 'and wishes to contribute to promoting better understanding between England and Germany.' As late as 1935 Lothian wrote to *The Times* to assert that 'Germany does not want war and is prepared to renounce it absolutely as a means of settling her disputes with her neighbours.'[13] With such convictions, it was inevitable that he should try to avoid any direct clash with the German government over the Scholarships and to keep the system going on the grounds that, though it might not be operating perfectly, it was a great deal better than nothing.

Allen supported him. 'As a group,' he told Lothian in 1937, 'the post-war German Rhodes Scholars have really been very satisfactory indeed.'[14] Not all of them were liberals; in a debate at the Bentham Society, Geoffrey Cox attacked Hitler and was challenged by Baron Harald von Oppen to join the

Nazi Youth Labour Service and discover the merits of National Socialism. (He did, and didn't.)[15] The only German Scholar who was an avowed and vociferous Nazi, however, was Karl Motz. Allen conceded that his selection had been the result of political pressure, but claimed that this was a one-off and that Motz had been widely disliked while at Oxford, by the other German Scholars as much as by the British.[16] In Allen's view, the more troublesome German Scholars came from the left. Adolf Schlepegrell had a Jewish grandmother, a fact which seemed of no particular significance until, in 1933, the Nazi government banned any employment of Jews in the public service. Allen accepted that Schlepegrell was outstanding – for a German to become Secretary of the Oxford Union was a remarkable achievement – but did not like either him or his socialist convictions: 'He is unmistakably a self-seeker and something of a self-advertiser, and I am afraid I must add that I regard him as definitely conceited. . . . In short, he is not to everybody's taste, and he is not eminently to my own taste. . . . It may be that Hitler is not so very far out after all and that the qualities which slightly jar are contributed by ancestry.'[17] In spite of these disobliging comments, Allen had been appropriately outraged when Schlepegrell applied for registration as an 'honorary Aryan' and was rejected: 'The case is as harsh and fantastic as one could imagine. . . . You and the Trustees might like to know of this, the first instance in which present German politics affect a Rhodes Scholar. Heil Hitler!'[18] But when Schlepegrell applied for help in finding work in Britain, Allen had doubts whether this would be proper: the question, he said, was whether 'he ought not to go back to his own country . . . and face the music'.[19] To be fair to Allen, he made this appalling comment in June 1934, when he had little if any idea what sort of music a Jew returning to Germany would have had to face. His attitude was hardly sympathetic, however, any more than Lothian's when he recommended to the Trustees that they should reject Schlepegrell's plea; anything else would 'open up an uncharted sea of possibilities if the Trustees are to begin to support Rhodes Scholars in after life'.[20]

Another German Rhodes Scholar strongly opposed to his country's policies was Ernst Schumacher. Peacock got Schumacher spectacularly wrong. 'I tremble to think of the volumes this plodding, indefatigable German will turn out,' he wrote when Schumacher applied for a third year[21] – hardly an apt description of the economist whose *Small is Beautiful* was to become one of the most influential tracts of the twentieth century. Allen, too, thought Schumacher a talentless trouble-maker, and Schumacher had little use either for the Warden or the Oxonian experience. When he moved on to the United States he dismissed the American Rhodes Scholars as being '"clever", "brilliant" but no use for anything. That really is one of the main factors in my life at the moment: to get away from the atmosphere of Oxford. . . . Thank goodness that I never fell in love with Oxford life: on no account would I return.'[22]

The Trust was not at its best in its handling of the German Scholars and Scholarships in the years before the Second World War. Allen subscribed to the jovial school of British upper-class anti-Semitism; never condoning persecution but inclining to the view that the Jews had to some extent brought their sufferings on themselves. Lothian was dedicated to the task of conciliating the Nazi government and was ready to accept any assurance of goodwill on their part even if their conduct belied their words. He talked to Ribbentrop about the independence of the selection committee and concluded that he could 'be relied on to prevent interference as far as he can'.[23] Of course, some of the Trustees were more robust, but Lothian and Allen were the machine that made the system move and it would have taken some very exceptional circumstances and much better information than was available to them to induce the Trustees to insist on another policy. It would not have changed the course of history if the Trust had suspended the Scholarships in 1935 or 1936; it would indeed have deprived some liberal-minded Germans of an Oxford education; but it would have cleared up a moral ambiguity and have proclaimed that the Trustees would not tolerate even a vestige of governmental interference with the workings of its selectors. On the whole it would have been better if they had done so.

CHAPTER TWENTY-SIX

THE SECOND WORLD WAR

'The whole situation is so different from 1914 that one has to readjust all one's ideas,' Allen told Aydelotte shortly after war broke out.[1] The main difference was that between 1,500 and 2,000 undergraduates were at Oxford throughout the war, but though there were still seventy-seven Rhodes Scholars in residence by the end of November 1939, the number was diminishing almost daily. The process could not go too fast for the American State Department. None of 1939's intake of American Scholars was allowed to leave for Oxford, while any who happened to be on vacation in the United States were forbidden to return. Meanwhile Allen was busily employed trying to track down members of his flock who were scattered around Europe and finding problems in returning to England. Two were in Russia; to escape they had to sell almost everything except the clothes they stood up in, which yielded just enough to buy two plane tickets to Sweden.[2] Allen was relieved to see them safely back but, as far as the Americans were concerned, eager to see them go again: 'They are going to have great difficulties, they will need much tolerance and endurance, and in other ways I doubt whether their position is going to be altogether comfortable.'[3] Aydelotte fully agreed. If the American Rhodes Scholars stayed in Oxford they would inevitably find themselves drawn into some kind of war service, in defiance of the American neutrality laws. 'I should sympathise heartily with any man who wanted to do this but . . . I don't want to get the Scholarships embroiled with American politics just now in view of our pro-German isolationist critics.'[4]

The Americans' discomfort was not to last for long. In June 1940 the last thirteen sailed from Ireland on their journey home. Three were on the point of taking their Honours examination and Aydelotte arranged for them to sit their papers at his own university of Swarthmore. To the astonished hilarity of the American undergraduates they paraded formally in white tie and gown and saw their completed papers despatched to Oxford. 'If any of us expected anything good from the German blockade,' wrote Gilmore Stott, 'it was simply the remote possibility of their granting our *magna opera* a speedy and blessed demise. Foiled again!'[5] That left the Scholars from the dominions. Elton was in two minds what to do about them. Many of them would be ill at ease, wondering whether it was their duty to return home and join up or to complete their studies. If they asked him for advice what should he say? He consulted the various High Commissioners and got no very helpful advice beyond the obvious comment that every Scholar would have to make up his own mind in the light of his circumstances. Allen was more robust. Ralph Harry from Tasmania was reluctant to do military service and asked the Warden if he could help find him some non-combatant role. 'I don't know whether it is consistent with my duty as an officer of the Trust to have any views in such cases,' Allen told Behan, 'but as an individual I decline to help any conscientious objector.'[6] Harry's objections cannot have been deeply felt; in the event he joined the Army and much later ended up as Australian Ambassador to the United Nations.

Selection committees did their work in all the Commonwealth countries in 1940, even though the successful candidates could not hope to come up to Oxford until after the war. This was worth while, Elton felt, since it would help 'keep the Rhodes idea alive' and, anyway, 'it is always an asset for a young man to have been elected to a Rhodes Scholarship even if he is unable to take it up'.[7] Aydelotte disagreed; if a student was awarded a Rhodes Scholarship it would inhibit him from trying to go anywhere else. There would be no elections in the United States until the end of the war. Elton and Allen were unconvinced but withdrew from the battle when they realised that Aydelotte's real reason was his fear of criticism in the anti-British press. That 'an endowment of such long standing should be thought compromising does seem somewhat perturbing', Allen wrote sadly. 'I suppose this only means that we do not fully realise in this country how much America still distrusts us.'[8] Aydelotte then suggested that the Scholarships should still be awarded but for study in the United States or, perhaps, in Canada. That would be getting pretty far from Rhodes's intention, commented Elton, 'which, after all, is to bring men to Oxford'.[9] The Trustees agreed and Aydelotte's bright idea was abandoned.

Inexorably the numbers dropped away. By July 1940, after the final American exodus, seventeen Scholars remained at Oxford; the following year there were only five; at the end of the academic year 1942–3 Allen told the Trustees that none was left. By then it seemed that there might be as many as 150 Scholars whose Scholarships were unspent, either in whole or in part, and who might want to return to Oxford, in addition to the influx of new Scholars. This would be even worse than after the First World War, and at the end of 1941 the Trustees suspended all further elections. Two exceptions were made and one made itself. Rhodesia was offered the chance to elect in 1942 but

refused in conformity with the rest of the Commonwealth. Malta, in recognition of the battering it had endured, was offered a similar opportunity and
accepted: the Maltese Scholars, Elton told the Colonial Office, had not been of
'a high academic level, but they have been men of excellent character and
personality', and he thought they would somehow be able to scrape up enough
suitable candidates to fill the bill.[10] Finally, the ever recalcitrant Bermudans
once more refused to let themselves be told what to do by Oxford. They let
1943 pass without selecting a Scholar, then in 1944 insisted that they must do
so. Elton was initially in favour of making a fight of it but finally accepted that
this would involve more trouble than it would be worth. 'I should be in favour
of letting Bermuda have its Scholarship – Danegeld if you like – on this occasion,' he told Peacock. 'Although I hate Danegeld in any form, I agree with
you,' Peacock replied regretfully.[11] Allen argued that, if an exception was made
for Bermuda, the same would have to be done for Jamaica. The Trustees
agreed but, as with Rhodesia, the Jamaicans decided that they too would
rather conform to the great majority of the Commonwealth and make no
further elections till the war was over.[12]

With many fewer, and eventually no, stipends to pay, the Trust found itself
almost embarrassingly rich. In July 1940 Elton reported that its income had
held up while expenditure had fallen, so there should be a surplus of at least
£50,000 by the end of the year. He urged caution in disposing of this bounty:
there was bound to be inflation at the end of the war and stipends would have
to be increased. By then savings on the Scholarship Fund had risen to
£373,000, investments in gilts and other securities were up from £2.53 million
to £3.32 million; the Trust's property holdings were probably worth another
£0.93 million: 'All things considered, this is a highly satisfactory showing, on
which we certainly could not have reckoned six years ago.'[13] This had been
achieved in spite of substantial grants made to organisations involved with the
welfare of dominion and American troops – the Salvation Army, the YMCA,
the Church Army – and the usual support to South African schools.

Elton talked the Trustees into commissioning a series of portraits of
worthies connected with the Trust to hang in Rhodes House. Sothern Holland
– by now a curmudgeonly sixty-seven-year-old and seeming at least a decade
older – took strong exception to this extravagance and threatened to resign; a
threat which, to the mild regret of his fellow Trustees, he did not carry
through. Allen objected on other grounds – that Wylie was not one of the
favoured heroes in this Rhodesian pantheon. 'Elton seems to favour men of
public note,' he told Aydelotte, 'and, consequently we have Baldwin, who has
never been, or even attempted to be, of the slightest use to the Trust.'[14]

One cause which the Trust had supported loyally for many years and was
called on to renew towards the end of the war was Lady Frances Ryder's system

for despatching Rhodes Scholars to stay in – so it was hoped – 'suitable' homes around the British Isles. Allen clearly disliked Lady Frances. She was, he told Elton, a 'very unsuitable person to be conducting a scheme of this kind'. She knew little about the dominions or the United States, and what she did know was out of date. She subjected Scholars to a patronising interrogation about their tastes and background and then sent them to the wrong sort of houses where they picked up ideas of 'English life and society which seem to me regrettable'. Her assistant and successor, Miss Macdonald of Sleat, was better but 'still not ideally appropriate'.[15] Allen was in favour of severing all links with Lady Frances; Elton drew back from this but agreed that the grisly assemblies at which Lady Frances inspected Scholars at Rhodes House should be discontinued. Allen later changed his views. When Miss Macdonald put in for an increased grant in 1951 he supported it enthusiastically. The Dominions Fellowship Trust, he said, was 'doing better work than it has ever done before'. The war had changed things for ever: 'hosts had learned to understand overseas men better than they did', while Scholars who had been ill at ease in grand houses were 'far happier when expected to muck in'.[16]

Elton thought that the Trust did not make enough of its work beyond the Scholarships. In the past when it had been supporting political causes in South Africa, there might have been a reason for secrecy, but now it could justifiably claim credit for its activities. The only reasons for avoiding publicity, he argued, were the 'well marked tradition of reticence', and the risk that the Trustees might be subjected to a lot of undesirable pressure from would-be beneficiaries. Amery clearly considered these were obstacles of some validity. He played for time; Elton was instructed to consider the possibility of issuing a report every five years, the first not to appear until after the war. The idea seems never to have been followed up.

Rhodes House itself cost a lot to run during the war. It was first suggested that it might become a hospital but it was totally unsuitable for such work. It then became a transit station for mothers and children on their way to the United States or Canada, accommodated a full quota of evacuees and finally, in September 1940, with every bedroom full, was hit by an influx of 115 refugees from Kent. The party, including sixty children and five babies under a month old, had been travelling for sixteen hours with virtually no food. There were no complaints about the rough-and-ready reception offered them: 'they were just pathetically grateful to us because we had food and hot drinks and beds, though only mattresses on the floor.'[17] Dorothy Allen, who recorded this, was a dynamo of energy, efficiency and warm-hearted goodwill. Under her auspices Rhodes House became a centre where any Rhodes Scholar in England could drop in and be sure of a welcome. Endless letters in the *American Oxonian* testify to her 'astonishing ability to perform a daily miracle of the loaves and fishes in entertaining hosts of visiting firemen on a wartime ration'. Every Thursday there was open house: 'There may be a crumb to eat and a drop to drink but don't count on it!' she warned her guests. 'As you know, we are also always in for tea on Sunday afternoons.'[18] Such entertaining was mainly for Rhodes Scholars, but the Allens also ran Leave Courses for Canadian troops with lectures, a brains' trust, visits to Stratford and a dance on each Tuesday night. All this was done with minimal help: the four living-in maids vanished soon after the outbreak of war. 'It would be tedious to list the decayed gentlewomen, the partial mental defectives, the kleptomaniacs, the neurotics, and all the other odd characters, both male and female, who passed through our house in the guise of domestic workers.'[19]

One thing which Rhodes House had to accommodate was the office of the General Secretary. Lord Elton and his staff moved down to Oxford during the war. The cohabitation was not entirely happy. Elton's failure to commission a portrait of Wylie to hang in Rhodes House was not the only source of criticism. In 1943 the Trustees hired G.T. Hutchinson to write a pamphlet on Cecil Rhodes for circulation to Rhodes Scholars. Allen found the exercise entirely pointless. 'It is not very surprising that the suggestion should have come from Sothern Holland,' he told Aydelotte, 'but it is to me surprising that the other Trustees should have accepted it. I somehow feel that it would not have happened if Lothian had been with us.'[20] Hutchinson, a friend of the Rhodes family and the Treasurer of Christ Church, had himself been a Trustee since 1940 – something else which, one suspects, Allen felt would not have happened if Lothian had been around. Hutchinson and John Lowe – the Dean of Christ Church and a former Rhodes Scholar – were appointed after H.A.L. Fisher had been knocked down by a lorry and died a few days later. Fisher, Warden of New College, was very much an Oxford man, but he had been Minister of Education and prominent on a wider stage. Hutchinson and Lowe were the first Trustees to be appointed whose world was primarily Oxford centred. It was a signal that there had been a change of policy; that dons were no longer to be kept at bay but instead given a full voice in the running of the Trust. The following year the Trustees reverted to a more traditional appointment, electing Lord Hailey, a former Governor of the United Provinces of India and editor of the renowned *African Survey*. The choice of Hailey was a reminder, if such were needed, that the Empire was still central to the Trust's thinking and would figure largely when the war was over.

As at the outbreak of the First World War, the Trustees had been bombarded with helpful suggestions as to how the German Scholarships should be reallocated. All were politely rejected, but early in 1940 it was decided that, in the first elections after the war, two Scholarships would be allocated to India. Though Jamaica had sent black men to Oxford on several occasions, this was the first time that candidates had been invited from a country where it was almost certain that they would not be of British stock. The Trustees were reluctant to rule out completely the possibility that an Englishman living in India might be selected, but, as Elton delicately put it: 'The selection committee would no doubt bear in mind the fact that it would be unfortunate to elect a British candidate in the first year or two of the Scholarship.'[21] The reigning Viceroy, Lord Linlithgow, and the Secretary of State for India were enthusiastic; surprisingly, the former Viceroy, Lord Halifax, and Lord Lothian both had reservations. Lothian argued that 'Two Scholarships is a negligible amount for so vast a population and will produce a sense of grievance in due time, unless it is greatly enlarged.' He had doubts about the wisdom of bringing 'Indian adolescents' to Oxford: 'If they don't fit in they become embittered; if they do, they never feel at home when they get back.'[22] He must have felt mild *Schadenfreude* when the *Bombay Chronicle* sourly commented that the Trust 'had been in existence for decades without being aware of the existence of India. The award may constitute a compliment to Hitler, but it is certainly no better than a cheap ironical gesture in India.' This was not the only acerbic comment, but on the whole the award was well received. No one doubted that there would be a superfluity of highly qualified candidates.

In the old Commonwealth Allen noted that it was the Canadian Rhodes Scholars who showed 'least impulse to serve, and there still seems to be a good deal of isolationist or lukewarm feeling among them'.[23] This was the opinion of J.V. McAnee, who commented with some satisfaction in the *Toronto Globe and Mail* that Canadian Rhodes Scholars had been freer than any others from 'the moulding hand of Oxford. . . . Certainly we should be hard put to it to point to any Rhodes Scholar who is an outstanding imperialist.' From a countryman of Parkin these were harsh words indeed. Peacock asked the proprietor of the paper, George McCullagh, what he thought of the Rhodes Scholars. McCullagh answered that all those of his generation had returned from Oxford 'quite spoiled for good Canadian life. . . . the best of them were anti-British, negative in their criticisms, and all the more destructive because of their great ability and their good training at Oxford'.[24] McCullagh wrote in the early 1940s; this was the generation whose Rhodes Scholars achieved the most spectacular breakthrough into public life. Norman Rogers was Minister of Defence until his death in an air crash in 1940; Arnold Heeney was Clerk of the Privy Council; Norman Robertson was heading irresistibly towards the top at External Affairs; J.T. Thorson was President of the Exchequer Court; Thane Campbell and J.B. McNair were provincial premiers; L.R. Sherman was Archbishop of Rupert's Lane; politically the left wing was largely in the control of Rhodes Scholar activists. Good imperialists they may not have been but they were making a formidable contribution to the running of their country.

The Australians were less distinguished nationally but, on the whole, better imperialists. A conspicuous exception was 'Inky' Stephensen, whose hatred for Britain and the British Empire had mutated into a championship of Japan so virulent as to make the Australian government deem him a danger to the country.[25] Allen's only concern was for the reputation of the Trust; it would be intensely humiliating, he wrote, if the Scholarships were to get any adverse publicity as a result of Stephensen's behaviour. He need not have worried; in fact the Trust probably got more attention as a result of the antics of the Tasmanian Scholar elected for 1939, Robert Baker. For reasons that were no doubt compelling at the time, Baker in the same year disrupted a commemoration ceremony by hoisting a placard announcing that war had been declared. An outraged Governor threatened him with gaol and insisted that he must be stripped of his Scholarship; the Trustees showed rather more sense of proportion and let him off with a severe reprimand. He survived the war to become captain of the Oxford tennis team and Professor of Law at the University of Tasmania.[26] Apart from a group of scientists, mainly working for ICI, who were in reserved occupations, an impressively high proportion of Australian Rhodes Scholars joined the armed forces. The most prominent among them was Edmund Herring who, as a lieutenant-general in charge of the Australian forces in New Guinea, achieved the highest rank of any Rhodes Scholar in the Second World War.

Except for a handful of extreme left-wingers, almost every Australian Rhodes Scholar supported the war. The situation was very different in South Africa, where a substantial group of Afrikaners believed that they should not have been involved at all and that, if anything, they were inclined to favour the Germans. Representative of them in Oxford in 1940 was Etienne Malan. 'My sympathies in this war,' he told Allen, 'make it absolutely incompatible to my own conscience to continue enjoying the wonderful privileges of an Oxford Scholarship. . . . The battle today is for the very ideals of Rhodes and, according to my point of view, it is the duty of every Rhodes Scholar either to uphold those ideals and fight for them or else to, well – just get out.'[27] He just got out, though eventually ending his career not as a Nationalist but as a member of parliament for the United Party. 'He is impulsive and woolly-minded,' Allen told Elton, 'and at one stage wanted to volunteer for service in Finland.' Back in South Africa the Trust's Secretary, P.T. Lewis – rather unexpectedly given his lack of mobility – was called to military service. Bram Gie, a former Scholar and distinguished lawyer, took over temporarily and was horrified by the paucity of records. Elton told the Trustees that he had long felt that things in South Africa would run more smoothly if Lewis was replaced by 'a somewhat younger and more energetic Secretary'.[28] Gie was the obvious candidate, but the problem was how to give him the job without displacing a much liked man, who within his limitations had given good and loyal service to the Trust. Fortunately, at the end of the war, Lewis decided to stay in England and the difficulty was resolved.

Meanwhile, in the United States, the Rhodes Scholars found themselves under attack. At the beginning of the war a small group of Scholars was strongly isolationist; a slightly larger but still small group was in favour of immediate intervention; the majority thought that war was possible and that America should prepare for it but did not feel they should fling themselves into what was primarily a European struggle. The events of 1940, culminating in the Blitz, weakened the isolationists, strengthened the interventionists, and left most Rhodes Scholars feeling that war was now almost a certainty and that it must be accepted with resignation if not actively striven for. The attack on Pearl Harbor, at the end of 1941, came in some ways as a relief. America went to war. And then, in the autumn of 1943, that doughty anglophobe and long-term critic of the Rhodes Scholarships, Colonel Robert McCormick, launched in his *Chicago Daily Tribune* a series of ferocious attacks on the Scholars as being 'imperialist trained Americans who invited suspicion by accepting the Rhodes gratuity', who should be made to register as suspects with the federal government – 'and it might be a good idea to have them finger-printed as well'. No fair-minded person, one of these articles generously conceded, would accuse *all* Rhodes Scholars 'of subversive activities or even intent to overthrow our government and substitute British dominion rule', but unless they promptly disavowed the whole pernicious system, this was how they must expect to be regarded.[29] The Trustees concluded that it was 'neither necessary nor expedient to add fuel, by any rebuttal, to the fires of Colonel McCormick's imagination'. The *American Oxonian* went even further. The articles should be welcomed, it declared, as constituting 'a diverting episode in a time of stress and sacrifice' and proving, for once and for all, that the Rhodes Scholars really did count for something in national life.[30] But, grotesque though the charges were, some would believe them and others feel that there could be no smoke without fire. A politician like William Fulbright could not afford wholly to ignore such attacks. In 1942 Fulbright had been asked to stand for Congress in his home state of Arkansas. He consulted his mother who replied: 'Well, why not? How do you justify a Rhodes Scholarship if you don't intend doing something useful with it?' Within a few months he was introducing a resolution advocating membership of an international peace-keeping organisation. McCormick was outraged. Fulbright, he claimed, 'in his formative years was sent as a Rhodes Scholar to Oxford to learn to betray his country and deprive it of its independence. In this instance, as no doubt in many others, Mr

Rhodes appears to have got his money's worth.'[31] Now Fulbright, together with fellow Scholars Congressmen Hale of Maine and Elmer Davis, who was running the Office of War Information, were back in the firing line.

Not all Rhodes Scholars incurred the Colonel's wrath. Alex Valentine, the President of Rochester University, was a vociferous isolationist. He testified against the Lend-Lease Bill and was condemned in a letter in *Time* by another scholar, Herbert Ford, on the grounds that anyone who, thanks to Rhodes, had enjoyed British hospitality had a duty to support aid to Britain in return. Ford's letter was deplored by most Rhodes Scholars because it suggested that their response was regimented and owed little to their personal convictions. Aydelotte agreed. He had himself 'advocated most vigorously the passage of the Lend-Lease Bill', he told Allen, '. . . and I do not want to be thought to be doing this merely because I was a Rhodes Scholar'.[32] The fact that Lothian, until his death in December 1940, was in Washington as British Ambassador heightened McCormick's conspiracy fantasies. Aydelotte got into trouble when he sent every American Scholar, in a Rhodes Trust envelope, a copy of a speech by Lothian setting out Britain's case. He was attacked by a Harvard economist and fellow Rhodes Scholar, R.M. Goodwin, who declared that it was inappropriate to spread British propaganda by such means. Most Scholars seem to have supported Aydelotte on this issue – if only because Goodwin's letter irritated them by suggesting that the Americans were 'peculiarly innocent, or ignorant, or both'.[33]

The war put an end to complaints that American Rhodes Scholars did not enter public life. In 1940 there were some fifty Scholars in Washington; by 1943 the total had risen to 125 and regular lunches were held on the second Thursday of every month. 'I suspect that Mr Rhodes might have regarded with mixed feelings the large number of American Rhodes Scholars who are being absorbed into the vast bureaucracy of Washington,' Allen told the Trustees, 'but this must rank as conscientious service to the state.'[34] In New York two Rhodes Scholars, Francis Miller and Whitney Shepardson, were instrumental in founding the Century Group – named after the club where they habitually congregated – a ginger group of editors, financiers, lawyers and churchmen dedicated to the cause of intervention. One of their number, another Rhodes Scholar and editor at Harcourt Brace, Frank Morley, was responsible for concocting the bogus memoirs of a twelve-year-old Dutch boy who had been a victim of the German invasion of The Netherlands. It proved a triumphant bestseller.[35]

And then there were the Germans. F.C. von Clavé-Brünig wrote from Geneva in October 1939 to express his regret that he had been unable to return to Oxford in time for the beginning of term. He hoped to get back soon. 'As I shall not be able to collect the cheque from you in the first days of term, I would be much obliged if you could kindly send it to Lloyd's National Provincial Foreign Bank, Geneva.' The Trustees rejected this somewhat importunate request, fortified by the report that at Christ Church Brünig had been considered a Nazi sympathiser. Most of the German Rhodes Scholars who were of military age fought for their country, though often with grave reservations. One at least of these demonstrated his reservations with spectacular courage: General von Senger und Etterlin consistently defied the orders of the Nazi leadership and saved the lives of many Italians who would otherwise have perished at German hands. Five died in action, two or perhaps three committed suicide.[36] Two, Bernstorff and Adam von Trott zu Solz, were executed by the Gestapo. Georg Rosen, a Rhodes Scholar diplomat who had been dismissed for having Jewish blood and was living in the United States, pleaded that the German Scholarships should be awarded to refugees from Germany who pledged that they would return there after the war. The Trustees considered the proposal with some sympathy but felt that it was not something they could envisage in present circumstances.[37]

Only one Rhodes Scholar, Schwerin von Krosigk, played a prominent role under the Nazis, being Minister of Finance for most of the war and, briefly, Foreign Minister in Dönitz's interim government. He was tried and found guilty at Nuremberg but let out within a few years. Hugh Trevor-Roper dismissed him as a misguided blunderer who thought he could influence Nazi policy by working within the party. Like all Nazis he misunderstood foreign politics, but he misunderstood Nazi politics too: 'It was perhaps because he misunderstood them so thoroughly that Schwerin von Krosigk was able to survive among them so long.'[38] Allen submitted an affidavit at Schwerin von Krosigk's trial claiming that he had done his best to keep the Rhodes Scholarships free of Nazi interference, and Wylie too supported him.[39] Certainly he was a great deal less culpable than most of those with whom he associated, but it is difficult not to agree with Schumacher's acid comment: 'It's not all that difficult to avoid becoming a Cabinet Minister.'[40]

As the war neared its end, those Rhodes Scholars who had never gone up to Oxford or whose studies had been interrupted began to speculate about their future. They had been promised that, if they wanted to, they could resume their studies, but would this be compatible with their new ambitions and commitments? Some of them were already nearing thirty; would they be allowed to spend only a year at Oxford before starting their careers? Allen thought not; two years seemed the practicable minimum: 'Apart from academic considerations, I doubt whether many Rhodes Scholars . . . are likely to derive much benefit from Oxford in twelve months, half of which is vacation.'[41] Could they defer their Scholarships until they had established themselves in their careers? This was not what the Rhodes Scholarships were for, responded the Trustees: it was no doubt admirable that mature lawyers or scientists should take a year off to study at Oxford, but they would have to find some other auspices under which to do it. Most urgent of all: what about the wives whom many of them had accumulated in the years since they had won their Scholarships? Out of 208 Scholars who were eligible to return to Oxford or had not yet taken up their Scholarship, seventy-five were known to be married. The precedent of 1919 suggested that a Scholar who had married while serving his country should not now be denied his Scholarship. The problem was logistical. Accommodation was always scarce in Oxford; after the war it would be worse than ever. Elton thought it might be necessary to ban wives from Oxford altogether, but this had to be a last resort: it must be made clear to married Scholars that the Trust could offer no extra stipend to meet their needs, nor could it accept any responsibility for finding accommodation.[42] So it was decreed. But Dorothy Allen did not delude herself that this was how it would work out in practice. For the last five years she had served the Trust as full-time housekeeper and hostess; now she would have to become a house agent as well.

CHAPTER TWENTY-SEVEN
PLAY RESUMED AGAIN

At the outbreak of the Second World War Allen had told Aydelotte how different things had been in 1914. In 1945 things seemed much the same as in November 1918. Thirty-two Rhodes Scholars had been killed, as opposed to seventy in the First World War, but for Allen the central problem was the same: how to accommodate the undergraduates who had been up at Oxford before the war and now wished to complete their studies; those who would have come up during the war and were now in a position to do so; and those who finished school in the summer of 1945 and wished to move on to university. Fortunately most of those eligible were slow off the mark and the mechanism of selection did not get going in time to have new Scholars in place by October 1945. By the beginning of term thirty-four Scholars were expected to be in residence, with another five listed as possible. Of these twenty-four were now in Oxford.[1] South Africa had been the fastest into action, with thirteen Scholars; there were no Americans. By the following year the number of deferred Scholars had risen to 150; the Rhodes Scholar population at Oxford peaked in 1948 at 220.

Half the first post-war wave of Scholars had wives. The proportion fell but the total rose over the following years till in 1948 there were eighty-one wives in Oxford. The Trustees in the past had been adamant in their opposition to married Scholars because they feared that the presence of a wife in Oxford would make impossible the collegiate life which Rhodes had so much valued. In some cases their apprehension was justified. Zelman Cowen, for instance, a future Governor General of Australia, lived in cramped quarters in North Oxford, and in so far as he had any college life found it was centred on Rhodes House.[2] Most of the Rhodes Scholars, however, managed to combine university and married life: one New Zealander got a first in Greats, a Rugby blue, a fellowship and three children; another accumulated a first, a doctorate, a reputation as an acrobat and five daughters under seven.[3]

Dorothy Allen sought to prepare married Scholars for the tribulations ahead by sending every wife a 'misery pamphlet'. Shopping, they were told, was 'a lengthy and exhausting business'. Hot water was only occasionally available, towels and sheets were unobtainable, an amplitude of warm clothing was essential. However, Mrs Allen concluded – cheerfulness characteristically breaking through – 'if you are prepared to forego luxuries, work hard, eat sparingly, and put up with possibly rather peculiar accommodation, you can be as healthy and happy here as at home. Our amusements have not been rationed, and we all manage to enjoy ourselves a great deal in a comparatively simple way.'[4] As anyone who knew her could have predicted, she worked endlessly to find Scholars the accommodation that they had been told they would have to find for themselves. The lodgings were almost always small and sparse, sometimes insalubrious, but in the end everyone was fitted in. Rhodes House became for the wives a place where they could turn for help, advice, encouragement or consolation. Every Wednesday they gathered there in force. This was 'a hectic but delightful occasion', remembered Dorothy Allen. 'Prams were parked in our hall and carry-cots in our dining room. . . . Older babies crawled or toddled everywhere, and the big children explored the house, or in the summer climbed about in the garden, and somehow emerged unscathed.' The Warden prowled nervously but benevolently around these gatherings, feeling 'like a lion in a den of Daniels. I do not behave like a lion; on the contrary, natural shyness compels me to run like a rabbit.'[5]

Allen never changed his view that marriage was incompatible with a Rhodes Scholarship in its full sense. By the end of 1948 he was longing for a return to normality. 'I think we have carried on the married regime just one year too long,' he told Aydelotte. He had to put up with it for a while longer; in the end it was decided that no married Scholars would be accepted after the academic year 1949–50. 'My only fear is that this might cause an ugly rush to the altar during the next twelve months,' he told Elton, 'but I suppose that cannot be helped.'[6]

By then the over-crowding at Oxford was beginning to ease. This had been one of the reasons why the Trustees tried to cut back on the number of Rhodes Scholars allowed to stay on for a third year: the other being a suspicion that often such third years were not being profitably used. Before the war almost anyone who had wanted to stay for a third year had been allowed to do so; now there was talk of cutting the numbers so that no more than half stayed on in any given year. Elton claimed that Aydelotte supported this, saying that, in their third year, many American Rhodes Scholars wasted their time.[7] He may have said something of the sort, but when Scholars began to protest at being denied what they thought of as their rightful due, he pleaded that the Trustees should be lenient: 'The third year meant more to them from the point of view of the ideas in which Rhodes was interested, than the first two put together.' Allen sympathised, and thought that the privilege of remaining at Oxford for a third year was rarely abused. 'I am afraid that we shall be sending away at the end of this year some embittered Rhodes Scholars,' he told Aydelotte. However, he added dutifully, 'I must of course be careful to remain merely an instrument of the Trustees' policy.'[8] The whole matter was quietly forgotten within a few years. When the next Warden described the procedure in 1954 he said that he knew of no case in which a worthy applicant had been turned down and some in which the marginally meritorious had been accepted: 'The practice seems to be, when in doubt, allow rather than turn down.'[9]

The demand for third years was to some extent linked to the increasing tendency of Scholars to do some sort of research and eschew the traditional second BA. This had been apparent even before the war – by 1939 some 30 per cent of Scholars were reading for research degrees. This grew to about 40 per cent in the decade after the war and in the 1960s became a flood. Both Elton and Allen deplored the tendency. Elton thought the North American universities were the cause of the trouble and bemoaned their inability to realise that 'for many if not most men' a Final Honour School at Oxford was 'a much more rewarding educational experience' than postgraduate research, however many additional letters the latter would allow the Scholar to put after his name.[10] Research degrees not merely gave the Scholar a worse education, they tended to obviate that immersion in college life which was at the heart of Rhodes's scheme. Elton was haunted by the dread that the liberal, collegiate character-forming experience envisaged by Rhodes might be subverted into narrow technical training of the sort that could be acquired anywhere. When a selection committee in Quebec enquired about the eligibility of a candidate who was already near the end of his medical training, Elton somewhat regretfully agreed that he would be eligible. But he was alarmed at a reference in the application to 'professional' training: to Elton that suggested 'the trail of the serpent – the idea, I mean, that a man goes to university primarily to qualify for some particular profession, rather than to be educated'.[11] It was an inchoate but deeply held conviction that humanities provided the only true education which led Elton to rejoice when statistics showed that while, before the war, only just over 30 per cent of Scholars from the Commonwealth had studied the humanities, by 1954 the proportion had more than doubled to 65 per cent. The equivalent figures for American students were 88 per cent before the war and 84 per cent in 1954.[12]

Most undergraduates in the years after the war were older, some much older, than their equivalents had been in 1939. The buildings and the clothes were shabbier, the graciousness of life had taken quite a beating. But essentially things were much the same. Curmudgeonly servants still did their bit to contribute to the folklore which Rhodes Scholars treasured. The head porter at University College, Douglas Millin, was especially zealous in this cause. When the three Scholars for 1982 arrived, Millin asked them if they would be attending chapel. The first admitted that he was a Roman Catholic, the second that he was a Jew. 'And you'll be a bloody Buddhist, I suppose?' Millin said to the third. Bernard Rogers had been a particular friend of Millin's. He rang him up at home many years later, by which time he was the Supreme Allied Commander in Europe and an honorary fellow. Millin was resolutely unimpressed: 'Oh, this is God's bloody gift to the defence of the Western Hemisphere, is it?'[13] Dons were still eccentric and absent-minded, inhaling snuff, forgetting appointments, producing comments of dazzling perception from what seemed the profoundest inattention. Public schoolboys still formed cliques and outraged the democratic instinct of their Rhodes Scholar contemporaries: 'I was astonished at their lack of sensitivity, their assertiveness and their self-obsession,' wrote Bryan Gould. 'I could hardly believe the braying tones in which they addressed each other.'[14] One change was that the University was notably more polyglot, indeed polychrome, than it had been before the war. 'A man of colour is really under no disability at all at Oxford these days if he is a good sort of chap,' Allen told Aydelotte. 'We have two coloured Rhodes Scholars at present from Jamaica, and two Indians, though I cannot bring myself to regard them as men of colour in the ordinary sense.' The Trust was resolutely colour blind. When Willem Hefer, at that point still a cautious advocate of apartheid, went to his first dance at Rhodes House, Dorothy Allen thrust him into the arms of a Jamaican girl. She was the first black woman he had ever embraced. The evening was a great success.[15]

Because of the influx of wives, Rhodes House took rather longer to return to normal than most Oxford institutions. Lord Elton with the General Office moved out early in 1947; they established themselves in nearby Beaumont Street, however – it shows how much the perception of the Trust had changed that the idea of a return to London was barely mooted. Amery was still an active and vigilant chairman, but the focus had switched. 'The Trust, after all, is more concerned with Oxford than with London,' as Elton put it.[16] Among the new Trustees Charles Howard Millis was a City man, but Kenneth Wheare, who like Millis was appointed in 1948, was an Australian Rhodes Scholar who had made his career as a constitutional historian in Oxford and was now Rector of Exeter College.

Rhodes House itself continued to provide its fair share of problems, not least those caused by the relentless benevolence of Lady Milner. Having failed to persuade the Trust to buy an extensive collection of silver objects presented

Cecil Rhodes
at Watts Studio
1898.

1 Cecil John Rhodes drawn by George Watts in 1898. Watts was responsible for the equestrian statue in Kensington Gardens, known as 'Physical Energy', which is also the centrepiece of the Rhodes Memorial in Cape Town.

2 Cecil John Rhodes, drawing by Mortimer Menpes.

3 Sir Leander Starr Jameson, one of Rhodes's few intimates.

4 Sir Alfred Beit, a German-Jewish diamond broker who was one of Rhodes's closest associates and a founder Trustee.

5 Viscount Milner, who dominated the Trust until his death in 1925.

6 Sir George Parkin, first Secretary of the Trust and passionate imperialist.

7 Philip Kerr, Marquess of Lothian. A Secretary of the Trust who, socially and politically, outranked his masters.

8 Dr Frank Aydelotte, first of the American Secretaries.

9 Sir Edward Peacock, the Canadian banker who, as a Trustee from 1925 to 1962, contributed signally to the Trust's prosperity.

10 John Baring, Lord Ashburton, Chairman of Barings Bank and of the Rhodes Trust from 1987 to 1999. A drawing by Daphne Todd.

"RHODES SCHOLAR, NO DOUBT"

11 A 1930s drawing by Robert Day, which originally appeared in *Punch*.

12 Three generations of Wardens: standing, from left to right, Lady Wylie and Sir Francis Wylie, Sir Carleton Allen and Lady Allen, and seated, Lady and Sir Edgar (Bill) Williams.

13 Successor Wardens. From left to right: Sir Anthony and Lady Kenny and Mrs and Dr Robin Fletcher.

14 Dr John Rowett, Warden from 2000 to 2004, who was in large part responsible for establishing the Mandela-Rhodes Foundation.

15 Sir Colin Lucas, former Vice-Chancellor of Oxford University, who took over as Warden in 2004.

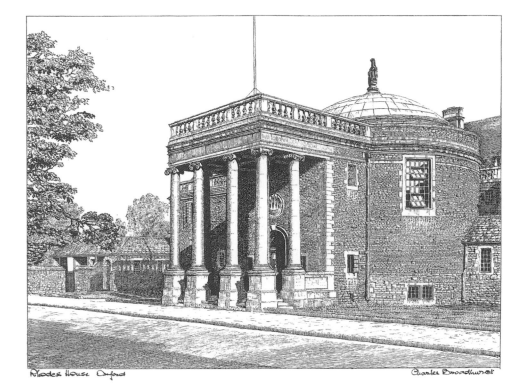

Rhodes House Oxford   Charles Broadhurst

16 Herbert Baker's massive Ionic portico to Rhodes House on South Parks Road. Pen and ink drawing by Charles Broadhurst.

17 The garden-front of Rhodes House. The Latin inscription reads 'This house stands forever as a reminder to the Oxford he loved of the name and example of Cecil John Rhodes'.

18 Tony Blair, Nelson Mandela and Bill Clinton at the centenary celebrations of the Rhodes Trust, Palace of Westminster, 2 July 2003. Photo © Marc Stanes

19 Nelson Mandela welcomed by an a cappella group of Rhodes Scholars on his first visit to Rhodes House, 1 July 2003. Photo © Marc Stanes

20 A coming-up dinner for Rhodes Scholars in the Milner Hall at Rhodes House.

21 Rhodes Scholars at the opening of the Scholars' Rooms at Rhodes House.

22 Second Meeting of the Trustees of the Mandela-Rhodes Foundation at The Mandela-Rhodes Building, Cape Town, February 2004. From left to right: Lord Fellowes (a Rhodes Trustee), Professor Jakes Gerwel (first chairman of the Foundation), Shaun Johnson (chief executive officer), Nelson Mandela, Baroness Deech and Julian Ogilvie Thompson (both Rhodes Trustees), Justice Yvonne Mokgoro, Dr John Rowett (then Warden of Rhodes House), Professor Njabulo Ndebele, Lord Waldegrave (Chairman of the Rhodes Trust since 2002) and John Samuel (Mandela-Rhodes Trust). Photo © Marc Stanes to her husband in the course of his career, she then presented it with a massive sarcophagus. 'It is one of the most hideous objects I have ever seen,' wrote Allen plaintively. All that could be done was to wrap it in baize and try to forget about it: 'I have acknowledged to her with insincere thanks.' Encouraged by this enthusiastic response, Lady Milner now offered the Trust nineteen silver trowels, three silver mallets and a spirit level – all relics of her husband's indefatigable laying of foundation stones. Evidently aware that the sarcophagus was not on permanent display, she specified that these new treasures were to be installed in a show case in one of the public rooms. When the Trustees regretfully explained that this could not be done, Grigg, now Lord Altrincham, emerged from the backwoods to express his dismay that Rhodes House should be unable to 'preserve any objects of value connected with Lord Milner's service in South Africa'. Amery would have preferred to conciliate Lady Milner, but Wheare resented the tone of Altrincham's letter: 'It is Rhodes House and not Milner House of which we are Trustees.' Peacock and Millis were ready to join Amery in some sort of compromise; Lowe, however, strongly supported Wheare. The trowels would be 'a perfect curse. As Trustees, I don't think we should let Rhodes House get cluttered up with ugly and useless junk. . . . The fact that Altrincham takes the opposite view confirms me in the opinion that our decision is right.' Amery ruled that the conciliators were in a majority but Lady Milner had by now taken offence and withdrawn the offer, saying that she would find 'some other body sufficiently interested in South African colonial history to be willing to care for these relics'. Though the incident was of trivial importance, it is not without interest as showing how far the Trust had grown away from its roots and, incidentally, how the Trustees would increasingly divide into an Oxford and a London camp, not usually at variance but looking at things from a different point of view and occasionally arriving at very distinct conclusions.[17]

Allen was having serious problems finding places in the various colleges for the swollen regiment of Rhodes Scholars. He was not just in competition with the post-war influx of British undergraduates; many more students from overseas were now converging on Oxford. Ironically the Fulbright Scholarships, introduced in 1945 by that most ardent of Rhodes Scholars William Fulbright, made Allen's task much more difficult. No one doubted that the Rhodes Scholar ranked higher in the pecking order of academic honours, but faced with a choice between what seemed to be a strong Fulbright Scholar and a weak Rhodes Scholar the Oxford colleges could not be relied on always to stick by their old connections. Many of the young fellows returning from the wars had little knowledge of or affection for the Rhodes Scholarships: 'It is somewhat disappointing', wrote Allen sadly, 'to find that after nearly fifty years the Rhodes Scholarships have not endeared themselves to Colleges more than they seem to have done.'[18] The expectation that a Rhodes Scholar would be above the average as an athlete still counted for something. John Lowe remonstrated strongly when a future Olympic runner from India was diverted from Christ Church, his college of first choice, to Brasenose. 'It is a little hard on us,' he protested, 'after acceding to a special request to take one of the first two [Indians] and getting a quite nice but thoroughly undistinguished little man, to be penalised for that when a real flyer comes along! Between ourselves, sending another athlete to BNC is sending coals to Newcastle, and sending a Christian there is almost cruelty.'[19] But athletic distinction was a dwindling asset. Even in 1948 Lowe seemed a little old-fashioned, by 1970 the Warden was complaining that it was hard to place people in a college when all they had to offer was 'hockey at a fairly high level. Now that St Edmund Hall has taken up literacy there are very few annexes of Vincent's* left.'[20]

New Rhodes Scholars made things more difficult for themselves by putting as their first choice the only colleges of which they had heard or which had been recommended by their predecessors. In 1947 more than half the new Scholars put Balliol or New College top of their list; seven or eight other colleges figured prominently but the rest were hardly mentioned. 'As you will readily understand,' wrote Elton, 'a college which seldom or never receives a first choice is likely to be less disposed, at a time such as this when it is compelled to turn away applicants almost daily, to put itself out to accept one of our men.'[21] A weak candidate, perhaps from one of the South African schools, might put Balliol as his first choice, Magdalen as his second, and then, rejected by both, present Allen with a testing problem as he tried to sell his unalluring package to a less well-known college or even one of the halls of residence that had not yet acquired collegiate status. Allen's suggested solution was that the award of a Rhodes Scholarship should be conditional on a place being found for the Scholar in an Oxford college; Aydelotte for one felt that this would impose an intolerable burden on the waiting Scholars and might, indeed, stop them applying for the Scholarship at all. Another approach, that the freedom to choose a college should be abolished and the Warden given discretion to place the scholars where he felt best, filled Allen with as much horror as it had Wylie before him. He was already in trouble enough with the colleges, he told Gie: 'Dealings with colleges, or at all events some colleges, about Rhodes Scholars are always somewhat delicate and really at times it is

*Oxford's most celebrated sporting club.

like dealing with a lot of rather highly strung children. I therefore find the policy of neutrality absolutely essential.'[22]

By the end of the war the assets of the Trust had risen in value to some £3.5 million, a satisfying increase but one which led the Trustees to wonder whether their terms of reference were set out with sufficient clarity. There were no problems about the Scholarship Fund and the Scholarship Capital Reserve Fund, but the residue of the Trust's assets, concentrated in the Public Purposes Trust and the Rhodes Trust of 1937, were more questionable. Obviously the running of the Scholarships, if the two funds designated for this purpose proved inadequate, must be the first priority, but the carping lawyers suggested that much of the rest of what was being done might be legally questionable. Geographically speaking, how far could the Trustees spread their largesse, and had they any right to hand over sums of money to other organisations? A private bill was prepared which, it was hoped – unavailingly, as is almost always the case in such circumstances – would establish for ever the rights and duties of the Trust. The Rhodes Trust Act of 1948 amalgamated the non-Scholarship assets of the Trust into the 'Public Purposes Fund' and empowered the Trustees to spend the income on 'the promotion or advancement in any part of the British Commonwealth of Nations or in the United States of America of any educational or other charitable purpose'. That seemed wide enough to cover almost any contingency; the fact that the Commonwealth was not necessarily a constant unit and that long-term commitments might therefore suddenly be put into question was a possibility that does not seem to have generated much discussion at the time.

Initially it seemed as if paying for the Scholarships might make major claims on the Public Purposes Fund, for the annual stipend of each Scholar was raised from £400 to £500 in 1946 and pressure was soon being applied to grant a further increase. The expectations of the Scholars diverged widely. The South Africans and the Australians seemed perfectly satisfied with the existing level; the Americans protested that they barely had enough to live on. Worse still, by the early 1950s the Rhodes Scholarship was worth less than its rivals, the Marshall or Fulbright. 'We must not be too optimistic', warned Elton, 'in assuming that, when most of our American applicants now apply simultaneously for the Fulbright and two or three other of the overseas awards, they will continue indefinitely to prefer our prestige and honor [sic] to the financial advantages of the other grants.' An even more compelling argument for an increase, in Elton's eyes, was the fact that some Rhodes Scholars were beginning to take vacation jobs: it was, he considered, 'an invaluable feature of an Oxford education that it allows a man a period of some months in which he can, and must, plan his own study, and in which it depends solely on himself whether he works or idles'.[23] His pleas led to an increase in the stipend to £600; by 1959 this had become £750, by 1963 £900. The age of explosive inflation was still to come but the comfortable stability of the first fifty years of the Scholarships seemed very far away.

If costs might exceed income, then perhaps new funding could be found. When Paul Havens came over to establish how Rhodes Scholars and other American Oxonians could best help the University – some £4,000 a year might be available – Elton pointed out that any such sum would be 'better administered by the Rhodes Trustees than by the University itself'. His appetite whetted by the thought of easy dollars, Elton turned to the great Foundations. Rockefeller rejected him as being outside their bailiwick, but the Ford Foundation was at first hopeful that they might take over responsibility for financing the administration of the Scholarships in the United States. Should not the American Rhodes Scholars first be asked to contribute, though? 'The Trustees would never wish to appeal to former Scholars for financial support,' replied Elton, with unconvincing squeamishness: 'If, however, Rhodes Scholars, unprompted by the Trustees, of their accord should ever feel moved to do anything of this sort I feel sure the Trustees would welcome it.' By now the former Rhodes Scholar Dean Rusk was President of the Rockefeller Foundation and Elton renewed the assault. 'To underwrite overheads for other philanthropics is not very appealing to Trustees,' Rusk replied. He too suggested that Rhodes alumni should be appealed to. 'We should never ask former Rhodes Scholars to contribute to anything and, in any case, we are not so hard up that we are in urgent need of five or six thousand a year,' was Elton's riposte. The American foundations did not find this combination of haughtiness and a begging bowl either appealing or convincing.[24] No aid was forthcoming. Nor was it needed. In almost every year the Scholarship Reserve Fund was able comfortably to cover any deficit there might be on the Scholarship Fund; the Public Purposes Fund continued to grow and the very occasional contributions it was required to make to the Scholarship Fund were never a serious curb on its ever more extensive benevolence.

CHAPTER TWENTY-EIGHT

END OF EMPIRE

Even by the time of Rhodes's death the flaws in his vision of empire were becoming apparent; the accession of the Indian sub-continent to independence in 1947 convinced even the most sanguine that it was never to be realised. It was, however, not until after the death of Amery in 1955 and the retirement of Elton as General Secretary in 1959 that the Trust finally shuffled off the last vestiges of its imperial role.

Elton, with the enthusiastic if detached support of Amery, envisaged Rhodes House not merely as a centre devoted to the study and preservation of imperial history but as an active agent in the dissemination of imperial ideals and, most significant of all, a forum in which the economic and political problems of Empire could be discussed in an atmosphere of academic calm yet by people closely involved with the shaping of policy in their respective countries. 'My own feeling is that the more Rhodes House can be developed as a centre of imperial studies, the more it becomes a "temple to Rhodes", he told Dawson.[1] The war had disrupted such ambitions – not just because it had fatally shattered the fabric of Empire in Southeast Asia and the Far East, but because it diverted the attention of those who should have been concerned with long-term imperial strategy to the more immediate problems of how to win the war. Elton, however, gallantly struggled to keep the Empire alive in the minds of the British people. At his instigation the Trust made grants to the Imperial Institute, the Royal Empire Society and the YMCA, all of which were running schemes designed to provide lectures on 'Empire topics' to elementary, secondary and public schools and to the armed forces. 'The Trustees feel', he told George Barnes of the BBC, 'that this is the psychological moment at which much can be done to repair the very dangerous and discreditable ignorance of the British Commonwealth which we have allowed to grow up in this country.' The Empire, he added, was 'a subject on which I am writing and talking a good deal myself at present, and if you should ever want a talk on this subject yourself, I should be glad to try my hand at it.'[2] His hand was already well in; by 1943, when he wrote this letter, he was at work on his *Imperial Commonwealth*, a history written with evangelistic fervour in which the humanitarian and trusteeship aspects of Empire were joyfully acclaimed and anything so vulgar as material benefits accruing to the conqueror were discreetly underplayed.

Today such fervour may seem disingenuous. In 1940 and 1941, before Pearl Harbor and the American entry into the war, Britain and a remarkably united Commonwealth really did stand alone against an unequivocally evil and all-conquering enemy. To promote the vision of an Empire which was liberal, progressive and bound by common ideals and values rather than by military force was both justifiable in terms of realpolitik and defensible in terms of history: Elton was a propagandist in the cause of Empire, but a propagandist who believed passionately in the cause he preached and who considered that the responsibilities and burdens imposed by leadership were far more significant than the privileges and advantages. He did not feel himself personally committed to South Africa but he fully accepted the assumption of the Trustees that this must be the focal point of their activities overseas. In the years directly after the war substantial grants were made to organisations encouraging emigration to Southern Africa as well as to the South African universities. Increased emphasis was put on the education and welfare of black South Africans, particularly at the college of Fort Hare, and grants and loans were made to the Bantu Press, a group which comprised almost all the newspapers published in the various African languages. But support was by no means confined exclusively to South African projects; or even to the Commonwealth in its more limited sense. The Trust, for instance, contributed to the establishment of a library at the Gordon Memorial College in Khartoum; the Founder's conspicuous admiration for General Gordon evidently outweighing any doubts about the propriety of selecting the Sudan as a recipient of Rhodes's bounty. To the gratification of the Trustees, a few years later the new Principal of the College turned out to be not merely a Rhodes Scholar from Australia but a son-in-law of Francis Wylie.[3] Rarely can the concept of the Rhodes Scholars operating as an international family have been more vividly exemplified.

The post-war Trustees happily went along with the Trust's imperial bias. Malcolm MacDonald, who was appointed at the same time as Wheare and Millis, was a quintessential Commonwealth man who had served it in a variety of roles – ministerial, administrative and diplomatic. His only drawback as a Trustee was that his peripatetic existence meant that he missed almost every meeting. George Abell, who joined in 1949, had been a pillar of the Indian Civil Service. Of the 1957 recruits, General Nye had been Governor of Madras and High Commissioner in India and Canada; Oliver Franks, though now Provost of Worcester College, had been Ambassador to Washington and was an ardent believer in the need for unity in the English-speaking world, while Lord Harcourt, though primarily a merchant banker, was the son of a former Colonial Secretary and had served as economic minister in the Embassy in Washington. By the time these men became Trustees, however, it was clear that the Empire was disintegrating at a speed which could not have been envisaged ten years before, and that the Commonwealth which was taking its place was, politically and socially, far less closely knit than men like Elton found compatible with their vision of the world.

It was in an attempt to stave off the complete collapse of the imperial vision and to provide the new Commonwealth with at least a handful of potential administrators and leaders that Elton appealed to the Trustees to create Scholarships for those emergent countries that seemed capable of producing suitable candidates. The initiative originally came from the Colonial Office, which wanted no fewer than twenty-five new Scholarships and hinted that it might be able to find the money to support them. Edgar Williams, who had taken over from Allen as Warden in 1953, was aghast. Like Allen, he was already having great difficulty in persuading colleges to take some of the weaker Scholars. Africa, he said, was fashionable at the moment, so it might not be impossible to accommodate a limited number but this would probably be at the expense of the traditional constituencies like Malta and Bermuda. On the whole the Rhodes community around the world supported Elton, though Bram Gie deplored a step which, he said, would offend Afrikaners and do untold damage to the image of the Scholarships in South Africa. It was no good expecting that a couple of years at Oxford would turn young Kenyans or Nigerians into supporters of the mother country, he argued; they were much more likely to pick up communist ideas and return as committed enemies of the Commonwealth.[4]

The relatively modest proposal as finally put to the Trustees was for five triennial scholarships for Ceylon, Ghana, the Malayan region, Nigeria and the Caribbean, staggered so as to ensure that there was not too large an influx in any one year. 'By its very nature the Rhodes Trust has a duty to the Commonwealth,' Elton pleaded. 'The multi-racial Commonwealth, if it establishes itself, may prove to be of incalculable benefit to the world; by providing the five new constituencies which are proposed with a small but steady stream of young men with qualities of leadership and well disposed to Britain we might render invaluable service to the new experiment.'[5] The argument begged many questions. The stream would certainly be slow but would it be steady? Would it bear the Scholars back to their homelands or to other countries where their talents would be more richly rewarded? Would they in practice be well disposed to Britain? Only time would provide answers; in the meantime the Trustees reckoned that the risk was worth taking and the new Scholarships were launched.

It was Elton's swan-song; when he ceased to be General Secretary in 1952 the heart went out of his crusade to keep the imperial flame alive. This did not mean that the Commonwealth ceased to be a major recipient of the Trust's bounty. As Anthony Kenny puts it in his brilliantly lucid analysis of the Trust's activities, the ghost of its past could still from time to time be discerned.[6] Gifts were made to schools in Swaziland and Botswana, to Makerere University in Uganda, even to make possible the publication of *Round Table*. But the Trustees increasingly fought shy of anything which might suggest they were proponents of the Empire or took what some might hold to be an improper pride in its achievements. In 1958 the Trustees agreed to help N.A. Nigumi by buying a hundred copies of his work on the British trusteeship of the Sudan, which painted the colonial administration in a favourable light. Abell doubted whether they should involve themselves in the distribution of such a book; the Americans, he argued, might well question its origins and its motives, 'they may even wonder, if it is sent out by the Rhodes Trust, whether the Trustees are propagandists'.[7] It is hard to conceive that such scruples would have deterred Lord Milner or Leo Amery.

More and more the Trust's interest in Empire became historical, even anti-quarian. Elton's dream of a forum in which active issues could be debated and policy formed did not survive his retirement, if indeed it lasted as long as that. It was still taken for granted, however, that Rhodes House was an appropriate venue for Commonwealth studies and that its library should be maintained as a centre of learning in this field. As late as 1994 the Trust made a grant of £150,000 towards the costs of the majestic five-volume *Oxford History of the British Empire*. The fact that the editor-in-chief of this History, Professor Roger Louis, was not merely the most eminent of historians of Empire but also an American caused outrage to some die-hards but gratified the Trustees as suggesting that the English-speaking world was indeed a unity in which scholarship and common values transcended national frontiers. A rather similar project was the cataloguing and conservation of the Milner papers. These belonged to New College, which was to deposit them in the Bodleian but was not legally entitled to transfer ownership. The Bodleian was delighted to house them, but was only allowed to work on papers which it owned. The Rhodes Trust came to the rescue, putting up £5,000 to pay for the necessary work. In both cases a signal service was offered to the cause of scholarship and an act of *pietas* rendered to the cause of Empire.

It was in a similar mood of historical propriety rather than imperial glori-fication that the Trustees considered the commissioning of a biography of

Cecil Rhodes which would draw on all the unpublished papers at Rhodes House. Their first choice, in 1944, was very much in the glorification school, but eleven years later Arthur Bryant had still not put pen to paper. Lowe's view was that Robert Blake would do just as good a job, if not a better one, but the other Trustees felt they should give Bryant another chance. What was essential, Bryant said, was that they should have a biographer who would be 'anxious to present the Founder as a great man whose creed still retains its significance in 1955'. Elton fully endorsed this view, but a year later Bryant had become deeply involved in the editing of Field Marshal Lord Alanbrooke's diaries and Rhodes was still in the pending tray. The Trustees finally despaired, and Elton began a hunt for a replacement. He was anxious to avoid an author whose attitude was 'faintly derisive or neutral or, even worse, would regard the whole story as a chapter to which the twentieth century has inevitably written *finis*'.[8] Neutrality in a biographer being evidently undesirable, Elton looked for one who might be deemed sufficiently partisan and ended up with J.G. Lockhart, who had already written a potted biography of Rhodes for a 'Great Lives' series. Lockhart died before the work was completed and the torch was finally handed to C.M. Woodhouse who contrived, without being 'faintly derisive', to achieve a level of objectivity which Elton would have felt undesirable if not sacrilegious.

In 1981 the then Warden, Robin Fletcher, in the context of suitable guests to invite to the annual dinners, raised the general question of the Trust's position in the world. 'It is probably a fair generalisation', he wrote, 'to say that the close links which bound the Trust to the Empire, and later to the Commonwealth, gave it a place in the political world which has gradually weakened as these links have been loosened. . . . the Trust's prestige is today centred round the concept of international exchange, in limited areas, through scholarship and education.'[9] To Milner such comments would have seemed incomprehensible; to Elton they would have been all too comprehensible but none the less anathema; today they seem unexceptionable. To take the Empire out of the Rhodes Scholarships has not deprived them of validity. There is still an English-speaking world, to whose cohesion and harmony Rhodes attached so much importance. There is still a 'world's fight', which today needs to be fought quite as vigorously as in 1904. There is still a need for young people of ability and goodwill who will 'esteem the performance of public duties' as their highest aim. Whether the Rhodes Trust has contrived to identify such people; whether their experience as Rhodes Scholars has in any way affected the pattern of their lives; whether, in short, the system has worked, must be the question to which the rest of this book primarily addresses itself. That those goals were now being pursued in a post-imperial age affected the appearance of the enterprise but essentially did not alter it a whit.

PART IV

Post-Imperial World

CHAPTER TWENTY-NINE

SOUTH AFRICAN TWILIGHT

In the immediate post-war years South Africa continued to be the most generously treated among the recipients of financial aid from the Trust; its Scholars
continued to be among the weakest in terms of performance. Bram Gie, the
Trust's Secretary in South Africa, was acutely conscious of these failings. Only
9.3 per cent of South African Rhodes Scholars took firsts, he told the *Cape
Times* – the corresponding figure for New Zealand was 34.2 per cent, for
Australia 32.9 per cent. Moreover, 5.2 per cent of South Africans failed to get
any degree – there were no such failures for New Zealand, only 0.7 per cent for
Australia.[1] The most obvious reason for this was that four of the South
African Scholars were still taken from schools which had only a tiny number
of possible candidates from whom to select. Gie placed the blame more on the
selection committees, which acted in isolation, with little reference to the
views of the Trustees, let alone to those of the national Secretary. In the Cape
Province the Chairman insisted on conducting the interview in Afrikaans; in
Natal he closed the meeting after an hour, saying that he had another appointment and that, as the committee knew the candidates, interviews were anyway
superfluous.[2]

Brian Bamford, one of the few South African Scholars to have made a reputation for himself in national politics, believed that the idiosyncratic approach
of the selectors was justified by the results. The Americans, he wrote, tended
to invest in scholars rather than genuine all-rounders: 'In contrast, the South
Africans are more truly all-rounders and, while they may be ... neither
academically nor athletically in the top flight, they perhaps more literally fulfil
Rhodes's ideal.'[3] However, what he saw as all-rounders Gie considered
respectable mediocrities. Gie's problems were compounded, in a manner
unique to South Africa, by the refusal of wealthy families to allow their sons
to go forward for a Scholarship. The Villiers de Graaf family, for instance, had
two boys who seemed ideally cut out to be Rhodes Scholars but who had been
discouraged from competing. Could they be awarded honorary Scholarships,

asked Gie? Allen could see no reason why a Rhodes Scholar need accept any emolument if he did not wish to but doubted whether this was the reason for a candidate not coming forward. In South Africa, in particular, a potential Scholar was more likely to be put off by a reluctance to accept the 'tainted' money of Cecil Rhodes: 'That certainly has happened in some cases and, actually, it ought to happen quite regularly in Stellenbosch if the Stellenbosch men were really honest!'[4]

Elton visited South Africa early in 1948 and concluded that things were not as bad as Gie represented. It was true that few Scholars had gone into public life – indeed, there were remarkably few opportunities for them to do so in the political climate of the day – but they still composed 'a respectable body of citizens, notably loyal to Oxford and the Scholarships, and capable of playing a useful part in the life of the Union'.[5] He fully supported Gie, however, in his campaign to improve the selection committees. There was not much to be done so far as the four schools were concerned, but the provincial selection committees were still under the chairmanship of the Provincial Administrator, an official appointed by the Nationalist government and therefore likely to be unsympathetic to the ideals behind the Scholarships. Evicting the Administrators and the Secretaries of Education from the selection committees proved a long and sometimes bitter business. It was not until the 1950s that Rhodes Scholar Secretaries had been everywhere installed and the committees were functioning to Gie's satisfaction.

Gie was a capable and energetic General Secretary but his instincts were conservative and his chief preoccupation was to keep Afrikaner candidates presenting themselves for the Scholarships and to remain on reasonably close terms with the Nationalist government. In this he was successful: on his first visit to South Africa as Warden-elect in 1951 Williams reported that, though the older Rhodes Scholars were anxious about political developments and many of the younger Scholars were joining the liberal Torch Commando, the 'growing Afrikaner xenophobia' did not yet seem to have stopped Afrikaner students coming forward as candidates.[6] Avoiding direct confrontation with the South African government was perhaps a reasonable aspiration, but Gie too often gave the impression that he thought government was in many ways pursuing a policy that was morally justifiable and of benefit to the country. He would never have defended apartheid, but still conceded that there were valid arguments in its favour. He was outraged when one of the more exuberant South African Scholars, David Bean, denounced apartheid in the *American Oxonian*. 'I sincerely hope that no members of the Nationalist Party see this article,' he told Elton. 'If they do, and it is taken up by their press I am afraid the consequences might be extremely serious. The political situation in South Africa is very delicate and it would be disastrous if the Scholarship Scheme were drawn into the political arena.'[7] The political arena was exactly where Bean thought it ought to be. His next enterprise was to try to organise Rhodes Scholars to stand as a bloc in elections for the City Council of Johannesburg: 'The Rhodes Scholars', Bean claimed, 'are perhaps the only body of citizens who could stand in this manner and command any substantial amount of public support.' Allen was inclined to agree with Gie about this particular enterprise but Elton supported it, admitting that 'I may have sowed the seeds of some such idea in Bean's mind myself.' He liked the idea of a body of Rhodes Scholars playing so active a role in South African politics, though, on reflection, he doubted the wisdom of their operating as 'a solid phalanx ... since it might well give the impression that Rhodes Scholars as a whole took one particular view!' Bean himself lost interest in the idea and the phalanx never formed.[8]

Gie was more concerned with maintaining his relationship with the Nationalist government than with opening up the Rhodes Scholarships to black, Indian or coloured candidates; nor was the Trust particularly active in this respect. When the Bantu Welfare Trust hoped that African students could be encouraged to apply for Scholarships, Elton replied merely that it would be a pity to urge people to apply if they 'were not likely to be up to the necessary standard'.[9] He was always quick to deny that the Trust exercised any sort of colour bar, pointing out to Abe Bailey's vigorously radical son Jim that there had been a succession of black Scholars from Jamaica, but it was not till the 1970s that the Trustees did anything very effective by way of countering the forces which made it almost impossible for a black South African to gain the necessary qualifications to compete successfully. In the years after South Africa left the Commonwealth in 1961 Gie was at least as much preoccupied by the folly of those who agitated for economic sanctions as by the iniquities of the government. To Williams he ranted against 'stupid politicians' who sought to destroy the traditional ties between South Africa and Britain. 'I cannot get into a general argument with you about the situation,' Williams replied cautiously. The businessmen who deplored sanctions and the political radicals who sought to impose them were talking about different things 'and the arguments are like ships which pass in the night and do not touch one another'.[10]

It was something of a relief when Gie retired in his seventieth year. He was replaced by Rex Welsh, a Vinerian Scholar who had become one of South Africa's leading advocates and differed sharply from Gie in his liberal ideas and disinclination to conciliate the prejudices of the Nationalist government. 'Welsh's appointment will not be universally popular in South Africa among those more wedded to apartheid,' wrote Williams with some satisfaction. 'I respect him very much.'[11] Among the first of the Augean stables which he tackled was the Natal selection committee, a body that was notoriously reactionary and sympathetic to apartheid, and which had recently turned down John Samuel – a future chief executive of the Mandela Foundation – allegedly on the grounds that he was a Jew.[12] Welsh deplored the absurd imbalance by which six out of South Africa's nine Rhodes Scholarships were drawn from the Cape and succeeded in slightly ameliorating the situation by getting the biennial Scholars for the Eastern Cape transformed into an additional annual Scholarship for the Transvaal. In one way he accorded with tradition – his two predecessors and his two successors were all lawyers; in another he broke with it – his predecessors had both been educated at SACS (South African College School), one of the four designated schools in the Cape, while he and his two successors all went to the Pretoria Boys' High School. The fact that he felt no particular reverence for or commitment to the Cape schools was to be a significant factor in the storms that broke in the 1970s and 1980s.

Most of the South African Scholarships had been designated as such under the Will and so were not affected when South Africa left the Commonwealth in 1961. Those created more recently were questionable. The Trust does not seem to have considered abolishing them but wished in some way to mark its disapproval of political developments. Around £10,000–£11,000 a year was available from the Rhodes Trust South Africa for any grants that the Trustees might wish to make to South African causes. It was decided that it would be inappropriate to make grants to a country in which the laws of apartheid were applied and which was no longer a member of the Commonwealth; the income therefore was freed to meet the cost of the post-Will Scholarships and the administration of the Scholarships in South Africa. Since the Public Purposes Fund was specifically restricted to the Commonwealth or the United States, all benefactions to South Africa ceased. Some worthy causes suffered as a result and Rhodes University and the four schools felt aggrieved at being cut off from what they had long regarded as the most reliable of milch-cows, but the Trustees never considered that they had made the wrong decision. It was to be some thirty years before South Africa once more benefited from the Trust's benevolence. As is the way of ill winds, it blew Oxford University a great deal of good.

CHAPTER THIRTY
THE WILLIAMS YEARS

If one was called upon to name the four individuals who made the profoundest mark on the development of the Rhodes Trust and Scholarships they would be Parkin, Aydelotte, Lord Milner and Edgar Williams.* Williams – 'Bill' to almost everyone – had had a brilliant war, rising at the age of a little over thirty to be a brigadier and Montgomery's Chief of Intelligence. He was a fellow of Balliol and, it had once been assumed, would one day have become Master; editor of the *Dictionary of National Biography* and Treasurer of the University Cricket Club. If the circumstances had been different he would himself have been an obvious choice as a Rhodes Scholar.

Inevitably he was compared with his titular superior Lord Elton, a man whom he found verbose and indecisive but liked well enough. Elton was a good man, generous and conscientious, taking endless pains to help people from whom he could expect no recompense, but he would ride his hobbyhorses almost to extinction and his judgment was uncertain. Williams, a man of wit, common sense and unshakeable integrity, could reach the right conclusion in half the time it took Elton to reach the wrong one. He cultivated an appearance of studied ordinariness. Edwin Yoder, an American Rhodes Scholar and Pulitzer Prize-winning author, remembered Williams meeting the arriving Scholars off the boat at Plymouth. 'My memory is of a nondescript overcoat, hat and glasses – and an imperturbable face in which concern and detachment, drollery and propriety mingled.'[1] Williams was conservative in his views but delighted in parodying himself as a strident reactionary: 'although, of course, I believe like mad in progress', he wrote in his Christmas letter, 'I'd rather it didn't happen until after my time'.[2] Willie Morris, another Rhodes Scholar author who found him a 'grand and flamboyant exemplar of the British Establishment', once asked him about his politics. 'I'm right wing

---

*Anthony Kenny would substitute Lothian for Milner; perhaps one should settle for a Big Five.

Tory,' Williams replied, 'which I understand is considerably further to the left than anything you have in the United States.'[3] Flamboyant was a word not often applied to him, but 'establishment' was certainly appropriate. Julian Ogilvie Thompson while still a Scholar became engaged to Tessa Brand, daughter of Thomas Brand, Chairman of Lazards and future Viscount Hampden. Ogilvie Thompson confessed to Williams that he was going to get married. Williams, who disapproved in principle of early marriages and assumed that in this case the delinquent Scholar had got some stray nurse into trouble, looked disapproving. 'To Tommy Brand's daughter,' Ogilvie Thompson added hurriedly. 'Oh, that's all right then,' exclaimed Williams with relief.[4]

He held certain fixed beliefs that guided his twenty-eight years as Warden. He was convinced that there were already more Rhodes Scholars at Oxford than was good for either Rhodes House or the University and he resolutely opposed the creation of any new Scholarships. Academically outstanding himself, he fully recognised the importance of sound scholarship but refused to accept that this was the be-all and end-all of an Oxford education. James Gobbo, an Australian Scholar, got a blue for rowing but promised Williams he would work really hard in his final year. He was then invited to become President of the Boat Club. 'Go for it!' advised Williams. 'As a lawyer it doesn't matter what degree you get, provided it's respectable, while the experience you'll get as a President will be far more valuable.' He was right: Gobbo ended up a knight, a Supreme Court judge and the Governor of Victoria.[5] Williams believed that every Scholar had the right to hold and to express his own opinions. When Peter Conrad told him that he planned to go to London to demonstrate outside the American Embassy against the Vietnam War, Williams's only advice was that he should avoid hitting a policeman, particularly if he happened to be on a horse.[6]

In almost any circumstances he could be relied on to support his Scholars. He could seem taciturn, even brusque. 'I'm fifty-five, establishment and white,' he told the *Los Angeles Times*. 'That's three strikes against me, you might say, and I find it infinitely more difficult to communicate.' But he found that the most active leaders of student discontent tended also to be the most talented and articulate, and he was genuinely interested in their views. 'If they are to be criticised,' he concluded, 'it would be to say that they're not awfully good listeners.'[7] Some people considered he was not an awfully good listener himself. Doug McCalla, the economic historian, recalled that several Canadian Scholars of his generation felt him to be 'aloof and uninterested'. But when McCalla had a sinus operation and was confined to an old people's home to recuperate, he was rescued by the Warden's wife, Gill, installed in Rhodes House and nursed devotedly. Another Canadian, Arthur Scace, found that Williams was extraordinarily good at looking after waifs and strays. Scace's girlfriend and future wife was in Oxford when her father died. She left at once and Williams let Scace use the telephone at Rhodes House so as to keep in touch and even gave him a key to allow him to come and go.[8]

Organised jollities were not his scene; he so disliked the fifty-year jubilee of 1953 that he contrived to avoid anything similar when the seventy-fifth anniversary came up and he was still in office. In fact, the 1953 jubilee included nothing very lavish by way of celebration; honorary degrees were conferred by the University on a group of Rhodes Scholars – a process which inevitably caused as much chagrin to those who did not receive degrees but felt they deserved one as it gave pleasure to the recipients – and the individual colleges gave Gaudies for their members. Two years later Amery died. He had been a Trustee for thirty-six years, Chairman for twenty-two. A disciple of Milner and a dedicated imperialist, he alone carried into the post-imperial age the ideals and convictions that had inspired the Founder. With him died the last link between the Trust and the ideology of Empire.

Williams had long ago decided that there was nothing Elton did which he could not do rather better himself, and that the time which he and Elton spent explaining to each other what they had both been doing would more than make up for the extra workload which would be involved if the tasks of Warden and General Secretary were amalgamated. Elton would not have put it quite like that (nor, publicly, would Williams), but he regretted the fact that, while as Secretary it was his duty to make sure that the best candidates were selected, he depended on the Warden for judgments on how the choice of the selectors had worked out in practice. If the jobs could be combined without putting an impossible burden on the incumbent, then he admitted there was a case for doing so. Peacock, who had taken over as Chairman on Amery's death, needed little convincing; he appreciated the economy involved in running together the two offices and, being a man of orderly mind, rejoiced in the fact that the occasional messiness involved when the Warden wished to swim one way and the General Secretary the other would henceforth be eliminated. In 1959 Lord Elton retired, the office in Beaumont Street was closed, and Williams assumed both functions. He was to continue to do so for the next twenty years: never dictatorial but increasingly autocratic and more than anybody else responsible for redefining the Trust's role as the Empire crumbled around it.

It had at first been envisaged that Williams would be provided with a deputy to share the load. It was not an easy slot to fill. Williams would have found it hard to put up with the second rate, yet had no intention of delegating any work of real importance. 'I am most unwilling', he admitted, 'to have a really able man my frustrated junior.'[9] Eventually a suitable subordinate was found, but he lasted only six years before moving on to another job. The experiment was not repeated; henceforth Williams ruled alone.

He was not the first Warden to conclude that, though Rhodes House provided reasonably convenient office space, its vast public rooms were likely to be under-used and the house posed almost insuperable problems as a residence. When Allen took over there had been seven full-time servants, now there was only one. The work involved in looking after a large and extravagant house, acting as surrogate mother to the Rhodes Scholars and tending to her own small children put Mrs Williams under almost unendurable pressure. 'The fact is,' Allen agreed with Williams, 'Rhodes House is not, and never was, well designed for modern purposes, because the Trustees in 1928 were not very clear in their own minds about the purposes for which they intended it. And the residential part was never convenient.'[10] The inconvenience was now redoubled; the purposes remained as vague as ever. Williams seized on the fact that the University was looking around for a new headquarters to suggest that Rhodes House would be ideal for such a purpose and would thus worthily commemorate the Founder's devotion to Oxford. As a *quid pro quo* the University would make over to the Trust a site then available in Holywell on which offices could be built and a small house provided for the Warden. The Trust would retain the right to hold its two annual dinners in Rhodes House; to escape all the other running costs would save it £10,000 a year at least. Elton, from retirement, wrote to support the idea. Remembering 'the ambitious plans for Rhodes House' which he had once cherished, he naturally felt regretful, but given the realities of life in 1961 he had to agree that to accept Williams's plan would be 'a wise and courageous decision.'[11]

The Trustees agreed, the University seemed enthusiastic, all was apparently set fair; then the problems began to emerge. Wadham, which had originally sold the site to the Rhodes Trust, now claimed that, if the property was disposed of, the college must receive the difference between the price the Trust had paid for it and the current market value. The Bursar of Wadham suggested that £50,000 would be about right, though the college might be prepared to lower that by a little provided the Trust recognised its right in principle. 'I take a very poor view of Wadham's attempt to profit by our gesture,' wrote Peacock angrily.[12] It seemed, however, that the college might be out-manoeuvred if the Trust did not transfer the property in the site to the University but merely allowed it to use the building under a revocable licence. Next the projected site for the new slim-line Rhodes House turned out to be impracticable; this hurdle too was surmounted when an alternative site in South Parks Road seemed to be on offer. Finally the architect, Sir William

Holford, pointed out that Rhodes House was unsuitable for conversion into offices, while it would be well adapted for 'something of a collegiate character'.[13] The Vice-Chancellor now suggested to the Trustees that they should hand over their building not as a headquarters, which would for ever link the name of Rhodes with that of Oxford University, but as a non-residential graduate college. Since at the same time it became clear that the South Parks Road site would not, after all, be available and that the suggested alternative was not satisfactory, the Trustees withdrew their offer. Williams had to settle for a remodelling of Rhodes House which left his wife with a rather less arduous domestic burden.

In the course of these negotiations, Kenneth Wheare had taken over from Peacock as Chairman of the Trust. Wheare was the first Oxford don to take the chair. He had been involved with the negotiations over Rhodes House from their inception: 'a tower of strength', Williams said of him, 'not least because he is a tower with a sense of humour, an unusual sort of tower, maybe, but he didn't entirely accept my suggestion that the only other one with the same combination is at Blackpool'.[14] Williams liked him, trusted him and worked closely with him. George Abell, Wheare's fellow Trustee and eventual successor as Chairman, described him as 'most unexpected, most intelligent and totally unpompous'.[15] As the head of an Oxford house and a man whose judgment Williams genuinely respected, he more nearly exercised control over the Warden than any of the other four Chairmen who came and went while Williams reigned at Rhodes House. He was usually dulcet in his approach but was capable of firmness when firmness was needed. Edward Boyle, the former Tory minister, was appointed a Trustee in 1965. He was already hopelessly over-committed and should never have taken on the task; over the next four years his apologies for non-attendance were so regular as to become something of a joke. 'My colleagues and I have talked it over informally,' Wheare told him, 'and they were in agreement that I should write and ask you whether in fact you might not feel that you had to give up your place as a Trustee. We should be sorry if you felt obliged to do so, but at the same time we should understand it.' Boyle resigned apologetically and with some relief; Wheare's letter, Williams considered, was 'a masterpiece of reflective delicacy; I shall keep it around in case I need to ask somebody to resign some day'.[16]

Boyle's expulsion shortly followed the appointment of an American Trustee: Don Price, a professor from Harvard and a former Rhodes Scholar. He would be particularly useful, Williams told him, as providing 'a different angle of approach. . . . All the Trustees at one time or another have been in the States, but it would be fun to stop them competing as experts.'[17] Price provided all the expertise that could have been expected but never pushed the American point of view with too much vigour. The experiment was considered a success, yet was not repeated until the former investment banker Thomas Seaman was appointed a Trustee in 2004 – and Seaman, though American, was also Bursar of All Soul's and thus quintessentially Oxonian. The American contingent was by far the largest among the Rhodes Scholars and the Association of American Rhodes Scholars was vociferous and well organised. Some among the Trustees may have felt that was enough, that an American voice within their ranks would risk giving too much emphasis to the point of view as formed the other side of the Atlantic. Nobody doubted that the policy of the Trust must be decided in England and not in Washington, but the Trustees were always alive to the possibility that the Commonwealth constituencies might feel neglected or treated as of secondary importance.

Williams was accustomed to refer to the Trustees as 'my masters' and was scrupulous in applying the proper procedures whenever any controversial issue was in question, but his authority grew with the years and while he was General Secretary there were not many significant points on which he did not get his way. Certainly he did over the creation of new Scholarships. 'The Warden has felt for a long time', he told the Trustees in 1979, 'that we have got just a few too many Rhodes Scholars to place in Oxford each year: and in recent years we have had to look elsewhere, outside Oxford, which is never satisfactory.' It was a little more satisfactory though far from perfect if Rhodes Scholars ended up at one of the new postgraduate colleges like Linacre: 'There is a certain sort of Rhodes Scholar who doesn't need a Boat Club, so to speak, and he may find his way happily to Linacre College.'[18] But this 'sort of Rhodes Scholar', he implied, was – not necessarily inferior but – a less complete example of the genus. The best solution was to keep the Scholarships at their present level or, better still, eliminate one or two of the more vulnerable.

For the greater part of his time as Secretary this called for a sustained rearguard action, since several of the Trustees were in favour of expansion and it was hard to argue that the funds for extra Scholarships were not there. Since the advent of Peacock in 1924 the Trust's wealth had grown substantially. Peacock himself, Millis, John Phillimore of Barings, Lord Harcourt, George Abell and most recently John Baring had proved themselves notably successful. In the first twenty years or so of Williams's Secretaryship the value of the Trust's investments rose from £5.5 million to £24.6 million, well ahead of any inflationary growth – an excellent result helped by the death of Georgia Rhodes, the last descendant of Cecil Rhodes's parents, and the addition of £250,000 from her estate to the Trust's resources. By 1979 the Trust's income was some £1.5 million a year, the cost of the Scholarships and their administration about £1 million – which left a lavish surplus for grants and the building up of reserves. It was not all rosy. In 1966, for the first time, the Trustees accepted that the fees required from the scientist were often so much larger than those of the student of the humanities that the only fair course for the Trust to follow was to take over the payment of fees direct and to pay a living allowance on top of that. This at once increased the total outlay, but more expensive was the government's ruling that foreign students must be charged higher fees. Oxford initially resisted this demand but eventually succumbed. The result was that, towards the end of Williams's Wardenship, the Scholarships cost the Trust considerably more, but still not so much as to put a serious dent in the overall surplus.

Then, in 1979, the new Education Secretary imposed a further steep increase in fees for overseas students. Williams was seriously alarmed at the implications for the Trust's finances – possibly, too, he felt that here was an opportunity to achieve his long-nurtured ambition to get rid of one or two of the least well-favoured Scholarships. He told the Trustees that, if no step was taken to curb expenditure, almost the whole of the Public Purposes Fund would have to be used to fill the hole in the Scholarship Funds. And yet, as Harcourt, who had become Chairman in 1974, had pointed out the previous year, the Public Purpose Fund must now be regarded as 'the principal reserve fund of the Trust as a whole, instead of being treated as of old as the Benefactions fund'.[19] The Trust seemed threatened, if not with bankruptcy, then at least with an excess of expenditure over income with no guarantee that this would be only a fleeting crisis.

Williams, who had always felt that the number of American Scholarships was disproportionately large and had been disappointed by the quality of some of the recent arrivals, at first suggested that their total should be cut from thirty-two to twenty-four. He was told by the lawyers that this was impossible unless it could be shown that the money could be found from no other source to pay for the Scholarships. Other possibilities were considered: the Maltese and Pakistani Scholarships could be suspended, the New Zealand and Indian Scholarships cut back to one a year. In the end Williams put forward a modest proposal that only two Scholarships should be cut back, one from the Canadian Maritimes, one from South Africa.

By now Williams was on the point of retirement. He had suffered a heart attack a few years before from which he had never fully recovered, and was less inclined to put himself out except where people or issues of particular interest were involved. No one doubted that he had done great things for the Trust and deserved well of it, but his word no longer carried the authority which it would have enjoyed even a few years before. When he called for cuts in the Scholarships the Trustees refused to be rushed; even the limited reductions which he had finally recommended were shelved until his successor was in office. As happened not infrequently in the history of the Rhodes Trust, a crisis which at one time seemed calamitous soon turned out to be not so bad after all. Within two or three years the way once more seemed open for expansion.

CHAPTER THIRTY-ONE
WHY NO PRESIDENT?

The Rhodes Scholars, wrote Andrew Sullivan in a bad-tempered article in a 1988 issue of *Spy* magazine, were America's titled nobility, but 'Rhodies possess none of the charms of the aristocracy and all of the debilities: feck-lessness, excessive concern that peasants be aware of their achievements, and a certain haemophilia of character'. They were 'high profile losers', who ended up in jobs 'where bland, mainstream intelligence is welcome; jobs that reward the very best of the second rate, those adept at nattering away at the country's problems, prescribing solutions of soulless reasonableness'. Sullivan's final and most crushing conclusion was that the White House would never by occupied by a Rhodes Scholar: 'How come? Because no other Rhodie has ever done it, so it must not be a thing Rhodes Scholars do; because the presidency is not appointive; because it's a job with a huge amount of real responsibility . . . because if you were President, you could never hope to put anything better on your résumé; and because that, to a Rhodie Scholar, is tantamount to death.'[1]

In spite of its silliness, the article stung, because many American Rhodes Scholars did suffer from a lurking sense of under-achievement. The prestige of the Scholarship in the United States after the Second World War was, in fact, as high as it had ever been. The *Atlantic Monthly* was perhaps less lively than *Spy* but it was taken a great deal more seriously. Seeking to boost its circulation, advertising letters were sent to a wide range of people. 'Because of some distinctly complimentary things ABOUT YOU that we have heard', the letter read, the recipient was being offered a few free issues. 'You may be an ex-Marine, a career-woman, a renowned lawyer . . . perhaps a *cum laude* – even a Rhodes Scholar. . . .' 'So now', commented one Scholar who received the letter, the Ambassador Stanley Hornbeck, 'we're even getting evens.'[2] Another Rhodes Scholar, the editor of the *New Republic*, Michael Kinsley, wrote that the Scholarship was 'the one college age credential that someone carries with him all through life. I have heard it said that the only two things you can do at the age of twenty-one that will become part of your identification permanently are win a Rhodes Scholarship or join the Marines.'[3]

And yet, when Sullivan wrote, there never had been a Rhodes Scholar President. There were the occasional senators and congressmen, generals and ambassadors, heads of universities, but most Scholars ended up as prosperous lawyers, successful doctors, second-rank academics: not failures, certainly, but not heroic figures. They were 'safe, respectable, able-bodied citizens just a little lacking in fire and color', wrote Milton Mackaye in *Scribner's Magazine*. 'One thing is obvious . . . the Scholarships have failed to produce national political leaders.'[4] In the *American Oxonian* Kenneth Keniston, an author and educationalist, congratulated his fellow Scholars in the class of 1951 for avoiding 'work where making money is the end' in favour of jobs 'where some goal of service, whether in government, education, science or elsewhere, is uppermost'. Cecil Rhodes, he surmised, would have been well pleased.[5] Perhaps he might have been, but one suspects Rhodes would have hankered after something a little more dramatic, and that many of the Scholars who were so worthily employed might have nourished similar cravings.

The post-war American Rhodes Scholars had plenty of excuses if their careers did not flow as smoothly as they might have hoped. The wave of ex-servicemen had hardly been absorbed by Oxford before the North Koreans crossed the 38th parallel and the United States was again at war. Most of the new Rhodes Scholars were able to arrange deferment, but the threat of military service hung over them and, even after an armistice was signed, conscription was still retained. The fact that they did not necessarily rush to war was taken as proof that they lacked patriotism by those who were predisposed to believe that everyone who took part of their education abroad was *ipso facto* suspect. In 1951 Colonel McCormick was back on the rampage with a series of articles in the *Chicago Tribune* alleging that Rhodes Scholars were not merely dangerous anglophiles but communists to boot. The main thrust of the articles was that the plot to reintegrate the United States in the British Empire was still being actively pursued and that the mafia of Scholars who dominated government and the academic world were promoting it with villainous assiduity. 'All these details about the success of the Rhodes Scholars in public affairs are in reality one of the finest tributes to the Rhodes Scholars that has ever been published,' commented Elton with satisfaction.[6]

Allegations that Scholars were communist sympathisers were more dangerous. Harold Velde, the House of Representatives' equivalent to Senator McCarthy, announced at the end of 1952 that the House Committee on un-American Activities was about to investigate 'communist influence in Rhodes scholarship matters'. Courtney Smith, who had just replaced Aydelotte as American Secretary, was seriously alarmed. In the mid-1930s, when the

Spanish Civil War and the rise of fascism meant that communism was in vogue in Oxford, a group of Rhodes Scholars had joined the Young Communist League. Some of them had done little more than add their names to a list, but one or two had been more serious about their commitments. Given the assumption that to have been an active member of the Communist Party was in itself treasonable, the House Committee was going to have some promising material to work on. Smith was anxious that the cases should be handled individually, thus averting 'any attempt to discredit Rhodes Scholars as a whole'. Allen was told of this threat to his former Scholars. 'That group was a headache to me,' he told Williams, '– not exactly a cell of disaffection but completely detached in a superior and slightly hostile way.' He had thought little of any of them. Daniel Boorstin had been 'clever enough' (somewhat tepid praise for a man who was to become one of America's most distinguished and prolific historians), but Allen had never thought him 'very deep in the water' and had suffered from his 'introspection and egocentricity (wh. I have noticed in a good many Jewish RS)'. As for the rest: 'If any of them joined the party, it would be little more than a sentimental gesture.'[7] Luckily for the individuals involved and the American Rhodes Scholars as a group, Velde concluded that they were not sufficiently interesting as a quarry and went off to hunt for communists in the Church. Two or three Scholars suffered setbacks in their careers but no serious harm was done to the Scholarships as a whole.[8]

For the Rhodes Scholars at Oxford the Vietnam War proved far more disruptive than any witch-hunt of their seniors in the United States. By the mid-1960s the threat of the draft again hung over them: a fate that would not merely disrupt their studies but might involve them in a dangerous and profoundly disagreeable campaign. Few Scholars had actually wanted to fight in Korea, but at least they knew that if they did they would enjoy the support of a united nation, indeed of the democratic world. The war in Vietnam was disapproved of by a substantial proportion of the American people and the great majority of their contemporaries at Oxford. To dodge the draft would be justified on moral grounds, yet it also exposed the Scholar to charges of cowardice and lack of patriotism. Most Oxford dons were as ambivalent as the Scholars, but Williams was unusually robust. He was 'a prig about the war', said William Fletcher. 'He once said to me: "Could you look yourself in the mirror in the morning if you didn't fight in it?"' Yet he too had his reservations. 'I am always, privately, distressed about those who wriggle around,' he told Abell, 'even though to some degree I understand their plight; it is rather different from 1939, after all.' Fletcher acknowledged that, after the Warden had had his say on the need to fight, he 'willingly wrote to draft boards explaining what important work the Rhodes Scholars were doing'.[9]

Most American Scholars at Oxford were inclined to think that the war was a mistake, if not actually immoral. Some preferred to keep their doubts to themselves and to defend their country's policy in public. Bill Bradley, international basketball player and future senator, deplored the war, 'but when an Englishmen or a Pakistani lambasted LBJ and our involvement, my visceral reaction was to defend the actions of my country'.[10] Whatever their attitude they could not escape the war. They talked about Vietnam, said James O'Toole, 'about twelve hours a day, seven days a week' – an obsession which inevitably distanced them from their fellow Oxonians.[11] The American Rhodes Scholars, Williams told the *Los Angeles Times*, 'were preoccupied by the draft, the ghettos and the election. . . . Much more than usual they are holding US Dialogs.'[12] They always had a propensity to cling together; in the late 1960s this became more marked than ever. Yet for the most part, largely because they themselves were divided in their opinions, they abstained from any collective action. One of the few exceptions to this came early in 1967 when a group of fifty American Rhodes Scholars presented Philip Kaiser, the Minister at the US Embassy in London and himself a Rhodes Scholar, with a letter to the President arguing against the war. Their action was deplored by the President of the Association of American Rhodes Scholars (AARS) – not, as he was careful to point out, because of their views but because they had 'attempted to put the prestige of the Rhodes Scholars behind a question of foreign policy'.[13]

In the five years between 1966 and 1970, thirty-nine Scholars either did not take up their Scholarships or left Oxford without gaining a degree; for the 1968 class alone the figure was nine – almost a third of the year's intake and the lowest graduation rate since the Second World War. One of them was William Clinton. It has been claimed that Clinton was a failure as a Rhodes Scholar and disliked his time at Oxford. Neither of those allegations seems true. His tutor, Zbigniew Pelczynski, thought him not cut out to be an academic but exceptionally able and sure to get his DPhil if he had persevered. As for Oxford, Clinton himself said that it exceeded his expectations: 'It was more beautiful, more steeped in history, more hospitable to what I wanted to do at that point in my life. . . . I liked England. I was a real Anglophile when I was there.'[14] Even allowing for politeness, these do not sound like the words of a resentful rebel. What is certain is that his second year was disrupted by the disappearance of Pelczynski on a sabbatical year and by Clinton's own ever increasing preoccupation with the Vietnam War. Should they try to evade the draft and if so how? Was their opposition to the war wholly disinterested or influenced by their reluctance to fight? These questions tormented a whole generation of American Rhodes Scholars. The marvel is not that so many dropped out but that some two-thirds saw their courses through to the end.

Aydelotte finally retired, after thirty-five years as Secretary, at the end of 1952. Elton had visited him a few years before and found his energy, organisational powers and zest for life almost unimpaired. One could not fail to be impressed, Elton wrote, by 'how completely Aydelotte has been the master-builder of the American Rhodes Scholarships, and how it is thanks to him that, more than in any other constituency, Rhodes Scholars in America possess a self-conscious solidarity of their own and are active both in maintaining their association with Oxford and promoting goodwill for Britain'.[15] But he was an old man – 'very much older than I expected', Williams told Elton in 1951, and most of the work was effectively being done by his deputy, Courtney Smith. Smith was the obvious choice to succeed him, seemed indeed almost predestined for the part when he also took over the role that Aydelotte had with such distinction filled, that of President of Swarthmore College. Lord Hailey met Smith, liked him, but doubted whether he would have the 'personal persistence or the solid weight' of his predecessor. 'Perhaps the position no longer requires this?' mused Hailey.[16] After the Creation, who needs a second Jehovah? But the American constituency required constant and close attention and in his long though tragically truncated reign Smith proved that he was fully up to it.

One of his prime preoccupations was to get black American Rhodes Scholars to Oxford, something that had not been done since the ill-fated experiment with Alain Locke in 1907. He courted the black colleges and was disconcerted to find some reluctance to take up his invitation to compete. 'Negro boys', he was told at Howard, 'are usually very anxious to get on with their professional careers . . . and the idea of foreign study has little appeal.'[17] It was 1962 before the first two black Scholars were elected and even after that there were rarely more than two each year and often one or none at all. 'All of us black Scholars attended predominantly white colleges,' wrote Randall Kennedy, who went to Balliol in 1977, 'where we were schooled in the ways of "cultured" white folks. The likelihood is remote of a black winning a Rhodes Scholarship who cannot adapt reflexively to the tribal mores of white upper-middle-class society.' When he got to Oxford he met no trace of racial prejudice within the University but was dismayed to hear 'Nigger, go home!' shouted from a passing car, a cry he hadn't heard since his childhood in South Carolina.[18] George Keys was warned not to go out into the town on Guy Fawkes night but set out regardless with two of his most muscular black friends and had no trouble. When he gave a party with his wife for Thanksgiving, however, some vandals smeared excrement all over his front door.[19] The larger the number of black Rhodes Scholars, the easier they found it to adjust. Five arrived in 1971. They seemed 'not only fairly settled', Williams told Abell, 'but to have made their two predecessors already in residence much more settled too: less edgy on the whole, curiously enough, than their white contemporaries'.[20]

Courtney Smith lasted till 1969 and would have been good for another decade or more if he had not died suddenly in the middle of the student unrest that was then ravaging the campuses of American universities. His successor was William Barber, a Harvard man at Wesleyan College. 'Large, crew-cut, bespectacled and calm. . . . He has plenty of humour and a broad bottom' was how Williams described him.[21] 'You were the only candidate presented,' Don Price told him. 'I don't know what happens if you refuse.'[22] He needed both the humour and the broad bottom because he was almost immediately pitchforked into an agitated crisis over the failure to admit women Rhodes Scholars. The details of this controversy are best considered elsewhere,* but the unfortunate Barber found himself so harassed that at one juncture he was on the point of recommending that the American Scholarships be suspended. Fortunately things never became so bad and long before he resigned his post the issue had been safely disposed of.

There were more than enough other problems left to plague him. One, which he inherited from Courtney Smith and was to bequeath to his successors, was the ever increasing predominance of Harvard, Yale, Princeton and the service academies. The boy from Wyoming who moved on to Harvard would find his chances of getting a Rhodes Scholarship far better if he contested as a candidate for his home state. Yet it was Harvard which gained, and probably deserved, the credit. One in 250 Harvard graduates became a Rhodes Scholar against one in 48,000 from the run-of-the-mill state universities. Surely, it was argued, this was contrary to Rhodes's wish that the Scholarships should be spread around the country? The short answer seemed to be that, whether or not it was regrettable that Americans should choose to continue their education outside the confines of their own state, nothing could be done to stop them. It was questionable whether the Oklahoman who had been to West Point was any worse an Oklahoman than one who had never left home; but he must be equally eligible for a Rhodes Scholarship in either case. 'We are dealing with individuals, not institutions' had been Aydelotte's guideline and it remained the golden rule.

The growing prominence of the Rhodes Scholars was made conspicuous when J. F. Kennedy formed his government early in 1961. 'We have all gained great exhilaration from the number of Rhodes Scholars who are being appointed to various posts . . . ', wrote Williams exultantly. 'There seem to be upwards of a dozen involved, which would, one supposes, give the Founder as

---

*See Chapter 33 below.

good a chuckle of pleasure as it would cause Colonel McCormick of the *Chicago Tribune* to be grinding his teeth.'[23] Walt Rostow made the same point when he wrote in the *American Oxonian*: 'As I look about and count the Rhodes Scholars operating in this town I find myself drafting the kind of editorial the late Colonel McCormick would have written. For this and other reasons Washington is a congenial place these days.'[24] Rostow, Chairman of the Policy Planning Council, was near the heart of the richest constellation of Scholars: Dean Rusk, as Secretary of State, had under him two other Rhodes Scholars as Assistant Secretaries as well as several Rhodes Scholar ambassadors. Others in proximity to the President included the Deputy Attorney General (later to be Attorney General), an assistant and a deputy Secretary of Defense, the Secretary of the Army, and the Budget Director. Thomas and Kathleen Schaeper have estimated that twenty-five Rhodes Scholars were working in Kennedy's administration. They rightly point out that none of these men was given his post *because* he was a Rhodes Scholar, but rather because of his intelligence and abilities. If he did not make the grade, Scholar or not, he would soon find himself out of a job.[25] Being a Rhodes Scholar, however, gave him the inside track, bolstered his reputation, made it more likely that he would be known to those who arranged the appointments. These men were not employed because they were Rhodes Scholars, but the fact that they were Rhodes Scholars made it more likely that they would be employed.

It was not only the ghost of Colonel McCormick who deplored this development. Lyndon Johnson was holding forth in awe-struck tones to Senator Rayburn about the brilliance of the President's entourage. 'Well, Lyndon, you may be right,' replied the Senator. 'They may be every bit as intelligent as you say. But I'd feel a whole lot better about them if just one of them had run for sheriff once.'[26] There was a suspicion that has never gone away, probably never will go away, that Rhodes Scholars are too smooth, too theoretical, too detached, that they are not prepared to get their hands dirty in day-to-day hard work. The record of those who worked for Kennedy does not give much evidence to support this thesis, nor did the reputation of Rhodes Scholars suffer from their exposure to public scrutiny. Andrew Sullivan's diatribe, which opens this chapter, was written more than twenty years after Camelot's fleeting glory had shed its radiance on the Rhodes Scholars. The effect had by then to some extent worn off. But, whatever Sullivan might have said, during these years the Rhodes Scholars achieved a prominence in American national life which would never be wholly forfeited. The advent of the first Rhodes Scholar President would fortify and immeasurably enhance that reputation.

CHAPTER THIRTY-TWO
THE GERMANS AGAIN

In the fifty-five years since 1914 there had only been nine years in which German Rhodes Scholars had come to Oxford. Some people thought that this was nine too many; more doubted whether it could make sense to revive the Scholarships for a second time. Among the Trustees there was usually a handful of irreconcilables who felt the German Scholarships had always been an excrescence on Rhodes's Will and that Germany had forfeited any right to have them restored. A larger group believed that the Commonwealth should come first and that, if extra Scholarships could be afforded, they should be awarded to the old faithfuls like Canada or Australia or to the new, emergent members. Finally there were usually some who felt that, whatever the shortcomings of the German government, German Rhodes Scholars had on the whole been a credit to the system and that the Founder's wishes should be respected. As the Second World War became more distant, the balance of power moved from the enemies to the champions of restoration. It proved a lengthy process, however.

The surviving German Rhodes Scholars had begun to show signs of collective life as early as 1948 when H.K. Mandt asked what the Trustees would think if the Association of German Rhodes Scholars was re-established. The Warden's response was notably non-committal. The Trustees, he said, would be neutral on the issue, but, 'if the real object of the Association was to press for the revival of the German Rhodes Scholarships, I did not think . . . that the effort was likely to succeed, at all events within any measurable time'.[1] He had good reason for his view. Among the Trustees, Peacock, Hailey and, most markedly, Amery were opposed to the restoration of the Scholarships. Elton was still more implacable. When Eric Warburg pleaded for resumption and even offered to raise some of the necessary money, Amery said he was impressed by the fact that 'a Jew and an exile from Hitler's tyranny' should champion such a cause. He could see no moral obligation on the Trust to make a gesture to Germany, Elton replied. 'It would seem that the world situation of 1901, which then made the codicil relevant to the main purpose of the Will, no longer exists.'² With the old guard of the Trustees and the General Secretary resolutely opposed, it did indeed seem that a resumption of the German Scholarships was far away.

The Germans certainly were not optimistic. When Adolf Schlepegrell announced that he was going to the 1953 reunion in Oxford, his ten-year-old stepson, Thomas Böcking, said that in time he too would become a Rhodes Scholar and would attend the centenary reunion (he was and did). 'There will never be another German Rhodes Scholar,' said Schlepegrell sadly.³ If so, it would not be for want of effort on the part of well-wishers. It became increasingly hard to justify the Trust's attitude on financial grounds: as well as Warburg, the great educationalist Robert Birley suggested that the Foreign Office might put up the money for two Scholarships; the German Ambassador promised that businessmen from his country would do the same; Antonin Besse, son of the founder of St Antony's College, offered to take on the responsibility. It was not just a question of money, Elton retorted. Places were hard to find in Oxford and priority should be given to citizens of the Commonwealth.

In the mid-1960s, with Amery, Hailey and Peacock dead and Elton retired, it seemed as if the way might be opening. Williams himself, initially against renewing the Scholarships, had now become a not particularly enthusiastic supporter. 'I can manage well enough without Germans,' he had told the Trustees in 1960, but he thought that at least one German Scholarship could be justified. He was amused when the first Ghanaian Scholar turned out to be called Lebrecht Wilhelm Hesse: 'The German Rhodes Scholars always say that the Trustees transferred their Scholarships to somebody else; now we can claim that they transfer their men to our Scholarships.'⁴ But any hopes Williams might have had that the issue would now be quickly disposed of were dashed when it became clear that two of the newer Trustees, Nye and Wheare, were quite as emphatic as their predecessors on the need to give priority to the Commonwealth. Nye was 'surprised and distressed' to find that he was in a minority among the Trustees in holding this view: 'It is evident that a great change in approach seems to be pending, and, so far as I can see, without any very clear reasons.'⁵ The change proved to be slow-moving. Edward Heath was in the forefront of those clamouring for renewal, writing a letter which suggested that the Germans had every right to be aggrieved at their exclusion from a scheme 'in which they formerly shared'. Williams was infuriated by the tone of the letter and copied it to the recently appointed Trustee, Derick Amory 'so that you may contemplate whether it reflects quite his customary astuteness'.⁶ His indignation was redoubled when Heath's letter was leaked to the *Daily Telegraph* before the Trustees had even had a chance to reconsider the question. Their immediate reaction was to dig in their heels, a resolution reinforced when the *Frankfurter Allgemeine Zeitung* accused the Trustees of violating the Will and having 'an inadequate concept of their duty'.[7]

But they could not hold out indefinitely against a consensus which included the government, the heads of almost every Oxford college and the Rhodes Scholars themselves. The death of Nye in 1967 left Wheare in a minority of one and in March 1969 the Trustees decided to create two annual German Scholarships. 'I did not agree with this,' Wheare wrote grimly, 'but I was finally voted down by my colleagues. I must hope that they were right.'[8]

Harald Mandt was the senior as well as the most zealous of the German Rhodes Scholars and seemed the obvious person to act as chairman of the first selection committee. Some time after he had first raised the question of reviving the German Rhodes Scholar Association, an intelligence contact had warned Allen that there was much in Mandt's past that looked unattractive. He was said to have been a party member from an early date and 'a 100% flag-wagging German, who took Nazism in his stride as being a good thing for Germany'.[9] He had been formally rehabilitated, however, and was an ardent anglophile. The Trustees decided to let this sleeping dog lie and never had cause to regret their decision. Mandt soldiered on till 1973 – 'I confess to a feeling of deep joy,' he told Williams, when invited to lead the selection committee – and established a record by exceeding by fifteen years the age limit of seventy set by the Trustees for people in his position.[10]

In spite of the furious lobbying that had preceded the restoration of the Scholarships and the rejoicing when at last they were renewed, the Rhodes Scholarships never recaptured the status they had once enjoyed in Germany. There are many reasons for this failure. It was thirty years since the last election had been made and only a handful of old Scholars remained to keep the flame alive. Of these, according to one of the most distinguished of them, Fritz Caspari, one was a literary recluse and another was ruled out as having been intimately linked to the Nazi Party.[11] Since then a torrent of German students has found its way to England by other means: by 1996 there were 368 Germans at Oxford alone – the second largest national group. In spite of this large Oxonian population, many German students preferred to continue their studies in the United States, or possibly France. They appreciated the intimacy between teachers and students, which they had rarely encountered in German universities, but deplored the 'museum-like unreality' and 'unjustified intellectual arrogance' which they found at Oxford.[12] The Secretary of the Trust in Germany, Thomas Böcking, told the Warden that many potential candidates were deterred by the requirement that any Rhodes Scholars must spend at least two years in Oxford; after the protracted education which was the norm in Germany a year's study in a foreign university was as much as they were prepared to contemplate. Others, he said, were put off by the unusual 'profile' demanded by the selectors or even by 'latent imperialistic connotations'.[13] Whatever the causes, the fact remained that many students who might have been expected to apply for Rhodes Scholarships did not do so: once the selection committee found it impossible to elect their full entitlement of Scholars, yet that same year over a hundred Germans found their way to Oxford.

Some German Scholars put the blame for this on Thomas Böcking, not for the way he did his job but because he operated from Coburg – 'a charming but somewhat out of the way town where most of us rarely have the occasion to pay a visit', as one of the Secretary's critics described it.[14] Böcking, he went on, did nothing to keep Rhodes Scholars in touch with each other and failed to co-operate with those who were trying to do so.

The Warden mildly pointed out that the fostering of a German Rhodes Scholars Association was not one of the Secretary's duties; as a servant of the Trust he should act as a conduit to any such organisation but not involve himself too closely with it.[15] The trouble was that nobody in Germany seemed disposed to take on the task with any energy, and the relatively small number of Scholars, widely dispersed around the country as they were, would anyway have made it uphill work. In 1985 Williams's successor as Warden, Robin Fletcher, told the Chairman of the Trust about the dissatisfaction among the German Scholars but concluded cheerfully: 'I hope that is now on the path to solution.'[16] His optimism does not seem to have been justified. German Rhodes Scholars over the last twenty years have gravitated towards management consultancy or the diplomatic service; they play no conspicuous role in national life and are as sluggish as ever in supporting a national association – 'unless I've missed something', Böcking wryly concludes.[17]

The reunification of Germany led to the creation of first one, then two additional Scholarships but also greatly increased the dispersion of the Scholars. The original plan was that one Scholarship should be reserved for an East German; there was no reason to believe that graduates from East German universities would be any less intelligent or well grounded than their West German counterparts, but the rigid educational system imposed under the communist regime and the fact that Russian had long been their second language meant that they would be far less able to cope at Oxford. Positive discrimination was essential if candidates from the East were to be in with a chance; and if they were not in with a chance then they would lose interest and a large part of Germany would in effect be closed to the Scholarships. It did not prove necessary to keep up the arrangement for long; within a few years candidates from the former East German universities were competing on equal terms with their Western contemporaries and holding their own. Academically there have been few complaints about the standing of German Rhodes Scholars since reunification, indeed since the Scholarships were restored. Whether they have necessarily been candidates of whom Cecil Rhodes would have approved as future leaders and fighters of the world's fight is another matter: if they are not, it is as much the fault of the demands put upon students by the Oxford colleges as of the choices made by the German selection committee. This is a theme which will become increasingly apparent as the history of the Rhodes Trust nears the new millennium. In so far as Germany was to some extent starting from scratch when the Scholarships were revived, the effects of Oxford's increasing insistence on academic excellence, with the other traditional criteria largely forgotten, were noticeable more quickly than in the more well-established Rhodes constituencies.

CHAPTER THIRTY-THREE
WOMEN AT LAST

The Trustees had been preoccupied by the question of whether Rhodes Scholars should be allowed wives long before much attention was paid to the possibility that women might become Scholars. No one could doubt what Rhodes himself would have thought on either issue. Women, whether as students or as appendages, had no place at Oxford; they would distract the men from the serious business of sport, examinations and societal bonding and might well pick up unsuitable ideas about the role that they should play in later life. For many years the Trustees were content to go along with this, after both world wars they accepted that it was only fair to let Scholars who had married while serving their country bring their wives to Oxford when they resumed their studies, but this was a temporary concession on no account to be extended to Scholars whose studies had not been interrupted by the call of patriotic duty. They agreed that American Scholars who were drafted to fight the war in Korea might enjoy the right to postpone their period at Oxford but did not extend this privilege to cover the acquisition of a wife: 'a Korean veteran will presumably not have been so long out of civil life as the World War veterans were', Elton told Aydelotte.[1]

But though the line seemed logical enough to the Trustees it proved increasingly difficult to defend. In the United States, in particular, it was claimed that many good candidates were deterred by the fact that accepting a Scholarship would mean that they would have to defer marriage by two or three years. Even if they did decide to make the sacrifice, an increasing number dropped out during their time at Oxford. Soon after he became Warden, Williams admitted that he hoped Scholars would eventually be allowed to marry in their third year, but he knew that it might be some time before this came about.[2] Four years later in 1957, when Courtney Smith urged him to bring the issue before the Trustees, he explained why he was reluctant to do so. 'If there is to be a change we must wait for it. If I table one and it is defeated I must wait in ordinary courtesy another five years to bring it up again. Sir Edward [Peacock] and Lord Hailey are 86 and 85.' It would be better to wait until the old guard had passed on.[3] Smith had suggested that Scholars be allowed to marry in their second year. Williams fluctuated in his views but was cautiously in favour of such a step. Elton was opposed to any concession, and was strongly against its extension to the second year. 'The Rhodes Scholarships being what they are,' he told Peacock, 'it would be wrong to risk taking our men out of the main stream of College life. . . . And if we do lose a certain number of good candidates, we can reflect that we are doing better in Oxford by those we get!'

As it turned out, the senior Trustees were not so obdurate as Williams had expected. By 1959 it had become clear that not merely all the Overseas Secretaries but a great majority of the heads of the Oxford colleges were in favour of marriage being permitted in the third year. Their attitude, Williams explained, was based on the fact that in their third year Scholars would almost certainly anyway be living out of college and that experience showed that at this point in their university career a wife was a stabilising influence who led to better rather than worse results in examination. Even Elton now favoured the reform, though admitting this was a 'change which would undoubtedly have surprised Mr Rhodes, and, indeed, would have been quite unjustifiable in his day'.[4] With remarkably little demur, the Trustees gave way. If they deluded themselves that this would end the matter, they were quickly proved wrong. Within two or three years the American Secretary was lugubriously citing cases of excellent potential candidates who had rejected the possibility of a Rhodes Scholarship because the prospect of two years' enforced celibacy was intolerable. Williams, with Elton now safely off the scene, once more hesitated. In 1963 he regretfully recommended against a change, though 'one feels sad about individual cases'.[5] Within a year he had changed his mind in favour of marriage being allowed in the second year. As on the issue of the German Scholarships, Nye provided the main opposition. 'I cannot be persuaded', he said, 'that a man who married in his second year can really contribute to the same extent to college and university life, nor himself gain from this life to the same extent.' When Williams pleaded that Balliol in particular favoured married students because the academic results were conspicuously better, Nye retorted that he was not impressed by any college primarily concerned with high academic achievement. That was not what Oxford, still less the Rhodes Scholarships, were all about.[6] Nye was speaking with the voice of the traditional Rhodes Trustee, indeed with the voice of the Founder himself. It was a mark of the extent to which the balance of power in the Trust had changed in favour of Oxford and academic values that he was supported only by the merchant banker, Phillimore; of the remaining Trustees, Wheare, Abell, Harcourt and Amory were all in favour. Oliver Franks missed the meeting, but the Provost of Worcester would certainly have joined his fellow head of house in supporting the change.

That was as far as they would go, however, and, while Williams was Warden, as far as they would be asked to go. When the Rhodes Scholars in residence began to press for a complete removal of the ban on marriage he painted a dismal picture of an Oxford in which disconsolate Scholars would arrive for the first time with a wife at their side, nowhere to live and no college where they were already known which might offer help and companionship. 'I welcome the wives,' he told the Trustees; 'I think they play a great part here; I don't welcome them until their husbands have made Oxford ready to welcome them.'[7] The Trustees unanimously supported him; it was to be another twenty years and a very different Oxford before the last barrier crumbled.

Meanwhile the battle for the election of female Rhodes Scholars had been fought and won (or lost, according to one's point of view). Like a dormant volcano that from time to time emits a threatening puff of smoke the issue of woman Scholars had always been present in the background. As early as 1921 the Secretary of Smith, a leading women's college in the United States, argued that since the status of women at Oxford had been changed it was no longer proper to reserve the Rhodes Scholarship for men. A few years later the President of Wilson, another women's college, took the same line.[8] Both were ignored, and could safely be so. But after the Second World War the clamour for equal rights for women became ever more vociferous and the Trustees realised that it was not going to go away. There were two questions: did they want women Scholars and, given the terms of Rhodes's Will, would they be allowed to have them anyway? If the answer to the first was 'no', then no time needed to be wasted on the second. Williams unequivocally thought that the answer must be 'no'; if he could have put back the clock he might have driven women from Oxford altogether; as it was, he shuddered at the thought of all the 'muscular jokes' which women Rhodes Scholars would have to endure. 'I certainly don't think Rhodes Scholarships for women are necessary or, I believe, even apt in terms of Oxford undergraduate education,' he told Courtney Smith.[9] But he realised that some sop would have to be thrown to the feminists, and so he devised and put to the Trustees a plan for Women's Visiting Fellowships, by which female graduates from Commonwealth universities would spend a year or two in the senior common room of one of the women's colleges at Oxford – to the benefit, it was hoped, of both visitor and college. The scheme got off to a promising start when Susan Kippax, an Australian psychologist, within half an hour of successfully confronting the selection committee at Lady Margaret Hall dived into the Cherwell and rescued a drowning man;[10] but though the Visiting Fellows and the colleges were on the whole well satisfied by their experience, any hope that it would avert the demand for women Scholars was quickly extinguished. It was 'a classic case of "tokenism"', stormed the physicist Stephen Brush; the more prestigious the Scholarships appeared to be, the more offensive it was to deny them to women.[11] Another suggestion for a compromise – that the Trustees might create parallel Scholarships exclusively for women – was dismissed almost without discussion; such an award, said Williams, would have an 'inevitably second eleven flavour' and would merely incite rather than appease criticism of the Trust's anti-feminism.[12]

One of the more convincing reasons for deprecating the election of women Scholars had been that there was only a handful of colleges at Oxford where they would be accepted; if they took anything like the number of Scholarships which the balance of the sexes suggested should be the case, it would be difficult to fit them in and they would tend to congregate in undesirably large flocks. In the 1970s even that defence was lost as the men's colleges began to open their doors to women. By 1977 there were still only five colleges which had taken the plunge, but the trend was irreversible and gathering speed. It might slightly have appeased the restless spirit of Cecil Rhodes if he had known that his own college, Oriel, was to be the last to accept women.

In 1972 the first shot in what was to be the decisive battle was fired when a woman from the University of Minnesota applied for a Rhodes Scholarship. She was refused an interview. Malcolm Moors, the President of the University, wrote sorrowfully to Williams: 'We clearly think the Rhodes program is one of the most respected and prestigious honours a student can attain,' he assured the Warden. But the United States had established national guidelines about equal opportunity and if the University was to retain its funding it must respect them. 'It is with some dismay, then, that I can foresee circumstances in the future that could force this University to withdraw from participation in the Rhodes Scholarship program.'[13] William Barber, the American Secretary, predicted that every American university would be compelled to take a similar line. At the moment the threat came only from the United States, but in Oxford the Rhodes Scholars, by almost ten to one, voted for the admission of women and it seemed inevitable that the Commonwealth countries would eventually join in the crusade.

Now the real problems started. The operation of the Trust was subject to the control of the Charity Commissioners. The terms of Rhodes's Will left no room for doubt that he intended its beneficiaries to be men. The Commissioners would agree to waive this clause only if it could be shown that the main purpose of the Trust was rendered impossible by its existence. They did not accept that this was so. There might be some falling off in American applications – though even this was speculative – but there was no reason to

doubt that enough candidates would still come forward to meet the purposes
of the Will. The Trust's application to open the Scholarships to women was
rejected. Immediate disaster was averted by the decision of the American
Secretary of Education, Caspar Weinberger, that the ban on funding for institutions which practised sexual discrimination would not apply if that
discrimination related only to benefits received under some foreign trust or
will – an exclusion clause more or less overtly intended to rescue the Rhodes
Scholarships. That was satisfying as far as it went and a remarkable tribute to
the importance which the American establishment attached to the
Scholarships, but nobody imagined that it would provide more than a
breathing space.

Fortunately another line of attack now opened. A White Paper was
published in 1973 setting out various forms of sexual discrimination which
were to be outlawed in the United Kingdom. At the request of the Trust a
clause was inserted in the bill which would enable the Trustees to change their
statutes so as to eliminate any discrimination against women. In December
1975 the Equal Opportunities Bill became law. The Trustees immediately
applied to the Secretary of State for Education, and the following year their
wish was granted and they were free to invite women to apply. By then the
various selection committees had been told that they should include at least
one woman among their members. Several had already done so – India and
Massachusetts, indeed, had females in the chair – but a few of the more traditional committees protested. The Governor of South Australia, Marcus
Oliphant, maintained that he was perfectly capable of judging any candidate,
irrespective of sex – 'which may well be true in his own case', Williams
conceded.[14] Sir Marcus was a renowned nuclear physicist who, at the age of
seventy-four, had announced that he would join any expedition designed to
interrupt French nuclear testing in the Pacific. He might have proved an
equally formidable opponent when it came to female selectors, but fortunately
for the Trust he retired in 1976.

A reform which had seemed cataclysmic before it happened, and which
certainly would have outraged the Founder, passed off without a tremor. Not
everyone believed that the change was more than cosmetic. A woman reporter
from the *Washington Times* phoned the American Secretary and asked him
how many women were going to be elected. He had no idea, Barber replied.
Come off it, said the reporter: 'Everybody knows that this is an "old boys club"
and you aren't going to let more than a token woman inside.' In the event, thirteen American women were elected against nineteen men.[15] There were
twenty-four women Scholars in all; four from Canada, three from Australia,
one each from India, New Zealand, South Africa and Germany. The following
year the total was twenty, and though there were marked fluctuations between

years it became the norm that some 40 per cent of successful candidates would
be female. Given the disproportion in numbers that still existed in most countries between male and female students, and the fact that the South African
schools selected only from male candidates, this meant that the women had
more than their anticipated share.

'It will be interesting to see how the women fit in next year,' Williams wrote
in March 1977. 'On paper they are very bright so the men will have to pull
their socks up. And the English women will be left standing when it comes to
organised sport. No doubt it will all settle down in quite a short time and then
we will wonder what any fuss was about.'[16] It did settle down, and what little
fuss there was passed quickly. But it was testing for the first arrivals. Alison
Muscatine, in time to become a distinguished journalist and presidential
speech-writer, found that she and her fellow Scholars were 'written about and
photographed, objects of interest and curiosity'. Both at the time and later she
felt under immense pressure to prove that she was worthy of her position, to
excel academically and professionally and also, in due course, to raise a
family.[17] The obligation to excel haunted every Rhodes Scholar of every generation. The problem of balancing the claims of family against career must
perplex every woman of ability, Rhodes Scholar or not, but that first generation of women Rhodes Scholars was uniquely vulnerable because of the iconic
status with which they were willy-nilly vested.

By the time first-year marriages were reconsidered it was therefore possible
that the spouse might be either male or female. The principle that such
marriages were anathema had in fact been subject to some attrition in the
1980s. In 1982 a South African Scholar reported that his fiancée was under
mental stress and the doctors had recommended that she accompany him to
Oxford. They were devout Christians and would not contemplate living in sin
together. The Trustees agreed that an exception might be made: 'It was questioned whether the rule concerning marriage could be maintained in view of
current habits of cohabitation, but it was decided that its retention was still
important in dissuading Scholars from marrying before they had enjoyed
some experience of college life.'[18] A few years later a Jamaican first-year Scholar
requested permission to marry on the grounds that his fiancée was pregnant.
The Trustees contrived simultaneously to stick to their guns and sell the pass
by refusing permission but offering an interest-free loan equivalent in value to
the forfeited Scholarship.[19]

At the end of 1994 the principle was reviewed. Much had changed over the
last twenty or thirty years; much was still the same. Rented rooms were now
relatively easy to find so the accommodation argument had lost its force. A
large majority of Scholars were doing postgraduate work, and many of them

were in postgraduate colleges, so the need for a traditional collegiate experi-ence no longer seemed quite so compelling. Some good potential candidates were certainly being deterred by the fact that they could not be accompanied by a spouse but it was impossible to say how many. A majority of Rhodes Scholars then at Oxford wanted a change to the rules, but not an overwhelming majority – about three out of five. 'The Trustees will make themselves roughly equally unpopular whichever decision they take,' the Warden prophesied gloomily. When it was put to the Trustees, one objected on the grounds that the unique advantage Oxford had to offer 'these highly strained students, is a college structure which has an academic dimension and is not simply a hall of residence'.[20] All the Trustees approved the change. Mary Moore, the Principal of St Hilda's College and the first woman Trustee, feared that this would complete the transformation of the Rhodes Scholar into 'just another grad-uate student living in a flat in Iffley', but still felt the Trust had no alternative.[21] The Rhodes Scholars had changed, Oxford had changed; ignoring the facts of life would not alter them. It remained to be seen how many of the traditional values of the Scholarships could be carried through to the next millennium.

CHAPTER THIRTY-FOUR
THE BROTHERHOOD

Of all the dignitaries who have adorned the Rhodes Trust, Lord Elton was the most messianic in his conviction that in accepting a Scholarship a Scholar was taking on not just two or three years at Oxford but 'life-long membership of a world-wide brotherhood'. Already within each of the main constituencies there existed Associations which would speed the departing Scholar on his way to Oxford, welcome him on his return and take a protective interest in his subsequent career. But more was needed, national institutions were not enough: 'the time may come when the need will be felt by a periodical, and conceivably an association, to do throughout the world what is already being done for the individual constituencies'.[1] He told Peacock that he relished above all this 'oecumenical aspect of the work' and on all his trips abroad he never missed a chance to urge Rhodes Scholars to shape their lives as part of a close-knit and strongly motivated community.[2] Exactly what he had in mind is hard to establish: Elton's ideas were habitually cloaked in a mist of well-meaning vapidity; when the mist dispersed only a damp patch was left where a noble concept had once seemed to be taking shape.

By the 1960s and 1970s the Associations in the larger constituencies had outgrown the phase when they were little more than skeletal bodies responsible for organising the occasional Old Boys' rally. With varying degrees of efficiency they had set up machinery for keeping tabs on the individual Scholars and perhaps bringing together potential employers with promising young men or women who had recently returned from Oxford. In some countries and at certain times, things were taken a stage further and the former Scholars sought to operate as a body, establishing what was being done and what needed to be done to improve the structure of society, co-operating in common enterprises and enlisting others to do the same. Such joint enterprises were usually the work of a single Scholar or a small group of Scholars and tended to wither if the driving force was removed. Nowhere was to be found the culmination of Elton's dream: an international fraternity which transcended the boundaries of the separate countries and worked as one in the pursuit of Rhodes's ideals.

This was not for want of effort on Elton's part. He preached his doctrine to the Trustees as assiduously as to the Scholars overseas and won from them a general statement that they 'wished the Secretary and the Warden to do anything possible to promote among former Rhodes Scholars a greater awareness of Rhodes Scholars from other constituencies'.[3] Elton canvassed opinion as to how this could best be done and passed his findings on to Williams. There had been some enthusiasm shown for a distinctive badge or button to be worn by Scholars. 'My own ideas, which do not run to charms or watchkeys, are beginning to take some kind of shape,' he announced. First priority, he thought, should be a newsletter, which would replace and be considerably livelier than the present Annual Statement.[4] Through this and other methods the local Associations should be made more active. 'It is quite clear that what is needed to keep them alive and healthy is as many active functions as possible, in addition to an annual dinner!' he told the South African Secretary. There were many useful things the Scholars could be doing: nominating Rhodes Scholar members of selection committees, holding conferences to discuss the selection process, occupying themselves with the welfare of their Scholars at Oxford, producing a newsletter, publicising the Scholarships, offering dinners for departing or returning Scholars.[5] When the selection committee in Rhodesia concluded that, as there was already an Oxford Society in the country, there was no need for a Rhodes Scholars Association as well, Elton wrote in dismay to the former Rhodes Scholar Chief Justice Sir Robert Tredgold. An Oxford Society was concerned at the best with maintaining contact between Oxonians and Oxford. A Rhodes Scholars Association could do much more than that. 'By maintaining an interest in the elections and in Rhodes Scholars newly returned from Oxford it can do a great deal to improve the quality of competition and also to promote that sense of coherence among Rhodes Scholars all over the world which the Founder would doubtless have desired to see.' 'Only connect!' one can almost hear him urging the reluctant Tredgold. That was the whole of Margaret Schlegel's sermon and it was close to being the whole of Elton's too.

Wherever he went Elton was dismayed by 'the surprising ignorance of most Rhodes Scholars as to Rhodes Scholars from every country save their own'. This was flatly against Rhodes's intentions, he concluded. When Dom Mintoff, the Prime Minister of Malta, was fêted at the same dinner party as Norman Manley, the Prime Minister of Jamaica, the two men discovered only by chance that they were both Rhodes Scholars. No member of the Massachusetts selection committee had known that Howard Florey, the Nobel Prize-winning inventor of penicillin, was a Rhodes Scholar.[6] A few Rhodes

Scholars did more than pay lip-service to Elton's international vision. The
New Zealand lawyer Jonathan Ross, for example, found that there was an
element of freemasonry about the Scholarships. When he had been in San
Francisco recently the Chairman of the American Association had given a
dinner for him and he would repay the compliment if he got the chance. If
there were two applicants of equal merit for a job, the fact that one was a
Rhodes Scholar would, in his eyes, tip the balance. But not everyone was so
enthusiastic. Andrew Moore, also from New Zealand, thought that there was
no real network nor any need for one; occasional social gatherings were quite
enough. Ian Pollard, an Australian businessman, while seeing a case for
Rhodes Scholars getting to know each other, especially across the generational
gap, did not feel the process should be institutionalised – that way, the tub-
thumper would be sure to try to make the other Rhodes Scholars join in the
thumping of his tub.[7] Elton's ambitions were made more inaccessible by the
fact that his successor did not share his views. 'Old Boy Dinners rather run
against the grain,' Williams told the New Zealand educationalist J. C. Dakin.
'Besides, I think Rhodes Scholars should be yeast in their own countries
rather than trying to make themselves a compact dough.'[8] Successive General
Secretaries felt it their duty to encourage the establishment of local
Associations, but after Elton the passion went out of the pursuit until it was
revived at the centenary celebrations.

Unsurprisingly, the Association of American Rhodes Scholars continued to
be the largest, richest and most vociferous. Professor Ted Youn of Boston
College, who with Karen Arnold has for several years been leading a team
enquiring into American elites with particular reference to the Rhodes
Scholars, has detected a sense of homogeneity and common purpose among
the latter not to be found in any comparable group. An indication of their
enthusiasm is that, when the researchers appealed for information, a phenom-
enal 87 per cent responded – a proportion vastly greater than could have been
expected from, say, Harvard graduates or some professional grouping such as
clergymen or surgeons. American Rhodes Scholars, Youn believes, have a
sense of social obligation more compelling than is to be found in any other
category of responsible citizenry. They also feel themselves bound by collective ties stronger than those that link, for example, other Oxonian Americans:
when they leave Oxford both groups feel themselves similarly unified, but the
machinery of the AARS ensures that the Rhodes Scholars will not be allowed
to forget their ties amid the welter of new interests in which their lives will
involve them.[9] The infinite variety of political and social opinions among
Rhodes Scholars ensured that the AARS would never try to establish itself as
a powerful lobby in national affairs, but when the members were united on

some issue relating to the Scholarships they would make sure that their views were loudly and clearly heard.

The marked difference of approach between Canada and the United States was no less apparent after the Second World War than before it. Elton accepted that the Canadians were never going to match their southern neighbours in either the size or the fervour of their Association – 'being more individualistic they are less disposed to be organised' – but he was still convinced that more could be done to promote the cohesion of the Scholars.[10] Michener was disposed to agree with him: of the 349 living Canadian Rhodes Scholars, he worked out, 272 were living in Canada. There were also eleven non-Canadian Rhodes Scholars in Canada, so the potential membership was 283, 'a goodly number . . . it may be that the time is ripe to develop an Association'.[11] In 1951, with Elton again present, the Association was duly set up. Its objects, it was said, were to further higher education, to help administer the Scholarships and to promote intercourse between Scholars. It survived and, in so far as it numbers a substantial minority of French Canadians among its members, can be said to have made a contribution to national unity. It performed at least one notable service when it pioneered a scheme for 'Scholarships in Reverse', by which an Oxford graduate, selected by the Warden, was sent to a Canadian university for a year or two. That the beneficiaries themselves appreciated the experience is shown by the number who elected to settle in Canada, a development very much in keeping with Cecil Rhodes's aspirations. But as the long-standing Canadian Secretary Arthur Scace admits, a smaller proportion of Canadian Scholars belong to their Association than is the case in the United States and 'it is generally taken a lot less seriously', though it helps administer the Scholarship by keeping in touch with those who might serve on selection committees.

In Australia and New Zealand enthusiasm was more evident. Australia seemed to Elton to provide a model for other countries, holding as it did a biennial conference at which such subjects as selection committees, publicity for the Scholarships and openings in the civil service for returning Scholars were debated and constructive action taken subsequently. 'I trust that each of the younger Associations, when they are, say, ten years old, will be equally active and useful,' wrote Elton appreciatively.[12] New Zealand, in due course, obliged. When Elton went there in 1958 he had to admit that, with only thirty resident Rhodes Scholars and immense distances between the various centres, it was going to be peculiarly difficult to get a proper Association established.[13] A start was made in organising participation in selection committees and providing farewell jollities for the new Scholars, but a proper newsletter was never produced. More than thirty years later, Hugh Templeton, who had been a minister in the government of Robert Muldoon, only learnt of the death of several New Zealand Scholars through the Warden's Christmas letter. He resolved to put the matter right. 'I believe we need an active Association as an expression of our identity,' he told the then Warden, Anthony Kenny. 'New Zealanders have some fear of elitism, but I see an active Association as a means of responding to our good fortune in being Rhodes Scholars. We cannot do that without keeping in touch.'[14] Within two years the Association was up and running, with Templeton as its President. The first annual dinner was held in December 1993 and when the centenary came to be celebrated an exhibition was organised to mark the occasion.

It was in the heartland of the Rhodes system, South Africa, that Elton's dream most signally failed to take on any substance. An abortive effort to establish an Association had been made in the 1920s in Cape Town, and Gie, once again at the prompting of Elton, decided to try again in 1948, recruiting the core of his membership from the galaxy of Scholars who worked in the Oppenheimer empire of Anglo American De Beers.[15] The enterprise quickly ran into squalls due to the attempts of its turbulent Secretary, David Bean, to draw the nascent Association into the political field.* When Bean was reproved for his indiscretion, he retorted that the Association had not been formally constituted, that he had never been appointed Secretary, and that therefore his activities had been conducted in a private capacity. In this it turned out that he was perfectly correct: 'I do not think that the Association can expect to survive long unless, and until, it constitutes itself in a formal manner,' wrote Elton reproachfully.[16]

For a time Gie deluded himself that these troubles had been left behind and that all was set fair for the Association. True, the Scholars in South Africa showed no particular interest in each other's activities or in the workings of the system, but 'I am still satisfied that Rhodes Scholars are interested in the Rhodes Scholarships scheme and there is a conscious feeling of association between them.' Whenever there was a real reason to meet, for instance when Elton paid a visit to South Africa, 'the response has been very, very good indeed'.[17] But the ability to attract people to an occasional gala event was thin evidence for the existence of a thriving Association. 'We are, in reality, a dormant body resuscitated once a year for our annual dinner,' the Anglo American executive Christopher Griffith told Elton, only two years after Gie had written so enthusiastically about the prospects.[18] It was Griffith who painted the truer picture, as Gie was sadly to admit. 'When I was appointed,' Gie wrote early in 1963, 'I assumed that . . . one of my duties was to create a corporate spirit among all past Rhodes Scholars. In this respect I have

*See p. 195 above.

failed. . . . One hoped that we could have annual functions, such as dinners etc, but somehow they have not materialised. The Rhodes Scholars Association has not really been a great success.'[19] A few years before, this confession would have provoked a trumpet blast from Elton, exhorting Gie to fresh efforts – holding more conferences, giving more dinners, circulating more news-sheets. But a new General Secretary was now installed and Williams was sceptical about the corporate spirit. Gie's lament went almost unremarked, and the Association continued to moulder. For thirty years, indeed, during the bleakest apartheid years, the Rhodes Scholar community found itself beleaguered, dissociated from but anxious to avoid too brutal a confrontation with the apparently invincible power of the Nationalist govern-ment and viewed with some suspicion by the African National Congress for bearing a name linked with old-school imperialism, capitalism and the exploitation of native labour. Many Rhodes Scholars left the country, others never returned from their period at Oxford. The reaction of most of those who remained was to lie low – some, as individuals, doing great things in the struggle for civilised values but, as an organisation, trying above all not to attract attention.

The long, long night is over. Today the South African Rhodes Scholars can confront the world with a new confidence. It is too early to say whether a Rhodes Scholars Association might be revived and, this time, flourish. If ever there was a country, though, in which the need for it was obvious and the potential for its usefulness limitless, it must be South Africa. It is conceivable that the linking of Cecil Rhodes and his Scholarships with the magic name of Mandela, discussed in Chapter 47, might lead to an Association in which ideas could be exchanged, initiatives launched, co-operation in the world's fight established on a lasting basis. It is a curious twist of fate that South Africa, so reluctant to move down the path towards true association, might yet prove to be the country where Elton's dream comes nearest to reality.

CHAPTER THIRTY-FIVE

PRIORITIES

'À Harvard j'ai appri,' a francophone Quebec prime minister was accustomed to say. 'À Oxford j'ai appri à vivre.' For the first sixty or seventy years of the Rhodes Scholarships it was taken for granted by the Trustees that, though a few other universities around the world, particularly in the United States, might from time to time boast technical facilities more sophisticated than those to be found in Oxford, there was still an almost mystic quality about the Oxford experience that made it superior to any other education. No students in their senses, certainly no students who might make convincing candidates for a Rhodes Scholarship, would contemplate accepting an award to any other university if the chance of going to Oxford was given them. Complacent at the best of times, this confidence became increasingly hard to justify in the 1960s and 1970s. The growing determination of Rhodes Scholars of the period to pursue postgraduate studies while at Oxford exposed striking deficiencies. During the 1950s twice as many Scholars were taking an undergraduate degree as were doing postgraduate work. Inexorably the balance switched, so that by 1966 the postgraduates were in a majority; today the Rhodes Scholar taking an undergraduate degree is something of a rarity. Yet, so far as provision to meet this new need was concerned, supply lagged far behind demand. Increasingly Scholars found that the courses they wished to follow were not to be found and that the facilities provided were inadequate compared with what was available in the United States or even, sometimes, at a Commonwealth university. The myth of Oxford's superiority was wearing thin.

At the end of 1966 Williams put the facts before the Trustees. 'Bluntly,' he said, 'from the point of view of the American Rhodes Scholarships, Oxford has got to remain good enough for Harvard men to want to come to it.' A second-rate Oxford would attract only second-rate Scholars; the academic good-health of the University must be a prime concern of the Trustees when considering how to spend whatever money was left after the Scholarships and their administration had been paid for. At that time the annual income of the

Trust was about £400,000 and of this three-quarters were needed to cover expenses related to the Scholarships. That left £100,000 uncommitted. Clearly Trustees could not devote all of this to Oxford; there were many other benefactions to which they were committed or towards which they felt a responsibility. As a rough rule of thumb, Williams suggested that the Trustees should spend half the money available on Oxford causes. There were many ways in which such aid might be applied – in help to the poorer colleges or the new graduate colleges, in providing tutors for subjects which colleges found difficult to cover unless new fellows were elected, in housing for students. But such a policy should be followed with caution: 'It is important not to get into the position of being relied upon by the University to get it out of a jam, as if the Rhodes Trust were an extension of the Higher Studies Fund.'[1]

The Trustees accepted Williams's recommendations in principle, but it proved difficult to decide how much could safely be given away. The fierce increases imposed by Mrs Thatcher on the fees charged to overseas students at one moment seemed calculated to drive the Trust to the verge of bankruptcy. The talk was of suspending Scholarships rather than increasing grants.* The panic quickly passed, however. By the time Robin Fletcher took over from Williams in 1980 the economic barometer was moving towards 'Set Fair'. The Trust's finances had entered a period of sustained growth which made possible generosity on a scale far more lavish than had been conceivable in the past.

By 1989, when Fletcher in his turn handed on Rhodes House to the Master of Balliol, Anthony Kenny, the total value of the Trust's holding was £67 million; the annual income had risen to £5.4 million, of which over £2 million was available for giving away or building up reserves. Even allowing for inflation this was a remarkable result. At one moment, indeed, it seemed as if it might be too remarkable for its own good. In 1986, after disbursements, a surplus of more than £1 million was shown in the Public Purposes Fund. The Charity Commissioners queried this: if the income was being accumulated rather than given away or spent on the Scholarships then it should be subject to tax. Without too much difficulty Fletcher persuaded them that the Public Purposes Fund should not be considered in isolation. Viewed overall, 82 per cent of the Trust's income had been spent, and the Scholarship Funds showed a deficit or were only just in the black. Given the Trust's commitments, it was essential that it should be allowed to build up its reserves. The explanation was accepted but a warning had been given. To

*See p. 203 above.

the natural inclination to be generous was now added the incentive that if they did not give away enough the Trustees might find themselves penalised for their frugality.

In 1961, when a grant to an Oxford cause was approved, Charles Millis had told Williams: 'I confess that I had not thought that in Peacock's lifetime a gift to the University would have been allowed to be contemplated!'[2] Twenty years later, with Peacock, Amery and Elton dead and the influence of Williams still potent at Rhodes House, it was gifts to anything other than the University which required justification. From 1964, when the Trustees gave £75,000 for the building of a gymnasium on the Iffley Road (something which, as Williams pointed out, 'would seem to fit in with the general notion that Mr Rhodes had of the sort of man he wanted'),[3] a stream of grants on an ever increasing scale was made to Oxford causes, including handouts to individual colleges. From time to time the Trustees were forced to accept that some project was beyond them. 'Hopes of a University swimming bath have foundered – it is just too expensive,' Williams wrote in his Christmas letter for 1975, but such moments of restraint were rare. 'The University and its Colleges have received well over half a million in the short time since Godfrey Elton retired,' reported Williams two years later, 'but it is not a bottomless pit.' Even if not bottomless it was remarkably deep; every year in the last two decades of the twentieth century very substantial funds were distributed to Oxonian causes.

It was taken for granted that individual Trustees would push the claims of causes to which they were particularly attached. Wheare advanced his own college, Exeter. He knew it was only one of many colleges in need, he admitted, but it was the college of Kingsley Fairbridge – 'generally thought of, I think, as among the greatest Rhodes Scholars' – and Exeter had always been especially favourable towards the Scholars and had tried to give them two years in college. This was in 1959, before the making of grants to individual colleges had been accepted as normal practice. It was a dangerous precedent, thought Peacock, 'for all the Colleges at Oxford could make claims', but he felt that in this case the risk was worth taking; after all 'Wheare was particularly valuable as a Trustee'.[4] They contributed £5,000. This *ad hominem* approach marked many of the Trust's deliberations. Sir William Paton, a Trustee since 1968, always supported any appeal connected with clinical pharmacology. 'I get a bit "engaged" in things,' he wrote apologetically to Williams. 'I hope it's known that even I recognise this, and hope only that my arguments and not my feelings are taken into account.'[5] The contrary was the case: the fact that one of their number felt passionately about a cause predisposed the Trustees to endorse it.

At least Paton and Wheare were both seeking grants for Oxford causes. In 1975 Robert Blake asked his fellow Trustees for £50,000 to be given to the University Press to help with the costs of editing Gladstone's diaries. It was, he admitted, an 'unusual application' but 'the circumstances are unusual too. Gladstone was, I suppose, one of the greatest, certainly one of the most remarkable figures ever to have been educated at Oxford University.'[6] That was true enough, but the thought of this imperial sceptic and adversary of General Gordon being commemorated by courtesy of his Trust to the tune of an eventual £106,500 must have caused the Founder's ghost some chagrin.*

Fifteen years earlier, General Nye had asked Elton on what principles the Trust decided whether or not a request fell within its bailiwick: 'I sometimes feel, in my very limited experience, we aren't always quite consistent – but perhaps I'm quite wrong.' He was quite right. The inconsistencies, Elton replied, were the result of changes in the composition of the Board of Trustees, but he thought that, though no tests or principles had ever been written down, 'like the British Constitution, we can perhaps claim to have evolved certain (rather vague) precedents and traditions'.[7] Vague they had been at the best of times, and with South Africa off the list of beneficiaries and Commonwealth causes of dwindling importance, they could by now hardly be said to exist at all. It was generally accepted that Oxford should have the lion's share, but after that it was every Trustee for himself, with the prizes going to those who had the greater eloquence or persistence.

The scope for inconsistency had grown at the same rate as the funds available for distribution. It was a grant to finance Paton's hobby-horse of a chair in clinical pharmacology which stung Price to protest. This was just one of a series of proposals, 'each one of which is very good but which seem to carry out no general policy and relate to no particularly well-defined purpose. . . . I suspect that my colleagues among the Rhodes Trustees would prefer not to start with a systematic definition of policy but to proceed by common law. But it does make me squirm a bit.' Price wanted all grants from the Public Purposes Fund to be designed 'to help Oxford do for the next generations what Rhodes thought that the Oxford of about 1900 could do in its day', to train people for the 'career services ("political" in its broadest sense)'. Williams professed to agree in principle, but showed little inclination

---

*This proposal was high on the scale of rhodocycles – a measure devised by Kenny when he was Warden to express the number of times any given innovation would cause the Founder to turn in his grave. Though the same personal rancour would not have been involved, William Waldegrave's success in securing a grant to enable John Grigg to complete his majesty biography of Lloyd George would also have set Rhodes spinning.

to do so in practice. 'You may think we eddy too much and there is no particular point in the Rhodes Trust going for Paton's chair,' he told Price, but this was still better than undue rigidity. 'Case law may produce an incoherence. Tram lines, on the other hand, lead to the terminus.'[8]

The hunger of the University for support was about to impose some measure of coherence on the Trust's dispensations. In 1983 Fletcher calculated that, at the present value of money, the Trust had given about £3.25 million to the University and the individual colleges over the previous thirty years. Of this, by far the larger part had been contributed in the last decade. Then it became known that the University was planning to launch an immense appeal, designed to put it back at the forefront of contemporary research and, *inter alia*, to provide a centre for study to which even the most sophisticated and demanding Rhodes Scholar would be proud to go. It was clear that the Trust would be expected to set the ball rolling with a massive contribution. Fletcher was uneasy in a way that Williams would probably not have been. He told Paton that he felt the Trust, 'with all its international prestige, has been retreating into an "Oxford shell". It has, indeed, occurred to me that it ought to double its assets through appeal and embark on an ambitious scheme matching the inspiration of the Founder.' To the Trustees he pointed out that in recent years almost all the major benefactions had gone to Oxford: 'An outsider would be surprised at (though he could not legally question) this emphasis on one institution, and not be reassured to learn that all the Trustees were members of that institution.'[9]

When the Vice-Chancellor duly fired his first salvo at the Trustees they responded more enthusiastically than Fletcher would have wished. True, they wanted reassurance on certain points. Who else had been approached at this preliminary stage? How far would benefactors be put off by being asked to contribute to a general fund rather than specific projects? How would the appeal be co-ordinated with the separate appeals being made by individual colleges, even by departments? But the Vice-Chancellor can have been in little doubt that help on the scale he was hoping for would be forthcoming. As a first step the Trust put up £0.5 million to meet the expenses of the development office responsible for the campaign; then they pledged a further £2.5 million as their main contribution to the appeal. The grant was not entirely without strings. The first priority was to top up the endowments for the four academic posts at Oxford which the Trust had sponsored in the past and which were now suspended for lack of funds. They did not lay down rigid criteria for the disposal of the rest of their contribution, and their targets changed as other donors adopted certain projects, but they expressed particular interest in a new building for plant sciences, the Pitt Rivers and the

Ashmolean museums and a new all-weather running track.[10] It was a princely donation and in the end they gave more than as much again: £1.675 million dedicated to the endowment of two University lectureships in management studies and £1 million for a proposed Institute of American Studies.

In spite of these immense commitments and a considerable increase in the number of Scholarships, the Trust seemed to get richer and richer. The collapse of Barings Bank, the asset-management wing of which had for many years handled the Trust's investments, caused some consternation, especially since the Bank held £2 million of the Trust's liquid cash, but in the end no more than temporary inconvenience was caused. By 1996 the Trust's assets were worth more than £150 million and the income was around £6.5 million. 'In the league table of British charities deriving their income principally from endowment,' Kenny announced in his Christmas letter that year, 'the Trust is edging up into the top twenty, up there with the British Heart Foundation.' By then the apartheid regime in South Africa had almost miraculously crumbled. The traditional beneficiary of the Trust's surplus income, for so long struck off the list of recipients, was suddenly restored to favour. Oxford could no longer expect to get by far the greater part of whatever was on offer. In June 1995 the Trustees formally endorsed the policy that approximately half the sum available for benefactions should be devoted to Oxford causes, the rest should be spent in Africa: 'Within Africa, it was thought that the emphasis should be on educational projects.'[11] At that time they assumed that this balance would be retained for a decade at least; long before then, however, the claims of Africa had begun to seem paramount and Oxford went almost by the board.

One expensive project that was on the agenda in 1992 was the conversion of Rhodes House into a club for the use of academic staff, mainly working in the scientific field, who were not members of any senior common room and had to rely for communal social life on a poky establishment called Halifax House, which itself was now under threat of being converted into laboratories. Though successive Wardens had struggled valiantly to convert Rhodes House from a white elephant into a useful asset to the University or a centre for Commonwealth studies, it was still grossly under-used. The Trustees liked the idea of the club, though deploring the proposal that it should be described as the University Hospitality Centre – they felt that the Rhodes Society would be a better name.[12] All went swimmingly: the University was enthusiastic, architects were commissioned, plans made for a new wing to be built containing twenty bedrooms, £2.67 million earmarked for the project. And then the Trustees discovered, as their predecessors had done on more than one occasion, how difficult it was to get anything done at Oxford. Wadham insisted that a change of freehold was involved and revived their claims for compensation, the University decided after all to keep Halifax House open for the foreseeable future, the project got entangled with plans to build a new Business School. It became obvious that no final decision could be made for several years. It was the debacle of 1964 re-enacted; once more the Trustees withdrew their offer and the Warden reluctantly resumed his struggle to make effective use of his mausoleum.

At least the collapse of the Rhodes Society meant that a large sum of money was available for another project close to the hearts of some at least of the Trustees. Plans for an Oxford Institute for American Studies had been germinating for several years, and the Trust was already committed to a grant of £1 million, conditional on an equivalent amount being raised in the United States. In 1997 Kenny proposed that this should be increased by a further £4 million. 'It may be felt', he admitted, 'that such a generous gift to an American Institute will make the Trustees appear to be leaning too far to gratify their US constituents.' The answer to this, he suggested, was that once the new Institute was operational the Bodleian's holdings of American books, which were now lodged in the Rhodes House Library, would be moved to this new home. This, in its turn, would free the Trust to develop the Library for the purpose for which it had originally been intended – as a centre for Commonwealth studies. The Trustees accepted the argument and approved the grant, though – mindful of their recent experiences – they made the offer conditional on work starting on the Institute within a year.

This time all went well, the work was completed more or less on schedule and the American material was duly transferred. With it went almost 90 per cent of the readers who had used to work in the Rhodes House Library. As long before as 1947 Allen had argued that the ideal solution would be to transfer *everything* in Rhodes House to the Bodleian: 'It would, of course, be a considerable economy to the Trustees if the whole thing was re-absorbed.' The problem with this was that the Library had 'acquired a definite identity of its own and there would be strong resistance, I think, to its going back into the general pool'.[13] Now that the greater part of its substance was departed and the Library seemed destined to join the list of cavernous and under-tenanted halls with which Rhodes House was already so generously provided, the question arose whether it might not be put to some different and more profitable use. Oxford being Oxford, it would have been surprising if any suggestion as to how that might be achieved was not met with contumely and derision.*

*See p. 322 below.

In a paper submitted to the Trustees at the end of 2000, the new Warden, John Rowett, quoted the Chairman as saying that the very large benefactions which had been made over the previous decades might 'be regarded as the end of an era'.[14] Rowett had clear ideas as to what shape the new era should take. Their working out will be, in a sense, the culmination of this story.

CHAPTER THIRTY-SIX

WHOM IS THE FIGHT AGAINST?

The world in whose fight Cecil Rhodes had wished his Scholars to engage looked radically different as the second half of the twentieth century wore on. Were different qualities therefore required? Should selection committees apply different criteria in sorting out the candidates? The most conspicuous change after 1945 was that the British Empire had disappeared. The basic assumption behind Rhodes's Will – that the world was best run by a coalition of that Empire and the United States – became increasingly irrelevant. But the countries that had once composed the Empire were still there, linked in a Commonwealth whose ties were far more tenuous than Rhodes would have hoped for, but still paying lip-service at least to certain values and codes of conduct. English was still the lingua franca of this vast area. The need to evolve a common policy with the United States was no less pressing than it had been in 1910 or 1930. The Rhodes Scholarships had never been conceived as a training ground for the administrators of Empire, but a significant number had nevertheless graduated into imperial service. The New Zealanders who had helped govern Fiji would no longer have that outlet for their energies, but the proliferation of international organisations meant that they would not be starved of opportunity if that was the direction in which their ambitions took them. Despite the end of Empire, by 1980 more rather than fewer Rhodes Scholars were working in what could loosely be called the developing world.

Essentially, therefore, the same sort of people would be facing the same sort of challenge, however much the circumstances of the world might have evolved. But those changed circumstances did demand certain adjustments to bring the concept of the late nineteenth century into accord with the realities of the late twentieth. The Trustees had always believed that, though Rhodes's ideals must continue to provide their lode star, it was their duty to reinterpret those ideals so as to make them relevant to the circumstances of the day. In 1956 a selection committee in New Zealand had debated to what extent the reference in Rhodes's Will to the desirability of a candidate having 'an interest in his schoolmates' applied in an age when the university experience was of so much greater immediate importance. 'I do not think that the committee need have gone back to the Will,' wrote Elton. 'What is really relevant for the committee's purpose is now not so much the Will as the Scholarships' Memorandum, in which the provisions of the Will are interpreted in the light of present-day requirements.'[1]

Williams made repeated efforts to dress the Founder's aspirations in modern garb. In 1961 he rewrote the memorandum for selection committees in words that seem as applicable today as when he wrote them:

> Quality of both character and intellect is the most important requirement for a Rhodes Scholarship and this is what the Selection committee will seek. The Rhodes Scholar should not be a one-sided man; or a selfish man. Intellectual ability should be founded upon sound character and integrity of character upon sound intellect. Success in being elected to office in student organisations may or may not be evidence of leadership in the true sense of the word. Cecil Rhodes evidently regarded leadership as consisting of moral courage and interest in one's fellow men quite as much as in the more aggressive qualities.... Physical vigour is an essential qualification for a Rhodes Scholar, but athletic prowess is less important than the moral qualities which can be developed in sports.[2]

Williams was acutely conscious of the contradictions that lay at the heart of the selection process. Successful scholars had to be winners, ambitious, energetic, determined to make a mark, yet they had also to be compassionate, attentive to the needs of others. It takes all sorts to make a Rhodes Scholar, Williams contended, 'but one sort it does not take: the man who is out for himself'. The very concept of a programme designed to promote the existence of an elite was open to challenge in the egalitarian society which increasingly prevailed, but the Rhodes Scholarships were aiming at something that was both morally more justifiable and more difficult to attain. 'We are seeking in our Rhodes Scholars outstanding ability married to unselfishness,' Williams told the Trustees. 'It is a tall order: to discover an elite with a conscience – with compassion and without arrogance.'[3] In picking their Rhodes Scholars, selection committees were looking to the future as much as assessing the merits of the men in front of them. When a Scholar from Stellenbosch was eager to get his doctorate, Williams commented: 'Ours is an investment in a human being who will be significant twenty years later, not a grant to a man who wants to better himself here and now. Of course they may coincide ... and they may not.'[4]

By 1945 the days had passed when a Scholar would be sent to Oxford with little prospect of getting even a moderately respectable degree but in the confidence that he would play cricket or row for the University. In 1946 the New Zealand selection committee turned down Martin Donnelly. He was already at Oxford when he applied for the Scholarship and when he presented himself to the committee he 'made no secret of the fact that his principal interest was sport' and that he planned to do only as much work as was necessary to scrape a pass. Unfortunately he had misjudged what was needed and failed his examinations. The committee felt, the New Zealand Secretary told Elton, 'that such an attitude was not up to Rhodes Scholarship standard'. There was a note of wistfulness about Allen's comment: 'Donnelly is one of the finest bats in the world. . . . I have met him and he is a very attractive young man. He is also a footballer and, therefore, perhaps, a double blue lost to the Rhodes Scholarships. Sad but true, and no doubt right.'[5] (Having thus stoutly defended the integrity of their Scholarships, the Trust proceeded to have it both ways by making Donnelly a grant for no particular reason except that he had served during the war and was both a good chap and a great cricketer.)[6]

Allen's mild regret was characteristic. At any rate until the age of Kenny the officials of the Trust tended to attach rather more importance to sporting ability than did most selection committees. This was particularly true where the Americans were concerned. In 1947, Allen complained, only ten out of forty-eight American Scholars had any athletic distinction, the Commonwealth doing rather better with seventeen out of thirty-six. 'This is an old and difficult subject,' Allen noted, 'and we do not want to revert to the days when too much emphasis was laid upon sport, but I can't help thinking that at present we may tend to other extremes.'[7] Of course the occasional outstanding athlete secured a Scholarship – Hamilton Richardson was for eight years in the American Davis Cup team – but such cases became increasingly rare. Cecil Rhodes would probably not have considered Richardson's prowess of decisive importance, but he would certainly have joined with Williams in his criticism of selectors who picked a candidate who was academically first rate and then looked round 'a little desperately and find in one of the testimonials that a man once opened a window, and this is taken as a clear evidence of his interest in the outdoors'.[8]

Williams also regretted the growing tendency to select Scholars who were in some way physically impaired, holding that they could not play a full part in the life of the University. In 1955 Ved Mehta was told that, as an Indian citizen, he was not eligible to compete for an American Scholarship, but that, having been educated in the United States, he could not put in his name for India. Elton wrote to him apologetically, explaining that his candidature would 'set up an insoluble administrative problem, as well as giving ground for legitimate complaint among Indians educated in their own country'.[9] The fact that Mehta was blind was deemed to be irrelevant. In 1992 the Newfoundland Secretary asked whether the reference to 'physical vigour' in the criteria might not be considered discrimination against the disabled. The Trustees replied that 'many disabled persons displayed conspicuous vigour and took part in demanding sporting activities'.[10] It was a far cry from the days when the 'Cincinnati cripple' had been so brusquely rejected.

More than any other official of the Trust, Williams was insistent that the Scholarships should not be awarded to pure academics, however brilliant, since there was already an abundance of ways by which they could get to Oxford. So long as a man could get a decent second, he told the Governor General of New Zealand, Lord Cobham, the academic side was adequate. 'What we want is a *man* who looks as if he'll be worth something to the community in twenty years' time. I believe the difficult word "distinction" has crept into selectors' judgment to our disadvantage. It wasn't Rhodes's word and it isn't mine. It comes to mean distinction of intellect because it is difficult if a man is still just over twenty for him to be distinguished in any other way, save perhaps as an athlete. Would you want him in your battalion? Would he be a good man to have with you in a jam? Is he unselfish?' What was needed, he concluded, was 'the all-rounder with a bulge – the bulge being one of personality'. The selectors must put their money into growth stock, not go for those who had written the best examination papers – 'a bit more emphasis on "guts" and a little less on distinction will help'.[11]

Williams's rejection of 'distinction', on the grounds that it must always relate to distinction of mind, was playing with words. When he told another New Zealand Governor General, Bernard Fergusson, that selectors should choose Scholars who were going 'to be outstanding in twenty years' time in whatever field it may turn out to be', he was saying that they must look for people who were in some way out of the ordinary. They were prone to take the safe option, which meant that 'the Scholars are all a bit cut to type and the eccentric does not stand much of a chance'.[12] The successful candidates, in a word, lacked distinction. Few if any selectors would have disputed his premise, that they must look for the Scholars who would make their mark in life twenty or thirty years ahead. But, even if that could successfully be established, the selectors still had to ask themselves what sort of mark the Rhodes Scholar should seek to make.

At a conference in Chicago in 1985 the future American Secretary, Elliot Gerson, raised this question. Were the selectors, he asked, to favour a 'wonderfully generous, unselfish, magnificent person who may, for example, spend the rest of his or her life working with the mentally retarded in a small community', or should they search for someone who was going 'to make a difference in the world for a lot of people', perhaps not winning many prizes for moral virtue, but a 'strong, ambitious dynamic figure' who would be likely to change the world? He cited the example of a contemporary Rhodes Scholar who had become a Buddhist monk and was 'living in a rain forest somewhere'. He might be a more perfect person, but was he what a Rhodes Scholar was supposed to be? Lord Blake, who was representing the Trustees, probably without much reflection, replied: 'I would have thought not.' If the Scholar in question, Harry Weinberg, had been cultivating his soul in seclusion, Blake's comment might have been to the point; as it was Kittisaro Bhikku, as he now styled himself, was running a Buddhist centre and hermitage in Natal and doing formidably useful work in the fields of AIDS and rural education. It would be disconcerting, indeed unsatisfactory, if every Rhodes Scholar became a Buddhist monk, but in terms of his contribution to the sum total of human happiness, or at least to the relief of human misery, Weinberg deserves to be included with Fairbridge and a handful of others in a pantheon of Scholar saints. Yet being a saint, at any rate in the Fairbridge mould, calls for a great deal of hard work, energy and organising ability. Robin Fletcher, at the same conference, urged selectors to look cautiously on idealistic candidates who 'haven't really got a career in mind but have a burning desire to go and help the world. These are easy to fall for. They are most excellent people, but Oxford is not the right place to start in indulging in helping the world.'[13]

'The fact is,' Williams wrote to a New Zealand Rhodes Scholar, '. . . right through the world we have people fitted to win Rhodes Scholarships who don't make it. . . . You have only got to think of, say, Massachusetts, which is a strong constituency, to realise that every year they have several men who would make far more than adequate Rhodes Scholars, but they are forced to choose between them.'[14] Every selector with any length of service, like a zealous fisherman, is haunted by the memory of the one that got away. The Trust, very properly, does not disclose the names of unsuccessful candidates and those who failed do not normally make much play with the fact in later life, but a few celebrated names are known from the post-1945 years. In 1947 Jimmy Carter was beaten in Georgia by a man who, Carter is supposed to have said, 'became, I am told, quite a good teacher'. In fact Leslie Youngblood had a distinguished career both as a naval officer and a businessman, but it would have been satisfactory for the Trust to have had two Presidents of the United States among its alumni.[15] William Styron, Pulitzer Prize-winning author of such novels as *The Confessions of Nat Turner* and *Sophie's Choice*, allegedly failed because he was weaker in physics than another candidate.[16] David Riesmann, author of the immensely successful and, in its day, influential *The Lonely Crowd*, was another casualty.[17] Sometimes rejection inspired the candidate to greater things. One young man was so put out that he retreated in a rage to his father's garage, brooding on how to change the world, and is now a dotcom billionaire and the first South African to go into space. Undoubtedly, thinks Charles Carter, who as assistant General Secretary sat in on the selection process, he was driven by his determination to prove the selectors wrong.[18]

The task of the selector is made more difficult by the proficiency of candidates in preparing a curriculum vitae which attests to a daunting range of talents and achievements and abounds in heart-warming accounts of enterprises carried out among the under-privileged. To detect how much of this is eyewash is a task calling for much experience, acumen and common sense, especially since the candidate may well have been coached intensively in techniques for dealing with sceptical selectors. This is particularly the case in the United States, where in certain universities likely Rhodes Scholars are identified in their second or even first year and subjected to mock interviews and cocktail parties and cramming on every aspect of current affairs likely to be brought up by the selectors. The practice is not only to be found in the United States; David Natusch, from Canterbury in New Zealand, studied the quirks of people he expected to be on the panel of selectors, and assembled groups of older people who quizzed him on issues likely to be raised at the interview.[19] It is no doubt gratifying for the selectors to know that the Scholarship is so highly valued, but the appalling proficiency of the would-be Scholar must sometimes leave their judges wishing that they lived in a more innocent age when the candidates had no idea what to expect and were spontaneous, ill-prepared and ingenuous.

Anthony Kenny as Warden attended many selection committees and was impressed by the skill, tact and fairness shown by the selectors. The one weakness, he felt, was inadequate probing of the candidates' reasons for wishing to go to Oxford or of the use they would make of their time if they got there. He wanted to ask: 'Yes, I see that you have done wonders in your life hitherto, and you have plans to do even more later: but what will you do in Oxford, and how will going to Oxford help you build on the strengths you already have?'[20] The problem was to distinguish between those candidates who saw the Scholarship primarily as a trophy, likely to be of value in their subsequent career, and those who would use their time at Oxford to full advantage and whose life would be enriched by what they learnt there.

It was made still more difficult for the selectors by the fact that they were picking Rhodes Scholars and that Rhodes Scholars were supposed to be different. They were looking not for mere bookworms, but for future leaders. And yet, more and more, the Oxford colleges seemed to be interested only in academic potential. Allen and Williams had felt that the selectors were going too far in favouring academic achievement over other qualifications; Kenny and Rowett found themselves under constant pressure to take the same line themselves. From the colleges they were bombarded with complaints about the intellectual inadequacy of their Scholars. After a visit to the United States Rowett reported indignation among selectors who were accused of sending too many stupid people to Oxford. 'They do not believe that they have . . . and point to a growing tension between the narrow professionalism increasingly valued by Oxford tutors and the requirements specified in the founder's Will.'[21] It would be a dispiriting conclusion to the first century of the Rhodes Scholarships if the scheme was marred not by the extravagance of the Founder's concept or the inability of the selectors to provide scholars of sufficient quality, but by the failure of the University which Cecil Rhodes revered to preserve the values which he, and once it, had held sacred.

CHAPTER THIRTY-SEVEN
LIFE AFTER WILLIAMS

It is always difficult to take over from a man who has been ensconced in office for more than a quarter of a century. When that man was as idiosyncratic, as autocratic and as much of a celebrity as Sir Edgar Williams, the task must be doubly difficult. Finally, when that man had let things slide to the extent that Williams had done over the last few years before his retirement in 1980, his replacement was bound to have a troublesome time while he was settling in.

Sir William Paton, doyen of Oxford's – indeed the nation's – pharmacologists was still Chairman of the Trustees when Fletcher was appointed. The principle had been established some years before that roughly half the Trustees should be drawn from Oxford and half from the world outside, but no attempt was made to apply this rule with any rigidity. To do so would indeed have been impossible. Robert O'Neill, for instance, who became a Trustee in 1995 and was himself a Rhodes Scholar, was the Chichele Professor of the History of War and a fellow of All Souls but the greater part of his career had been pursued in the field of international defence studies outside Oxford; Robin Butler was Secretary of the Cabinet when appointed in 2001 and thus clearly in the London camp, yet became Master of University College on leaving Whitehall and so technically transferred his allegiance to Oxford. What was invariable since the time of General Nye was that all the Trustees should have been educated at Oxford; those appointed while Williams was still in office included Marmaduke Hussey, Chief Executive of Times Newspapers, Chairman of the BBC and sometime scholar of Trinity, and Robert Armstrong, Secretary of the Cabinet, Head of the Home Civil Service and sometime scholar of Christ Church. Not until Robert Fellowes, a former private secretary to the Queen, became a Trustee in 2000 was the rule again breached.

The balance of power among the Trustees and between the Chairman of the Trustees and the Warden fluctuated according to the personalities involved. The appointment of Robin Fletcher had been largely Williams's doing. In 1970 he had written: 'If I had died ten years ago I would have told the Rhodes Trustees to appoint him from my death bed. Now, since I appear to have survived I would look (and I haven't yet looked) for someone younger.'[1] By 1980 he had still found no more suitable candidate. Fletcher's qualifications were obvious. He was a Greek scholar of distinction, he had served with small boats in the Mediterranean and won the DSC in the Second World War, he had been a senior proctor and was thus very much part of the University establishment, he had played hockey for England and won a bronze medal at the Olympic Games, he had a wife who was eminently well equipped to bring some warmth and a sense of fun to Rhodes House. Equally obviously he did not have the stature or the reputation of Bill Williams. In the opinion of two at least of the younger Trustees, he was not enough of a personality to take on so public and demanding a role. His appointment was settled between Williams, Paton and Lord Harcourt and presented to the other Trustees more or less as a *fait accompli*. Hussey, who had been at Trinity with Fletcher and was assumed by the new Warden to be responsible for his appointment, had in fact not even been consulted.[2]

Fletcher was found by most of the Scholars to be slow in initiating contacts and apt to lurk unobtrusively on the fringes or disappear altogether at Rhodes House parties, but always ready to help when need arose. His reports, laconic yet sympathetic, suggest that he knew rather more about his charges than most suspected. He was sympathetic to the plight of the unfortunate girl who 'to the detriment of her studies, cannot rid herself of an infatuation for a character quite unworthy, by all accounts, of her affection. She is off home this vacation to sort things out.' She went and did, returning the following year. Nor was he less understanding of the two Scholars who were hauled before magistrates on a charge of attempting to steal a motor car. They were, he explained to the Trustees, 'only indulging in an irresistible desire, brought on by a high degree of inebriation, to push a motor car up the road'.[3] They were acquitted, the Trust contributing to their costs.

One of the first of Fletcher's duties was to organise for the eightieth birthday of the Trust the celebration that might reasonably have been expected five years before. Fifteen hundred people attended the 1983 Reunion, 850 Scholars and 650 spouses. There was a dinner under marquees on the lawns of Trinity, a service in Christ Church Cathedral, a conference in the Sheldonian and a garden party at Rhodes House. The 89-year-old Chancellor, Harold Macmillan, delivered a deeply moving after-dinner speech of exquisite artistry which for many was the most memorable feature of the festivities. The garden party, attended by the Queen, provided one of the few controversial notes of the reunion, since to accommodate the guests a hole had to be punched in the wall between the gardens of Rhodes House and Wadham.

Only five years earlier, when the same wall had been repaired after the fall of a copper beech, Harcourt had written: 'I infinitely prefer the look of the wall without any gate and I really can't see that a gate between you and Wadham is in the least necessary.'[4] He died the following year. If he had lived to attend the party he might have doubted his prescience. Installing a temporary gate cost £10,000, a fact that was widely reported in the press and caused some ribaldry in the United States. Among those who were awarded honorary degrees were the former Governor General of Australia, Zelman Cowen; the novelist and poet Robert Penn Warren; and the Supreme Allied Commander in Europe, General Bernard Rogers. The list was uncontroversial; more troublesome was the conference in the Sheldonian when a black American Rhodes Scholar, George Keys, attacked the policy of the Trust in South Africa. In so doing he stoked a fire which had been smouldering for decades and which was to do serious damage over the next few years.*

The historian Robert Blake became Chairman in 1973. Early the following year he remarked that there was a case for having a woman Trustee, and suggested the former diplomat and Principal of St Hilda's College, Mary Moore. For the London Trustees John Baring suggested the name of John Sainsbury: 'We would have liked to include the name of a woman but we felt that in the first instance the appointment of a woman Trustee might best be made from Oxford. We do unanimously feel that with quite a proportion of lady Rhodes Scholars it is a bit surprising that the Trustees should remain exclusively men. The name which springs to our minds, which is perhaps obvious, is that of Mary Moore.'[5] With such impressive unanimity it was not surprising that Mrs Moore was elected. She feels that she was chosen because she could be relied on to stick up for women's rights but would do so without too much stridency. She only once found herself in a minority of one: over an issue concerning a Scholar's pregnancy. Mrs Moore felt that the rules should be applied, while all the other Trustees were for making an exception. 'Men go goofy when you mention a baby,' she explains tolerantly.[6]

In 1965 the Trustees had made certain rules to regulate their own existence: every Trustee should retire at the end of the financial year following their seventieth birthday; the Chairman should act for only five years, after which he would be ineligible to serve for a second term until at least a year had elapsed.[7] The latter provision was quickly forgotten: John Baring replaced Wheare as Chairman in 1987 and served until 1999, by which time he had succeeded his father as Lord Ashburton. He and John Sainsbury presented a uniquely powerful pair of London overlords, and in so far as a balance of

---

*See Chapter 38 below.

power between Oxford and London could be said to exist, in these years it shifted back to the metropolis. In his quiet way, however, Fletcher was effective at getting what he wanted on matters relating to the Scholars. He was liberal on most issues, though he stood firm on the principle that the Scholarships were intended primarily for work in Oxford and should certainly never be used to cover periods of study in the country from which the Scholar had come. When a Scholar from Natal pleaded that her field of research made it essential that she should spend some months in South Africa, Fletcher retorted that she should have chosen another subject. 'In an imperfect world,' he concluded, 'the rich are able to afford many things which the poor cannot. Has it occurred to you that all Rhodes Scholars on full stipend and with grants available for good cause, are sometimes seen by fellow students, let alone by others less fortunate, as falling into the rich rather than the poor?'[8]

One issue which caused Fletcher particular trouble was the distribution of the Scholarships around the various colleges. Scholars in the 1980s were no less prone than in the past to apply for the fashionable colleges of which they had heard or which were recommended by the loyal alumni to whom they applied for advice. In the five years ending 1983, Fletcher told the Trustees, eighty-one Scholars had made Balliol their first choice, forty-seven Magdalen, thirty-three University, thirty-one New College, twenty-four Merton and St John's. The other twenty-six colleges only had twenty-four first choices between them. 'This is a very far cry from the expressed wish of the Founder that the Scholarships should be distributed amongst the colleges and not result in undue numbers to one or more colleges.' There was a real risk that a privileged group of 'Rhodes Scholar colleges' might be established. This would be damaging to the Scholarships and would make it increasingly difficult to place those weaker candidates who had been turned down by their first and second choices and now had to be farmed out to less favoured colleges. The Trustees agreed that this was regrettable but did not see that much could be done. The Secretaries in the various countries involved should try to persuade their scholars to cast their net more widely, and the Warden should point out that the differences between the various colleges were much less marked than they had been in the past; but it was not believed that such measures would make any substantial difference to the outcome.[9]

The Conference of Colleges felt that the Warden should play a more proactive role. The Rector of Exeter suggested that a ceiling – perhaps three – should be put on the number of Rhodes Scholars any college could take in one academic year. The Principal of Brasenose thought that any such regulation would be unacceptable to the Scholars but hoped that Fletcher would do all he could to direct them 'to colleges where they would be best provided for' – Brasenose, by implication, being high on any such list. Blake, who was Provost of Queen's, a college which at the time did not have a single Rhodes Scholar, saw some force in such pleas; so did Mary Moore, who, at St Hilda's, had only one. But the colleges which took the lion's share of Scholars were not disposed to agree. Richard Johnson, a don from Magdalen who spoke with all the authority of a senior bursar as well as a former Rhodes Scholar, argued that any quota system would be unfair. 'I am opposed to the notion that the Rhodes Scholar, alone of all students applying to Oxford, will not be able to exercise a free preference for the college of his choice.' Besides, Rhodes Scholars operated more happily in a society where there were others like them: 'Those I know who live more isolated lives in colleges with fewer Rhodes graduates seem to me more lonely people. . . . The question I would ask is whether the interests of Rhodes Scholars themselves are being considered in the proposed "reform". I can see no sign of it at all.'[10] In the *American Oxonian* Barton Gellman, a former Scholar at University College and so himself from one of the most favoured colleges, protested that the Conference of Colleges should realise that Rhodes Scholars were not 'like libraries or playing fields and do not belong on the agenda in this way'. If the smaller colleges felt that they were being overlooked then it was up to them to change the perceptions of the successful candidates.[11]

A fresh element was added to the brew when Duncan Stewart, a New Zealand Rhodes Scholar who was the first male Principal of Lady Margaret Hall and had become a Trustee in 1986, wrote indignantly to complain that the American Secretary, David Alexander, had 'in the strongest possible terms' urged a new Rhodes Scholar to go for one of the traditional colleges rather than Lady Margaret Hall. 'Specifically to condemn one college, on grounds not clearly given, seems to be a piece of black propaganda straight from the Department of Dirty Tricks.' Anthony Kenny, who was by now Warden-elect, replied soothingly that Alexander was no doubt merely passing on information from an unofficial prospectus prepared by undergraduates which, *inter alia*, said that Lady Margaret Hall was not recommended for PPE.[12] The Trustees stopped short of endorsing even such an informal quota system, but the Warden managed nevertheless to get a better spread of scholars. By 1997 every college except Mansfield had at least one Scholar, though Balliol, Magdalen and Merton continued to attract the greatest numbers. The problem of placing the weaker candidates was not solved, however. In July 1996 Kenny reported that there were more new Scholars still unplaced than ever before: 'I think it is damaging the reputation of the Scholarships having Scholars hawked around as late in the year as this.'[13] He felt that it would be necessary to limit the number of applications the Warden made to colleges, and that the successful candidates should be warned that, in spite of their award, there was a real risk that their Scholarship might not be confirmed.

That year the scholar from Bermuda proved impossible to place. Kenny applied to every college and eventually acknowledged defeat. The Scholarship was not confirmed.

Kenny had already been Master of Balliol for ten years when he applied for the Wardenship in succession to Fletcher. The Trustees were grateful to have a candidate of his stature, and his election was almost a formality. He was asked how he felt about being associated with the notorious Rhodes and replied cautiously that, though he was not an unequivocal admirer of the Founder, he had known and admired many Rhodes Scholars. On reflection he felt he should have retorted that, having long been associated with the robber baron John de Balliol, Rhodes offered no new horrors.[14] Kenny was one of those individuals, discomfiting to the generality of mankind, who cram into a year what most people would need a decade to accomplish. He contrived, while still Warden, to serve as Chairman of the British Library, become President of the British Academy and publish eight books. The Trustees were mildly disconcerted by so much extra-mural activity, but since he was so obviously on top of the job and doing more than could be expected of him, resolved to say nothing and bask in the reflected glory. John Baring, as Chairman, had expected to work closely with the new Warden; in fact he was quickly satisfied that there were no problems which Kenny could not sort out for himself and adopted a hands-off attitude until he himself retired in 1999.

One innovation that Kenny introduced was to take reading parties of Rhodes Scholars to the chalet on the spur of Mont Blanc which the celebrated Balliol don 'Sligger' Urquhart had used for this purpose between the world wars. Balliol was one of the three colleges which traditionally used the chalet and Kenny knew it well already. The parties – featuring private study in the morning, bracing mountain treks in the afternoon and discussion around a given theme in the evening – involved ten or so Scholars chosen with an eye to the subject of the discussions. On the first reading party, for instance, the main theme for debate was post-apartheid South Africa. Five male and four female Scholars attended, drawn from the United States, South Africa, Canada, Zambia, Kenya and New Zealand.[15] Those who attended invariably valued the experience highly; as is the inevitable hazard of such enterprises, some of those who did not felt that they were being unfairly excluded and resented the existence of a favoured inner circle.

When John Ashburton finally retired in 1999 it was taken for granted that the next Chairman should be drawn from the Oxford Trustees. It fell to Richard Southwood, a Trustee since 1986 and a former Vice-Chancellor of the University. Southwood had been closely involved in the proposed conversion of Rhodes House into a club building and if he had served rather longer as

Vice-Chancellor might well have seen the project through. From Oxford he had been joined as a Trustee in 1987 by the historian and Warden of Merton, John Roberts; Roberts in his turn being succeeded by Colin Lucas, another historian and Master of Balliol (creating curious problems of precedence, with an ex-Master of Balliol as Warden serving a subsequent Master of Balliol as Trustee); Robert O'Neill from All Souls, and in 1996 Ruth Deech, the Principal of St Anne's, as a replacement for Mary Moore. From London came William Waldegrave, Conservative Cabinet minister and fellow of All Souls, John Kerr, then head of the diplomatic service, and a banker, Rosalind Hedley Miller.

The years in which Kenny was Warden were marked by a formidable growth in the Trust's wealth and also by the sharpest increase in the number of Scholarships in the century since Rhodes's death. The Trustees had taken, if not a dramatic new direction, then at least a decisive step forward. Kenny would be one of the first to wonder whether the step had been entirely wise.

CHAPTER THIRTY-EIGHT

THE SOUTH AFRICAN WAR

From the moment at which South Africa left the Commonwealth the Scholarships went into a state of suspended animation. Rex Welsh, the Rhodes Trust Secretary, was anxious to do what he could to open the Scholarships to all races. He succeeded in alleviating if not curing the hidebound conservatism of the selection committee in Natal. By 1971 a coloured musician had been included in the short list for Cape Province and a black medical student for Natal: neither was chosen but, as Williams told the Trustees, at least it meant that 'some men of colour regard it as worth having a go'. But the selectors were battling against the entrenched obduracy of an all-powerful state, determined that non-whites were unfit to share the benefits of higher education and must therefore be deprived of all possibility of advancement. As for the four schools designated for Scholarships under Rhodes's Will, the Trustees were in a position of considerable embarrassment. The phrase in Rhodes's Will which specified that no student should be disqualified 'on account of his race or religious opinions' seemed incompatible with the existence of Scholarships reserved for all-white schools, but this had been Rhodes's unequivocal intention, and the Trustees were unable to change it without an act of Parliament. It was unlikely that the government would be prepared to override the clear intentions of the testator unless it could be proved that the system had broken down. 'The Will may be reprehensible,' concluded Williams sadly, 'it is not unworkable.'[1]

Left to themselves the Trustees would have become resigned to the inevitable and left the schools to their own devices. They were not left to themselves, however. This was an age of protest and the 'present generation of "students"', Williams continued cynically, 'have found South Africa the cushiest "demo" available'. The sentiment had been whipped up by the arrival of black Rhodes Scholars from America who, having broken through themselves, now wanted to extend the benefits to their brothers who were suffering under the apartheid regime in South Africa. The chief instigator was George

Keys, a Rhodes Scholar at Balliol who came from the Air Force Academy. Keys was unaware of the existence of apartheid till he asked a Xhosa friend who seemed to be permanently short of money why he had not applied for a Rhodes Scholarship. The friend just laughed. With two or three other black Scholars Keys went to call on Bill Williams, who was sympathetic but gave no impression that the Trustees planned any action on the question. 'Confrontation was on our minds,' recalled Keys. 'The Warden kept trying to suggest that we were not "acting like one of the chaps". I suppose we didn't feel like one of the chaps.' He set about organising a petition urging the immediate suspension of the schools' Scholarships.[2] Williams viewed his activities with equanimity but was less pleased when he found the petitioners were accompanied by representatives of the press and Radio Oxford and still more put out when a few nights later stones were thrown through the windows of Rhodes House. 'It was probably by Saturday night drunks,' he observed, 'but it was calculated, not casual; and it was rather disagreeable.' What made it worse was that, though he deplored their methods, his sympathies were with the demonstrators. 'The Secretary must state to the Trustees at once that, however tiresome the Term has been, however distasteful some of the ways of going about the matter, in short, however old-fashioned he is, he shares with the petitioners their very real disquiet about the question. . . . When the roll is called he remains fussed that there is a built-in white privilege which makes the general notion of the Scholarships of which he has been the servant for twenty years, not entirely satisfying.'[3]

The Trustees accepted that something must be done. However slim the chances of persuading the government that the schools' Scholarships might be abolished, they resolved that they must go through the motions. In the meantime they would introduce a new South-Africa-at-Large Scholarship which, it was hoped would normally be taken up by some non-white victim of apartheid. The petitioners were invited to meet a group of Trustees and were told what was planned. 'The three young men', Williams noted urbanely, 'were evidently surprised to find themselves dealing with such wise and nice men. Until then, they had only met the Warden.'[4] As Kenny later pointed out to the American Secretary, it was ironic that in the history of the Trust there had only been two occasions when American Scholars had waited on the Trustees in person. The first time, in 1907, it had been to protest against the election of Alain Locke, a black from Pennsylvania. The second time, in 1970, it was to protest against the non-election of blacks from South Africa.[5]

Keys was left with a vague feeling of dissatisfaction, but he had to concede that the Trustees were taking steps to address the petitioners' concerns and that there was nothing much more the Scholars could do about it. They kept the pressure up, but the venom had gone out of their campaign. Williams felt even more disconsolate. He knew that in going into battle against the schools the Trustees were doing the right thing, yet still he regretted it. 'It is all rather miserable,' he told the Chairman of the Trustees, George Abell. 'I hate conceding to pressure, I hate turning my back on all those good School Scholars . . . and yet when the crunch comes, the non-discrimination clause in the Will is in the upshot the most respectable.' He soon found out that, though he might have resigned himself to turning his back on the schools, the schools had no intention of turning their backs on him. Sir Richard Luyt, the Vice-Chancellor of the University of Cape Town, travelled to London to register the schools' determination to resist in the courts any attempt to abolish their Scholarships. When the Trustees turned to the Secretary of State for Education, Margaret Thatcher, to abolish the schools' Scholarships on the ground that they were contrary to the spirit of the English Race Relations Act, her reply was – as Williams had predicted – that there was no justification for overturning what was clearly the intention of Cecil Rhodes. They still had the possibility of promoting a private act of Parliament but the Trust's money could only be used for this if the Secretary of State agreed, and there seemed every likelihood that she would refuse. An appeal to the Attorney General would then be possible, but this too would probably be rejected. Frustrated, the Trustees told the schools that they did not intend to take the matter any further. Williams found some consolation in the fact that the long-standing ties with the schools had not after all been severed, but the wounds were not easily healed. If he had been a Trustee at the time the decision was taken to attack the schools' Scholarships, said Robert Blake, he would probably have been against it. In retrospect he certainly was, 'for we have now got the worst of both worlds, having distressed and annoyed the Whites and failed to placate the Blacks!'[6]

Though the blacks may not have been fully placated, they were sufficiently appeased to take no immediate steps to renew the conflict. Meanwhile the Trustees sought to ameliorate the situation by setting up a multiracial selection committee to pick a South-Africa-at-Large Rhodes Scholar. Williams's first thought had been that it would be better to start with an all-white committee: 'The break-through would then be less vulnerable in South Africa itself, quite apart from the possible political difficulties which a mixed committee might itself encounter.'[7] In the end, however, they decided to go for the bolder course, which involved holding the meeting at the Holiday Inn Hotel at Jan Smuts airport near Johannesburg – the only venue open to mixed-race gatherings without a special licence. Later Welsh moved the meetings to the Carlton Hotel where the licence issued by the Secretary of Justice specified that the participants might dine but not dance together – a ban which caused little inconvenience to the all-male participants.[8] First results were disappointing if unsurprising; only two non-whites applied in 1971, both Indian and both ineligible as being too old. It was not till 1976 that the first non-white – again an Indian – was awarded a Scholarship and only in 1978 did a black South African gain the prize. Loyiso Nongxa had achieved the best results ever recorded at the black university, Fort Hare, and faced the selection committee with little knowledge of the Rhodes Scholarships and in the sublime certainty that he would win. Only many years later did he fully appreciate how remarkable a trail he had blazed.[9] That trail grew no less hazardous as the political storms grew fiercer in the 1980s. Kumaran Naidoo arrived prematurely at Oxford having fled South Africa with the security police on his tail and a charge of subversion hanging over him. The Trustees agreed to take him on stipend immediately, even though his Scholarship officially did not start for another six months.[10]

Ramachandran Govender, the first Indian Rhodes Scholar from South Africa, was also the first to have previously benefited from one of the Rhodes Trust Scholarships which had been instituted in 1973 to help non-white students secure a university education. It had been hoped that the ten to fifteen students given one of these would provide a pool from which Rhodes Scholars proper might eventually be drawn, but in the first few years the Scholarships were monopolised by medical students, who were too old to qualify for a Rhodes Scholarship when they had finished their course. Govender bucked this trend, but neither from this nor from any other source did successful black candidates, or indeed any black candidate, emerge. By the mid-1980s there had still only been two black Rhodes Scholars from South Africa while of the four schools SACS and Paul Roos still admitted no blacks – were, indeed, legally unable to do so – while the Diocesan College and St Andrew's, though professing the most liberal intentions, remained substantially unchanged.

It was this slow and uncertain progress towards genuinely colour-blind Scholarships which provoked the next explosion of protest on the part of the Scholars. Once again it was George Keys who was in the forefront. As part of the 1983 reunion at Oxford a conference was held in the Sheldonian. Against the wishes of Fletcher, Keys seized the opportunity to renew the battle. Twelve years before he had raised this issue, he said, and had been told that everything possible was being done to increase the number of black South African Rhodes Scholars. Since then only two had been selected, and only one of these was black in the sense of being of African blood (the correct figure was four – two Indians, one African and one coloured). The South-Africa-at-Large Scholarships merely mirrored the doctrines of apartheid; they should be abolished and transferred to other Third World countries which could make better use of them.[11]

The Rhodes Scholars at Oxford now took up the cause. In 1984 a group of fifty of them met to discuss the issue and called for the establishment of a committee of Trustees and Scholars which would report on how best to get rid of the schools' Scholarships, to improve secondary education in South Africa and to disinvest from the South African economy. The Trustees replied emolliently that, while they did not think a formal committee was the best way to proceed, they would be happy to keep in close contact on the subject. So as to increase the chances of black candidates they announced that they were raising the maximum age up to which students could apply for a Natal or South-Africa-at-Large Scholarship from twenty-five to twenty-seven. This went down well with the Scholars; their representative said that they looked forward to working with the Trustees 'as adjuncts rather than adversaries'.[12] But though some of the bitterness had gone out of the battle, the confrontation continued. In 1985, 171 Rhodes Scholars up at Oxford, including twenty-seven from South Africa and six from the four schools, petitioned for the abolition of the schools' Scholarships on the grounds that two of them excluded blacks and – broadening the base of their attack – that none of them accepted women. Somewhat gloomily, the Warden concluded: 'It will be prudent, although it may hasten the Secretary's retirement, to continue the debate with the Rhodes Scholars. It may not be easy to continue for long without the promise of an approach to the Charity Commissioners.'[13]

Across the Atlantic the storm raged quite as fiercely. George Keys renewed battle in the *American Oxonian*, calling for the immediate suspension of all the South African Scholarships and their reallocation to Third World countries, the invention of a special Scholarship for a non-resident black South African national and the creation of new Scholarships tied to black universities such as Fort Hare.[14] The Trustees chose to ignore this challenge but could hardly do the same when Senator Lugar, former Rhodes Scholar and Chairman of the Senate Committee on Foreign Relations, urged action 'on the question of Rhodes Scholarships for black South Africans'. He wrote on the official paper of the Senate Committee and Blake wrongfooted him by replying blandly that he assumed Lugar was writing not as a Senator but as a Rhodes Scholar: 'The Trustees are, of course, always pleased to learn the views of past Scholars on matters affecting the business of the Trust.' As to the substantive point, Blake wrote that, when Lugar referred to 'Scholarships for black South Africans', he presumably meant Scholarships for which blacks could compete on equal terms with whites. 'The Trustees cannot agree to a policy of ear-marking Scholarships for persons of particular race, and it was precisely because they regarded the Scholarships allocated to the four schools as "Rhodes Scholarships for whites" that they sought their removal.'[15]

Now the Association of American Rhodes Scholars moved into action. A formidable questionnaire was submitted to the Trustees: how many blacks had been awarded Scholarships; how many had served on selection committees; how many had been selected from the two schools that purportedly did not practise apartheid? The Association's object, the Trustees were assured, was 'to be helpful in a situation which may have adverse consequences for the selection process in this country'. Fletcher was uncheered by this affirmation of goodwill. He was reluctant, he told the Trustees, to 'act as post office for passing details of each other's working from one constituency to another'. He prepared an enormously long and pretty evasive draft reply, which he suggested that he should send, so that the Trustees could then disown him if they felt it desirable.[16] The Trustees did nothing of the sort but instead ruthlessly threw the Secretary to the wolves by despatching him, in October 1986, to meet the AARS. To make the meeting still less congenial, they refused to allow the South African Secretary, Rex Welsh, to attend as well and were equally reluctant to let the Americans see their submission to the Charity Commissioners asking for permission to suspend the four Scholarships. His impression after the meeting, Fletcher told the Trustees, was that 'Mr Welsh is the blue-eyed boy, the Secretary is a suspicious character and the Trustees are definitely bad eggs.'[17] It could have been worse, but the Trustees reckoned that the sacrifice of their Secretary had not been enough fully to appease the wolves and despatched their Chairman after him. John Baring met the AARS in October 1987 and, according to the American Secretary, David Alexander, explained how things stood 'in so sincere a manner that the members ... appear to be thoroughly convinced about both the difficulties and the actions taken by the Trustees.'[18]

By this time Welsh had retired as Secretary in South Africa, to be replaced by Laurie Ackermann. Ackermann was an urbane oenophile of courage, wit and academic distinction, who had resigned as a judge rather than administer apartheid legislation and had become Professor of Human Rights at Stellenbosch. He was quite as convinced as his predecessor that the schools' Scholarships, as at present constituted, were an affront to the system as a whole and that the Trustees must do anything within their powers to change them. What they actually could do, however, remained as uncertain as ever; the political climate might have changed but the rules imposed by the Charity Commissioners remained inflexible. At the end of 1990, with the action against the schools due to be heard early the following year, the Trustees were told that costs were likely to amount to some £100,000 on each side and that, whatever the outcome, the Trust would probably find itself paying the full £200,000.

But at the same time the situation in South Africa was evolving at astonishing speed. Suddenly it seemed as if the problem was not merely going to be solved but was about to disappear. As apartheid crumbled, so the schools adapted to the new political realities. Early in 1991 a large majority of parents at Paul Roos, traditionally a bastion of racial prejudice, voted to open the school to all races. The approval of the Minister was being sought. SACS had already taken the same step. With immense relief the Trustees congratulated them on this bold step and prepared to drop the legal proceedings. Somewhat ungraciously, the AARS suggested that the schools were still guilty of discrimination in that they did not admit girls. The Trustees refused to follow them down this path, at least for the present: after all, as they pointed out with some satisfaction, they accepted Scholars from single-sex institutions in the USA and sent them to single-sex colleges at Oxford.[19]

Everything was not yet as the Trustees would have wished. Ackermann encountered the same difficulty as his predecessor when it came to persuading suitable black candidates to come forward, whether because they lacked confidence in their abilities, had a wrong perception of the sort of people who won the Scholarships, or simply did not fancy the idea of two or three years at Oxford. Even if they could be persuaded to apply, however, the selection committees would still be faced, in exacerbated form, with a problem that confronted committees in every country and at every period. How far should allowances be made for a candidate's inadequate education or social deprivation? How far could the selectors go in backing a hunch, and choosing undeveloped potential at the expense of a more mature and safer candidate?

In principle Ackermann was in favour of a measure of 'positive discrimination': the selection of a black candidate in preference to an Indian or white, provided the disparity was not too great, just *because* the candidate was black. Black Scholars were needed, and it could not be expected that black candidates, in their early twenties, would be as immediately impressive as their rivals from a more privileged background. But he did not wish to push this argument too far; he knew well that Oxford had no support programme for disadvantaged students and had no intention of providing one. To select Scholars who could not hold their own at Oxford would be disastrous from every point of view.[20] Fletcher was more inclined to share Ackermann's reservations than his original premise. In his experience, indulging what he felt to be a particularly American predilection for picking 'the underprivileged boy or girl from "the sticks", particularly if black', rarely produced good results. Any sort of discrimination on the basis of race seemed to him unwise: in South Africa in particular, it raised almost insuperable problems. Discrimination in favour of non-whites would favour the Indians; in favour of black as opposed to Indian or coloured would probably favour the Zulus.[21] Much better avoid this hornets' nest by ignoring race altogether.

The problem was not going to go away; indeed, though its nature was modified, it was in some ways to be made worse over the decade after South Africa discarded apartheid and rejoined the Commonwealth. The miracle had happened, however – South Africa had been reborn. In the 1990s the Trust fully renewed its involvement in the continent where it had been conceived.

CHAPTER THIRTY-NINE

A PASSAGE FROM INDIA

Anglo-Indian relations, Malcolm MacDonald told Lord Elton, were 'the key to the future of both Asia and the Commonwealth'.[1] Indians had for many years been prominent at Oxford – even by 1914 there were seventy Indian under-graduates – and between the world wars dignitaries of various colours and professions had pleaded with the Trustees to add India to the list of those providing Rhodes Scholars. It was not till 1946, however, that two Scholarships were allotted to the sub-continent and the first selection committee met, under the chairmanship of the Chief Justice of India, who happened also to be the Vice-Chancellor of Delhi University, Maurice Gwyer. Its task was not easy. Two hundred and fifteen applications were received, of which eighty-five could promptly be rejected as being women, married, over-age or not having gained a first-class degree. Others failed to list their academic qualifications, which the committee took to mean that they did not have any. In the end eighteen were selected for interview. The first choice was Asim Kumar Datta. 'We were all agreed that we had seldom come across a young man with so attractive a personality,' Gwyer told Elton. 'He had charming manners and I think will go far.'[2] He did, in due course becoming Principal of the College of Arts in Calcutta.

By the time the next selection committee met, the only Muslim candidate had to travel to Delhi under police protection. On 15 August 1947 the state of Pakistan had come into existence. Any hope that the Rhodes Scholars might somehow straddle the frontier and be selected on a sub-continental basis had quickly to be abandoned; if they were not divided, Gwyer pointed out, they would 'be regarded as grossly biased and partial by one Dominion or the other'. He was in favour of creating a third Scholarship and giving two to India and one to Pakistan, in recognition of India's far larger population.[3] The Trustees feared that this too might be thought 'grossly biased and partial' and were swayed by Allen's insistence that there should be no change for the moment at least. 'I think we ought to go very carefully with the Indian

Scholarships altogether until we know what sort of people they are going to provide,' he told Elton, 'and also, of course, what the general situation in India is going to be.' He was himself pessimistic about the prospects. When the decision was made to split the Scholarships evenly, he wondered what the response would be in India. 'I don't suppose it matters,' he concluded, 'because anything the Trustees did would inevitably be wrong in Indian eyes. . . . Let us hope that they will not all be assassinated before the elections take place.'[4]

Gwyer left India at the end of 1947. Allen, still pessimistic about the prospects for the sub-continent, wondered how the selection committee could survive: 'It is my own private hope', he admitted to Elton, 'that after an experimental period of, say, five years, the Indian Scholarships will prove to be unworkable, and I shall see them go without regret.'[5] Some of his worst qualms were laid to rest when Gwyer's place was taken by the distinguished civil servant and historian Penderel Moon, a man whom not even the most censorious observer could accuse of any sort of bias. Moon soldiered on till 1961, by which time the Scholarships were firmly established and even Allen, if he had still been Warden, would have conceded that it was proper for an Indian to take on the chairmanship.

In fact Allen had long before recanted on his condemnation of the Indian Scholarships. In 1950 he told Elton that he had no hesitation in saying that they had fully justified themselves. 'These Indian Scholars', he handsomely admitted, 'have been a very good lot indeed, and in point of character and conduct they have all been quite exemplary.' He would strongly have supported the decision of the Trustees to mark the Queen's visit to India in 1961 by creating a second Scholarship. Indeed, given the immense population and the abundance of highly educated students to be found in India, even two Scholarships was a derisory total. Elton had described the award of the first Scholarship as 'primarily a symbolic gesture' and much the same could be said of the second. It was only a beginning, however, and the total rose steadily until it reached a rather more respectable six. In 2006 one of these had to be suspended because of financial pressures, but there was nobody who doubted that the larger number was fully justified and that India could have produced as many again without too much of a sacrifice in quality.

At one point the Indian government, eager to repudiate any form of foreign tutelage, made a bid to take over the running of the Scholarships. The Indian High Commission wrote to Williams to explain that it was official policy to administer all foreign Scholarships through a central agency. The government proposed to hand over the selection process to the University Grants Commission. 'A representative of the Rhodes Trust', the High Commissioner generously added, 'would, however, be associated with the selection committee in case it is so desired.' Williams gave this proposition short shrift.

His Trustees, he replied, would be strongly averse to surrendering control to anybody. 'We have managed over the sixty odd years of the Rhodes Trust's history to keep free from governmental influence most deliberately and I want to make it quite clear that we could not have the selection of our Scholars taken out of the hands of the Trust.'[6] Possibly the Indians had expected some such rebuff; at any rate the assault on the Scholarships was not renewed.

Though the Indian selection committees consistently produced Scholars of high quality there was always some lurking doubt in the minds of the Trustees about the methods by which they were chosen. When Gwyer left India he stressed the need to find another Briton to take over: 'For a long time to come an Indian Chairman would find himself exposed to such pressure from outside that he might not always be impartial. Nepotism is very rampant today in India.'[7] Nor was it only nepotism; Elton was told of one Vice-Chancellor who happened to have a son at his university who was eligible for a Rhodes Scholarship and therefore put up no notices advertising the selection process in case they encouraged others to compete.[8] General Nye, a Trustee of much Indian experience, confirmed the risks. The real difficulty, he said, was to find 'chaps whose integrity is proof against pressure, which is usually very heavy and often directed from high places. . . . Few, very few, would resist such pressure.' There was also, he went on, another bias of class and state.[9]

That that is still true today is the view of Anita Mehta, an Indian Rhodes Scholar of 1978. The selection committee is dominated by cliques, she believes: students she had encouraged to apply had told her they felt it was unlikely they would get in unless they were at St Stephen's College in Delhi, or had read English at Calcutta, or were lawyers from Bangalore or Hyderabad. She herself, when she had served on selection committees, had had to fight hard to ensure the best potential Rhodes Scholars were not passed over in favour of inferior candidates whose friends or relations knew how to work the system. She had several times been approached by people who turned out to be parents or uncles of candidates.[10] Recent statistics suggest that there is some truth in her words. Of the Rhodes Scholars selected in the decade beginning in 1996 – fifty-five in all – nine went to St Stephen's College, eight more to other Delhi institutions, and thirteen to the Bangalore Law School. This, of course, does not prove undue partiality, let alone corruption, but it does suggest that the system is so weighted as to mean that the students of a relatively small group of colleges are more likely to know about the Rhodes Scholarships, to apply for them and, eventually, to win them. When Kenny attended a meeting of the Indian selection committee in 1994, however, he had expected the proceedings to be courtly rather than searching but found that he was entirely wrong. 'Of all the interviews we had sat in on in many countries, these were some of the tightest and best calculated to expose superficiality and strip off pretence. . . . I could not detect any ideological agendas or personal prejudices among the selectors.'[11]

A more serious cause for worry was the tendency of Indian Rhodes Scholars not to return home after they had finished at Oxford. The reason was much the same as that which had kept New Zealanders away from their homeland before 1939: the opportunities did not exist for them to make full use of the skills that they had acquired. Particularly in the case of medical students, however, those skills were desperately needed. As a rule selectors would ask candidates whether they proposed to return to India after Oxford. All, no doubt sincerely, said they did. But then the lure of better jobs, better facilities, a better standard of living, began to tell. Today 60 per cent of Indian Rhodes Scholars live in the United States, only 10 to 20 per cent go back. Virander Chauhan, the present Secretary of the Rhodes Trust in India, admits that, especially in the case of doctors, he sometimes wonders whether there is any point in giving people Scholarships so that they can make a lot of money abroad. But the fact that Indian Rhodes Scholars work overseas does not necessarily mean that they are lost to India for ever or that they are not doing work of which Rhodes himself would thoroughly have approved. Virenda Dayal spent many years with the United Nations but is now back in India. He believes that many of the younger Scholars feel a need to prove themselves on the world stage before returning home. Opportunities for doing fulfilling work in India are also increasing rapidly; there are already signs that Scholars of the present generation are more likely to make their life at home than would have been true of their parents and grandparents.[12]

The proliferation of foreign Scholarships available to clever young Indians meant that the Rhodes Scholarship never acquired the almost mystic significance which it possessed in those countries where it had been established since the beginning of the century. It also posed a considerable problem for the selectors. The original rule had been that any candidate must have graduated from an Indian university. Was it proper for Indians from Harvard or the London School of Economics to compete? If so, did the Trust have to pay to fly them back to India to face the selection committee? Ranjit Bhatia, who was Secretary of the Trust for thirty-five years from 1962, felt that they should not: 'The Harvard or LSE based Indian who has opted out of the Indian university stream, for one reason or another, and then at a later stage wishes to add the Rhodes Scholar label does not quite fill the bill.'[13] The Trustees at first accepted this, but in 1980 Fletcher returned to the charge when a particularly worthy Indian student from Harvard pleaded to be admitted. The Indian selection committee did not relent: 'Opening doors to those Indians who have not studied in an Indian university would create a very complex situation, apart from deviating from the spirit of the whole thing.' Eventually a compromise was reached; Indian citizens studying abroad *were* eligible for Rhodes Scholarships but they had to make their own way back to India to face the selection committee.[14] The cost involved, plus the fact that they were likely to find selectors prejudiced against them, effectively ensured that only a handful of émigré students would think it worth their while to compete.

Bhatia, in 1990, noted the view of Rhodes House that, though on academic terms the Indian Scholars were among the best, some of them fell short in their 'lack of involvement in other aspects of life at Oxford'.[15] Certainly the emphasis on sporting achievement, which had been taken seriously by the early selection committees, was largely abandoned. The criticism was anyway not too seriously meant. Kenny considered the Indian Scholars 'by far the most successful of the new Commonwealth constituencies' and Kenny's successor, John Rowett, believed they could stand comparison with any of the original constituencies as well.[16] The Scholarships can never hope to enjoy in India the prestige that is bestowed on them in Australia or the United States (though Aveek Sen, a Scholar from Bengal, believes that in Calcutta it is most highly esteemed and that he owes his job as leader writer on the *Times of India* in part at least to his having won a Scholarship), but the Indian Scholars at Oxford can fairly boast that they do all that could be asked of them and more besides.

Sadly, the same cannot be said for Pakistan. Though Allen radically revised his views about the Indian Scholars, he never relented towards the Pakistanis. They were, he judged, 'definitely exotics, who have much more difficulty in acclimatizing themselves'.[17] Of the two with whom he had been most recently concerned, 'one is stupid, the other a congenital liar'. The latter was eventually arrested for stealing £100 from a priest in London and, though acquitted for lack of larcenous intent, had to be sent back to Pakistan in disgrace. Elton blamed the inadequacy of the Pakistani Scholars largely on the selection committee involved. The European members had unanimously voted against the 'congenital liar' but had had a majority against them. At one meeting, reported Elton, a member, 'a charming man with an impeccable record, quite embarrassed his colleagues by his strenuous support of the candidature of his own nephew'.[18] The European selectors do not seem to have been perfect either. The Bishop of Lahore must have caused Elton some disquiet when he prided himself on rejecting 'bookworms, office wallahs, research students. . . . In this part of India we produce a fine, manly, robust type which Cecil Rhodes would have approved of. The Punjabi Mussulman is not over-brainy, but he is a man of character and action.'[19]

By 1971 the record of the Pakistani Scholars was so deplorable that, when the government followed the example of the Indians and made a bid to take over the work of the selection committee, Williams suggested that this be made a reason to suspend the Scholarships altogether. He put the blame for the low quality of the Scholars not so much on the selectors as on the deterioration in the standards of the universities – 'A light pause would, in my view, be no bad thing.'[20] For a time the Scholarships alternated between Pakistan and the newly independent Bangladesh, but the former East Pakistan proved unable to produce candidates of the required quality. Another chance to extinguish the Pakistani Scholarship came in 1974 when Pakistan left the Commonwealth, but after some hesitation the Trustees decided to continue it, though on a triennial basis. In time this became annual, and then two a year, but the record of the Scholars was still not entirely happy. Pakistani Scholars proved as likely as Indians to desert their native heath. One caused Lord Hailey great offence by writing to complain that he was unable to get a decently paid job in his own country; would Hailey please find him a place in a commercial firm in Britain? As a Trustee, Hailey told him, he would be more interested in seeing a Pakistani Scholar following 'an honourable career in his own country rather than earning a little more money in a commercial firm in England'. Hailey's indignation was redoubled when he found that the Scholar had sent identical letters to Williams and to all the other Trustees. 'I am dealing with the matter,' Williams pronounced sternly.[21] The Pakistani Scholars, Kenny concluded, 'are in general no more than respectable and have made little contribution to the life of college and university'.[22] There are, of course, honourable exceptions. Wasim Sajjad, Secretary of the Trust in Pakistan, excelled at Oxford and went on to become Chairman of the Senate and, on several occasions, acting President. But such cases are sadly few. The efforts of the Trustees to spread the benefits of the Scholarships to the new Commonwealth were to meet with many setbacks; in Pakistan they might reasonably have hoped for better things.

CHAPTER FORTY

THE DEVELOPING WORLD

From the end of the Second World War, those responsible for the future of the Rhodes Scholarships fell broadly into two camps: those who believed that, if any new Scholarships were to be created, they should be concentrated in the core constituencies – Australia, Canada, New Zealand and, though with increasing doubts, South Africa; and those who believed that the Trust should extend its activities to the new Commonwealth, where education was so sadly deficient and the Scholarships might make a fundamental difference. Lord Elton was the arch-expansionist; Williams was for restraint and for capitalising on what was there already.*

Rhodes's original foundation was based on his belief in the Anglo-Saxon peoples, Elton told the news editor of the *Daily Telegraph*. Now that they were embarked on the 'hopeful yet hazardous experiment of a multi-racial Commonwealth' it would have been Rhodes's wish that his Scholarships should contribute to 'the success of this great adventure'.[1] He quickly discovered that the Scholarships posed problems which had not arisen in the past. The new members of the Commonwealth guarded their independence jealously and were suspicious of a system of Scholarships founded by an arch-imperialist and controlled from England. The first reaction of 'all the "new" countries seems to be that it will be for them to frame the regulations, if not to appoint the Scholars', Elton told Millis.[2] The Prime Ministers of Ceylon and Malaya in particular found it difficult to accept that the selection committees were to be free of official control; in Ghana the Trustees were advised not to include Europeans among the selectors since this would inevitably give rise to charges of covert colonialism. To Elton's relief the Ghanaian Prime Minister, Nkrumah, showed no signs of wanting to interfere, 'although in a speech the other day, he threatened the University that if it

*See p. 202 above.

continued to produce opposition-minded undergraduates, he would clear the whole lot of them out'.[3]

Ghana was the first country to alert the Trustees to the difficulties they had taken on. The Post Office's failure to deliver more than a small proportion of the letters meant that the first elections had to be postponed by several weeks, then the man designated as Rhodes Secretary was purged and disappeared abruptly, then the Ghanaian government made an effort to put forward to the selection committee only candidates whose work would be useful to the country. 'We are not interested in being involved in the man-power problems of Ghana,' wrote Williams.[4] The situation was not helped by the intervention of the Irish firebrand Conor Cruise O'Brien, who was Vice-Chancellor of the University of Ghana. Williams invited him to join the selection committee. He would be less than frank, O'Brien replied, if he concealed the fact that he thought the title of the Scholarships 'anachronistic and unhelpful'. Rhodes was considered by most Ghanaians to have been not a benefactor but one 'who cheated and robbed Africans'; anyone who accepted a Scholarship with such an origin would be guilty of great cynicism. In that case, retorted Williams, you had better not serve on the committee. 'It's not my decision, it's yours!' replied O'Brien. He thought the advertisement listing the qualities Rhodes had expected to be found in his Scholars pushed 'hypocrisy even further than I would have expected. Candidates are expected, I see, to have a regard for "truthfulness" and "consideration for the weak". From an acknowledged master of the deliberate lie and calculated crushing of all in a weaker position than himself, the requirement of these particular qualities is perhaps best ascribed to a touch of cynical humour.'[5]

In spite of these vicissitudes, the Ghanaian selection committee managed to find a perfectly respectable candidate for their first election, Lebrecht Hesse, who went on to run the nation's broadcasting service. The record was not to be sustained. In 1963 only three candidates turned up for the selection committee's meeting, 'all were pathetic', none was selected.[6] Of the next two Ghanaian Rhodes Scholars, one got a third in PPE, the other was packed off home heavily in debt, having achieved nothing. 'It would seem better to let the dust settle before proceeding to organise another election there,' concluded Williams.[7] For five years the Scholarship was suspended. 'The long hiatus was most unfortunate and totally unnecessary,' wrote Hesse when it was rein-stated,[8] but shortly afterwards he in his turn was in temporary disgrace. Once again the Scholarships were suspended, and though the Foreign and Commonwealth Office in 1994 suggested that the risk of nepotism and polit-ical favouritism had receded, the Trustees concluded that they had burnt their fingers twice and did not feel disposed to take the risk again. 'It is one of the Trust's principles that it sees a constituency once established as an on-going commitment and does not chop or change,' Fletcher wrote proudly in 1988.[9] He forgot that in Ghana conditions had failed to change and the Trustees had felt bound to chop.

The Ghanaian experience was uniquely dreadful, but things did not run altogether smoothly in the other countries of the new African Commonwealth. Nigeria got off to a faltering start. The first Scholar found life at Oxford difficult but managed to get a doctorate; no suitable candidate was found when the selection committee met again; the second Nigerian Scholar, when one was elected, failed to last the course. When William Paton attended the selection committee in 1975 he found that there were few applications and that only two of those who had got so far as an interview were remotely suitable. One problem, he concluded, was that there was a plethora of other awards available and the Rhodes Scholarship enjoyed no particular prestige. The name was not a positive deterrent – to the Nigerian schoolboy, Rhodes seemed as remote from reality as King Alfred and the cakes – but the scheme was badly advertised and to some students the courses at Oxford seemed unduly restrictive.[10]

Things did not get better. When Kenny visited Nigeria in 1991 he found that regional tensions made the work of the selection committee uniquely difficult. Overall, he told the Trustees, 'it was difficult to feel great confidence in the selection procedures in Nigeria'. He thought it likely that, in a year or two, it would be necessary to suspend the Scholarships.[11] And so it proved. The 1991 Scholar could not be placed at Oxford or any British university. The 1992 Scholar got off to a 'difficult and troubled start'. For the 1993 selection the committee interviewed only a single candidate. The Rhodes Secretary was 'eccentric, sometimes inefficient, and often difficult to communicate with. . . . It will be difficult to have confidence in the selection committee while it is organised by the present Secretary,' concluded Kenny.[12] Suspension followed. When asked, the Trustees confirmed that it was their intention eventually to reinstate the Scholarship, but doubts remained about the possibility of setting up a selection committee that would be fully independent and impartial. Those doubts had still not been resolved when the economic problems of the new millennium forced the Trustees to think more in terms of cutting back on existing Scholarships than inventing new or reinstating old ones.

The old East Africa Rhodes Scholarships, reserved exclusively for whites, had expired in the early 1950s, but Kenya was given a Scholar in 1984 and a second in 1991, while the scheme was extended to Uganda in 1995. John Silvester, the Rhodes Secretary in Kenya, told the Trustees that his government was strongly opposed to South Africa and would take great exception to money for the Scholarships being derived from a South African source. 'The Rhodes Trust is a private Trust and adopts what policy it pleases within the terms of an Act of Parliament,' was Kenny's robust response. 'If the Kenyan Government interferes in any way, the Trustees will cease to offer the Scholarships.'[13] After that skirmish, things settled down. 'The Kenyan Rhodes Scholars presently in Oxford seem to be doing well,' Kenny assured Silvester in 1990. His overall judgment was more cautious. Kenya had produced some problematic Scholars, he told Ashburton a few years later, 'one had a long career here of mental illness, one achieved a failure in a Final Honour School (almost unheard of) and several have wanted to spend much of their course in or near Kenya'.[14] The record was good enough, however, to ensure that when the recession forced economies in 2006 the two Kenyan Scholarships survived inviolate. Uganda was less fortunate: in the few years that its Scholarship existed its Scholars had too often failed to come up to an acceptable standard and it was inevitably numbered among the victims when the cut-back came.

Zambia was different to the other African constituencies to its north in that, as the former Northern Rhodesia, its Scholarship was enshrined in Rhodes's Will and thus could not be suspended. Its record, however, was as disastrous as that of any other African country. 'We have had a run of charming Zambians who are all without exception very ill prepared for Oxford,' observed Williams,[15] and both the charm and the academic inadequacy persisted. Of the thirteen elected Rhodes Scholars from Zambia, Fletcher wrote in 1984, one had never taken up the Scholarship, three had not been placed in Oxford, two had been placed only after a period at another university, one had disappeared and one was in prison. Zambia, concluded Kenny fourteen years later, was 'the weakest constituency academically'.[16] If the Trustees could have shed this burden they undoubtedly would have done so.

In spite of this dismal record, a group of African Rhodes Scholars in 1996 protested that the Trust paid too little attention to Africa. They were particularly alarmed by rumours that new Scholarships might be under consideration for Asia. The first priority, they claimed, should be to restore the Nigerian and Ghanaian Scholarships and to introduce a new one for Tanzania; more should follow as soon as possible thereafter. It should be the aim of the Trustees to further, by more peaceful means, Rhodes's integrationist dream, by bringing together as many as possible of the future leaders of Africa and so to help develop 'the co-operative alliances that Cecil Rhodes intended'. The Trustees, Kenny replied, were distressed by the suggestion that they were neglecting Africa. Under Rhodes's Will, 14 per cent of the Scholarships had been allocated to Africa; the proportion was now 17 per cent. In addition, vast sums had been devoted to charitable purposes in South Africa and at the moment some 250 non-whites there were being educated through the Trust's support.[17] Kenny made no promise about the restoration of Scholarships to

Nigeria and Ghana, or the provision of new Scholarships for other African countries.

It would have been hypocritical if he had. As early as 1982 Fletcher had argued that only from Kenya and possibly Nigeria was there any chance of getting a stream of consistently able Scholars. 'Apart from the countries to which Scholarships were given in the Will, it cannot be said that any firm foothold has been established in Africa. Political as well as educational factors are no doubt responsible.'[18] Two years later he questioned whether Rhodes Scholarships were appropriate for most potential black African candidates. What was important was to pick those candidates who would benefit most from their time at Oxford: 'The Secretary sees no logic in the argument that the Trust has a special obligation to African countries other than those particularly associated with Cecil Rhodes.'[19] The Trustees were not prepared to face the moral obloquy of appearing too overtly to discriminate against Africa, but the force of Fletcher's arguments was recognised and the last decade has seen a noticeable lack of enthusiasm for projecting ill-prepared black African students into an environment in which they are likely to founder and do little good either to Oxford or to themselves.

Zambia was not the only long-established constituency to cause concern. Malta had enjoyed a Scholarship since 1921 and its successful candidates had on the whole been adequate but unexceptionable. 'Malta has had the brave wisdom to make no election,' Williams reported with characteristic acerbity in 1969. 'Sometimes one thinks it a pity that they don't do that every year.'[20] Things changed abruptly for the worse when one of the most talented and forceful of Maltese Rhodes Scholars became Prime Minister. Mintoff was of the extreme left, said to be a communist, and fiercely opposed to any connection with Britain and its Empire. Since his return home he had eschewed any connection with his fellow Rhodes Scholars, and Elton had been surprised to be fêted by him when the General Secretary visited Malta in 1950. 'There is certainly much potential good in him,' Elton concluded, adding prudently, 'though it is possible that good will not come out of his political career.' It did not. Mintoff delighted in tilting at the establishment, and the Rhodes selection committee in Malta was establishment to the core, including the Governor, the Lieutenant-Governor, the Archbishop, the Minister of Education and the Rector of the University. Elton wondered whether any other Scholarship committee was entitled to be addressed as 'Your Excellencies, Your Grace, Your Honour and Gentlemen'.[21] When Mintoff took power in 1971 he set to work to revolutionise the educational system. The University had been 'castrated', reported Williams; 'it would be tempting to say we should suspend the Scholarships in protest'.[22] The Trustees delayed for a year, but then succumbed to the temptation. After Mintoff had disappeared from the scene and a measure of autonomy had been restored to the University, the Maltese Foreign Secretary – another Rhodes Scholar – pleaded that the Scholarships should be renewed. Briefly this was done, in 1993, to mark the fiftieth anniversary of the award of the George Cross to the island, but Malta was no longer part of the Commonwealth and the experiment was not repeated.

Bermuda continued to be a thorn inextricably embedded in the flesh of the Trustees. Allen visited the colony in 1947 and found that all the Rhodes Scholars were white and drawn from a tiny social group linked by inter-marriage and monopolising most of the best jobs on the island. The selection process was run on sternly official lines – the annual announcement of the competition appearing in the press under the heading 'Government Notice'.[23] Allen believed that there was no chance of a black man even competing under these circumstances, though they had good educational facilities and might well have coped better with the demands of Oxford than some of their successful white counterparts. Things gradually improved, however, and the appointment of Chester Butterfield as Secretary heralded a more businesslike and open era. The first black Bermudan was elected in 1964, the only black candidate in the previous five years and one of the very few in the history of Bermuda. At Michigan State University, where Arthur Hodgson had spent the last four years, he had earned the reputation of being 'an extremely political animal'. Back in Bermuda, wrote Butterfield, he 'spent more time canvassing for and agitating in the local Teachers' Union than he did in attending to his duties'. Butterfield accepted that the selection committee was taking a chance, but they believed Hodgson 'if properly directed . . . might do a great deal for this Colony in these crucial years of developing racial relations'.[24] Hodgson himself believes that he owes his Scholarship to the luck of being the first credible black candidate to come forward at a time when attitudes towards racial segregation were changing.[25] He duly entered politics and, as Butterfield predicted, played a valuable part in rebuilding Bermudan national life after the social revolution of the 1960s and 1970s.

Bermuda had turned the corner. By the closing decades of the twentieth century more than a hundred Bermudans a year went to foreign universities and the academic quality of the Scholars stood comparison with all but the cream of each year's Oxford intake. 'It remains our rotten borough,' remarked Williams in 1979, 'but like many rotten boroughs it has produced some very good candidates.' They were still capable of idiosyncrasy: in 1992 they sent as their Scholar a young man who had not yet got a first degree. 'I hope that in future the Bermudan committee will come into line with all the others,' Kenny wrote, but since Simon Draycott went on to get a first and an MPhil in crim-inology it seems that the selection committee's judgment was not too faulty.

When Kenny himself attended a meeting of the Bermudan selection committee the following year, his experience was 'unexpectedly favourable. . . . The best two candidates', he concluded, 'could well stand comparison with the typical pair nominated by middle-sized states for consideration by US district committees.'[26]

In one respect, though, Bermuda suffered from the same malaise as the other smaller constituencies. In 1977, out of the thirty-two or so Scholars elected since the Second World War, only thirteen had returned to the island. The same is true of that other beneficiary under Rhodes's Will – Jamaica. Nearly two-thirds of Jamaica's Scholars remain abroad; nearly all of them intend to return when they accept the Scholarship; many of them later think that they will come back after acquiring a few years' experience, but it becomes harder and harder to abandon security and prosperity for the uncertainties of Jamaican life. Peter Goldson, the Rhodes Secretary, is one of the exceptions. He finds that some selection committees stress that there is an obligation to come back; others consider that a contribution to society can be made as well overseas as in Jamaica. He himself would feel prejudiced against candidates who clearly had no interest in the region but understands too well the pressures they are under to condemn them if they eventually make their life elsewhere.[27] As with Bermuda, the quality of Jamaican scholars has improved considerably. In 1946 Allen despaired of finding a college prepared to take them: 'My only hope is that black men are now so popular in Oxford that, possibly, if the Jamaicans are dark-skinned that will be their chief attraction.'[28] Within ten years, with the Prime Minister Norman Manley and the Finance Minister Noel Nethersole both Rhodes Scholars, the system enjoyed unique prestige and the success of the University College of the West Indies ensured a regular supply of worthy candidates. No one would be likely to describe Jamaica as the most stable of environments, but it is still united, reasonably democratic and racially relaxed. The Jamaican Rhodes Scholars have done as much to make this come about as their counterparts in any other country.

Fortunately the Scholarship for the Caribbean, which was set up in 1962, was never linked to the short-lived West Indian Federation. The Trust's Scholarship, Williams told Peacock, 'was formulated for people and not for political arrangement'. Williams's main regret when the Federation perished was that the Governor General, Lord Hailes, could not become chairman of the first selection committee. This deprived the committee of the services of a leader who would have been both capable and prestigious, but, Williams consoled himself, 'I think the prestige of the Trust will see it through anyway'.[29] At first the Scholars – initially one every three years, then one annually, then two a year and finally once again one a year – came mainly from Barbados, but in the new millennium Trinidad has made dramatic progress. Yet though the

Caribbean Scholars were individually of good quality, they were too scattered to allow the creation of any sort of Rhodes community. John Rowett, who had succeeded Kenny as Warden in 1999, visited the area and found 'a strong sense that the Scholars resident in the Caribbean did not feel connected to the Trust and its activities. I encountered some feeling that no connection with the Trust could be expected once Scholars returned to the Caribbean.'[30]

With the exception of India, the same is true of the Asian Scholarships. The Scholars from Ceylon and Malaya had been exemplary, Williams reported in 1966; those from Hong Kong were 'respectable' if undistinguished, said Kenny; but that was as far as it went. Academically they deserved a place at Oxford but they 'do not display any of the other characteristics which Rhodes called for in his Will'.[31] Ceylon – or Sri Lanka as it had by then become – lost its Scholarship in 1975 and Hong Kong followed a few years after it was taken over by mainland China, but Singapore remains the exemplar of the strength and weaknesses of the Asian Rhodes Scholarships. The great majority of Singapore Scholars had been awarded some form of government scholarship abroad in the years before they confronted the selection committee; more than half of them ended up in government service.[32] Some had already been at Oxford. 'Obviously,' Fletcher observed, 'support of students who have already had Oxford experience raises questions in terms of the purpose of the Scholarship.'[33] Often the best potential candidates were studying abroad at the time when they might have been meeting the selection committee in Singapore. Even when they were available for interview they were not necessarily of the type the selectors in the more traditional Rhodes constituencies would have found most suitable. Greig Barr, a Trustee who visited Singapore in 1985, complained that the educational system there tended to produce the 'mere bookworms' whom Rhodes had been anxious to avoid. Rhodes Scholars were – or should be – distinct from other academic groups thanks to their idiosyncrasies, their unpredictability, the diversity of their enthusiasms and their talents. Singapore ironed out any such characteristics in its Scholars so as to produce a smoothly crafted bureaucrat calculated to fit snugly into the machinery of government. The result was perhaps more likely to make a useful contribution to the running of the state than the products of Zambia or Bermuda, but it was far indeed from Rhodes's aspiration.[34]

In 1981 Professor David Fieldhouse, who had just become Professor of Imperial and Naval History at Cambridge, wrote to Fletcher to urge that there should be a fundamental reallocation of the Scholarships. There was no cause now for white students, particularly from the United States, to come to Oxford to read a first degree. 'The modern equivalent of the US and colonial student of Rhodes's day is the graduate from an Anglophone university in one of the "new Commonwealth" countries where standards are much lower than they are in Britain. . . . These also are the countries whose future relations with Britain may be determined by the attitudes of an indigenous elite.' Most of the American Scholarships should be abolished and conferred instead on African, Asian and Caribbean countries.[35]

If only because of the legal problems involved, the Trustees do not seem to have taken much account of Fieldhouse's somewhat drastic proposition. Increasingly, indeed, there was a tendency not to advocate the creation of new Scholarships in the developing world but to question whether Rhodes Scholarships were appropriate to the needs of that section of humanity. For successive Wardens the question was brought into sharp focus by the problems met in placing the weaker Scholars in Oxford colleges. In 1996 Kenny had to tell the Trustees that the Malaysian Scholar could not be placed at Oxford but was taking a course in Industrial Relations at the London School of Economics. Neither of the Zambians had been placed; one had gone to Reading to study Urban Land Appraisal, the other would try again next year. The Bermudan Scholar had failed to find a college and had decided to abandon the Scholarship. The Ugandan had similarly failed to find a college; he too would try again the following year. This catalogue of disasters raised the question of whether Scholars of sufficiently high calibre were being found in the developing world. It also, more pertinently, caused doubts about whether, whatever their academic ability, Oxford was the right place for them to be or – even if it was – whether a Rhodes Scholarship was the right vehicle to carry them there.

Kenny for one found much cause for reflection. At the end of 1998 he told the Trustees that he had once been proud that more new Scholarships had been created during his tenure of office than under any other Secretary. 'Now, as I near the end of my term, I have begun to wonder whether that pride has been misplaced. I have begun to question whether the creation of new Rhodes Scholarships is the most appropriate way for the Trustees to spend money.' Nobody doubted that Kenya, Zambia and Malaysia benefited from access to British universities, but were Rhodes Scholarships – expensive, restricted to Oxford, lumbered with strict residential requirements – necessarily the best way to bring this about? Their loss would not seem so grievous to the Third World countries as they would have in the old dominions or the United States. If the Trust were to abolish the Scholarships in Pakistan, Kenya, Singapore, Hong Kong and Malaysia and channel the money saved into a general fund to bring students from those countries to the United Kingdom, then the developing countries would quickly be consoled. In the academic year 1997–8 the cost per student under the Scholarship schemes operated by the University of Oxford had been £5,077. The equivalent figure for a Rhodes Scholar in 1998–9 was expected to be over £20,000. Nearly four times as many foreign students would therefore benefit from the Oxford scheme as did at the moment through Rhodes Scholarships. If the principle was accepted, he suggested, this would be a good time to put it into practice. 'Abolition of Scholarships is bound to be unpopular: responsibility for suggesting it could remain with the present Secretary, who could then carry the odium with him harmlessly into retirement.'[36]

It was a handsome offer but, as almost every committee does when confronted by a revolutionary proposal, the Trustees procrastinated. For the moment they decided that they would leave the distribution of the Scholarships unchanged but that the matter must be constantly reviewed. The cogency of the Warden's arguments was acknowledged; the conclusions that he drew were too drastic for immediate application. In the meantime they agreed that the Trust should contribute £250,000 a year for four years to the Vice-Chancellor's scheme 'to enable the University to offer Scholarships and financial aid for overseas students'. It was to take an economic crisis a few years later to impel the Trustees to accept some at least of the cuts in Scholarships that Kenny had suggested.[37]

CHAPTER FORTY-ONE

CLINTON AND AFTER

After the glory years of Kennedy's administration, the Rhodes Scholarships continued to enjoy high renown in the United States. David Alexander, the President of Pomona College, was American Secretary during most of this period. Robin Fletcher had stayed with him a few months before the new Secretary was chosen, liked what he saw, and urged his appointment when he got back to Oxford. He never had cause to doubt his judgment. He visited the American Secretary again at the end of 1986 and admired the aplomb with which he brushed off an importunate VIP who was trying to bully his way on to a selection committee. 'Not only does he remain very efficient and enthusiastic,' Fletcher told the Trustees, 'he is also courteous but firm.'[1]

But though Fletcher was happy with the American Secretary he was less satisfied with the calibre of some of the Scholars from the United States. A small but significant proportion of these were below the minimum standard expected by Oxford. Fletcher believed the selectors indulged in an unwarranted degree of 'social engineering', favouring 'women, blacks and Mexicans'. This no doubt reflected well on the warmth of their hearts but meant that Scholars arrived in Oxford without the abilities required if they were to make good use of their time there.[2] Alexander accepted that there was something in the charge but felt that as much was due to the imbalance between the pools of potential candidates available in the different electoral districts. The carving up of the United States into eight regions had never been wholly equitable, and demographic changes and the growth of new universities since 1930 had made the imperfections of the system still more evident. With the support of Fletcher's successor, Kenny, Alexander now put forward plans for a drastic reform which would abolish the two-tier system of nominations by states followed by elections by a district committee and substitute direct election of two or three Scholars each year by fourteen regional committees. The plan proved too radical for most of the American Rhodes Scholars who rose in furious protest against the abolition of what

Kenny told the Trustees was 'the cumbersome and unfair two-tier system'.[3] Alexander lost heart and, though urged on by the Trustees, retreated to a more modest proposal for the realignment of the eight existing districts. The Trustees imposed this without further consultation. Satisfied by their victory on the main issue, even the most conservative of the American Scholars accepted the *fait accompli* with little demur. The first election under the new system was held in 1996. Alexander reported that the quality of the candidates seemed higher and their provenance more varied than under the previous dispensation.

By this time Bill Clinton had already been four years in the White House. During his electoral campaign prurient journalists had lurked around University College and Rhodes House trying to establish that he had fornicated, taken drugs or otherwise behaved improperly during his time at Oxford.[4] Bill Bradley, the former star basketball player and US Senator, was called upon to defend Clinton against charges that he had betrayed his country by visiting Russia when a Rhodes Scholar. Bradley said that he had done the same himself. There was nothing unpatriotic about it. 'What hogwash! I thought education was learning about the world first-hand as well as from books.'[5] When Clinton's victory was announced, all the Rhodes Scholars at Oxford were invited to Rhodes House to toast their new President. A toast was also drunk to the second Rhodes Scholar President who was perhaps among those present. The Master of University College was so delighted that he proposed to fly an American flag with the college flag above it, as the British Navy did when it had captured an enemy frigate. He was persuaded that this would be ill judged: the Americans were sensitive about their flag and fund-raising might be seriously affected.[6] The Rhodes community in the United States rejoiced, though conducting themselves with commendable sang-froid. The Class Letter for 1968 in the *American Oxonian* recorded: 'Bill Clinton writes that Chelsea's ballet skills have reached a new level of perfection. . . . Bill notes that in early November he was elected President of the United States.'[7]

Even if Clinton had not been a Rhodes Scholar there would have been an influx of Rhodes Scholars into the White House after his victory. The same thing had happened under Kennedy, Johnson and Carter. Rhodes Scholars tend to be Democrats, probably by a margin of at least two to one. In the 1988 election forty-six members of the class of 1950 planned to vote for Dukakis, only nine for Bush (though thirty-eight expected Bush to win against only seventeen for Dukakis – a statistic which suggests that Rhodes Scholars temper their liberalism with a dash of realism).[8] Partly this was a matter of temperament: the Democrat emphasis on the beneficial power of government and the value of a career in the public service appealed strongly to the average

Scholar. Partly it was social origins: Rhodes Scholars tend to be drawn from the middle-class professional families who incline traditionally towards the Democrats as opposed to the more affluent entrepreneurs who favour the Republicans.[9] Rhodes Scholars were also geographically well placed for an assault on the White House when the opportunity offered; in 1990 of the 1,550 living American Rhodes Scholars, more than two hundred were in Washington. Most of them were lawyers by training, but a high proportion of these were doing jobs that brought them closely into contact with government.[10] Given this, there was nothing extraordinary about the number of Scholars connected with the new administration. Thomas and Kathleen Schaeper reckon that about fifty or so Scholars could claim to have served Clinton in the White House during his period as President – a substantial number certainly but far removed from the 'army of fellow Rhodies . . . poised to take over the world', whom the Washington Post claimed to be advancing under Clinton's banner.[11] Of these only a handful, notably Robert Reich, the Secretary of Labor, and Strobe Talbott, the Deputy Secretary of State, were among Clinton's contemporaries at Oxford. Almost all those who were appointed would have been strongly in the running for their jobs whether or not they had been Rhodes Scholars. The fact that they had been Scholars may have helped them to reach that point in their career; it is possible that, other things being equal, their Scholarship might have given them the edge over a less fortunate rival; but in practice other things almost never were equal. Clinton's appointments, like Kennedy's, were made because he believed the men or women in question were best for the job, not because they had been Rhodes Scholars. Nor did the Rhodes Scholars in the White House operate as a group. The New American claimed that, since Clinton occupied the Oval Office, 'the Oxford influence in the Executive branch of the federal government has attained unprecedented heights'.[12] That a significant proportion of those who mattered in the White House had spent two or three years at Oxford is incontestable; to argue from this that there was any coherent attempt to impose upon American political life values peculiar to Oxford or to the Rhodes Scholars is to retreat into the fantasy world of Colonel McCormick. Those working in the White House under Clinton were far too busy doing their designated jobs to have time to weave conspiracies or follow any hidden agenda.

But, whatever the reality, the popular perception was that a Rhodes Scholar President was presiding over a Rhodes Scholar administration. The prestige of the Scholarships, already high, was still further enhanced and remained at an inflated level. This was not just the judgment of excitable journalists or of the man in the street: the Dean of Harvard told John Rowett in 2000 that 'for America's leading universities the blue riband of student achievement remained the Rhodes Scholarship'; at West Point Rowett was assured that there was 'no finer way for a US Army officer to begin his career of service than as a Rhodes Scholar at Oxford'.[13] The competition to secure a Scholarship became ever more ferocious. At the University of Arkansas talk about possible candidates began in the freshman year. At the beginning of the senior year there was a two-day retreat at which potential candidates could listen to lectures on foreign affairs and be coached on how to write an essay. The four students on the short list met for three hours every Sunday afternoon, they were bombarded with e-mails containing relevant articles from *Foreign Affairs* and invited to a mock selection-committee cocktail party. One candidate had ten mock interviews. When President Clinton visited the campus his advice to would-be candidates was: 'Just read *Time* and *Newsweek* and get plenty of sleep the night before.' The students listened deferentially but were assured later that the President was out of date. This anecdote appeared in an article in the *New York Times*, under the headline: 'At 100 years old, it's the grand-daddy of fellowships: the most prestigious, most arduous, most selective. Start prepping now.'[14] Oklahoma State University was no less eager to ensure its share of the Scholarships; from their second year potential candidates were given bi-weekly seminars on current affairs. An alumnus of Indiana University, Pennsylvania, was said to have promised to pay $1 million if it produced a Rhodes Scholar in 1999 – if it failed to do so the President had to buy the alumnus a box of Cuban cigars.[15] Even an institution as renowned as West Point admitted that it coveted Scholarships, not just because they helped produce good officers but because they earned prestige for the establishment responsible.[16]

More than ever before, the fact that an American had been a Rhodes Scholar became an important factor in his subsequent career. Like the Scholars' domination of the White House, this was as much a matter of popular perception as of reality, but when Anthony Kenny conducted a survey among American Scholars he found that a third of them felt that their award had been 'very important' in getting them their job, while another third felt that it had been a significantly useful factor. Inevitably, the lustre wore off as the years went by – middle-aged Scholars would be judged primarily on their performance, not on the fact that they had succeeded in impressing a selection committee favourably more than twenty years before – but for the young men or women starting a career the fact that they had been Rhodes Scholars was taken to guarantee a high level of intelligence, ambition and forcefulness.[17] Stan McGee, a Scholar from Alabama who went to Oxford in 1992, claimed to know many people who applied 'not just to get into Oxford but because it is a very significant accolade in the United States. You have basically already won before you come over here.'[18]

In his novel *I Am Charlotte Simmons*, Tom Wolfe, that Hieronymus Bosch of contemporary American fiction, described a clever young undergraduate, Adam, who was resolved to advance rapidly in life. There was a new type of intellectual, he told his girlfriend Charlotte, 'the bad-ass. The bad-ass is a sort of rogue intellectual. . . . You're an intellectual but you want to operate on a higher level. This is a new millennium, and you want to be a member of the millennial aristocracy, which is a meritocracy, but an aristo-meritocracy.' The first step was to pick some insalubrious part of the world in which to do good works – Africa would be ideal – then to try for a Rhodes Scholarship. 'If you get one, you go to Oxford and get a DPhil degree, and then it's like magic. Every door opens.' Rhodes's idea had been to bring bright young American barbarians over to England and make them citizens of the world. He wanted to lift them up to a higher plane and extend the reach of the British Empire with its American cousins in tow. 'The British Empire is gone, but a Rhodes still lifts you to a higher plane. You're not doomed to being some obscure college teacher. You become a public intellectual. Everybody talks about your ideals.' What if you don't get a Rhodes Scholarship? asked Charlotte. 'In that case you go after a Fulbright. That's a pretty long way down from a Rhodes, but it's okay. There's also the Marshall Fellowships, but they're the last resort. I mean that's bottom-fishing.'[19]

Though it was gratifying for the Rhodes Trustees that their Scholarships should be so highly esteemed, their enthusiasm was diminished by the fact that some – perhaps even most – of the American Rhodes Scholars considered the winning of the award to be far more important than its subsequent enjoyment at Oxford. Kenny in 1991 attended two selection committees in the United States. It was, he reported, difficult to avoid the conclusion that 'not only many of the candidates, but also some of the interviewers, regard election to a Rhodes Scholarship not as an opportunity to benefit from the educational riches which Oxford has to offer, but rather as a glittering prize for previous performance, which carried with it a not altogether welcome obligation to study at a particular overseas university'.[20] Oxford, in the starkest application of this analysis, became an institution where the Scholar was committed to spend two or three years of relative idleness, before the real business of life began on his return to the United States.

American Rhodes Scholars had long had a propensity to complain about poor food and accommodation, old-fashioned libraries, inadequate equipment. Visiting the United States in 2000 John Rowett was unsurprised to encounter complaints about the lack of computers and the poor standing of certain science departments but was disconcerted when the criticism was extended to 'certain of the humanities faculties'.[21] John Cloud, an American Rhodes Scholar at Brasenose, had five years earlier contributed an article to the *American Oxonian* which denounced the manners and mores of contemporary Oxford and was so offensive about his tutor that the Trustees considered whether a formal rebuke should be delivered.[22] Rosa Ehrenreich was a Marshall Scholar rather than a Rhodes but her 1994 novel *A Garden of Paper Flowers* involved the Trust in possible legal difficulties. Ehrenreich too ridiculed Oxford practices and portrayed the heroine's tutor as idle, silly and unresponsive to his pupil's needs. Cloud reviewed the novel in the *American Oxonian* and identified Ehrenreich's real tutor, who, he claimed, was clearly the model for his fictional counterpart. The unfortunate tutor threatened legal action, telling Kenny that he would include the Trust in the action as distributors of the offensive material. The matter petered out inconclusively, but it left an unpleasant taste in the mouths of the Trustees and of the Oxford authorities.[23]

Oxford for its part felt that the American Rhodes Scholars clung too closely together and made little effort to contribute to the life of the University. In 1997 Kenny questioned whether the Trust should pay for the 'sailing luncheon' given before the American Scholars flew to England, quoting complaints that this occasion – which had by now become merely the final episode in a weekend of jollifications – encouraged the participants to view themselves as a group apart when they got to Oxford. Robert Edge, the President of the Association of American Rhodes Scholars, rejected the charge: getting to know the other Scholars was an important part of the Rhodes experience, and 'Until someone can show me that one cannot simultaneously have strong American friends and also be active in the broader range of Oxford experience, I will be hard to convince.'[24] He might have been shaken if he had studied the comments of the class of 1991. The best thing about their time at Oxford, most of them agreed, was the opportunity to associate with other Rhodes Scholars, particularly American; the worst, as one disaffected Scholar put it, was 'Britain – sorry, I know it's rude'. As the compiler of the survey blandly concluded: 'it is only right to point out that Rhodes's concern about American Scholars being overly susceptible to the charms of Oxford is today as misplaced as his imperialist dreams'.[25]

It would be easy to make too much of this. The majority of American Rhodes Scholars enjoy their years at Oxford, work hard while they are there and make efforts to mix outside their own community. But academically, and indeed in other respects, they have been outshone by the Scholars from Canada, Australia or South Africa. In the 1990s nearly 12 per cent of American Scholars failed to get a degree. This is not necessarily proof that they had not worked but it does suggest that an Oxford qualification is not considered a particularly significant addition to the curriculum vitae of ambitious young men and women, even those who plan to pursue a career in academe. The

Oxford experience is still valued, but today it bulks less large in the lives of American Rhodes Scholars than in those of Scholars from the other main constituencies. Whether the Scholarships fulfil Rhodes's other prime intention, of creating in the upper levels of American society a spirit of goodwill towards Britain and a predisposition to co-operate on a common policy, is still more difficult to establish. The verdict of the class of 1991 would hardly suggest this, but there are still plenty of anglophiles among the Rhodes Scholars and the lot of a British Ambassador in Washington is made notably easier by the existence of this powerful and well-disposed network. Christopher Hitchens put the value of the connection pretty low. 'The subliminal influence of the Rhodes Scholarships', he wrote, 'is rather like the subliminal influence of the etchings in the men's room at the Harvard Club, which happen to be of Peterhouse, Cambridge, Ely and Durham cathedrals and the West Highlands of Scotland. They act as a reinforcement of English taste and manners upon the American condition.'[26] Even that is something, and coming from Hitchens it can safely be accepted as the blackest exposition of the case for the Scholarships. It does not seem too much to claim that, though the view of Britain held by the American establishment today may not be all that might be hoped for in London, it would be still more jaundiced if Rhodes had not made the Will he did.

Since 1998 the American Secretary who has had to face this situation has been Elliot Gerson, a distinguished lawyer who went on to a highly successful career in business. Gerson's particular ambition is to encourage the candidature of students from those universities which not only could claim few if any Rhodes Scholarships from the past but did not even think it worth encouraging their members to compete. When Kenny visited the United States in 1996 he found that almost a third of Rhodes Scholars over the last decade had come from Harvard, Yale and Princeton; in 1988 Harvard alone had won ten out of the thirty-two available awards (most of them, of course, gained by candidates standing for their own home states rather than Massachusetts). Only at Berkeley did he find that the undergraduate ethos discouraged candidates from coming forward; it was felt that the Scholarships were 'an East Coast kind of thing'.[27] The weaker universities, in principle, were enthusiastic about the idea of the Scholarships but did not think that it was something to which they could aspire. By developing the Trust website in the United States and by a personal crusade, Gerson has made it his business to ensure that all such universities have the necessary information about the Scholarships and are encouraged to put forward suitable candidates.[28] There is still some way to go, but much has been achieved. One cause for regret among the more traditional American Rhodes Scholars is that the Oxford colleges now put so much emphasis on academic ability that Rhodes's all-rounder is becoming progressively less likely to find a place: Clinton, on this analysis, *might* have scraped through the selection process and found a college; Bill Bradley, the sporting hero and highly influential Senator, almost certainly would not. Gerson's other notable achievement is to have pushed through the reform which Alexander had tried but failed to secure. The two-tier system has now been abolished: the United States has been divided into sixteen areas roughly comparable in population, and would-be Scholars, with their universities' backing, apply directly to the appropriate selection committee. Opinion had changed in the years since Alexander's foray; the reform met with remarkably little opposition and seems to be working well.

Gerson also had occasional problems with the other scholarship schemes open to American students. Tom Wolfe's Adam had asserted that a Fulbright was 'a long way down', while the Marshall was 'the last resort'; as the new millennium dawned the Gates Scholarships promised to provide sterner competition. Bill Gates, founder of Micosoft, envisaged 120 awards a year for graduates to go to Cambridge who had 'demonstrated extraordinary academic accomplishments and outstanding leadership ability' – a clear echo of Rhodes's criteria. The Dean of Harvard, whose university was another conspicuous beneficiary of Gates's generosity, assured Rowett that no challenge to the Rhodes Scholarships was intended; Gates realised that to try to undermine them would be a public-relations disaster in the United States and was anyway wholly contrary to his intentions.[29] Even though, or perhaps sometimes because, most Gates Scholarships would last only a year, they clearly offered an attractive extra possibility for Americans who fancied the idea of a term of study in Britain. The Vice-Chancellor of Cambridge proposed the setting up of a working party to ensure that the two Scholarship schemes were 'as far as possible . . . complementary and work to the benefit of our universities, of the Scholars, and of the countries from which they come'.[30] Though so far no formal arrangements have been made, the Trustees welcomed the initiative and there have been no indications that graduates who would have been natural Rhodes Scholars have been seduced by the lure of Gates and Cambridge.

The relationship with the Marshall Scholarships, administered by the British Embassy in Washington, has at times proved more abrasive. The established pattern had been that the winners of the Marshall Scholarships were announced first; the Rhodes results were published a few days later, so that if anyone had gone for and won both he or she could decide which they would rather take. Except for one candidate who was particularly anxious to follow a course at Bath, this in practice meant that the Rhodes Scholarship was invariably accepted. (In the case of the one misguided delinquent, Alexander told her sternly that 'her name would be stricken from our records and that she could not claim to be a Rhodes Scholar'.)[31] In 1990 and again in 2002, the administrators of the Marshall Scholarship demanded an immediate response from the successful candidates, several of whom, on the principle of a bird in the hand being worth two in the bush, accepted the award and withdrew their names from the Rhodes list of would-be Scholars. On each occasion, acrimonious exchanges between the two organisations were followed by a patched-up settlement. At the moment Marshall winners can still hold on until the Rhodes selection committees have done their work before committing themselves to accept the lesser prize.

A roll-call of the positions of distinction held by American Rhodes Scholars proves little but would no doubt have gratified the Founder. One President; seven Senators; fourteen Congressmen; a bevy of senior ministers, state governors, judges, mayors of major cities, ambassadors, generals, admirals, heads of universities; Robert Penn Warren for poetry and fiction; Hubble and his telescope; Kris Kristofferson for popular music – the list could be indefinitely protracted. A few blotted the Rhodes copybook. First actually to end up in prison was Henry Isaacs, for misappropriation of Trust funds. 'The only time I met him,' remembered Allen, 'he was in England on what seemed to be a wild-cat scheme for turning water into motor-fuel. I confess at that time I formed an unfavourable impression of him.'[32] On the whole, however, success in terms of their career has been the hallmark of the American Rhodes Scholar, though the success has often enough been employed in ways valuable to society to justify the claim that the Scholarships are not just about worldly prestige. They are still 'the grand-daddy of fellowships: the most prestigious, most arduous, most selective'. And if they sometimes seem a little frayed at the edges and out of date, uncertain of their status in a rapidly changing world, then that is the way of grandparents the world over. There is good reason to believe that in the United States they will keep their essential qualities for many years to come.

CHAPTER FORTY-TWO

THE OLD COMMONWEALTH

It was not only in the United States that people began to question whether two or three years at Oxford were necessarily the high point of any civilised education: in the countries of the old Commonwealth, however, the growth of such doubts was slower and more muted. Canada was closest in outlook to its southern neighbour. From the point of view of the Trust, administrative problems were eased in 1948 when Newfoundland became a province of Canada and this notoriously idiosyncratic Rhodes constituency lost its independence. 'This will mean it comes under the jurisdiction of Michener, which will be all to the good,' Elton observed with satisfaction.[1] Michener had been the Trust's Secretary in Canada since 1936 and no safer pair of hands was to be found. 'He is liked and respected by all and I hope that he will remain our Secretary for a considerable time to come,' wrote Elton.[2] He did, even though he entered federal politics and became Speaker of the House of Commons. He only resigned when he was sent to India as High Commissioner and continued to take a keen interest in the Scholarships even after his final transmogrification into a much respected Governor General.

In the United States the increasing prominence of the Rhodes Scholars had been demonstrated when they were denounced by Colonel McCormick in the *Chicago Tribune*. Canada's McCormick was Elmer Sopha, who in 1965 told the Ontario legislature that the Rhodes Scholarships were 'foreign, and associated with the age of colonialism'. He wanted a new 'Canada Scholarship' to be created, which would displace the Rhodes Scholarship as Canada's highest academic honour.[3] His outburst marked a remarkable period in which the Canadian Rhodes Scholars not only became prominent in national life but, in certain fields, seemed almost to take it over. In the Department of External Affairs, for instance, Sopha would have observed with disapproval that the Deputy Minister, the Ambassadors in Washington, Moscow and Tel Aviv and the High Commissioner in London were all Rhodes Scholars. In federal politics, Michener was replaced as Speaker by another Rhodes Scholar, there was

a Minister of Justice and two Ministers without Portfolio, and John Turner
was Finance Minister in the 1970s and briefly Prime Minister in 1984. But the
climate in Canada was changing; by the time Bob Rae became Premier of
Ontario in 1990, fellow Rhodes Scholars were already thin on the ground in
the upper reaches of the political world. In an entertaining fantasy Michael
Howarth, who understudied Michener as Rhodes Secretary, imagined Cecil
Rhodes visiting Ottawa in 1961 and finding that some sixty of his Scholars
were on the national payroll. He was delighted by their eminence yet also felt
some disquiet. 'Can there be too much of a good thing? Have his Colonial
Scholars taken his espousal of "public duties" too seriously or too narrowly?'
When he returned towards the end of the century, however, he found that
things had moved abruptly in the other direction. 'Today, members of the
public would be hard put to it to identify a single Scholar who could be
described as a mover or shaker in Ottawa.' He would have met with the same
disappointment in the provincial capitals.[4] Doug McCalla, doyen of Canada's
economic historians, reckons that this reflects more on the nature of the state
and politics than on the skills and proclivities of the Scholars. Today there is
much more cynicism about government service, bureaucracy is all important,
promotion goes strictly by seniority – in such circumstances Rhodes Scholars
look elsewhere. Arthur Kroeger, for many years a deputy minister and
Chancellor of Carleton University, thinks that it was the government which
lost interest in recruiting bright young men and women into its service and
left them to drift away into the more lucrative world of management consultancy.[5] Whatever the reasons, in the last few years the pendulum seems again
to have swung and there are once more young Rhodes Scholars vigorously
climbing the governmental ladder.

Michener remained as Secretary till 1964; John Stewart, his successor, died
after only six years in office and Arthur Scace took over. His most significant
contribution was to restructure the Scholarships so that three Scholarships
were awarded each year to the Prairies instead of one each to Alberta,
Manitoba and Saskatchewan, and two to the Maritimes instead of one each to
Nova Scotia and New Brunswick. This long-overdue reform met the same
outraged opposition as Aydelotte had encountered when he changed the
system in the United States in the 1920s; prudently Scace presented the change
as being a diktat from the Trustees which he was bound to implement.[6]

Saul Panofsky, the narrator's son in Mordecai Richler's *Barney's Vision*,
waited until he had been awarded a Scholarship before rejecting it with scorn.
'Cecil Rhodes', he told the selection committee, 'was a vicious imperialist
and his Scholarship Fund would be more honourably used making restitution
to the blacks he exploited.'[7] Few other Canadians would have matched
Panofsky's fervour. The French Canadian Scholars were notably free of ideo-

logical hang-ups. 'A scholarship is a scholarship' was Yves Fortier's conclusion, though he feels that his winning the award definitely affected his attitude to public service. Without it he might well have refused the invitation to become Canada's representative at the United Nations. Gerard Coulombe went to Oxford at least in part on the principle of 'knowing thy enemy' but he enjoyed his time there greatly, made many friends and found London far more welcoming than Paris.[8] Most French Canadian Scholars tend to be proudly conscious of their French roots without being separatists. But the name Rhodes does not resonate so loudly, nor does Oxford have the same appeal, as for the English-speaking Canadian. If offered a Rhodes Scholarship or a place at Harvard or Massachusetts Institute of Technology most English-speakers would opt for Oxford and hope the American offer would still be open later; the francophone Canadian might well choose the United States.

No Rhodes Scholar of either group would like to see the Rhodes community in Canada become no more than a sub-section of the American Association. When the direct sailings from Montreal to England ended in 1971 the Canadian Scholars on their way to Oxford were packed off to New York to join the American party. The practice continued long after aeroplanes had taken the place of boats. Arthur Kroeger felt it improper that young Canadians should be fêted in New York under American auspices when often they had never visited their own capital. He insisted that the ceremony should be repatriated, and in 1998 the first Canadian 'sailing dinner' was held. The result was the invigoration of the Canadian Association and the setting up of a mentoring programme under which former Rhodes Scholars who had established themselves in Canadian society would give advice and a helping hand to their juniors when they returned from Oxford.[9]

Canada, Kenny told the Trustees in 1998, sent some of the best Rhodes Scholars, though there were occasionally weak choices from the Prairies and the Maritimes. Like all previous Wardens, he went on, he found 'the Australian Scholars the best; they have clear academic goals, they generally work hard, and most of them are all-rounders in Rhodes terms'.[10] Somehow it seemed that even the more frail among them were destined to make good. Elton complained about the 'distinctly unpromising impression' made by the dossier of a Tasmanian Scholar; he seemed 'a weak candidate' and had been rejected by several colleges with unflattering comments – he should never have been selected. Ronald Gates went on to become President of the Economic Society of Australia and New Zealand, Chairman of the Institute of Urban Studies, Vice-Chancellor of the University of New England and author of many significant books including detective stories in Esperanto.

After thirty years as Secretary Sir John Behan, as he had become, was approaching seventy. He was anxious to carry on regardless, but Elton, though conceding that he was still doing his job efficiently, felt he was too precise and humourless to be ideal for his role.[11] George Paton was selected to replace him, only to be appointed Vice-Chancellor of the University of Melbourne. Despite his initial feeling that the two jobs could hardly be combined, he concluded that after two years learning the work at Melbourne he would be able to perform the role alongside that of Rhodes Secretary. Behan secured a respite of two years and then retired disconsolate. Williams visited him in retirement. 'Jock Behan is old and melancholy,' he told Elton, 'and I think the arrival of a young Warden-elect reinforced his feeling that his world is coming to an end.'[12]

Williams saw no harm in the tradition that the Governors of the various states presided over the local selection committee; Elton saw things differently. In 1945 he tried to persuade Behan that the practice was pernicious. The additional prestige of involving the Governor in elections was no longer necessary and there was always a risk that 'by the very nature of his position, the Governor may exercise disproportionate influence with the Committee'. It was not a question of prestige, retorted Behan, but of 'public confidence in the fairness and impartiality of Selection Committees'. No Governor in Australia had ever exercised or sought to exercise undue influence on the committees.[13] When Paton took over, Elton renewed the attack. It depended on the Governor, Paton replied. Sir Dallas Brooks, for instance, was 'worth his weight in gold'. The fact that the Chairman of the selection committee was unlikely to know any of the candidates personally forced the other members to clarify their views. 'I think the general opinion is that it is still useful.'[14] Elton was again frustrated; on the whole to the benefit of the Scholarships. Governors could generally be relied on to inject some sturdy common sense into the proceedings. When Bob Hawke, a future prime minister, faced the selection committee he was harassed by a member who would not accept his reply that, while he knew he wanted to perform some sort of public service in his life, he didn't yet know what it would be. Eventually Hawke appealed to the Chairman, saying that he had given an honest reply and was not prepared to concoct some spurious but more acceptable formula. Later the Governor told him that any doubts he had had about Hawke's suitability had been settled by 'the way you dealt with that blithering idiot'.[15]

As in every constituency where Scholarships were allotted to individual states or institutions, Australia was plagued by the fact that the most populous state, New South Wales, could elect only one Scholar – the same as Tasmania which was only a thirteenth of its size. To mitigate this the Trustees in 1975 approved an additional Scholarship for Australia-at-Large. The next problem was to decide what sort of animal this was. Was it a super-Scholarship competition to find the national champion or a consolation prize for the best of those who had failed to win selection at the state level? 'Between the Scylla of superiority in repute and the Charybdis of inferiority in status,' as Paton's successor as Secretary, John Poynter, put it, 'the strait for the new award was narrow indeed.'[16] In the end they settled for the principle of picking the Scholar from the best runners-up; the demographic facts were such that, even if it could be said that the selection committees had invariably chosen the strongest candidate, it would be rarely indeed that the Australia-at-Large Scholar would be obviously inferior to all the Scholars chosen by the individual states.

Poynter succeeded Paton as Secretary in 1973. 'I will brook no refusal,' Williams told him.[17] He inherited a situation in which applications for Rhodes Scholarships had failed to grow in proportion to the increase of the student population and in some cases had actually declined. The fact that there were many more opportunities for doing postgraduate work in Australia and that some university professors appeared to think that it would be unpatriotic on the part of young graduates to pursue their further education outside the homeland was an element in this malaise. Even when the graduates did decide to go abroad, there was no guarantee that Oxford would seem the most desirable destination. The new universities in particular, with no tradition of Rhodes Scholarships behind them and a rich variety of other awards to choose from – some of them financially more enticing – showed no great enthusiasm for putting forward candidates. 'One can certainly no longer assume that the best people will apply for the Rhodes Scholarships,' said Geoffrey Kennedy, Chancellor of the University of Western Australia, at a reunion of Scholars in 1988. 'We have had the experience of some academics actively discouraging possible candidates from applying, on the ground that the candidate's area of study is not strong at Oxford.' At the same reunion Poynter said that he doubted whether they were getting applications 'from all those parts of Australian society which will be producing the leaders of Australia in the twenty-first century'. Excellent candidates were still coming forward but there was 'a need to make the Scholarship known to groups and institutions which might not normally aspire to consideration for selection'.[18] There was a real risk that the Rhodes Scholarships might be progressively sidelined – either not known about or, when they were brought to the attention of potential candidates, dismissed as 'a relic of a disreputably conservative past'.[19]

In the United States the election of Clinton had raised the profile of the Scholarships among those who had previously been only dimly aware of their existence. In Australia, the election of Bob Hawke as Prime Minister in 1983, perhaps because he was so very far from being 'disreputably conservative' himself, seems to have had something of the same effect. There were three Rhodes Scholars in his government and three more on the opposition front bench; a Rhodes Scholar was Governor of Victoria, another High Commissioner in London, a third headed the Department of Foreign Affairs. Hawke himself had had little to do with the Scholarships since leaving Oxford but he went back there for the centenary celebrations. Fifty years before, at University College, he had broken the record for a 'sconce' – a fine exacted in a college hall and paid by draining a gigantic tankard of ale in the shortest possible time. Now the Master of the College and Rhodes Trustee, Lord Butler, challenged him to repeat the feat. An American alumnus who was also present egged him on. Hawke climbed on to the table and – though in non-alcoholic beer, for he was off alcohol at the time – manfully emptied the tankard at a gulp. He was not quite so fast as in the past but he took only a highly creditable thirty-five seconds. It must be the first time that a former Prime Minister of Australia has stood on a table and drained a tankard of beer to the applause of a former President of the United States and a former Secretary to the British Cabinet. It seems unlikely that there will be a repeat performance.[20]

The episode was typical of the bravura with which Hawke conducted his eight years at the head of government. The fact that he had been a Rhodes Scholar did not figure so prominently in the public consciousness as had Clinton's similar experience, but it was still much commented on. In Australia today, the man in the street – at least if he is not a recent immigrant – will probably be aware of the existence of the Scholarships. If wishing to express his intellectual limitations, he is as likely to say 'I'm no Rhodes Scholar but . . .' as 'I'm no rocket scientist' or 'I'm no Einstein'. But the threat to the preeminence of the system remains. There are still many graduates who are potentially strong candidates for a Scholarship but who reject the opportunity, either because they do not feel it is appropriate for a progressive Australian in the twenty-first century or because they doubt whether Oxford would give them the sort of further education for which they are looking. Whether that perception can be changed depends as much upon the conduct of affairs at Oxford as it does upon the public-relations skills of the Rhodes Secretary in Australia and the enthusiasm of those former Scholars who second his efforts.

New Zealand is to some extent Australia writ small, with the isolation, the restricted size of the Rhodes community and the lack of economic opportunity all potent if diminishing factors against which the Trust and its servants have to battle. In 1958 the Governor General, Lord Cobham, told Elton that 'Ambition is not in the air in this country . . . nobody *wants* to lead, or to excel, or to make a fortune.' Cobham was wrong, Williams commented; New

Zealand might not produce Scholars of prodigious talent, but it turned out many who were eminently well qualified to 'fight the world's fight'.[21] Certainly any New Zealand student with even a glimmer of ambition would have been stirred by the glamour which a Rhodes Scholarship bestowed on those who won it. It was 'the pinnacle of any student's achievement', Bryan Gould's mother told him; when he attained that pinnacle it became national news and he received telegrams of congratulation from 'everyone from the Prime Minister downwards'. David Williams went to a school the walls of which were lined with boards commemorating the triumphs of miscellaneous cup-winners: the list of those who had won Rhodes Scholarships had to be memorised and recited.[22]

Post-war New Zealand Scholars were at first no more likely to return home after their time at Oxford than had been their parents before 1939. Donald Schultz, at the 1953 Reunion, told a BBC interviewer that, as an electrical engineer, he had always assumed he would make his career in New Zealand, but that now he had realised he couldn't 'go back to my own country because there's no opportunity for me to do the work I've learned to do here. Much as I'd like to go back to my country, and plough back, as it were, some of the things I've gleaned here . . . I find myself . . . forced to find employment somewhere else.'[23] At Oxford the University Press became almost a New Zealand fief: Kenneth Sisam becoming chief executive, Dan Davin deputy secretary to the Delegates and R. W. Burchfield chief editor of the Oxford English dictionaries and therefore uncrowned king of British lexicographers. Lord Porritt, who was the first man to be president simultaneously of the British Medical Association and of the Royal College of Surgeons, and who only went back to New Zealand when appointed Governor General, cheerfully advised David Williams at his selection committee: 'Don't rush back. It took me forty years.' When Williams told his namesake, the Warden, that he planned to go to teach in Tanzania, Bill Williams commented that this was just the same as the idealistic New Zealand Scholars who had joined the colonial service between the wars. David Williams was rather affronted by the comparison but on reflection had to admit that the motivation was much the same.[24] By the mid-1950s, of the sixty-seven living New Zealand Scholars, twenty-nine were in Britain, only twenty-five at home.

The charge that New Zealanders lacked ambition never wholly disappeared. In 1980 Fletcher found that good possible candidates preferred to study for their PhDs at home so as to make sure of getting the best jobs. 'There seems a natural conspiracy against ambition and enterprise,' he stormed. 'Somehow somebody needs a jolt.'[25] Perhaps the energetic new Rhodes Secretary, David Baragwanath, helped administer the jolt. Certainly within a decade of Fletcher's visit, economic growth had turned the country into a far more attractive environment for young Scholars wondering what to do after Oxford and thus made it safer for them to risk a period away.

By the new millennium a large majority of Scholars were coming back to New Zealand to settle. No less than in Australia, young New Zealanders wonder whether they want to study abroad at all and, if they do, whether Oxford is necessarily the best place to do it, but the Scholarships continue to enjoy unique renown. A Rhodes Scholarship is no longer automatically the dream of every eager young New Zealand student, but that it is easily *primus inter pares* cannot seriously be disputed.

CHAPTER FORTY-THREE

SOUTH AFRICA COMES IN FROM THE COLD

The crumbling of apartheid and the triumphant election of Nelson Mandela had little immediate effect on the four schools designated for Scholarships under Rhodes's Will. The headmaster of Bishops took pride in the fact that on several occasions one of his boys, who had failed to get the Scholarship reserved for his school, had gone on to win a South Africa-at-Large Scholarship, thus demonstrating that even Bishops' second best was better than anybody else in South Africa.[1] Malicious critics suggest that this was because Bishops deliberately passed over their strongest candidate in the confidence that he would gain the at-Large selection. Even if they did pursue so riskily devious a course, however, it would still follow that their boys were among the stronger candidates for a Scholarship. Sometimes, indeed, they were, but units as small as the four schools could not hope consistently to produce Scholars who could meet the demands of Oxford at the end of the twentieth century. In 1996 Kenny told Ackermann that he had been unable to place the Bishops Scholar in any college. Should he try the London School of Economics? Or should the Trustees refuse to confirm the Scholarship? Ackermann favoured the latter: 'After all, it is the *Oxford* experience that was paramount for Rhodes and I have always found it uncomfortable to speak of a Rhodes Scholar who has not been to Oxford.' It would be disagreeable for nominated Scholars to have to wait for weeks or even months before their Scholarship was confirmed, but the rejection of a Scholar would be a stark warning to the schools that they should never put forward a candidate unless certain he was of the necessary calibre.[2] Two Scholars from Paul Roos had also failed to find a college in the past few years; on average the Scholars from the four schools were below the level of other South African Scholars. To make matters worse, Oxford colleges were beginning to question the propriety of accepting the beneficiaries of closed Scholarships at a time when such exclusive arrangements had been abolished in the United Kingdom.[3]

Legally, the schools' Scholarships seemed impregnable; morally they were on increasingly shaky ground, both because Paul Roos and SACS at least were closed to black and coloured pupils and because they excluded girls. The first restriction was obviously not going to last long in a South Africa about to be run by a black government. It was Paul Roos, traditionally the redoubt of the Afrikaans-speaking nationalist, which took the lead. In a ballot, an over-whelming majority of parents voted in favour of making the school open to all races. One reason for this was probably that the parents, 35 per cent of whom were academics, were afraid that the school would lose its cherished Rhodes Scholarship if it did not mend its ways.[4]

Paul Roos was also notably progressive in another field. In 1999 Kenny had found a general expectation in the schools that they would soon find them-selves under fresh attack on the ground that they practised sex discrimination. Here it was St Andrew's, Grahamstown, which took the lead; they paired with a neighbouring girls' school and in December 1998 selected their first female Scholar.[5] Paul Roos followed in 2006. They shared certain courses with two Stellenbosch girls' schools and decided that any girl who participated in such a course – probably as many as 120 by 2006 – could compete for the cherished Scholarship. They were trying to be as blind to sex as they already were to colour: the headmaster complained mildly that the only people who took a keen interest in the racial origins of pupils at Paul Roos were the officials of the Ministry of Education, presumably in case integration was not proceeding fast enough.[6]

In terms of both race and sex the two Cape Town schools, Bishops and SACS, have lagged behind. About one in five of the boys at Bishops is now non-white, the majority of these Cape Coloured; they hope to double this proportion but are reluctant to lower standards by accepting boys who will not be able to cope with the work. As for sex, they claim that they have no girls' school conveniently located near by with whom they could easily form a partnership. Further afield there are many possibilities; arbitrarily to pick one would be unfair to the rest and cause unnecessary offence. At SACS the road to reform was for long blocked by a conservative headmaster who was reluc-tant to push the case for non-white boys to be admitted in face of opposition from the government, his argument being that it would be unfair to the boys to treat them as political footballs. The race issue is now, in principle at least, resolved; the headmaster has retired; it seems certain that there will be movement on the sex issue as well. But, however impeccably liberal the schools might become, there will always be critics who will maintain that in the twenty-first century there should be no Scholarships tied to particular schools with a field of potential candidates only a few score strong in any given years. Edwin Cameron, the immensely impressive Judge of Appeal and now

Secretary of the Trust who defied South Africa's refusal to confront the terror of AIDS by proclaiming that he was HIV positive and had overcome the disability, feels that sooner or later this problem must be tackled and the Schools' Scholarships converted into awards for South Africa-at-Large.[7] The Trustees, twice bitten, may fight shy of embarking on yet another legal battle, but it would be surprising if this particular sleeping dog was allowed to lie in peace indefinitely.

What is demonstrably true is that, through men like Ackermann and Cameron and through the resolute colour-blindness of the Trust, the Rhodes Scholarships have been a positive force, first in keeping lines open between the races during the blackest days of apartheid and then in aiding the task of reconciliation. Fanie du Toit, an Afrikaner student from a conventional background, had seldom spoken socially with a non-white until he stood in a queue waiting to be inoculated before taking off for Oxford. Near him he saw Chris Landsberg, a coloured Rhodes Scholar from Johannesburg, who was known to be an activist in the African National Congress. Plucking up his courage, he introduced himself. 'Our government has made a mess of it,' he declared – the most left-wing comment he could manage. 'You must look at it in the context of the times,' replied Landsberg, the most right-wing comment *he* could manage. The two men shared rooms at Oxford and became firm friends. It was friendships such as that which helped save South Africa.[8]

But except in the four schools, where the awards still possess a talismanic quality, the Rhodes Scholarships do not have the cachet in South Africa which they enjoy in the other main constituencies. For Michelle Norton, for instance, who competed in 1984, it was just one of a set of more or less similar scholarships which would all have got her to Britain or the United States. When told she had won she asked Edwin Cameron, then Assistant Secretary, how long she could have to make up her mind. Cameron's reply made it clear that awe-struck gratitude was the expected response, not hesitation over whether to accept. Loyiso Nongxa, who was in time to become Vice-Chancellor of the University of the Witwatersrand, only realised how remarkable his achievement had been when he spent a year at Harvard and found that his Rhodes Scholarship gave him heroic status. As for Shaun Johnson, the highly successful political journalist who took over the Mandela–Rhodes Foundation, he found that his editorial masters assumed his Rhodes Scholarship meant merely that he had been educated at Rhodes University.[9]

Nongxa was doubly exceptional, in that not only did he win a Rhodes Scholarship but he was one of the very few black South Africans to compete. In the past the reasons for this had been partly ideological – the name of Rhodes was associated with colonialism and capitalism; it was an elitist award inappropriate for the new South Africa, and partly psychological – people from the under-privileged background common to most of them could not possibly be suitable for so establishment a system. Now fresh reasons were added. There was a galaxy of other scholarships to be won, a fair number of which were reserved for black South Africans who might otherwise have tried for a Rhodes. Many of these scholarships took the winners to the United States, a distinction that seemed to offer more in the way of economic advancement than Oxford and was likely to be less demanding in terms of academic accomplishment. But even these were sometimes under-subscribed. Another factor which has become increasingly evident over the last few years is that current legislation makes it incumbent on South African businesses to take on a growing proportion of young black employees. Any black men and women of ability leaving a South African university are likely to find them-selves overwhelmed by lucrative offers. To study abroad for another two or three years would be financially much less rewarding and might involve missing opportunities that would never recur. Kuseni Deamini, a leading spirit in the Rhodes Scholars' Southern African Forum, angrily protested that there must be 'many black students in Southern Africa who meet and exceed the Rhodes Scholarship criteria but ... are unsuccessful in the selection process'. 'Crass,' Ackermann found the charge; if only there were, how much easier things would be.[10]

In the dying days of apartheid it was unsurprising that young men and women of ambition and liberal ideas should look elsewhere to make a life for themselves. In 1988 the South-Africa-at-Large selection committee was told that of the 450–500 living Rhodes Scholars elected from South Africa, little more than half were at home; when only those chosen by the at-Large committee were considered the equivalent figure was a quarter. Things have improved notably since then; many more South African Rhodes Scholars now return home, but the economic temptations to stay away are still substan-tial. Cameron and his assistant, Isaac Shongwe, when they meet the successful new Scholars, stress that they have taken on responsibilities as well as privi-leges: 'There is a moral contract between you and the Trust.' There are many ways in which Rhodes Scholars can perform their part of the bargain but, unless there are compelling reasons to the contrary, Cameron believes that they should do so by serving their country in public or private life.

With the end of apartheid the Trust renewed its involvement in South Africa. The biggest single grant which it made was for the construction of All Africa House at the University of Cape Town, a building designed to enhance academic contact with faculty members and graduate students from all over Africa. When announcing the benefaction the Vice-Chancellor of UCT, Mamphela Ramphele, paid tribute to the vision of Cecil Rhodes, Smuts and their peers. 'It is sad', she went on, 'that their vision failed to acknowledge the inhumanity of racism and sexism. They must, however, find peace. . . . This installation ceremony presents us with an opportunity for ritual cleansing of the UCT community to enable us to tackle the future with greater confidence.'[11] It was only the most prominent of many similar grants. The Trust made up for the years of necessary neglect by lavishing more than £4 million on South African causes in the last decade of the twentieth century. A total of £450,000 was devoted to bursaries for disadvantaged students; £250,000 to under-privileged pupils; £300,000 to the Alexandra Health Centre. In the year 1995–6 there were more non-whites being educated in South Africa through the Trust's support than there were Rhodes Scholars at Oxford.[12] In 1994 George Parkin's granddaughter, Charity Grant, wrote to urge that the present South African Scholarships should be abolished and the money saved devoted to higher education for Africans. The Trustees were bound by the Will, Kenny replied. 'You will be glad to learn, however, that nearly 200 black Africans are being funded through High School and University in South Africa by funding from the Rhodes Trust.'[13] The greatest enterprise was still to be launched, but by the end of the century the debt that the Trust owed to the source of Rhodes's wealth was already being lavishly recognised.

As South Africa came back into the sunshine, so Rhodesia retreated into the shadows. In the decades after the Second World War its potential had seemed unlimited: prosperous, secure, with a growing black middle class and what promised to be a smooth passage to a country run by Africans yet in which the Europeans would have a role of economic and political significance. In theory the Rhodesian Rhodes Scholarships had always been open to black candidates, though in 1949 Elton admitted that he thought it unlikely that there would be a black Scholar in the near future 'for when it comes to the point, Selection Committees will probably fear to rouse prejudices and will more rationally feel that a negro needs to be very specially qualified if he is to fit happily into Oxford'.[14] Robert Tredgold, the forthrightly liberal Rhodes Scholar Chief Justice, saw no reason for selection committees to be so squeamish, but was alarmed when the South African universities were closed to black students. Since this was almost the only route by which a black Rhodesian could hope to compete realistically for a Scholarship, it seemed as if he would be effectively excluded before any selection committee could screw up its courage sufficiently to select him.[15] By the time he wrote to Elton on the subject, however, the University of Southern Rhodesia had been established. It was 1960 before the first Rhodesian won a Rhodes Scholarship direct from his national university, but higher education was now available in the country and Tredgold's worst fears were allayed.

They were soon revived; a right-wing government cut back on the country's progress towards black majority rule and the inexorable march was on towards the 1965 Unilateral Declaration of Independence and the calamities that followed it. The selection committee refused to be cowed and the following year chose its first non-white Scholar, an Indian medical student called Ramanial Gokal. 'That you should have the guts to do it at this juncture and where you are stationed, commands my admiration,' Williams wrote to the local Rhodes Secretary. 'Let us all pray that he does well: it will be so needful.'[16] (Gokal did do well but, unsurprisingly, never returned to Rhodesia.) By then the short-lived federation of the two Rhodesias and Nyasaland had perished. Zambia, as Northern Rhodesia had become after independence, refused to have anything to do with its southern neighbour, so the three Scholarships were eventually administered separately – one to each and one alternating between them.

Ian Smith's UDI in 1965 involved another Rhodes Scholar Chief Justice, though of a very different political bent to Tredgold. Three years after Smith had decided that Rhodesia should go it alone, Sir Hugh Beadle announced that the *de facto* government which had then taken control was now permanently established and should be recognised *de jure*. The Rhodesian Scholars, who for the most part deplored the attitude of Smith's regime, increasingly remade their lives abroad. The ripples caused by the disturbances in Rhodesia even lapped at the doors of Rhodes House in Oxford. Traditionally the Anglo-Rhodesian Society had always been allowed by the Warden to hold its meetings there. In 1970, alarmed by the hostility which the policy of Smith's government had aroused in the University, the Society asked for police protection at one of its meetings. Unfortunately, it omitted to consult the Warden before doing so. Williams was concerned by the fact that the politically less-informed tended to associate the Rhodes Trust with the Rhodesian government. Rhodes House had already been the scene of demonstrations. When he found a police car parked outside his front door protecting a meeting of a body that was supposed to support Smith's activities, he was infuriated. He banned the Society from meeting in Rhodes House again. Robert Cranborne, whose family had long been associated with Rhodesia and whose ancestor had given the capital its name of Salisbury, was in his turn affronted. 'I find the attitude of the Trust extraordinary,' he wrote, 'in that, because they have received highly illegal treatment from unauthorised persons, they are prepared to be bullied into a course they would otherwise not have adopted. . . . I wonder whether you pause to consider what Cecil Rhodes himself would have thought of such an attitude. I should have thought it was an insult to his memory.'[17] Rhodes, who was strikingly pragmatic when it came to matters constitutional, would probably have thought that Smith was an ass to have put himself into an untenable position and that the Trust was well advised to dissociate itself from his activities. For Williams, however, who deplored extremism whatever its political hue and who had doubts about the future of Rhodesia if a black government took over, Cranborne's rebuke must have made painful reading.

In due course the inevitable happened; Smith fell and a black government took over. Visiting Zimbabwe, as it had by then become, in 1989, Kenny found it 'an invigorating constituency'. The Rhodes Scholars, whatever their attitudes had been during the civil war which had raged over the preceding years, 'were now fully reconciled and full of optimism'. Race relations were 'excellent'.[18] If the Rhodes Scholars had been put in charge they would have remained excellent. But already there were signs that the reconciliation had been less than total. Statues of Rhodes in Harare and Bulawayo were pulled down and Rhodes's grave in the Matopos hills became a political issue. Robert Mugabe, Prime Minister and then President of Zimbabwe, was in favour of leaving it where it was as an encouragement to tourism: the bones did nobody any harm, he said, but 'we want to make them pay taxes'.[19] On less cosmetic issues he took a harder line; shortly after Kenny visited Harare the University of Zimbabwe was closed, only to reopen when purged of any elements that Mugabe deemed subversive. Today, with the economy destroyed and only a simulacrum of democracy allowed, a mere handful of Rhodes Scholars remain in the country. They try gallantly to keep the system going and continue to operate a selection committee which each year sends two Scholars to Oxford. Zimbabwe provides 'a stream of excellent Scholars', wrote Kenny in 1998,[20] and the supply of talented and enthusiastic candidates shows no signs of drying up. But the selectors know that, unless things change dramatically, it is highly unlikely that any of the successful Scholars will return to Zimbabwe. A Rhodes Scholarship has become a passport, allowing the best of Zimbabwean youth to make its future somewhere else. No one can blame the Scholars or the selectors but, far more than the expulsion of the Anglo-Rhodesian Society from Rhodes House, this tragic situation is an insult to the memory of Cecil Rhodes.

CHAPTER FORTY-FOUR

THE EUROPEAN EXPERIMENT

From time to time in the past there had been desultory efforts to persuade the Trustees that the Scholarships might legitimately be extended to Europe. In 1920 a group of Swiss industrialists said they were eager to reduce German influence on their country and urged the creation of a Rhodes Scholarship for Switzerland. Money, it was hinted, would be no problem. Edward Grigg torpedoed that initiative, arguing that it would be impossible to create Scholarships outside the Empire 'without raising some very invidious questions as to other countries'.[1] Twenty-five years later Grigg's son, John, raised the possibility of a Scholarship for France. 'Quite impracticable,' ruled Elton. 'The Founder's whole concern was for the British Commonwealth and the Anglo-Saxon world.'[2] After Britain joined the European Community the issue was again revived. This time Fletcher opposed the idea, holding that to extend the Scholarships to Europe would be 'contrary to the terms of the Public Purposes Trust'. It was to take the signing of the Treaty of Maastricht and the advent of the expansionist Kenny as Warden to move the Trustees towards Europe. Kenny argued that the Public Purposes Trust was not exclusively reserved for the benefit of Commonwealth and United States citizens. In 1963 counsel's opinion had been that the Fund could properly be used to pay for the German or other foreign Scholarships. With the last instalment about to be paid to the Trust's commitment to the Oxford Appeal there was money to spare for a dozen or so new Scholarships. Where would they be more valuable than in Europe?[3]

It is at least questionable whether Cecil Rhodes would have supported Britain's entry into the Community, let alone the signature of the Maastricht Treaty, but that supreme pragmatist would almost certainly have come to terms with the fact of Europe and have sought to incorporate it into his vision. That, anyway, was the view of Kenny, strongly supported by Robert Armstrong. Baring hankered after Scholarships for Arabs but was prepared to accept the case for Europe; with varying degrees of enthusiasm the other

Trustees agreed that the experiment should be made. Certain preliminary questions had first to be answered. On the analogy of the at-Large Scholarships in Australia or South Africa it could be said that Germans who had failed to secure a Rhodes Scholarship in their own country should be allowed to compete in the European arena. The Trustees decided, however, that a fourth German Scholarship should instead be created and Germany excluded from the new competition. Then there was the problem of picking the European Scholars. If the scheme prospered and became established it was hoped that selection committees might eventually be set up in all the countries of the Community, but in the short term that seemed impracticable. Instead it was decided that the Scholars should be drawn from that large and rapidly increasing body of European students who had already secured a place at Oxford. Applicants from this group would be sifted in Rhodes House and those on the short list interviewed by a panel of Trustees. It was decided that eight Scholars a year would be elected for three years: after that the future of the European Scholars should be reviewed.

Even among the Trustees there were doubters who felt that this was an improper use of Rhodes's money; among the wider Rhodes community there was some indignation. Wieland Gevers, a professor at the University of Cape Town and one of South Africa's most eminent scientists, complained that 'the emphasis of the Trust on the former or present dominions is being lost or at least down-graded in favour of . . . recruiting elite students from the developed world'.[4] The concept of the 'developed world' is flexible – it could reasonably be contended that a large majority of Rhodes Scholars come from developed countries – but Gevers articulated a view held by many that this was not what the Scholarship scheme was supposed to be about. The Trustees were committed, however, and by February 1992 more than 130 applications had been received. In so far as the question had been considered, the expectation had been that the largest number of the candidates would come from France, Italy and perhaps The Netherlands; in fact fifty came from Ireland, twenty-seven from Greece and only seventeen from France. In the event eight Scholarships were awarded: three to Greece, two to Ireland and one each to France, Italy and Denmark. The qualifications of the successful candidates were almost a parody of the genre: Barbara Crostini was planning a dissertation on the eleventh-century monastic author Paul of Evergetis – 'she is active in half a dozen sports and enjoys mosaic-making and singing Gregorian chant. She worked for Ethiopian refugees in Rome and has a keen interest in Christian scholarship'. Ioannis Kelemanis was a concert pianist who had won the Homerian award for young poets, was a long-jumper at the Pan-Hellenic Games and was a member of the basketball team which had twice won the Aegean Cup.[5]

In 1992, after the preliminary sifting, the final list of serious applicants had been cut down to forty-six; the following year it was only twenty-two. Again the largest groups were Irish or Greek; where candidates came from other countries there was sometimes confusion over nationality – a French winner turned out to have an American mother and to have spent much of her life in the United States. Eight worthy Scholars were elected, but in 1994, though applications were slightly more numerous, the Trustees responsible for selection felt that only six candidates deserved a Scholarship – two from Ireland, one each from Greece, Italy, France and Spain.

The time had come to reconsider the future of the European Scholarships. It was obvious that the scheme had failed to make the hoped-for impact in the larger countries. Even the Director of the British Council in Paris early in 1995 professed never to have known that Rhodes Scholarships were open to French citizens: 'perhaps it is a new development', he ventured.[6] Kenny reviewed the situation and sadly concluded that the scheme had not fulfilled the hopes of the Trustees. Academically the scholars had performed well, but the distribution of the Scholarships bore no relation to the size and power of the eligible countries: in three years, seven Scholars had come from Ireland, six from Greece, only three from France. 'Four years ago the Trustees would have been very unlikely to approve a proposal to set up two-Scholars-a-year competitions for Ireland and for Greece, but the effect achieved has been the same.' Often the successful candidates were by background more British or North American than European; one alleged Dane 'appeared to the uninformed eye a typical Harvard Iranian, and he has now gone to Washington to work on the *New Republic*'. Few of the European Scholars had contributed to sporting or any other extra-curricular life and the process of selecting them had proved haphazard and difficult to organise.[7] The Trustees decided to try for one more year, but though the total number of applications went up the imbalance continued; four of the successful candidates were Irish.

In the late summer of 1996 the moment of truth arrived. The Trustees were canvassed for their opinions and by a majority of five to three decided that the European Scholarships should be ended. The Trust, said William Waldegrave, should 'stick to its last, which should be trans-Atlantic and old Commonwealth with a growing concentration on Africa'. Mary Moore considered that the Rhodes system was not suited to continental Europeans 'who don't want to be good at competitive sport, don't necessarily want to "take an active part in college life", don't need to be introduced to the concept of formal dinners – and whose homes are sometimes closer to Oxford than those of many Scots undergraduates'. Kenny admitted that, having once been an enthusiast for the European Scholarships, he had become lukewarm as a result of the experiment.[8] There was some tentative support for a compromise which would have involved setting up selection committees, initially only in France and Italy, to pick an annual Scholar, but even this was too much for John Sainsbury, who did not think the Scholarships should be carried on in any form: 'Their contribution unavoidably detracted from the Trustees' ability to promote causes more germane to the purposes of the Trust.'[9] Before anything could be done to implement the compromise a benefaction from elsewhere provided for twelve students from the European Community to study each year at Oxford. With some relief the Trustees reckoned that this let them off the hook. To appease their consciences they made substantial grants to support the *entente cordiale* Scholarships, a scheme devised by a former British Ambassador in Paris, Christopher Mallaby, for an exchange of students between Britain and France.

The European Scholarships did not die unmourned. A group of European Scholars pleaded that to abandon the scheme would be to proclaim that the Trust was hostile to the idea of Europe. The fact that so many of the successful candidates were Irish or Greek was a reason for trying harder in the other countries, not for giving up altogether. Rhodes himself would have 'wanted his Scholarship to be the vehicle for bringing European students closer to Britain and its culture, rather than shutting them out'.[10] Athena Tsingarida, prime mover in the bid to save the Scholarships, claimed that the European Scholars had 'all forged inextricable ties with Britain, her culture and her people'. Surely all that should not be thrown away?[11] The answer, of course, was that those links could have been formed without the intervention of the Trustees; it was their responsibility to concentrate on those who might otherwise not have been able to come to Oxford and to build up those links within the English-speaking world which had been the chief preoccupation of the Founder. This had been as true in 1992 as it was in 1996; it took the failure of the European Scholarships to remind the Trustees of their roots.

In the sixty-odd years since the Second World War the concept of a Commonwealth bound by strong ties that are economic and political as well as emotional has grown increasingly hard to sustain. Should the Trustees, therefore, conclude that the intentions of Cecil Rhodes are irrelevant to the present day and that his Scholarships should be redeployed to serve the interests of Britain in the twenty-first century? Or should it be their concern to foster what ties remain, among the most potent of which are the Rhodes Scholarships? The Trust today does little actively to promote the Commonwealth; if it supports any organisation working to such an end it is more as a nostalgic gesture to the past than with hopes of reversing the tide of history. But the English-speaking world is very much a reality. Canada, Australia, India, Kenya cannot be expected to shape their policies to suit Great Britain, but Canadians, Australians, Indians, Kenyans can still be encouraged to look to Britain to sustain certain shared cultural and social values. Numerically, the Rhodes Scholarships may not be enough to make a significant difference to this work; historically and psychologically they remain of the first importance. The abandonment of the European Scholarships in 1996 showed that in the minds of the Trustees, though the world has changed, some at least of the old values still prevail.

PART V

Present and Future

CHAPTER FORTY-FIVE
CAREERS

Rhodes's wish, as set out in his Will, was that his Scholars should 'esteem the performance of public duties' as their highest aim. What did he mean by 'public duties'? That a Scholar should become Prime Minister of South Africa and add two new countries to the British Empire might have been his reply, but in spite of Dr Jameson's insistence that Rhodes's ideal Scholar would have been a clone of himself it does not seem that he had any such extravagant expectations. It was enough that they should serve the society in which they lived and, by one means or another, contribute significantly to its well-being.

Though the careers that the former Rhodes Scholars followed varied from time to time and from country to country the overall pattern remained remarkably constant. By far the largest number – almost a third of the whole – worked in the field of education; the great majority of these in higher education. Rhodes viewed university dons with a curious mixture of reverence and contempt. Though he would certainly have felt it proper that some of his Scholars should make the education of the next generation their prime occupation, it seems likely that he would have considered things had gone too far: the world's fight was best fought in the streets and market places, not in the dusty corridors of academe. And yet that view would also have been modified as he realised that the world of the great universities was no longer, if it ever had been, cut off from public affairs. When a Rhodes Scholar became President of Harvard he was taking on a role of importance outside his own campus; far from living 'secluded from the world' he was at the very heart of national life. In the United States in particular, but also in every developed country, senior academics can wield influence if not power as considerable as that of the politician and civil servant. The 'remote and ineffectual don' whom Hilaire Belloc derided is today as likely as not to be also a shrewd businessman or an adept performer on television.

Nevertheless, over the last decades there has been a perceptible movement away from the universities and schools. The second most favoured profession, that of the law, has suffered from no such loss of popularity. The concept of a lawyer is infinitely elastic. Lawyers may be primarily academics; some of the most distinguished professors of jurisprudence have been Rhodes Scholars. They may move into business – at first, probably, to advise on legal issues, often continuing to become a major force in the making of policy. They may become politicians; more Senators, Congressmen, Members of Parliament, have started their life as lawyers than in any other occupation. Most Rhodes Scholar lawyers, however, passed their lives within the bounds of their profession. Those who become judges were by any criterion performing public duties. Others were patently concerned with issues that transcended their own careers. Cecil Rhodes might not have shared the political views of Bram Fischer, but he could only have admired the courage and self-sacrifice of this South African lawyer who eschewed the rewards which his talents and privileged background would have guaranteed him and instead defended the accused at some of the country's most significant political trials, saved Nelson Mandela from the death penalty and eventually himself died in prison. Where Rhodes might have felt regrets was at the number of his Scholars who earned good money and respectable reputations in legal practice but did little outside it. They did nothing wrong but, in Rhodesian terms, not much that was right; it was not for this that they had been picked out from the pack as the daring young spirits who would create a new society.

Rhodes might have had similar reservations about the third-largest group among his former Scholars, the government employees. Even more than was the case with the academics and the lawyers, the number of Rhodes Scholar civil servants in each country varied according to the vagaries of the times. In Canada in the 1950s and 1960s there was a higher incidence of Rhodes Scholars at or near the top of the administration than was the case in any other country at any other period. Michael Howarth imagined Rhodes visiting Ottawa in 1961 and finding some sixty Scholars on the national payroll.* Twenty years later and they would almost all have vanished. Probably he would have concluded that the former state of affairs was better than the latter: hard-working, incorruptible and intelligent public servants, keeping their country running, were doing work in which any Rhodes Scholar could take pride. But, as Howarth suggests, Rhodes would not have been satisfied if his Scholars had *all* been civil servants; he was himself a buccaneer and a crusader and he would have hoped that some at least of those who followed him would eschew the conventional path and seek out new worlds to conquer.

Probably he would have felt some sympathy for the increasing number of Scholars who, in the last decades of the twentieth century, moved to the world

*See p. 286 above.

of business. More than anything else, this movement can be associated with the vast and insatiably acquisitive management consultant firm of McKinsey and Company. In the mid-1980s this company decided that, in terms of both ability and prestige, Rhodes Scholars provided prime material for a recruitment programme. A team descended on Oxford, at one point even being allowed to instal itself in Rhodes House, tempting the Scholars with visions of mouth-watering starting salaries and unbounded prospects. Tom Wolfe's bad-ass intellectual Adam* explained to his girlfriend Charlotte how the new aristo-meritocrat today had no obvious slot in public life so instead went into 'consulting for like . . . McKinsey. That's the one thing they shoot for, McKinsey.' Charlotte was puzzled. 'I still don't understand consulting,' she said. 'What do you consult *about*?' 'You get sent to these corporations and you tell them how to improve their . . . oh, I don't know, management techniques, I guess.' Charlotte was still not satisfied: 'How could they know how to do that if they've just graduated from college?' Adam floundered. 'Well, I suppose they . . . uh . . . have some kind of – to tell you the truth I don't know. I've wondered the same thing. But I know they do it, and they make a lot of money.'[1] Many Rhodes Scholars believed they had 'some kind of –' and the recruiters for McKinsey were not being naive when they calculated that it was worth investing in these young men and women. Even though some fell swiftly by the wayside, most of those who joined McKinsey or other organisations of similar stature, like the investment bankers Goldman Sachs, quickly picked up the tricks of their trade and were worth the 'lot of money' which Adam confidently predicted they would earn.

Whether they were thereby doing work which fulfilled the expectations placed on them by the Rhodes Trust is another matter. Having at first offered McKinsey a cautious welcome, Rhodes House soon concluded that a career in management consultancy was not a proper crown to a Rhodes Scholarship. One recent American Rhodes Scholar remembers Kenny complaining about the pressure that had been brought to bear by McKinsey on another Scholar and exhorting him to remember the injunction of Cecil Rhodes that the highest aim of the Scholar should be to take up public service. Those who nevertheless succumbed to the blandishments of McKinsey or the like could protest that a successful career in business did not preclude active involvement in charity or community affairs. Perhaps more convincingly, they could plead that they took a job with McKinsey so as to build up a little capital and acquire useful experience before starting on the real work of life. Often this claim could be justified. Roy Bahel took a job with McKinsey but within a few years

*See p. 280 above.

had abandoned it to work with Mayor Bloomberg in New York as an economic development policy adviser, part of a group charged with creating the city's vision for rebuilding downtown.[2] Ross Garland started with Lehmann Brothers but rapidly moved into the film world in South Africa and was responsible for *Carmen in Kyalitsha*, a film that was both brilliantly entertaining and contained a strong social content.[3] Susan Dando from Tasmania was an idealist who rejected the overtures of McKinsey to work in the public sector. Now she is employed by a business which pays her a salary far larger than that earned by her two teacher parents put together, but she intends this to be for a few years only; if she marries and has children she will find a job in the public service, if she does not, she will go into politics.[4]

There is every reason to believe that she will be as good as her word. But though many Rhodes Scholars who have accepted lucrative posts in the business world do so with the best possible intentions about the future conduct of their life, by the time they are in their thirties, used to a comfortable style of living and with children to support, the arguments against a change of career in favour of something more altruistic can appear compelling. Though a change in the economic climate of the developed world over the last decade has meant that fewer Scholars are being drawn away into the world of business, there are many from the 1980s and 1990s who are now firmly ensconced in the more prestigious boardrooms and who seem unlikely to venture back into a more rugged world.

Successful businessmen are relatively common among Rhodes Scholars, yet there are few indeed who can stand comparison with the Founder when it comes to the amassing of a fortune. It is curious that a system which has nurtured a President of the United States and a crop of Prime Ministers should have produced scarcely any business tycoons of truly heroic standing. John Templeton, who acquired a gigantic fortunate through the mutual fund business, is one of the exceptions. Through his Foundation he gives away millions of dollars every year, his benefactions have ensured that his name was given to an Oxford college, his yearly Templeton Prize for Progress in Religion is more valuable than the Nobel Prize and has been won, *inter alia*, by Mother Teresa, Brother Roger of Taizé and Billy Graham. He can legitimately claim that a career in big business is compatible with the moral obligations imposed on those who have won a Rhodes Scholarship. Another more recent recruit to the ranks of the billionaires is the Canadian John MacBain, who has built up the world's largest company in the local classified advertising sector. Local advertising, like mutual funds, does not immediately appear to provide the sort of field in which Rhodes would have expected his Scholars to excel, but MacBain proposes to rival Templeton in his altruism. He is in the process of selling out his companies so as to establish a giant charitable foundation which will concentrate its spending on the needs of Africa.[5] There have been and are other Scholars of considerable, even gigantic wealth and most of them have made similarly responsible use of their fortunes. On the whole, though, it does not seem that the selection process is calculated to produce that curious combination of qualities which is to be found in the economic empire builder.

When the class of 1931 reviewed its experiences in the *American Oxonian* one contributor, a politician, claimed that he had found the label of 'Rhodes Scholar' positively a disadvantage in his career. In this he was exceptional if not unique. Some say that the fact that they had won a Rhodes Scholarship made little difference in their working life; most admit that the prestige attached to the award was certainly a help in getting started and in some cases retained its potency for a lifetime. Delroy Chuck, prominent in Jamaican politics, found that it was taken for granted that he must be brilliant. Sometimes this caused resentment – 'You damned Rhodes Scholar,' a political opponent had called out when he opposed the death penalty in a recent debate – but always too it commanded respect. 'We expect better than that from a Rhodes Scholar' had been a minister's response when Chuck criticised his policies.[6] In the Canadian parliament a member commented on the number of Scholars in the higher ranks of the civil service. The reason they advanced so quickly, he said, 'lies not only in the talent that they have but through their prestige and status, given by Scholarships. There is a label on them when they go into the public service to the effect that these boys are good, so they get somewhere.'[7] He might have added that the label meant that others in the public service recognised them, knew about their abilities and gave them a helping hand. Not many Scholars have been appointed to posts for which they were ill-qualified because they travelled under the flag of Rhodes, but, other things being equal, there was a natural tendency to pick the man or woman whose Scholarship gave them an established position, a guarantee of quality. Sometimes the tendency was still more marked; there is one case at least in which a high official charged with setting up a new governmental agency simply circularised all the Rhodes Scholars in the country who were of more or less the right seniority and offered them jobs. By the time he finished, five out of the six most important positions were held by Scholars. At West Point, George Lincoln ensured that there were never fewer than six Rhodes Scholars with him in the Department of Social Sciences. Since, with a wartime break, he was there from 1937 to 1968, a considerable number of Scholars enjoyed his patronage.[8]

A great many Rhodes Scholars do not fit into one of the three most favoured categories. There is a bevy of politicians; many members of the

armed forces; doctors and surgeons; religious figures of various denomi-
nations; scientists; writers; economists. Some preferred to have no career at
all: Roger Sorrell informed the *American Oxonian* from Honolulu that he
continued 'to enjoy life on the Islands where he is playing the piano and
singing nightly with his long-term partner, David'.[9] But such eccentrics are
rare – Sorrell, indeed, may well have been indulging in a playful fantasy. The
vast majority of Rhodes Scholars diligently pursue careers of dignity and some
importance; they are either employed in public service or devote a fair
proportion of their energies to working in some way in the public interest.

The advent of women does not seem notably to have affected the balance of
Scholars among the various professions, though it has reduced the incidence
of worldly success. Professor Youn has noted that, of the twenty-four female
American Rhodes Scholars in the classes of 1997 and 1998, only one appeared
in *Who's Who*. Of the forty men from the same period, thirteen did.[10] A
mention in *Who's Who* is not an essential corollary of worldly success, but in
the United States it is a significant indication of how well established an individual is in his or her profession. What is true in the United States seems *a
fortiori* to apply in the other Rhodes constituencies. Yet at Oxford no similar
imbalance was to be found; in so far as comparisons are possible it could even
be said that women have tended to outshine men. For some reason they fail to
build upon this foundation in later life. It is still, of course, a man's world; even
in the comparatively civilised surroundings in which most Scholars work, the
dice are loaded against the women. Driving ambition is far from being a
uniquely masculine attribute, but it does not so often seem to be so dominant
in the female. Most important of all, the almost impossible demands of
combining conscientious motherhood with a full-time job were imposed on
many of the women Rhodes Scholars at a stage in their careers when total
dedication was most called for. In September 2002 a hundred or so assembled
in Washington for an American Women Rhodes Scholars reunion (in itself a
curious concept when, to a mere male, it seems that the whole point of the
Scholarships since 1976 is that there should be no sexual discrimination).
Woman after woman spoke about her successes, her failures, her problems,
her aspirations. Then came a woman who said that she had given up her
career for her children and felt that, by the standards of the Rhodes
Scholarships, she had been a success. The applause was tumultuous and heart-
felt; almost every woman there felt some sympathy for the speaker. It is harder
to be sure how many of them shared her conclusion or felt moved to act upon
it. It is perhaps some presage of this conflict which explains why, though 54
per cent of US students are women, the proportion of female applicants for
Rhodes Scholarships is about one in three. Women's colleges in America do

not seem to encourage their students to apply, and women Scholars are notably slower to join the Association of American Rhodes Scholars. As Martina Vandenberg put it in 1991: 'The stereotypical Rhodes Scholar is male, white, went to the Olympics or plays professional sport, plans to enter politics and graduated from Harvard. Enough evidence supports this stereotype to make it daunting.'[11]

CHAPTER FORTY-SIX

NEW WORLDS

Early in 1999 Anthony Kenny sought to establish what, at the end of the millennium, an ideal Rhodes Scholar should be. He would, Kenny concluded, be someone able 'to get at least an upper second in Schools, or a pass in an MPhil, or to complete a dissertation; who competes in at least one sport at least at College level; who takes part in University societies of some social value (eg concerned with the welfare of the Third World); and who takes some part in the MCR [middle common room] government or the leadership of other Oxford organisations'. It was still the expectation of the Trustees that, as well as enjoying 'an opportunity for making international friendships', the Scholar should gain 'an experience of College life' and 'an immersion in British culture'.[1] By the time Kenny wrote, it was open to question whether this was something to which the Scholars themselves would aspire and whether the policies of Oxford and the individual colleges made such an aspiration practicable.

For one thing the admissions policy of the colleges ensured that the good all-rounder would less often be acceptable. The fact that if they did not excel academically one candidate was an almost certain cricket blue, another a pianist of repute, a third had done wonders among Eritrean refugees, was picturesque detail which might impress the members of a selection committee but meant less to the average tutor for admissions. For them the academic standing of the candidates was the thing that counted most; the painstaking evaluations of the selectors went for little. Even if potential all-rounders gained a place in an Oxford college they would find academic demands had to be satisfied before they could indulge in any serious display of their talents. In 1959 the *American Oxonian* had reported of the singer and musician Kris Kristofferson that 'He is reading English, writing a novel, boxing for the university and – if you will forgive my quoting *Time*, is "in a fair way to become wealthy as a guitar-thwonking singing idol". A half century later it is unlikely that even if his college, Merton, had accepted him he would have found so much time to box, write his novel or even thwonk his guitar.

The collegiate experience, the principal reason Rhodes gave for assigning his Scholarships to Oxford, plays a smaller part in the life of today's Scholars. They live in a middle common room where a high proportion of their companions will be foreign; they see little of undergraduate life, play fewer games and often, though by no means invariably, take a relatively small part in the life of the college. The e-mail and cheap air travel ensure that they remain far more closely in touch with friends and relations at home than would have been true of their parents or grandparents. This is not always the case. Juliana Horseman, a Scholar from Bermuda who was at St John's in the early 1990s after four years at Stanford, had expected to make most of her friends among the postgraduates but found that this meant spending her time 'secluded with thirteen Germans talking about Wittgenstein'. She reverted to undergraduate life, finding her new companions far more mature than their American counterparts.[2] Nor need the shift to postgraduate work and the existence of a middle common room inevitably weaken the collegiate tie. Prosser Gifford, one of a succession of Rhodes Scholars who, over several decades, have helped run the Library of Congress, believes that his college, Merton, has been markedly successful in accommodating postgraduates and junior fellows within the college and involving them in college life.[3] Oxford itself has changed and is changing and inevitably the experience of the Rhodes Scholars must change with it. As the postgraduate world – to which the overwhelming majority of Rhodes Scholars now belongs – becomes more solidly established, so the Scholars themselves will become less isolated. One can reasonably hope that fewer Scholars will share the experience of Sarah Kelly, a South Australian who rejected the overtures of McKinsey and is now working in the Cabinet Office in Canberra. She had no contact with the undergraduates and very little with the British postgraduates, not from any prejudice on her part but because she found that the British had usually been undergraduates at Oxford, had already formed their groupings and showed little enthusiasm for looking further afield.[4] Given a chance, she would have been happy to integrate with the local community. The same cannot be said for another Australian Rhodes Scholar, Richard Flanagan, who, in an intemperate interview with the *Sunday Tasmanian*, denounced English students as 'ignorant bores'. Oxford, in his view, was a 'fairly despicable place. They have made mediocrity a virtue and called it a tradition.' The way to get on was 'to socialise and sodomise with the right people', though even without recourse to such measures it was almost impossible to fail academically: 'I have met people who sit their exam in a drunken stupor and who had done no work, and they still pass.' If the Rhodes system was intended to make friends for Oxford and Great

Britain, it conspicuously failed with Flanagan; to be fair he found his fellow
Scholars almost equally repellent – 'the common denominator was crude
ambition'.[5]

Flanagan's denunciation of Oxford was exceptionally rancorous, but other
Rhodes Scholars were critical of what they found there. The Americans were
particularly quick to denounce the University's deficiencies. Susan Craighead,
in the *American Oxonian*, claimed that many first-year Americans were
'astounded by the inefficiency of the library, sleepy graduate seminars, the
high proportion of useless lectures, the inadequacy of laboratories, the eccentricity of some of the famed Oxford dons and the general unhurried pace of
the place. Oxford was nothing like the efficient corporations that had so
recently produced us.' But these were first impressions; with time, she
believed, would come a change of heart. The Scholar would discover that 'If
one is able to capitalise on Oxford's academic strengths, this can be a very
exciting place to be indeed. It is a question of bringing expectations in line
with reality.' Within a few months she had been seduced still further: 'Oxford
turns out to be a place where most of us are happy (where else can you drink
poetry and read red wine till all hours of the night? I recently revealingly
observed to a friend).'[6] Craighead wrote in 1988; two decades later she would
have found the laboratories and library rather more efficient but she might
have had less time for poetry and red wine.

The Rhodes Scholar at the end of the twentieth century was certainly more
ready to criticise and to challenge the establishment. In 1998 Julia Seirlis from
Zimbabwe proposed that the distribution of research grants should in future
not be decided by the Trustees but 'determined democratically by a general
assembly of Scholars'. She also demanded that the Trustees allow Scholars to
return to research in their home countries.[7] This last suggestion was one
that the Trust had always resisted. Some Americans, felt Kenny, already
considered the need to study at Oxford a slightly irritating price that had to be
paid for the privilege of describing themselves as Rhodes Scholars; nothing
would please them more than to claim the honour, accept the stipend and
then spend the next years in a library at Harvard. The Trustees considered the
possibility of relaxing the rule when Scholars from some developing country
put forward a strong case for following a line of research in their home
country, but decided against it. The Scholarships, they reaffirmed, should be
seen 'primarily as opportunities to study at Oxford, and secondarily as opportunities for broadening one's horizon by making acquaintance with cultures
other than one's own'.[8] Kenny, indeed, felt that the whole business of academic
tourism was getting out of control. 'I don't understand why people explore the
world before they explore Oxford,' he complained. 'It's true that Cecil Rhodes
thought travelling abroad was a means of broadening both your own horizon

and those of others, and that experience with other cultures was the way to world peace. But he meant a lot of the cross-cultural mixing to occur by bringing scholars here, rather than sending them elsewhere.' The requests of Scholars became ever more exotic: 'We are still waiting for the application to study the tourism industry in Bali.'[9]

There had always been an assumption at Rhodes House that a Rhodes Scholarship was the ultimate honour, which no one in their senses would contemplate refusing. The authorities at Oxford were not wholly immune to a similar belief about their University. By the end of the twentieth century both assumptions were being challenged. Reporting to the Trustees on a meeting of the Rhodes National Secretaries in June 2001, the recently appointed Warden, John Rowett, spoke of 'puzzlement over what appeared to be a lack of recognition in Oxford that those chosen as Scholars have, because of their quality, opportunities to study at the best universities in the world'. John Hood, Secretary in New Zealand, Vice-Chancellor of the University of Auckland and soon himself to plunge into the minefield by becoming Vice-Chancellor at Oxford, had emphasised that Harvard, Yale and Stanford were competing for those chosen for Rhodes Scholarships and that 'there was an increasing danger that we should begin to lose them to those universities'.[10] Though the Rhodes Scholarships had become reserved for candidates of high academic ability, this was not necessarily perceived by those in American or Commonwealth universities who were responsible for pointing their students in what they thought to be the most appropriate direction. In the United States Kenny several times encountered the perception that the really outstanding academic candidate should apply for a Marshall Scholarship rather than a Rhodes.[11]

Oxford had in fact changed substantially since Rhodes had known it. In 2000 it was still a federation of largely autonomous colleges, the main function of most of which was the teaching of undergraduates by the tutorial method. But, no doubt to Rhodes's posthumous regret, it is now substantially dependent on government funding, it is no longer devoted almost entirely to the liberal arts, it is no longer overwhelmingly British (although there are well over two hundred Rhodes Scholars in residence at any time, this is still less than 10 per cent of the overseas student body) and it contains a large number of graduate students. If it had not evolved in this way then, in spite of the prestige of the brand image, Rhodes Scholars would no longer wish to come to Oxford in any numbers; the changes, of course, cause some dismay to the traditionalists, but they are inevitable, even overdue. The Rhodes Scholars of today do not want to live the collegiate life of a glorified schoolboy which had given such gratification to their parents. The proportion of Scholars reading for a second BA grows ever smaller: partly because the Scholars hanker for something more sophisticated and tailored to their own requirements; partly because, as a notch on an academic curriculum vitae, it carried little weight in other countries. The National Secretaries, though careful to leave the decision in the hands of the Scholars, have been known to direct the abler student towards postgraduate work. The result is that, with some conspicuous exceptions, those taking BAs tend to be the weaker candidates. In 1990 Kenny said that, if Rhodes House had been graded as a college on the Norrington table, it would have come twentieth out of twenty-eight: 'As usual, it is the PPE results which pull us down – seven 2–2s and two 3s this year.'[12]

For the postgraduate, Oxford now offers a bewildering treasure-house of courses, many of them designed to meet the requirements of an individual. Zimbabwe, though consistently producing Rhodes Scholars of ability, is not among the most intellectually evolved of the constituencies. Over the last few years the subjects Zimbabwean Scholars have studied include 'Jewish, Classical and Christian allusions in some of St Jerome's writing', 'Super-novas and gamma ray bursts', 'Factors affecting fish distribution in the Virgin Islands' and 'Afromontane snakes: species boundaries, phylogenetics and physogeography'. (In contradiction to the thesis that Rhodes Scholars today seldom play any prominent part in college or University life it should be said that this same group of scholars produced one half-blue for rowing, two marathon runners, the vice-president of an MCR, a half-blue in rugby, an organiser of tsunami relief and a social officer for the Oxford African Society.) The one-year courses that Oxford now offers are attractive to many Scholars but less welcome to the Trustees, who are concerned lest Scholars should wish to call it a day after their first year's course. In the end they accepted that the Warden should authorise such courses, but only on condition that the Scholars agreed to pursue some other study in their second year. This is hard to enforce, particularly in the case of the MBA – Master of Business Administration – a course which has the additional disadvantages of being extremely expensive and of withdrawing students almost entirely from the life of their college. Of the five Scholars who read for the MBA in 1996–7, four had left Oxford by March 1998, though in several cases proclaiming an intention to return to take a doctorate within a few years. A possible solution was to authorise an MBA only for a second year, but in the end the Trust adopted the simpler if more drastic solution of banning the course altogether.

Faced by a new Oxford and new Scholars, with different needs and expectations, the Trust itself felt the need to adapt. Fletcher had believed that it should adopt a higher profile. Rhodes House should become better known as a centre, more distinguished guests should be invited to its celebrations, the

Warden should keep a fatherly eye on the other international Scholarships which to some degree owe their existence to Rhodes's original inspiration – 'all without trumpeting', he added anxiously, in a thoroughly British bid to avert a charge of soliciting publicity.[13] Robert O'Neill, the Australian Rhodes Scholar who was Chichele Professor of the History of War and had become a Trustee in 1995, believed that there was a growing gulf between the Trust and the National Secretaries, and even more between the Trust and the former Scholars. He proposed that some highly placed American living in the United States should be asked to become a Trustee: 'It is in North America that the Trust's interests are most powerfully served and where its reputation is most vulnerable – not least due to the impact of competition by other schemes.'[14] Nothing much seems to have been done about either of these suggestions, but the Trustees were left with a nagging sensation that, with the Empire gone, Oxford no longer the undisputed queen of the world's universities, and with a host of rival awards available, the Scholarships had lost their unique prestige. The Trust had somehow to redefine its role. Philip Whitcomb, a remarkable old gentleman who had become a Scholar in 1911, written more than twelve million words as a foreign correspondent and then, at the age of eighty-nine, secured a PhD in metaphysics, expressed their inchoate doubts when he complained that the Trustees had 'not yet found a modern equivalent for Cecil Rhodes's idealistic objective. Until they find it, the Rhodes Scholarships will drift closer and closer to becoming Nobel prizes for the exaltation of individualism, Olympic games with advanced degrees instead of medals.'[15]

Something was missing. Rough-and-ready though Rhodes's morality might have been it had still possessed a crude integrity. George Steiner, in rather different language, made the same point as Whitcomb. 'For all its talents, privileges, assiduities,' he wrote,

> our bunch has done damn little, if anything, to improve upon, to amend, to reduce, the political risks and follies which surround us. Many of us may have achieved lovely private lives, professional esteem, even a piece of schol-arship or argument worth putting forward. But is that what Rhodes had in mind? Or are the archaic ambiguities and myopias in his own initial programme now, ironically, confirmed by the temper and careers of those of us of whom he hardly would have approved?[16]

Certainly Rhodes would not have approved of Steiner: a cosmopolitan Jew born with a withered right arm, intellectual, iconoclastic, a 'mere bookworm' to end mere bookworms. Yet Steiner was saying something to which Rhodes would have responded and in which the Trustees saw much force. They were not looking for conspicuous reforms – indeed they rejected one candidate who proposed a radical change of direction – yet they sensed that something needed to be done. It was their feeling that a page had to be turned that in part led them in 1999 to appoint as Kenny's successor a historian from Brasenose, Dr John Rowett.

CHAPTER FORTY-SEVEN

MANDELA–RHODES

When the time had come for the Trustees to contemplate the appointment of a new Warden, Kenny set down for their benefit the main factors which he felt they had to consider. The General Secretary of the Trust and Warden, he observed, was 'the chief executive of a charitable Trust which is now about twentieth in size among those charities in the United Kingdom which depend on endowment'. It was his responsibility, apart from administering the Scholarships, ensuring the welfare of the Scholars and running Rhodes House, to sift and make recommendations on all the benefactions of the Trust. He had to maintain contact with the Scholars after they had left Oxford and liaise regularly with the Associations of Rhodes Scholars in the larger constituencies. Kenny stressed in particular that the domestic management of Rhodes House was a considerable task: 'It cannot be taken for granted that the spouse of an incoming Warden would be available or willing to take on these tasks.'[1]

John Rowett was younger and less well established than most of his predecessors; he had, however, served as a proctor, had been tutor for admissions at his college, Brasenose, and was very much at home in the labyrinth of Oxford government. The Trustees admired his energy and determination; he seemed to them the man to meet the needs of the times. He believed no task beyond him and disliked delegating anything but the most trivial chore – these two factors, taken together, were in time to subject both him and the organisation for which he worked to strains that were always uncomfortable and at times intolerable.

In the past, Wardens had always been careful not to build up Rhodes House as a centre to which Scholars could resort in preference to their college. Rowett took the view that this was largely a thing of the past. Whatever the Trustees might hope for, he felt that many Rhodes Scholars were enjoying little in the way of collegiate life. Not much, therefore, would be lost if they were encouraged to look to Rhodes House for the conveniences and for the companionship that were not available elsewhere. As a first step, the Warden developed in the basement of Rhodes House an IT centre open to all Rhodes Scholars.

The transfer from the Rhodes House Library to the newly opened Rothermere American Institute of the American collections belonging to the Bodleian opened the way for a still more radical reorganisation. Though the arrival of the papers of the Anti-Apartheid Movement was likely to attract researchers, the net result would inevitably be that the Library's reading room would be much less frequented than in the past. Rowett proposed that one end of the reading room should be converted into a centre where Rhodes Scholars could meet and other activities sponsored by the Trust take place. Fifty years before, Allen had predicted strong resistance if any attempt were made to change the nature of the Library.* It proved to be no less potent at the end of the century. More readers than the librarian had known existed rallied in defence of the status quo, a squall of protest blew up, and the Trustees postponed any radical change for the foreseeable future.

Another of Rowett's recommendations, which caused some alarm in Oxford, was that grants to colleges should be reduced so as to finance an increase in the Scholars' stipends. One head of house, he told the Trustees, had remarked that it had 'become a taken-for-granted assumption that the Trust can always be looked to for significant benefactions when colleges are mounting appeals'. The money, he believed, could better be directed to helping postgraduate Scholars who were in colleges that could or would do little to support them. An Indian scholar at St Peter's, for instance, was in dire financial difficulties; he saw his contemporaries in Magdalen doing much better and not unnaturally felt aggrieved.[2] In this case Rowett would have been perceived by the Scholars as acting in their interests; they felt less enthusiastic when he enforced the Trustees' growing opposition to their frequently expressed desire to take a third year of their Scholarship but to spend it at some other university – for instance, at the University of East Anglia for the celebrated course in creative writing. Courses of this kind were costing the Trust £70,000 a year, and, the Trustees felt, should be discontinued.

The radical departure with which Rowett was above all associated, however, related to Southern Africa. The idea seems to have had its genesis in 1998 in a letter to Kenny from the Rhodes Scholars Southern Africa Forum, a body which had once been the Rhodes Scholars against Apartheid but had changed its name when there was nothing left for them to be against. With the centenary less than five years away, the Forum felt that 'Rhodes Scholars around the

*See p. 236 above.

world have a unique opportunity to reflect upon the legacy and impact, on their own lives and on others through them, of Cecil John Rhodes.' It would be valuable 'to create an opportunity for every Rhodes Scholar, past and present, to participate in returning some benefit to the land and people of southern Africa'. What was needed was a 'Rhodes Centenary Trust fund, to enable the establishment of a significant and long-term sustainable development project in southern Africa. . . . We feel that it would be important to our sense of community that this should be a project fundamentally supported by individual scholars.' What they had in mind was some kind of Technology Resource Centre, in which the skills of Rhodes Scholars around the world could be recruited and put to use.[3]

Once installed as Secretary, Rowett eagerly took up the suggestion. He agreed that the emphasis should be on Southern Africa but felt that what was most needed was 'a bursary scheme in universities and a fellowship scheme focussed on academic staff in sciences and medicine, to enhance teaching and research capacity'. Then came the master-stroke. 'With a view to closing the circle of history in South Africa', Rowett suggested that both the bursary and the fellowship schemes should be named Mandela–Rhodes. The proposal was instantly accepted: the Trustees felt that such an enterprise would provide a thoroughly worthwhile focus for the Trust's activities in South Africa.[4] The coupling of the names of Mandela and Rhodes, from the point of view of public relations, was brilliantly conceived. In South Africa in particular Rhodes was associated with imperialism, exploitation of labour, cutting back the political rights of black Africans. If Mandela was prepared to enter into partnership with the ghost of Rhodes, then the Founder would become respectable, even honourable. One of the factors that discouraged black South Africans from putting themselves forward as candidates for Scholarships would have been removed. First Mandela had to agree, however. His more radical followers implored him not to do so, claiming that it would do grave harm to his reputation. In the unexpected pages of the *Daily Telegraph* Anthony Thomas exploded: 'To link the Rhodes name with Mandela is a blasphemy. It's unbelievable. It's linking the architect of apartheid with the exponent of its destruction. It shows terrible insensitivity.'[5] Mandela was unmoved. 'Pecunia non olet'* – a remark by the Emperor Vespasian which William Waldegrave drew to Mandela's attention while in Cape Town – seemed to him as valid in the twenty-first century as it had been in the first. He felt that the creation of a Mandela–Rhodes Foundation would complement the work that he was already doing and ensure that very substantial amounts of Rhodes

*Money doesn't smell.

Trust money would be channelled into the sector of South African education where it could do most good. The partnership between Mandela and Rhodes would express dramatically the reconciliation between the different races and cultures of South Africa which he had made the supreme purpose of his life since he had left prison.

The Trustees agreed that they would contribute £1 million a year for ten years, a sum which even in the heady days at the start of the new millennium, when the stock market seemed endlessly buoyant and the Trust was almost embarrassingly well-to-do, represented a considerable commitment. Rowett recognised that, both in Oxford and in the other Rhodes constituencies, the project might need some skilful selling. When he had urged the cessation of grants to Oxford colleges in favour of increased stipends for Scholars, one of his arguments had been that this would answer any concern that 'by developing Mandela–Rhodes we are weakening our commitment to our core business'.[6] In this he was successful: both among the Rhodes Scholars at Oxford and around the world, the initial reaction to Mandela–Rhodes was enthusiastic. But over the previous thirty years the University and its colleges had been accustomed to figuring also in the 'core business' of the Trust. 'It was agreed that care would be needed in the public presentation of the initiatives within the University of Oxford,' noted the Trustees with some apprehension. On the whole the colleges accepted with resignation, even with approval, the disappearance of this lucrative milch-cow from their byre. But there were complaints. Nor was the welcome given to the initiative in the other main constituencies as whole-hearted as Rowett at first believed. He claimed that in New Zealand, Australia and, most of all, the United States his exposition of the project had met with 'an amazingly positive response'. The President of Princeton had expressed the view of almost every university principal when he commented that Princeton had wished to try to operate such a scheme but had concluded that it would not be cost-effective to establish the necessary infrastructure. 'If the Rhodes Trust could meet that need he was certain that all major American universities would wish to be involved.' But when it occurred to people that the diversion of so much of the Trust's money to South Africa might mean that less was available for the Scholars, some critical voices were heard. A few American Rhodes Scholars were sharply opposed to the project, arguing that the Trust had already put back an extravagant amount into South Africa and that no further debt was owed to that constituency.

The Trustees were unworried by such symptoms of dissent, which, indeed, amounted to little. As the structure of Mandela–Rhodes evolved, its relationship to the Trust became more apparent. The first priority was to select Scholars who would attend a South African university and, if all went well, one day compete for a Rhodes Scholarship to Oxford. 'Proven intellectual and academic achievement of a high standard is the first quality required of applicants,' read the Concept Document, 'but they will also be required to show integrity of character, interest in and respect for their fellow human beings, the ability to lead, and the energy to use their talents to the full.'[7] 'Manly outdoor sports' were missing, but otherwise the sentiments would have been recognised and approved by Cecil Rhodes. The Trustees contemplated their creation with satisfaction. When Mandela–Rhodes was given its final approval in the autumn of 2001, they recorded their view 'that a decision of great historical significance had been taken both for the Rhodes Trust and for South Africa and that it was one that would echo down the ages' – a form of words which perhaps reflected the style of the Warden and writer of the minutes more than that of the Trustees themselves, but still conveyed their conviction that something momentous was being undertaken.[8]

The Foundation was formally unveiled when 750 Rhodes Scholars and their spouses met in Cape Town in February 2003 to celebrate the centenary of the Trust. It was a splendidly organised occasion, with banquets in some of South Africa's most beautiful houses, pilgrimages to Robben Island to visit the prison where Mandela had for so long been incarcerated and speeches by many of the most eminent and forward-looking of South Africans, admitting the fearful difficulties that lay ahead but striking so strong a note of hope and resolution that it was impossible not to share their faith in the future of their country.

The concept of Mandela–Rhodes was at the forefront of the festivities in South Africa – most markedly of all in the words of Mandela himself when he said: 'Combining our name with that of Cecil John Rhodes in this initiative is to sign the closing of the circle and the coming together of two strands of our history.' Considering the place and the circumstances, few if any questioned the prominence given to the new Foundation. Some doubts, however, were voiced when the festivities moved on to England. The highlight of the celebrations was a meeting in Westminster Hall. Clinton, the Prime Minister, Tony Blair, and Mandela were all on the platform. It was a cast list no other similar organisation could have matched and John Rowett could justifiably take pride in this crown placed upon his great enterprise. But a few Scholars wondered whether this was the most appropriate way to celebrate the Trust's centenary. He did not begrudge a penny of the Trust's beneficence towards South Africa, explained a West Australian Scholar; he warmly supported the Mandela–Rhodes Foundation; but was this all that the Rhodes Scholarships were about? No one complained, though, about the presence of Mandela at a reception for Rhodes Scholars in residence at Buckingham Palace later the same year: two monarchs from dramatically different backgrounds but meeting each other with obvious affection and respect amid the splendours of the State Apartments.

The small, dedicated and extremely hard-working staff of the Mandela–Rhodes Foundation set to work under the inspiring leadership of a Rhodes Scholar journalist, first editor of the *Sunday Independent*, Shaun Johnson. Johnson's first priority was to set up machinery so that the best young South Africans could be selected for university courses, his second to raise endowments so that this and other programmes could be continued and expanded. Primary targets for this second operation, Rowett told the Trustees, would be the corporate sector, philanthropists and other foundations as well as certain Commonwealth governments. Individual Scholars would, of course, be especially welcome contributors, but for reasons of time and practicality they must be a secondary target. The emphasis in Cape Town had been on participation; this was an enterprise in which Rhodes Scholars from all over the world could share. Inevitably there was some disappointment when it turned out that the signing of a cheque and the assurance of approval was all that the majority would be able to contribute, and even that would be delayed.

The fact remains that the centenary celebrations were rightly deemed to have been a great success. The Mandela–Rhodes Foundation is now well established and has already done good work in the field of tertiary education. It was not intended to be and could never have been run as an exercise in participatory democracy around the world. If any Scholars left Cape Town under the impression that this was what was intended, then they have been disillusioned. There is every reason to hope that, as the work done by the Foundation becomes more conspicuously valuable, any disappointment that might have been felt will die away. For the Rhodes community at large, the most dramatic manifestation of this will come when the first student nurtured by Mandela–Rhodes wins a Scholarship to Oxford. It would be surprising if such a development was long delayed.

John Rowett had played an enormous part both in organising the centenary celebrations and in setting up the Mandela–Rhodes Foundation. His dedication, his formidable energy, his refusal to take no for an answer, his persuasive powers, were all essential if the Trust's aims were to be achieved. The achievement was bought at a high cost, however. With benefit of hindsight one can see that it would have been difficult for any one man, impossible for a man as single-minded as Rowett, to undertake these massive responsibilities and yet perform the normal duties of Warden of Rhodes House. In the circumstances, the Trustees would have done better to hand over the setting up of Mandela–Rhodes to someone else or to have appointed a deputy Warden; a reversion to the old tradition of a separate Warden and General Secretary to the Trust might even have been a temporary expedient. There are plenty of reasons why this did not happen. For one thing, Rowett himself saw no need for such a move and was confident that he could manage the operation single-handedly. Sir Anthony Kenny and Lord Ashburton had retired almost simultaneously shortly before the conception of Mandela–Rhodes. Ashburton's successor and Vice-Chancellor of the University, Sir Richard Southwood, was a sick man who retired prematurely in 2002. By the time William Waldegrave took over, the damage had been done. The Scholars at Oxford felt they were being neglected. A storm of protest blew up. Rowett's last years at Rhodes House were not happy ones.

As if this was not enough there were serious financial problems. The large number of new Scholarships which had been added under Fletcher and Kenny, coupled with the lavish grants to Oxford causes and later to South Africa, meant that the Trustees no longer enjoyed the cushion of surplus funds to which they had grown accustomed. The formidable extra commitment to Mandela–Rhodes would have pushed them close to the limit even if the value of their investments had continued to rise. Instead, the stock market went into a sharp fall. The Trustees found themselves financially straitened at a time when university fees and all the expenses connected with the Scholarships were rising with disproportionate speed. Sir Colin Lucas, who succeeded Rowett as Warden in 2004, took over a leaky ship in what briefly threatened to become a full-blooded typhoon.

Lucas is a historian and leading authority on the French Revolution. He had been a Trustee since 1995 and had just handed over after a term of office as a highly esteemed Vice-Chancellor of Oxford (being replaced by John Hood, a Rhodes Scholar from New Zealand). Apart from the mending of bridges with the current Scholars and the various Associations of Rhodes Scholars abroad, urgent steps had to be taken to balance the books. There was, Lucas told the Trustees, a need to save £500,000–£600,000 a year. Something could be achieved by cutting down on third years, but he was against pushing this too far: 'I have to say that I don't like the strategy of trying to pressure Scholars into leaving earlier than they might.' Grants, other than the inescapable commitment to Mandela–Rhodes, should be cut back as far as possible. But the main economy had to be made in those Scholarships which were not enshrined in Rhodes's Will. The Hong Kong Scholarship, since Hong Kong had left the Commonwealth, was an easy target and was abolished. (It has subsequently been reinstated as the result of a benefaction from the Lee Hysan Foundation. It will be administered as a Rhodes Scholarship but will be distinct from the main Trust.) After much agonising it was decided by the Trustees that eleven more should be suspended: the victims being selected from those that had been most recently created – two each from Australia and

Germany; one from Bangladesh, the Caribbean, India, Malaysia, Pakistan, Singapore and Uganda.

Whether all these Scholarships will, or even should, be revived is a matter for conjecture. The economies have achieved their objective; the Trust's finances are already on a far more even keel. The value of its investments is almost back to what it was before the crash. The new generations of Scholars are intellectually a match for any of their predecessors, their range of interests and athletic pursuits have not been unduly restricted – if anything they seem still more altruistic and resolved to make some contribution to the betterment of the world. Morale within the organisation and in the Rhodes community at large has fully recovered; the new Warden has rebuilt relationships which had never broken down but had been severely strained. That the Trust will survive in all essentials inviolate has never been in doubt. It does not seem unduly optimistic to prophesy that a period of relative calm and even renewed growth lies ahead.

EPILOGUE

At the beginning of this book I said that there were two questions on which I hoped my work would throw some light. The first was 'What happens to a system inspired by a passionate imperialist and run for its first fifty years by men almost equally dedicated to the idea of Empire, when that Empire to all intents and purposes ceases to exist?' The second question, or rather group of questions, was 'Has it worked?' Has anything been achieved by bringing to Oxford this group of talented young men and later women which would not have happened if the Scholarships had never been created? Has the fact that they got to Oxford by means of a Rhodes Scholarship in any significant way distinguished them from those who found their way there by other means? And, as a corollary of this, have the Rhodes Scholars worked together in later life in a way which has made their contribution to society more effective than it would have been if they had acted only as individuals? Are the Rhodes Scholars now, have they been, will they ever be, what Cecil Rhodes believed they should be, a force that would change the world?

The disintegration of the British Empire seems to have made remarkably little difference to the operations of the Trust. In the first twenty or thirty years of its existence it expended considerable money and effort on South African causes which were avowedly political in intent, but once that phase was over it indulged in nothing similar. The fact that by far the largest of its constituencies was the United States was in itself enough to inhibit the Trust in any overt proselytisation of an imperial nature. It supported and was closely connected with the Round Table and gave sometimes quite generous grants to bodies whose object was, one way or another, to foster Commonwealth links, yet even by the end of the Second World War the Commonwealth as such had ceased to be an important factor in the Trust's deliberations. As a geographical unit defining the area in which it was legally possible for the Trust to make grants or create Scholarships the Commonwealth, of course, was still of importance, but for all other purposes it had become more a subject for historical enquiry or nostalgic regret than practical politics. Today the Trust does not consider the fostering of closer Commonwealth ties to be among its more serious responsibilities.

The second question is more complex and far more difficult to answer. Rhodes in his Will stated that one of the reasons for bringing young colonials to Oxford had been to instil in their minds 'the advantage to the Colonies as well as the United Kingdom of the retention of the unity of the Empire'. That had never been more than part of his grand design, however; the disintegration of the Empire did not affect his conviction that 'educational relations make the strongest tie' and that the fact that the great powers were bound by such ties would 'render war impossible'. Nor would it have changed his view that the highest aim to which his Scholars could aspire should be 'the performance of public duties'. How far he envisaged their working together in the performance of such duties, whether he supposed that former Rhodes Scholars responsible for making policy in Britain, Germany, the United States, would actively collaborate in the pursuit of peace, can never be finally established. The fact that the Trustees were required to provide opportunities at which former Scholars could meet and discuss 'their experience and prospects' suggests at least that he hoped they would act collectively as well as individually. He nowhere specified that he planned to establish an international brotherhood working to further his ends, but it would have been out of character for him not to hope and expect that this would happen.

If such, indeed, was his intent, he would consider the Trust had failed. Within each country, particularly within the United States, a degree of cohesion has been attained. Elton went to Washington in 1947 and found that among the Scholars permanently or temporarily living there 'a numerous group, meet regularly twice a month for a buffet lunch, after which there are usually a dozen or more two-minute speeches on a set subject, the main *motif* of the gatherings being the desire to cement Anglo-American friendship. . . . I could not help thinking', he mused, 'that if the Founder could have been present he would have felt that his Scholarships were indeed producing the result he would have desired.'[1] Elton was notoriously inclined to see what he wanted to see; even in 1947 it seems unlikely that the Scholars in Washington were as preoccupied by Anglo-American friendship as he believed; certainly today they would have other matters on their minds. But American Rhodes Scholars do still meet with some regularity and are more likely to formulate an agreed policy on controversial issues that any other national Association. Though there may be friendships between Scholars of different nations, however, even loose associations to deal with mutual problems, there has never been any systematic attempt to set up an international body which would co-ordinate the activities of Rhodes Scholars to a common end. Nor,

Fletcher at least would say, should there be. In his valedictory speech at the Leavers' dinner in June 1989 he said it was his belief that 'promotion of the well-being of the Scholarships is the single obligation of former Rhodes Scholars to the benefaction they enjoyed. The concept that corporately they have some mission to influence the world has always seemed to me erroneous, in that they are neither numerous enough nor homogeneous enough to exert much influence; and to smack of arrogance, in that it suggests that they are a race apart.'[2] The Mandela–Rhodes initiative has demonstrated both the valuable contribution Scholars can make if they work together in a defined area and for a defined end, and the limitations of the system if the Trust seeks to harness the international body of Scholars in support of such an enterprise.

The success or failure of the Rhodes Scholars must therefore be judged not by their corporate achievement but by their performance as individuals. In his tour as Warden-elect in 1951–2, Williams was impressed to find how often the Scholars he met were 'men who count in their communities. Mr Rhodes's experiment, one feels, is showing results. One's memory of his Scholars met on our journey is not only of their ability, in many cases their marked ability, but especially of their likeability. We scarcely met any that we did not like and we were delighted with the extraordinary number we could not help liking immensely.'[3] To possess both marked ability and immense likeability is an excellent start but by their fruits ye shall know them. Worldly achievement is not in itself enough to constitute 'good' Rhodes Scholars, yet it opens the way for doing the great things which Rhodes expected of them and it indicates the success which the selectors have achieved in picking men with the 'instinct to lead' required by the Will.

Applying such a test, Rhodes would probably have been mildly disappointed that there were so few world-shaking figures among the Scholars. There has, for instance, been only one President of the United States. But there have been half a dozen national or provincial Prime Ministers: Bob Hawke of Australia; John Turner of Canada; Norman Manley of Jamaica; Dom Mintoff of Malta. There have been two Nobel Prize-winning scientists, Florey and Eccles; and Hubble of the telescope. There have been writers and thinkers: John Crowe Ransom; Robert Penn Warren; the polymathic George Steiner; Ernst Schumacher of *Small is Beautiful*. When Kenny conducted a survey of living Rhodes Scholars in 1991–2 he found that of those who could be graded in a hierarchical system, 13 per cent said they had reached a level of a field marshal or full general, 29 per cent lieutenant- or major-general. When one considers how many Scholars had not yet attained the summit of their careers, the level of achievement is prodigiously high.

Impressive in a different way are the maverick spirits who lent a new lustre to Rhodes's estimation of the all-round man. Edward Selig was asked by the

Library of Congress whether he was really responsible for writing a book on the seventeenth-century love poet Thomas Carew and a later one on the economic incentives for pollution control. He admitted he was but pointed out 'the underlying continuity, since both books were essentially concerned with nocturnal emissions'.[4] The Canadian Rhodes Scholar Roy Leitch for his part died in his tarpaper shack in Nova Scotia in 1957. He had served in the Serbian Army in the First World War and the Belgian mercantile marine in the Second. He fought in the Spanish Civil War, and wrote and published a newspaper called *Storm* devoted to attacking all forms of government, international politics and religion. He spent his declining years running his private troop of Boy Scouts, taking them on hunting and fishing trips and teaching them forest lore.[5]

The influence and renown of the Rhodes Scholars varied widely from country to country and from decade to decade. At a luncheon given for Fletcher in Washington in 1980 there were present five Senators, one Senator Emeritus, the Chief Majority Whip in the House of Representatives, the Director of the CIA, an Economic Advisor to the Administration, the editor of the *Washington Star* and the Librarian of Congress. A Supreme Court judge and the Supreme Allied Commander in Europe were unfortunately unable to be present.[6] Twenty years before a galaxy of similar distinction if on a smaller scale could have been assembled in Canada. In South Africa in the apartheid years two members of the National Cabinet but also one of the bravest and most prominent champions of the African National Congress were Scholars; the great mining companies were largely in their hands. Two South African Rhodes Scholars were appointed Lord Justices of Appeal in the UK in 1992. Lake Success, where the United Nations took shape after the Second World War, was just the sort of place where a prominent Rhodes Scholar presence could be hoped for. High on the staff of the American Secretary of State, Dean Acheson, were Dean Rusk (himself one day to be Secretary of State), Walton Butterworth, a future American Ambassador to the European Community, and George McGhee, Ambassador to Turkey and Germany and tycoon in the oil industry. Escott Reid, a future High Commissioner to India and Ambassador to Germany, and George Ignatieff, Chancellor of the University of Toronto, were equally well established in the Canadian delegation. John Hood, a Scholar from Tasmania, was among Australia's representatives while Thomas Hamilton covered proceedings for the *New York Times*.

But a roll-call of celebrities is not what the Rhodes Scholarships are about; many Scholars who never achieved or even desired a high public profile did all that could have been hoped of them, others of great prominence did little that accorded with the Founder's wishes. What is evident from any study of the Rhodes Scholars, celebrated or born to blush unseen, is that an extraordinarily high proportion devoted a considerable part of their talents and energies to working for the benefit of others. Whether or not they esteemed the performance of public duties as their *highest* aim, they accepted that it was an important aim and one which they were morally bound to pursue. Public duties did not necessarily imply a political career, or working for the state, or even entering a busy world of lobbying and committees; it did involve the acceptance of an obligation to society and a determination to contribute in some way to the betterment of the lot of one's fellow men.

What is cause and what effect? Do Rhodes Scholars perform public duties because they are Rhodes Scholars, or are they selected as Rhodes Scholars because they seem the sort of people likely to perform public duties? No doubt a bit of both; but an extraordinarily high proportion of Scholars insist that their experience as Rhodes Scholars gave them an added sense of responsibility and a resolve to pay back to society some of the benefits their privileged education had bestowed on them. Joseph Nye, one of the most distinguished of American academics and a leading authority on the nature of power and international conflict, claims that he would have loved his time at Oxford and the wide range of friends he made however he had got there. But he would have missed the extra dimension of being a Rhodes Scholar; his already strong idealistic instincts were enhanced and refined by that experience.[7]

Idealism alone can be of doubtful value. Peter Beinart, a Scholar from Massachusetts who was made editor of the *New Republic* in 1999, was quoted by the *New American* (a paper notoriously ill-disposed towards the Rhodes community) as saying: 'In America, where idealism is the yardstick to judge a generation's collective virtue, Rhodes Scholars are its masters. . . . Not all want to run for elective office; but the bulk think their talents can be most fully realised through public service. Like Clinton, my peers believe earnestly in government. Above all, they believe in themselves in government.' He went on to say that this belief was not linked to 'a clear vision of what government ought to do. . . . Idealism masks an ideological vacuum.'[8]

There is enough truth in the charge to give the ambitious young Rhodes Scholar food for thought. There are certainly some among them who are convinced that their destiny is to rule and that society is fortunate that they should be ready to make themselves available, but have no clear idea of what they will do when power is theirs. Most of them are modest in their ambitions however, and not disposed to overrate the value of the contribution that they can make. Jeremy Kirk, an Australian Rhodes Scholar, left Oxford a less rather than a more ambitious person. Before becoming a Rhodes Scholar he had been keenly interested in politics; by the time he left he knew he would never be a politician. But his urge to serve had not been weakened. As a lawyer he makes a point of taking on ill-paid work for juvenile criminals, yet still asks himself whether he is concentrating too much on his own career. Delia Marshall from South Africa has found that her Scholarship has shaped her in a way that she had not expected. Seeing so many around her, Rhodes Scholars included, striving for greatness and the prestige of playing a prominent part, she became more focused on doing something humble which would not necessarily constitute success in the eyes of the world.[9] Indeed, Rhodes Scholars are often charged not with arrogance or excessive ambition but with a lack of the killer streak, the hunger to get to the top. Ranjit Chaudhury is one of the most eminent of Indian pharmacologists and a scholar of international repute. He sees himself, though, as an adviser to ministers, not as a minister himself. 'Rhodes Scholars,' he says, 'make good Number Twos.'[10]

Who then is the ideal Rhodes Scholar? The admiral who became head of the CIA or the Buddhist priest working in the field of AIDS? The President of the United States or the professor in the unfashionable university content to inspire generations of students with a love of learning and a respect for their fellow human beings? The *American Oxonian* 1985 suggested that the perfect scholar might be William Stevenson: Olympic gold medallist, prominent lawyer, director of Red Cross operations in England and North Africa in the Second World War, President of Oberlin College, Ambassador to the Philippines, President of the Aspen Institute of Humanistic Studies.[11] Certainly few could more perfectly fulfil Rhodes's idea of the all-round man. But apples cannot be rated against oranges, roses against violets. The search for the ideal Scholar is as pointless as it is misguided. It is the glory of the Rhodes Scholarships that their holders excel in an infinite variety of talents and pursuits. Some of them do not seem to excel at all, and they are not necessarily the least among them.

Are Rhodes Scholars better than any other comparable group? There is no other comparable group, so the question is an idle one. What, anyway, does 'better' mean? More successful in worldly terms, more influential, contributing more to solving the problems of society, giving more pleasure to their fellow humans, better parents, better friends? All one can say with confidence is that among the seven thousand or so Rhodes Scholars who have passed through Oxford there is to be found an astonishing range of talent and a mountain of achievement. A few have brought discredit on the system, some have done no harm but little good, the majority, in a multiplicity of ways, have made a positive contribution to the world they live or lived in. Almost all of them have been to some extent marked by their Rhodes experience; and almost all of those who have been so marked have been strengthened by it. And this we owe to the vision of that extraordinary man who made a killing in diamonds in South Africa towards the end of the nineteenth century. There is much which we may legitimately deplore about Cecil Rhodes, but this is his true legacy.

RHODES'S WILL

I THE RIGHT HONOURABLE CECIL JOHN RHODES of Cape Town in the Colony of the Cape of Good Hope hereby revoke all testamentary dispositions heretofore made by me and declare this to be my last Will which I make this 1st day of July 1899.

1. I am a natural-born British subject and I now declare that I have adopted and acquired and hereby adopt and acquire and intend to retain Rhodesia as my domicile.

2. I appoint the Right Honourable Archibald Philip Earl of Rosebery K.G. K.T. the Right Honourable Albert Henry George Earl Grey Alfred Beit of 26 Park Lane London William Thomas Stead of Mowbray House Norfolk Street Strand in the County of London Lewis Loyd Michell of Cape Town in the Colony of the Cape of Good Hope Banker and Bourchier Francis Hawksley of Mincing Lane in the City of London to be the Executors and Trustees of my Will and they and the survivors of them or other the Trustees for the time being of my Will are hereinafter called 'my Trustees'.

3. I admire the grandeur and loneliness of the Matoppos in Rhodesia and therefore I desire to be buried in the Matoppos on the hill which I used to visit and which I called the 'View of the World' in a square to be cut in the rock on the top of the hill covered with a plain brass plate with these words thereon—'Here lie the remains of Cecil John Rhodes' and accordingly I direct my Executors at the expense of my estate to take all steps and do all things necessary or proper to give effect to this my desire and afterwards to keep my grave in order at the expense of the Matoppos and Bulawayo Fund hereinafter mentioned.

4. I give the sum of £6,000 to   Kahn of Paris and I direct this legacy to be paid free of all duty whatsoever.

5. I give an annuity of £100 to each of my servants Norris and the one called Tony during his life free of all duty whatsoever and in addition to any wages due at my death.

6. I direct my Trustees on the hill aforesaid to erect or complete the monument to the men who fell in the first Matabele War at Shangani in Rhodesia the bas-reliefs for which are being made by Mr. John Tweed and I desire the said hill to be preserved as a burial-place but no person is to be buried there unless the Government for the time being of Rhodesia until the various states of South

Africa or any of them shall have been federated and after such federation the Federal Government by a vote of two-thirds of its governing body says that he or she has deserved well of his or her country.

7. I give free of all duty whatsoever my landed property near Bulawayo in Matabeleland Rhodesia and my landed property at or near Inyanga near Salisbury in Mashonaland Rhodesia to my Trustees hereinbefore named Upon trust that my Trustees shall in such manner as in their uncontrolled discretion they shall think fit cultivate the same respectively for the instruction of the people of Rhodesia.

8. I give free of all duty whatsoever to my Trustees hereinbefore named such a sum of money as they shall carefully ascertain and in their uncontrolled discretion consider ample and sufficient by its investments to yield income amounting to the sum of £4,000 sterling per annum and not less and I direct my Trustees to invest the same sum and the said sum and the investments for the time being representing it I hereinafter refer to as 'the Matoppos and Bulawayo Fund' And I direct that my Trustees shall for ever apply in such manner as in their uncontrolled discretion they shall think fit the income of the Matoppos and Bulawayo Fund in preserving protecting maintaining adorning and beautifying the said burial-place and hill and their surroundings and shall for ever apply in such manner as in their uncontrolled discretion they shall think fit the balance of the income of the Matoppos and Bulawayo Fund and any rents and profits of my said landed properties near Bulawayo in the cultivation as aforesaid of such property And in particular I direct my Trustees that a portion of my Sauerdale property a part of my said landed property near Bulawayo be planted with every possible tree and be made and preserved and maintained as a Park for the people of Bulawayo and that they complete the dam at my Westacre property if it is not completed at my death and make a short railway line from Bulawayo to Westacre so that the people of Bulawayo may enjoy the glory of the Matoppos from Saturday to Monday.

9. I give free of all duty whatsoever to my Trustees hereinbefore named such a sum of money as they shall carefully ascertain and in their uncontrolled discretion consider ample and sufficient by its investments to yield income amounting to the sum of £2,000 sterling per annum and not less and I direct my Trustees to invest the same sum and the said sum and the investments for the time being representing it I hereinafter refer to as 'the Inyanga Fund' And I direct that my Trustees shall for ever apply in such manner as in their absolute discretion they shall think fit the income of the Inyanga Fund and any rents and profits of my said landed property at or near Inyanga in the cultivation of such property and in particular I direct that with regard to such property irrigation should be the first object of my Trustees.

[2]

10. For the guidance of my Trustees I wish to record that in the cultivation of my said landed properties I include such things as experimental farming forestry market and other gardening and fruit farming irrigation and the teaching of any of those things and establishing and maintaining an Agricultural College.

11. I give all the interest to which I may at my death be entitled in any freehold copyhold or leasehold hereditaments in Dalston or elsewhere in the County of London to my Trustees hereinbefore named Upon trust that my Trustees shall lease or let and generally manage but not sell the same and pay all requisite outgoings usually paid by me in respect thereof and maintain the same in proper repair and insured against fire And upon trust that my Trustees shall so long as any one or more of my own brothers and sisters (which does not include my sister of the half blood) shall be living pay the net income derived from the said hereditaments to such of my own brothers and sisters aforesaid as shall for the time being be living and while more than one to be divided between them in equal shares And shall after the death of the survivor of them such brothers and sisters hold my interest in the said estate and the rents and profits thereof Upon the trusts hereinafter contained concerning the same and inasmuch as those trusts are educational trusts for the benefit of the Empire I hope the means will be found for enabling my Trustees to retain my interest in the said estate unsold and with that object I authorize and require them to endeavour to obtain at the expense of my estate a private or other Act of Parliament or other sufficient authority enabling and requiring them to retain the same unsold.

12. I give the sum of £100,000 free of all duty whatsoever to my old College Oriel College in the University of Oxford and I direct that the receipt of the Bursar or other proper officer of the College shall be a complete discharge for that legacy and inasmuch as I gather that the erection of an extension to High Street of the College buildings would cost about £22,500 and that the loss to the College revenue caused by pulling down of houses to make room for the said new College buildings would be about £250 per annum I direct that the sum of £40,000 part of the said sum of £100,000 shall be applied in the first place in the erection of the said new College buildings and that the remainder of such sum of £40,000 shall be held as a fund by the income whereof the afore-said loss to the College revenue shall so far as possible be made good. And inasmuch as I gather that there is a deficiency in the College revenue of some £1,500 per annum whereby the Fellowships are impoverished and the status of the College is lowered I direct that the sum of £40,000 further part of the said sum of £100,000 shall be held as a fund by the income whereof the income of such of the resident Fellows of the College as work for the honour and dignity of the College shall be increased. And I further direct that the sum of £10,000 further part of the said sum of £100,000 shall be held as a fund by the income

[3]

whereof the dignity and comfort of the High Table may be maintained by which means the dignity and comfort of the resident Fellows may be increased. And I further direct that the sum of £10,000 the remainder of the said sum of £100,000 shall be held as a repair fund the income whereof shall be expended in maintaining and repairing the College buildings. And finally as the College authorities live secluded from the world and so are like children as to commercial matters I would advise them to consult my Trustees as to the investment of these various funds for they would receive great help and assistance from the advice of my Trustees in such matters and I direct that any investment made pursuant to such advice shall whatsoever it may be be an authorized investment for the money applied in making it.

13. I give my property following that is to say my residence known as 'De Groote Schuur' situate near Mowbray in the Cape Division in the said Colony together with all furniture plate and other articles contained therein at the time of my death and all other land belonging to me situated under Table Mountain including my property known as 'Mosterts' to my Trustees hereinbefore named upon and subject to the conditions following (that is to say)—

(i) The said property (excepting any furniture or like articles which have become useless) shall not nor shall any portion thereof at any time be sold let or otherwise alienated.

(ii) No buildings for suburban residences shall at any time be erected on the said property and any buildings which may be erected thereon shall be used exclusively for public purposes and shall be in a style of architecture similar to or in harmony with my said residence.

(iii) The said residence and its gardens and grounds shall be retained for a residence for the Prime Minister for the time being of the said Federal Government of the States of South Africa to which I have referred in clause 6 hereof my intention being to provide a suitable official residence for the First Minister in that Government befitting the dignity of his position and until there shall be such a Federal Government may be used as a park for the people.

(iv) The grave of the late Jan Hendrik Hofmeyr upon the said property shall be protected and access be permitted thereto at all reasonable times by any member of the Hofmeyr family for the purpose of inspection or maintenance.

14. I give to my Trustees hereinbefore named such a sum of money as they shall carefully ascertain and in their uncontrolled discretion consider to be ample and sufficient to yield income amounting to the sum of one thousand pounds sterling per annum and not less upon trust that such income shall be applied and expended for the purposes following (that is to say)—

[4]

(i) On and for keeping and maintaining for the use of the Prime Minister for the time being of the said Federal Government of at least two carriage horses one or more carriages and sufficient stable servants.

(ii) On and for keeping and maintaining in good order the flower and kitchen gardens appertaining to the said residence.

(iii) On and for the payment of the wages or earnings including the board and lodging of two competent men servants to be housed kept and employed in domestic service in the said residence.

(iv) On and for the improvement repair renewal and insurance of the said residence furniture plate and other articles.

15. I direct that subject to the conditions and trusts hereinbefore contained the said Federal Government shall from the time it shall be constituted have the management administration and control of the said devise and legacy and that my Trustees shall as soon as may be thereafter vest and pay the devise and legacy given by the two last preceding clauses hereof in and to such Government if a corporate body capable of accepting and holding the same or if not then in some suitable corporate body so capable named by such Government and that in the meantime my Trustees shall in their uncontrolled discretion manage administer and control the said devise and legacy.

16. Whereas I consider that the education of young Colonists at one of the Universities in the United Kingdom is of great advantage to them for giving breadth to their views for their instruction in life and manners and for instilling into their minds the advantage to the Colonies as well as to the United Kingdom of the retention of the unity of the Empire. And whereas in the case of young Colonists studying at a University in the United Kingdom I attach very great importance to the University having a residential system such as is in force at the Universities of Oxford and Cambridge for without it those students are at the most critical period of their lives left without any supervision. And whereas there are at the present time 50 or more students from South Africa studying at the University of Edinburgh many of whom are attracted there by its excellent medical school and I should like to establish some of the Scholarships hereinafter mentioned in that University but owing to its not having such a residential system as aforesaid I feel obliged to refrain from doing so. And whereas my own University the University of Oxford has such a system and I suggest that it should try and extend its scope so as if possible to make its medical school at least as good as that at the University of Edinburgh. And whereas I also desire to encourage and foster an appreciation of the advantages which I implicitly believe will result from the union of the English-speaking peoples throughout the world and to encourage in the students from the

[5]   B

United States of North America who will benefit from the American Scholarships to be established for the reason above given at the University of Oxford under this my Will an attachment to the country from which they have sprung but without I hope withdrawing them or their sympathies from the land of their adoption or birth. Now therefore I direct my Trustees as soon as may be after my death and either simultaneously or gradually as they shall find convenient and if gradually then in such order as they shall think fit to establish for male students the Scholarships hereinafter directed to be established each of which shall be of the yearly value of £300 and be tenable at any College in the University of Oxford for three consecutive academical years.

17. I direct my Trustees to establish certain Scholarships and these Scholarships I sometimes hereinafter refer to as 'the Colonial Scholarships'.

18. The appropriation of the Colonial Scholarships and the numbers to be annually filled up shall be in accordance with the following table:—

Total No. appropriated.	To be tenable by Students of or from	No. of Scholarships to be filled up in each year.
9	Rhodesia	3 and no more.
3	The South African College School in the Colony of the Cape of Good Hope ... ...}	1 and no more.
3	The Stellenbosch College School in the same Colony	1 and no more.
3	The Diocesan College School of Rondebosch in the same Colony ... ...}	1 and no more.
3	St. Andrews College School Grahamstown in the same Colony ... ...}	1 and no more.
3	The Colony of Natal in the same Colony	1 and no more.
3	The Colony of New South Wales	1 and no more.
3	The Colony of Victoria	1 and no more.
3	The Colony of South Australia	1 and no more.
3	The Colony of Queensland	1 and no more.
3	The Colony of Western Australia	1 and no more.
3	The Colony of Tasmania	1 and no more.
3	The Colony of New Zealand	1 and no more.
3	The Province of Ontario in the Dominion of Canada	1 and no more.
3	The Province of Quebec in the Dominion of Canada	1 and no more.
3	The Colony or Island of Newfoundland and its Dependencies ... ...}	1 and no more.
3	The Colony or Islands of the Bermudas	1 and no more.
3	The Colony or Island of Jamaica	1 and no more.

19. I further direct my Trustees to establish additional Scholarships sufficient in number for the appropriation in the next following clause hereof directed and those Scholarships I sometimes hereinafter refer to as 'the American Scholarships'.

[6]

20. I appropriate two of the American Scholarships to each of the present States and Territories of the United States of North America. Provided that if any of the said Territories shall in my lifetime be admitted as a State the Scholarships appropriated to such Territory shall be appropriated to such State and that my Trustees may in their uncontrolled discretion withhold for such time as they shall think fit the appropriation of Scholarships to any Territory.

21. I direct that of the two Scholarships appropriated to a State or Territory not more than one shall be filled up in any year so that at no time shall more than two Scholarships be held for the same State or Territory.

22. The Scholarships shall be paid only out of income and in the event at any time of income being insufficient for payment in full of all the Scholarships for the time being payable I direct that (without prejudice to the vested interests of holders for the time being of Scholarships) the following order of priority shall regulate the payment of the Scholarships.

(i) First the Scholarships of students of or from Rhodesia shall be paid.

(ii) Secondly the Scholarships of students from the said South African Stellenbosch Rondebosch and St. Andrews Schools shall be paid.

(iii) Thirdly the remainder of the Colonial Scholarships shall be paid and if there shall not be sufficient income for the purpose such Scholarships shall abate proportionately; and

(iv) Fourthly the American Scholarships shall be paid and if there shall not be sufficient income for the purpose such Scholarships shall abate proportionately.

23. My desire being that the students who shall be elected to the Scholarships shall not be merely bookworms I direct that in the election of a student to a Scholarship regard shall be had to (i) his literary and scholastic attainments (ii) his fondness of and success in manly outdoor sports such as cricket football and the like (iii) his qualities of manhood truth courage devotion to duty sympathy for and protection of the weak kindliness unselfishness and fellowship and (iv) his exhibition during school days of moral force of character and of instincts to lead and to take an interest in his schoolmates for those latter attributes will be likely in afterlife to guide him to esteem the performance of public duties as his highest aim. As mere suggestions for the guidance of those who will have the choice of students for the Scholarships I record that—

(i) My ideal qualified student would combine these four qualifications in the proportions of 4/10ths for the first 2/10ths for the second 2/10ths for the third and 2/10ths for the fourth qualification so that according to my ideas if the

[7]

maximum number of marks for any Scholarship were 100 they would be apportioned as follows:—40 to the first qualification and 20 to each of the second third and fourth qualifications.

(ii) The marks for first qualification would be awarded by examination for the second and third qualifications by ballot by the fellow-students of the candidates and for the fourth qualification by the head master of the candidate's school; and

(iii) The results of the awards would be sent simultaneously to my Trustees or some one appointed to receive the same. I say simultaneously so that no awarding party should know the result of the award of any other awarding party.

24. No student shall be qualified or disqualified for election to a Scholarship on account of his race or religious opinions.

25. The election to Scholarships shall be by the Trustees after consultation with the Minister having the control of education in such Colony Province State or Territory except in the cases of the four schools hereinbefore mentioned.

26. A qualified student who has been elected as aforesaid shall within six calendar months after his election or as soon thereafter as he can be admitted into residence or within such extended time as my Trustees shall allow commence residence as an undergraduate at some college in the University of Oxford.

27. The Scholarships shall be payable to him from the time when he shall commence such residence.

28. I desire that the Scholars holding the scholarships shall be distributed amongst the Colleges of the University of Oxford and not resort in undue numbers to one or more Colleges only.

29. Notwithstanding anything hereinbefore contained my Trustees may in their uncontrolled discretion suspend for such time as they shall think fit or remove any Scholar from his scholarship.

30. My Trustees may from time to time make vary and repeal regulations either general or affecting specified Scholarships only with regard to all or any of the following matters (that is to say):

(i) The election whether after examination or otherwise of qualified Students to the Scholarships or any of them and the method whether by examination or otherwise in which their qualifications are to be ascertained.

(ii) The tenure of the Scholarships by scholars.

[8]

(iii) The suspension and removal of scholars from their Scholarships.

(iv) The method and times of payment of the Scholarships.

(v) The method of giving effect to my wish expressed in clause 28 hereof and

(vi) Any and every other matter with regard to the Scholarships or any of them with regard to which they shall consider regulations necessary or desirable.

31. My Trustees may from time to time authorize regulations with regard to the election whether after examination or otherwise of qualified students for Scholarships and to the method whether by examination or otherwise in which their qualifications are to be ascertained to be made—

(i) By a school in respect of the scholarships tenable by its students and—

(ii) By the Minister aforesaid of a Colony Province State or Territory in respect of the Scholarships tenable by students from such Colony Province State or Territory.

32. Regulations made under the last preceding clause hereof if and when approved of and not before by my Trustees shall be equivalent in all respects to regulations made by my Trustees.

33. No regulations made under clause 30 or made and approved of under clauses 31 and 32 hereof shall be inconsistent with any of the provisions herein contained.

34. In order that the scholars past and present may have opportunities of meeting and discussing their experiences and prospects I desire that my Trustees shall annually give a dinner to the past and present scholars able and willing to attend at which I hope my Trustees or some of them will be able to be present and to which they will I hope from time to time invite as guests persons who have shown sympathy with the views expressed by me in this my Will.

35. My Trustees hereinbefore named shall free of all duty whatsoever at such time as they shall think fit set apart out of my estate such a Scholarship fund (either by appropriation of existing investments or by making other investments or partly in one way and partly in the other) as they shall consider sufficient by its income to pay the Scholarships and in addition a yearly sum of £1,000.

36. My Trustees shall invest the Scholarship fund and the other funds hereinbefore established or any part thereof respectively in such investments in any

[9]

part of the world as they shall in their uncontrolled discretion think fit and that without regard to any rules of equity governing investments by trustees and without any responsibility or liability should they commit any breach of any such rule with power to vary any such investments for others of a like nature.

37. Investments to bearer held as an investment may be deposited by my Trustees for safe custody in their names with any banker or banking company or with any company whose business it is to take charge of investments of that nature and my Trustees shall not be responsible for any loss incurred in consequence of such deposit.

38. My Trustees shall after the death of the survivor of my said brothers and sisters hold my said interest in the said Dalston estate as an accretion to the capital of the Scholarship fund and the net rents and profits thereof as an accretion to the income of the Scholarship fund and shall by means of the increase of income of the Scholarship fund so arising establish such number of further Scholarships of the yearly value of £300 each as such increase shall be sufficient to establish. Such further Scholarships shall be for students of such British Colony or Colonies or Dependency or Dependencies whether hereinbefore mentioned or not as my Trustees shall in their uncontrolled discretion think fit. And I direct that every such further Scholarship shall correspond in all respects with the Scholarships hereinbefore directed to be established and that the preceding provisions of this my Will which apply to the Scholarships hereinbefore directed to be established or any of them shall where applicable apply to such further Scholarships.

39. Until the Scholarship fund shall have been set apart as aforesaid I charge the same and the Scholarships upon the residue of my real and personal estate.

40. I give the residue of my real and personal estate unto such of them the said Earl of Rosebery Earl Grey Alfred Beit William Thomas Stead Lewis Loyd Michell and Bourchier Francis Hawksley as shall be living at my death absolutely and if more than one as joint tenants.

41. My Trustees in the administration of the trust business may instead of acting personally employ and pay a Secretary or Agent to transact all business and do all acts required to be done in the trust including the receipt and payment of money.

42. My intention is that there shall be always at least three Trustees of my Will so far as it relates to the Scholarship Trusts and therefore I direct that whenever there shall be less than three Trustees a new Trustee or new Trustees shall be forthwith appointed.

[10]

IN WITNESS whereof I have hereunto set my hand the day and year first above written.

Signed by the said Testator The Right Honourable ⎫
    Cecil John Rhodes as and for his last Will and ⎪
    Testament in the presence of us both present at ⎬ C. J. RHODES.
    the same time who at his request in his presence ⎪
    and in the presence of each other have hereunto ⎪
    subscribed our names as witnesses ⎭

                CHARLES T. METCALFE.

                P. JOURDAN.

                ARTHUR SAWYER.

                      Jan/1900

                [Really January 1901.]

On account of the extraordinary eccentricity of Mr. Stead though having always a great respect for him but feeling the objects of my Will would be embarrassed by his views I hereby revoke his appointment as one of my executors.

Witnesses   C. J. RHODES.

    LEWIS L. MICHELL.

    H. GODDEN.

This is a further Codicil to my Will. I note the German Emperor has made instruction in English compulsory in German schools. I leave five yearly scholarships at Oxford of £250 per ann. to students of German birth the scholars to be nominated by the German Emperor for the time being. Each scholarship to continue for three years so that each year after the first three there will be fifteen scholars. The object is that an understanding between the three great powers will render war impossible and educational relations make the strongest tie.

America has already been provided for. C. J. R.

Witnesses   C. J. RHODES.

    G. V. WEBB.

    W. G. V. CARTER.

              ENDORSED ON BACK OF ABOVE.

A yearly amount should be put in British Consols to provide for the bequests in my Will when the Diamond Mines work out: the above is an instruction to the Trustees of my Will.

                          C. J. R.

                  [11]

Jan/1901.

As a further Codicil to my Will I leave J. Grimmer ten thousand pounds and the use of my Inyanga farms for his life. This bequest takes the place of the previous written paper given to him.

C. J. RHODES.

Witness

W. G. V. Carter.

H. Godden.

THIS IS A CODICIL to the last Will and Testament of me THE RIGHT HONOURABLE CECIL JOHN RHODES of Cape Town in the Colony of the Cape of Good Hope which Will is dated the First day of July One thousand eight hundred and ninety-nine. I appoint the Right Honourable Alfred Lord Milner to be an Executor and Trustee of my said Will jointly with those named in my said Will as my Executors and Trustees and in all respects as though he had been originally appointed one of my Executors and Trustees by my said Will. And I associate him with my residuary legatees and devisees named in clause 40 of my said Will desiring and declaring that they and he are my residuary legatees and devisees in joint tenancy. I revoke clauses 23, 24 and 25 in my said Will and in lieu thereof substitute the three following clauses which I direct shall be read as though originally clauses 23, 24 and 25 of my said Will:—

23. My desire being that the students who shall be elected to the Scholarships shall not be merely bookworms I direct that in the election of a student to a Scholarship regard shall be had to (i) his literary and scholastic attainments (ii) his fondness of and success in manly outdoor sports such as cricket football and the like (iii) his qualities of manhood truth courage devotion to duty sympathy for the protection of the weak kindliness unselfishness and fellowship and (iv) his exhibition during school days of moral force of character and of instincts to lead and to take an interest in his schoolmates for those latter attributes will be likely in afterlife to guide him to esteem the performance of public duties as his highest aim. As mere suggestions for the guidance of those who will have the choice of students for the Scholarships I record that (i) my ideal qualified student would combine these four qualifications in the proportions of 3/10ths for the first 2/10ths for the second 3/10ths for the third and 2/10ths for the fourth qualification so that according to my ideas if the maximum number of marks for any Scholarship were 200 they would be apportioned as follows— 60 to each of the first and third qualifications and 40 to each of the second and

[12]

fourth qualifications (ii) the marks of the several qualifications would be awarded independently as follows (that is to say) the marks for the first qualification by examination for the second and third qualifications respectively by ballot by the fellow-students of the candidates and for the fourth qualification by the head master of the candidate's school and (iii) the results of the awards (that is to say the marks obtained by each candidate for each qualification) would be sent as soon as possible for consideration to the Trustees or to some person or persons appointed to receive the same and the person or persons so appointed would ascertain by averaging the marks in blocks of 20 marks each of all candidates the best ideal qualified students.

24. No student shall be qualified or disqualified for election to a Scholarship on account of his race or religious opinions.

25. Except in the cases of the four schools hereinbefore mentioned the election to Scholarships shall be by the Trustees after such (if any) consultation as they shall think fit with the Minister having the control of education in such Colony Province State or Territory.

IN WITNESS whereof I have hereunto set my hand this Eleventh day of October One thousand nine hundred and one.

Signed by the said Cecil John Rhodes as and for a ⎫
    Codicil to his last Will and Testament in the ⎪
    presence of us all present at the same time who ⎪ C. J. RHODES.
    in his presence at his request and in the presence ⎬
    of each other have hereunto subscribed our names ⎪
    as witnesses. ⎭

       GEORGE FROST,
       FRANK BROWN.
         Servants to Mr. Beit,
             26, Park Lane,
              London.

TRUSTEES AND PRINCIPAL OFFICERS OF THE RHODES TRUST

Trustees

The Earl of Rosebery 1902–17 (chair)
Earl Grey 1902–17
Alfred Beit 1902–6
Sir Lewis Michell 1902–17
Bouchier Francis Hawksley 1902–15
Viscount Milner 1902–25 (chair 1917–25)
Sir Leander Starr Jameson 1902–17
Sir Otto Beit 1917–30 (chair 1925–30)
Lord Lovat 1917–33 (chair 1930–3)
Rudyard Kipling 1917–25
The Rt Hon. L. S. Amery 1919–55 (chair 1933–55)
Earl Baldwin of Bewdley 1925–47
Sir Edward Peacock 1925–62 (chair 1955–62)
Geoffrey Dawson 1925–44
Sir Douglas Hogg (Viscount Hailsham) 1925–9
The Rt Hon. H. A. L. Fisher 1925–40
Sir Reginald Sothern Holland 1932–48
The Very Revd John Lowe 1940–60
Capt. G. T. Hutchinson 1940–8
Lord Hailey 1941–64
The Rt Hon. Malcolm MacDonald 1948–57
Charles H. G. Millis 1948–61
Sir Kenneth Wheare 1948–77 (chair 1962–9)
Sir George Abell 1949–74 (chair 1969–74)
Lt Gen. Sir Archibald Nye 1957–67
Sir Oliver Franks (Lord Franks) 1957–73
Viscount Harcourt 1957–79 (chair 1974–9)
Viscount Amory 1961–9
John G. Phillimore 1961–74
Sir Edward Boyle (Lord Boyle of Handsworth) 1965–9
Professor Don K. Price 1968–78
Sir William Paton 1968–87 (chair 1979–82)
Sir John Baring (Lord Ashburton) 1970–99 (chair 1987–99)
Lord Blake 1971–87 (chair 1983–7)
Marmaduke Hussey 1972–92
W. Greig Barr 1975–87

Sir Robert Armstrong (Lord Armstrong of Ilminster) 1975–97
Sir John Habbakuk 1977–85
Mrs Mary Moore 1984–1996
Sir John Sainsbury (Lord Sainsbury of Preston Candover) 1984–98
Sir Richard Southwood 1986–2002 (chair 1999–2002)
Duncan Stewart 1986–96
Dr J. M. Roberts 1987–95
The Rt Hon. William Waldegrave (Lord Waldegrave) 1992– (chair from 2002)
Sir Colin Lucas 1995–2004
Professor Robert O'Neill 1995–2001
Dame R. L. Deech 1996–2006
Sir John Kerr 1997–
Rosalind Hedley Miller 1999–
Lord Fellowes 2000–
Lord Butler 2001–
Julian Ogilvie-Thompson 2002–
John Bell 2002–
Thomas Seaman 2004–
Sir Roderick Eddington 2004–
Elizabeth Fallaize 2006–
Sir John Vickers 2006–

Secretaries of the Trust

Organising Secretary of the Scholarships

Sir George Parkin 1902–20

London Secretaries

Douglas Brodie and Charles Boyd 1902–5
Charles Boyd 1905–8
Mrs Dorothea Mavor (Lady Butterworth) 1908–16
Thomas L. Gilmour 1916–19

General Secretaries

Sir Edward Grigg (Lord Altrincham) 1919–21, 1923–5
Geoffrey Dawson 1921–3
Philip Kerr (Marquess of Lothian) 1925–39
Lord Elton 1939–59

Oxford Secretaries (Wardens of Rhodes House)

Sir Francis Wylie 1903–31
Sir Carleton Allen 1931–52
Sir Edgar Williams 1952–9

Secretaries to the Trust and Wardens of Rhodes House

Sir Edgar Williams 1959–80
Dr Robin Fletcher 1980–9
Sir Anthony Kenny 1989–99

Dr John Rowett 1999–2004
Sir Colin Lucas 2004–

Principal Overseas Secretaries

American Secretaries

Frank Aydelotte 1918–52
Courtney Smith 1953–69
William Barber 1969–81
David Alexander 1981–98
Elliot Gerson 1998–

Canadian Secretaries

J. M. Macdonnell 1921–36
Roland Michener 1936–64
J. J. Stewart 1965–71
Arthur Scace 1973–

South African Secretaries

P. T. Lewis 1921–46
A. H. Gie 1946–67
Rex Welsh 1967–88
L. W. H. Ackermann 1988–2003
Edwin Cameron 2003–

Australian Secretaries

(Sir) John Behan 1922–53
(Sir) George Paton 1953–73
John Poynter 1973–97
Grahame Hutchinson 1997–

NOTES

RT indicates that the document concerned is to be found in the Archives of Rhodes House. Most of these are RTF – Rhodes Trust File followed by a number. There will also be found RTA (America), RTC (Canada), RTAU (Australia) and other variants. RTM means that the reference is to the minutes of the meeting of the Trustees on the given date. Styles varied over the years and though Caroline Brown imposed a high degree of order on the material some complications inevitably remain. I have sought always to produce an entry which will enable the interested reader easily to locate the particular document. I hope I have succeeded.

In my frequent citations from Anthony Kenny's *History of the Rhodes Trust* I have put first the author of the particular essay: for example 'McCalla. Kenny. *Rhodes Trust*.' If no name precedes that of Kenny, it means that he wrote the piece himself.

Chapter 1: Building a Fortune

1. Throughout these opening chapters I am deeply indebted to Robert Rotberg's *The Founder: Cecil Rhodes and the Pursuit of Power*. Revised edition. Johannesburg, 2002.
2. Paul Maylam. *The Cult of Rhodes*. Claremont, 2003. p. 126.
3. G. K. Chesterton. *A Miscellany of Men*. London, 1912. pp. 203–4.
4. Rotberg. p. 44.
5. Lewis Michell. *The Life of the Rt Hon. Cecil John Rhodes*. London, 1912. Vol. 1. p. 184.
6. Rotberg. p. 678.
7. Ibid. p. 86.
8. John Ruskin. *Lectures in Art*. Oxford, 1870. pp. 41–4.
9. Colin Newbury. 'Cecil Rhodes and the South African Connection', in *Oxford and the Idea of Commonwealth: Essays Presented to Sir Edgar Williams*. ed. Frederick Madden and David Fieldhouse. London, 1982. pp. 79–80.

Chapter 2: The Imperial Dream

1. *The Last Will and Testament of Cecil John Rhodes*. ed. W. T. Stead. London, 1902. p. 83.

2. Ibid. p. 98.
3. Rotberg. p. 132.
4. L. H. Amery. *My Political Life*. Vol. 1. London, 1953. p. 182. For a strongly hostile interpretation of Rhodes's views on race see Stanlake Samkange's *What Rhodes Really Said About Africans*. Harare, 1982.
5. Sarah Gertrude Millin. *Rhodes*. London, 1933. p. 221.
6. Rotberg. p. 362.
7. Ibid. p. 334.
8. Ibid. p. 523.
9. 'En ma fin est mon commencement'.

Chapter 3: Life after Death

1. *Last Will and Testament*. p. 98.
2. Amery. *Political Life*. Vol. 1. pp. 181–2.
3. Rotberg. p. 670.
4. Ibid. p. 385.
5. What appears to be the original of the 'Confession' is in the archives of Rhodes House. The fullest published text is to be found in John Flint. *Cecil Rhodes*. London, 1976. pp. 248–52.
6. *Last Will and Testament*. pp. 61–2.
7. Rotberg. p. 234.

8. Herbert Baker. *Cecil Rhodes: by his Architect*. London, 1934. p. 48.
9. Maylam. *Cult of Rhodes*. p. 64.
10. The text of Rhodes's seventh and final will is at Appendix I.
11. *American Oxonian*. 2 (1944). pp. 68–9.
12. See Sheppard in Kenny. *Rhodes Trust*. p. 357.
13. *Last Will and Testament*. p. 39.
14. *The First Fifty Years of the Rhodes Trust and the Rhodes Scholarships*. ed. Lord Elton. Oxford, 1955. p. 4.

Chapter 4: Setting up the Scholarships

1. George Parkin. *American Oxonian*. 2 (1918). pp. 48–50.
2. Rotberg. p. 279.
3. *The Milner Papers*. ed. Cecil Headlam. London, 1931. Vol. 1. p. 105.
4. Grey to Milner. 19 April 1902. MS Milner Dep. 467.
5. Milner to Boyd. 30 October 1903. RTF 2286(1).
6. *Last Will and Testament*. p. 109.
7. Lady Butterworth to Lord Elton. 1 January 1959. RTF 1451.
8. 30 March 1904. RTF 1850.
9. 27 December 1905. RTF 2285.
10. Boyd to Rosebery. 5 September 1905; Hawksley to Rosebery. 20 September 1905; Michell to Rosebery. 3 November 1905. RTF 2351(A) (originals in National Library of Scotland).
11. RTM 1276; Kenny. *Rhodes Trust*. pp. 12–13.
12. 31 December 1915. cit. Richard Symonds. *Oxford and Empire*. London, 1986. p. 169.
13. Gale Christianson. *Edwin Hubble*. New York, 1995. p. 76.
14. Amery. *Political Life*. Vol. 1. p. 38.
15. Sir John Willison. *Sir George Parkin*. London, 1929. pp. 152–3.
16. RTF 1985(1).
17. RTF 2326.
18. RTM 20 September 1906.
19. RTM 20 February 1903.
20. 18 March 1903. RTF 2044/1.
21. Parkin to Hawksley. 9 September 1903. RTF 1628/1.
22. Wylie to Parkin. 30 January 1904. RTF 1985/1.
23. *First Fifty Years*. p. 11.

Chapter 5: The Criteria

1. *First Fifty Years*. p. 8.
2. Anderson to Parkin. 22 March 1909; Memo to Trustees of 28 April 1909. RTF 1296.
3. RTF 1256(A).
4. RTF 1256(A).
5. *First Fifty Years*. p. 53.
6. *American Oxonian*. 1 and 2 (1972). p. 52.
7. *First Fifty Years*. p. 9.
8. William Plomer. *Cecil Rhodes*. Edinburgh, 1933. Africasouth edition. p. 168.
9. George R. Parkin. *The Rhodes Scholarships*. London, 1913. p. 120.
10. 22 September to 8 October 1909. RTF 1066.
11. Report to Trustees. End 1902. RTF 3675.
12. R. J. Challis. *Vicarious Rhodesians. Problems Affecting the Selection of Rhodesian Rhodes Scholars*. Salisbury, 1977. p. 2.
13. Report of October 1903. RTF 1219.
14. R. M. Ewen to Governor of Jamaica. 22 May 1908. RTF 1986(1).
15. Memo by A. H. Miles. 7 September 1908. RTF 1986.
16. Parkin memo of 29 April 1912. RTF 1296; *Sun*. 28 July 1912.
17. Parkin. *The Rhodes Scholarships*. pp. 100–1.
18. Kenny. *Rhodes Trust*. p. 35.
19. Report on visit to South Africa, 1910. RTF 3675.
20. 30 January 1905. RTF 2044(1).
21. Poynter. Kenny. *Rhodes Trust*. p. 325.
22. Brian Bamford. *The Substance*. Cape Town, 1960. p. 112.
23. Wilson to A. L. Smith. 4 May 1910. RTF 1296.
24. 11 April 1910. RTF 1296.
25. Parkin to Acting Secretary. 22 November 1912; Acting Secretary to Parkin. 14 December 1912. RTF 1250.
26. Parkin to Aydelotte. 29 August 1918. RTA 2(2).
27. 3 March 1908. RTF 1268.

Chapter 6: Surplus Funds

1. Milner to Michell. 24 August and 9 October 1909. Milner Papers. 468. ff. 67 and 92.
2. Michell to Milner. 27 September 1909. Milner Papers. 468. f. 84.
3. RTM 216.

4. Report by Boyd, 15 August 1904. RTF 1067.
5. Donald McIntyre. *A Century of 'Bishops'.* Cape Town, 1950. p. 45.
6. R. F. Currey. *Rhodes University.* Grahamstown, 1970. p. 8; Maylam. *Cult of Rhodes.* p. 65.
7. 5 May 1902. RTM; Darwin. Kenny. *Rhodes Trust.* p. 468.
8. Boyd to D. E. Brodie. 11 June 1903. RTF 1038.
9. 17 October 1903. RTF 1038.
10. John Marlow. *Milner: Apostle of Empire.* London, 1976. p. 178.
11. RTF 2773.
12. Marlowe. *Milner.* p. 208.
13. Milner to Geoffrey Robinson. 21 September 1906. RTF 1210.
14. 25 August 1901. Copy on RTF 2709(5).
15. July 1899. Copy on RTF 2709(5).
16. Milner to Richard Feetham. 6 September 1912. Milner Papers. 468. f. 172.
17. Nuttall. Kenny. *Rhodes Trust.* p. 257.
18. Michell to Parkin. 31 May 1915. RTF 2509.
19. *First Fifty Years.* p. 61.
20. Ibid. p. 92.
21. RTM. 217.
22. RTM. 945.

14. *American Oxonian.* 3 (1978). pp. 108–13.
15. *Varsity.* 17 November 1904.
16. *American Oxonian.* 4 (1964). p. 240; Thomas and Kathleen Schaeper. *Cowboys into Gentlemen.* New York, 1998. pp. 46–7.
17. *American Oxonian.* 2 (1951). p. 85.
18. *American Oxonian.* 2 (1970). p. 387.
19. Ross Galbraeth. *Scholars and Gentlemen Both.* Wellington, 2000. p. 140.
20. Wylie. Speech at Farewell Dinner. RTF 2044.
21. Parkin's Report on US Qualification Exam for 1907. RTF 3675.
22. Ibid.
23. Wylie to Professor Osler. 12 December 1910. RTF 1874.
24. Grey to Wylie. 18 January 1905. RTF 3676.
25. Michell to Joint Secretaries. 29 May 1903. RTF 2009.
26. 9 February 1911. RTF 1628.
27. Meeting of 11 July 1902. RTF 1066.
28. Parkin to Masson. 30 January 1913. RTF 1066.
29. 3 November 1904. RTF 1066.
30. Alan Paton. *Hofmeyr.* Oxford, 1964. p. 17.
31. Ibid. p. 331.
32. *American Oxonian.* 1 (1959). p. 6.
33. *American Oxonian.* 1 (1914). pp. 3–20.

Chapter 7: First Arrivals

1. *First Fifty Years.* p. 77.
2. Wylie to Hawksley. 29 April 1911. RTF 1682.
3. Karl Alexander von Müller. *Aus Garten der Vergangenheit.* Stuttgart, 1951. pp. 26–8.
4. RTF 1617.
5. Dawson to Millar. 24 January 1933. RTF 1617.
6. *First Fifty Years.* pp. 65–7.
7. Bissett to Woods. 24 April and 3 June 1903. RTF 1219(A); Boyd to Woods 18 April 1903 and to Duthie 11 December 1905; Wylie to Hawksley 24 April 1903. RTF 1219.
8. Wylie to Hawksley. 27 January 1905. RTF 1296.
9. *First Fifty Years.* p. 10.
10. *Varsity.* 29 April 1902.
11. *Isis.* 3 May 1902.
12. L. E. Jones. *An Edwardian Youth.* London, 1956. pp. 66–9.
13. Alexander. Kenny. *Rhodes Trust.* p. 105.

Chapter 8: Trust and Empire

1. Kenny. *Rhodes Trust.* p. 518.
2. David Gilmour in *The Long Recessional* (London, 2002), provides a lucid and stimulating analysis of this question.
3. Sir David Smith's address as Chancellor of the University of New Zealand on 1 September 1953 has interesting reflections on this theme. Copy in RTF 2790.
4. 21 June 1912. RTF 2109.
5. 20 September 1916. RTF 1294(1).
6. Amery. *Political Life.* Vol. 1. p. 184.
7. Grey to Boyd. 1 June 1905. RTF 1400.
8. May 1907 and 16 December 1921. RTF 1400.
9. Parkin to R. Carr Harris. 2 October 1907. RTF 1191.
10. For a discussion of this issue, see Symonds. *Oxford and Empire.* p. 45.
11. 18 August 1906. RTF 1038.
12. 20 November 1907. RTF 2031.
13. 4 November 1907. RTM 765.
14. 23 July 1912. RTF 2285.

15. 22 March 1907 to 1 October 1908. RTF 2031.
16. Carroll Quigley. *Tragedy and Hope*. New York, 1966. pp. 131–3. See also David Billington's telling comments in *American Oxonian*. 4 (1994). pp. 225–32.
17. Amery. *Political Life*. Vol. 1. p. 347; Darwin. Kenny. *Rhodes Trust*. p. 463.
18. Deborah Lavin. *From Empire to International Commonwealth*. Oxford, 1995. pp. 71, 118–19.
19. Parkin. *Rhodes Scholarships*. p. VII.
20. 5 November 1907. RTF 3676.

Chapter 9: Lesser Mortals

1. July 1899. Copy on RTF 2709(5).
2. Rotberg. p. 667.
3. A. C. Leroy to Boyd. 11 July 1903. RTF 1362; 22 July 1903. RTM 116.
4. 21 December 1912. RTF 1985(1).
5. 7 November 1916 and 15 May 1918. RTF 1362.
6. Boyd to Hawksley. 21 March 1907. RTF 1122.
7. Boyd to Wylie. 24 April 1907. RTF 1122.
8. Report by Parkin. RTF 3675.
9. Memo of June 1903. RTF 1122.
10. 19 July and 17 November 1904. RTM 188 and 224.
11. Boyd to Wylie. 21 March 1907. RTF 3676.
12. Rosebery to Boyd. 22 March 1907. RTF 1122.
13. Wylie to Boyd. 17 March 1907. RTF 1122.
14. Challis. *Vicarious Rhodesians*. p. 23.
15. June 1908. RTF 1617.
16. Wylie to Boyd. 20 March 1907. RTA 1122.
17. Report of 30 September 1910. RTF 1296.
18. Wylie to Provost Hamilton. 18 April 1909. RTF 1122.
19. Wylie to Boyd. 24 April 1907. RTF 1122.
20. Arthur Feez to Wylie. 5 March 1910. RTF 1113.
21. Wylie's Annual Report for 1910–11. RTF 1122.
22. Wylie to R. H. Roe. 12 March 1912. RTF 1113.
23. 6 April 1908. RTM 857.
24. Challis. *Vicarious Rhodesians*. p. 22.
25. Parkin to Hawksley. 18 May 1905. RTF 1269; McCalla. Kenny. *Rhodes Trust*. p. 206.
26. Parkin to Hawksley. 17 September 1909. RTF 1269.

27. Parkin to Hawksley. 17 November 1909. RTF 1269.
28. Parkin to Mrs Mavor. 5 November 1913. RTF 1985(1).
29. Wylie report for 1908. RT 1617.

Chapter 10: Americans are Different

1. 30 October 1906. RTF 2285.
2. 28 October 1909. RTF 1296.
3. *American Oxonian*. 2 (1962). pp. 64–72.
4. Schaeper and Schaeper. *Cowboys into Gentlemen*. pp. 46–7.
5. *American Oxonian*. 2 (1927). pp. 29–36.
6. Wylie to Parkin. 22 November 1904. RTF 2044(1); 1909. RTF 1256(A).
7. David Munro to A. L. Smith. 15 April 1910. RTF 1296.
8. E. C. Norton to Parkin. 27 December 1911. RTF 1296.
9. Paton. *Hofmeyr*. p. 64.
10. Thomas Daniel Young. *Gentleman in a Dustcart*. Baton Rouge, 1976. p. 41.
11. Schaeper and Schaeper. *Cowboys into Gentlemen*. p. 65.
12. *Alumni Magazine of the Alumni Association of American Rhodes Scholars*. September 1910. p. 7.
13. *Literary Digest*. Vol. XLV. October 1912. p. 620.
14. Max Beerbohm. *Zuleika Dobson*. London, 1911. pp. 120–2.
15. *First Fifty Years*. p. 89.
16. *Daily Mail*. 11 October 1910.
17. John Crowe Ransom. *Selected Letters*. ed. T. D. Young. Baton Rouge, 1985. p. 35.
18. *Alumni Magazine*. August 1911. p. 16.
19. D. R. Porter to Parkin. 18 March 1910; Michell to Mrs Mavor. 30 April 1910. RTF 1296.
20. 7 July 1913. RTM 1854.
21. Alexander. Kenny. *Rhodes Trust*. pp. 166–7.
22. *Alumni Magazine*. April 1913. pp. 4–7.
23. Memo of 6 October 1907. RTF 1265.
24. Memo of 31 January 1912. RTF 1296.
25. *American Oxonian*. 3 (1918). pp. 81–96.
26. Report of 31 October 1911. RTF 1296.

Chapter 11: The Colonials

1. C. K. Allen. *Forty Years of the Rhodes Scholarships*. Oxford, 1944. p. 3.
2. Galbraeth. *Scholars and Gentlemen Both*. p. 135.

3. Record of meeting of 4 September 1903. RTF 1628(1).
4. Parkin to Grey. 30 October 1906. RTF 1985(1).
5. Peacock to Parkin. 18 April 1911. RTF 2357.
6. Christianson. *Hubble.* pp. 65 and 132.
7. Parkin memo of 2 February 1910; Parkin to Parrock. 15 March 1910. RTF 1247(1).
8. Nuttall. Kenny. *Rhodes Trust.* p. 260.
9. Report on tour of 1910. Nuttall. Kenny. *Rhodes Trust.* p. 260.
10. Paton. *Hofmeyr.* pp. 32–5.
11. Michell to Parkin. 12 June 1909. RTF 2009.
12. Report for 1910. RTF 3675.
13. Morgan. Kenny. *Rhodes Trust.* p. 411.
14. Parkin to L. Foggin. 31 January 1912. RTF 1219.
15. Memo of 24 November 1914. RTF 1219.
16. Parkin memo of 24 April 1912. RTF 1296.
17. Parkin to Boyd. 19 April 1904. RTF 1546.
18. McIntyre. *A Century of 'Bishops'.*
19. Report for 1908–9. 28 October 1909. RTF 1296.

Chapter 12: First Impressions

1. Williams to J. G. Phillimore. 15 November 1962. RTF 3190.
2. RTF 1256(A).
3. *Alumni Magazine.* April 1908. pp. 2–3.
4. RTF 1617.
5. Report of 30 September 1910. RTF 1296.
6. *First Fifty Years.* p. 85.
7. *The Times.* 9 September 1918.

Chapter 13: The First World War

1. 23 February 1915. RTA 2(2).
2. Parkin to Wylie. 1 September 1914. RTF 3676.
3. 5 September 1914. Milner Papers. 469. f. 133.
4. Parkin to Wylie. 3 September 1914. RTF 3676.
5. Report for 1914–15. RTF 1296.
6. Wylie to Allen. 6 October 1939. RTF 2985.
7. *American Oxonian.* 1 (1915). pp. 47–9.
8. Parkin to Aydelotte. 3 March 1916. RTA 2(2).
9. Parkin to Grey. 20 February 1917. RTF 2285.
10. *The Fatherland: Fair Play for Germany and Austria-Hungary.* ed. George Viereck.

cit. Alexander. Kenny. *Rhodes Trust.* p. 183.
11. *American Oxonian.* 3. (1915). p. 138.
12. Parkin to Wylie. 27 August 1917. RTF 3676.
13. *American Oxonian.* 4 (1917) p. 144.
14. Parkin to Cundall. 7 March 1916. RTF 1986.
15. *Winnipeg Tribune.* June 1926. Copy on RTA 2(2).
16. Parkin to George Duthie. 20 November 1914. RTF 1219.
17. 21 August 1914. RTA 2(2).
18. 2 February 1915. Milner Papers. 470. f. 7.
19. 15 March 1916. RTF 1682.
20. 13 April 1916. RTF 1682.
21. Michell to Parkin 22 May and 2 August 1916. RTF 1682.
22. Michell to Milner. 15 March and 5 April 1916. Milner Papers. 470. ff. 173 and 189.
23. Wylie to Gilmour. 31 August 1918; Brocksma to Wylie. 2 December 1918. RTF 2252.
24. April 1916. RTF 2367; *Oxford and the Idea of Commonwealth.* ed. Frederick Madden and D. K. Fieldhouse. London, 1982. p. 91; 6 April 1916. RTF 2370.
25. Milner to Wylie. 9 December 1914. RTF 3676.
26. Kenny. *Rhodes Trust.* pp. 15–16.
27. W. M. Macmillan. *My South African Years.* Cape Town, 1975. p. 105.
28. Bernstorff to Wylie. July 1915; Wylie to Gilmour. 22 January 1915. RTF 1296.
29. 14 December 1915. RTF 2351(A).
30. 7 May 1917. Milner Papers. 470. f. 31.
31. 7 May 1915. Milner Papers. 470. f. 58.
32. 31 December 1915. Milner Papers. 470. f. 60.
33. Ibid.
34. 8 July 1917. Milner Papers. 471. f. 84.
35. Kipling to Mrs Hill. 8 April 1902. Copy on RTF 3709J(1).
36. Entry for 27 August 1917. Ibid.

Chapter 14: Play Resumed

1. Wylie's report to Trustees. 19 August 1919. RTF 1296.
2. Wylie to Grigg. 10 March 1920. RTF 1296; *American Oxonian.* 4 (1969). pp. 230–9; Parkin to Aydelotte. 15 April 1920. RTA 2(2).
3. Wylie to Gilmour. 11 July 1916. RTF 1296.
4. Memo by Wylie. 26 November 1918. RTF 1432.

5. Kipling to Gilmour. 8 December 1918. RTF 3676.
6. *First Fifty Years.* p. 107.
7. Allen to Lothian. 16 November 1931; Aydelotte to Lothian. 15 January 1932. RTF 1432; Allen to Lothian. 23 November 1931. RTF 1296.
8. David Lewis. *The Good Fight.* Toronto, 1981. p. 18.
9. Joseph Blotner. *Robert Penn Warren.* New York, 1997. pp. 87–92.
10. Wylie to Gilmour. 26 February 1919. RTF 1296.
11. Grigg to Behan. 18 November 1921. RTF 1296.
12. *South African Review.* 17 October 1924.
13. Beit to Grigg. 5 November 1924. RTA 2(2).

Chapter 15: The Trust between the Wars

1. Rosebery to Milner. 14 April 1916. RTF 3709(1).
2. Milner to Gilmour. 7 July 1916. RTF 2342.
3. 11 January 1919. Milner Papers. 472. f. 4.
4. Grigg to Milner. 7 October 1920. RTF 2500.
5. See, in particular, David Faber. *Speaking for England.* London, 2006. p. 138.
6. Amery to Elton. 10 November 1941. RTF 3000.
7. Wylie to Aydelotte. 7 March 1921 and 28 May 1925. RTA 5.
8. J. R. M. Butler. *Lord Lothian.* London, 1960. p. 15.
9. Symonds. *Oxford and Empire.* pp. 71–2.
10. H. A. L. Fisher Papers. 59. ff. 8–12.
11. Butler. *Lothian.* p. 127.
12. Edward Grigg. *The Faith of an Englishman.* London, 1936. pp. 232 and 246; Symonds. *Oxford and Empire.* p. 77.
13. Kipling to Beit. 22 June 1925. RTF 3709J(1); *Letters of Rudyard Kipling.* ed. T. Pinney. Iowa, 1999. Vol. 4. p. 509; *The Leo Amery Diaries.* ed. John Barnes and David Nicholson. Vol. 1. London, 1980. p. 415; Kenny. *Rhodes Trust.* p. 25.
14. Copy on RTF 3709J(1).
15. Amery. *Diaries.* Vol. 1. p. 415.
16. 23 December 1932. Copy on RTF 3709J(1).
17. 4 April 1930. RTA 11.
18. Beit to Kerr. 10 March 1929 and subsequent correspondence. RTF 2773.
19. Kerr to Beit. 30 May 1929. RTF 2773.

20. Beit to Kerr. 1 June 1929. RTF 2773.
21. Lothian to Allen. 21 February 1939. RTF 2978(1).
22. Fisher to Lothian. 29 November 1938. RTF 2657(B).
23. 1 May 1939. RTF 2978(1).

Chapter 16: The Oxford Experience

1. Allen to Lothian. 1 February 1938. RTF 1296.
2. Frank Milligan. *Eugene A. Forsey.* Calgary, 2004. p. 65; cf. Eugene Forsey. *A Life on the Fringe.* Toronto, 1900.
3. J. L. Granatstein. *A Man of Influence: Norman A. Robertson.* Toronto, 1981. p. 13.
4. Report on visit to United States. March–June 1931. RTF 3675.
5. RTF 1460A; Memo by Kerr. 19 July 1929. RTF 1296.
6. Report for 1930–1. RTF 1296.
7. Allen to Warden of Merton. 31 January 1937. RTF 2326(A)
8. *First Fifty Years.* p. 31.
9. Paul Gérin-Lajoie. *Combats d'un révolutionnaire tranquille.* Montreal, 1989. p. 17.
10. Report for 1926–7. RTF 1296.
11. RTF Minute No. 3131 of 4 October 1920.
12. John King Fairbank. *Chinabound.* New York, 1982. p. 30.
13. Memo by Lothian. 17 November 1933. RTF 2709(3).
14. Wylie to Aydelotte. 25 May 1927. RTF 2326; Wylie's report for 1926–7. RTF 1296.
15. Report for 1930–1. RTF 1296.
16. RTM 18 July 1924. Grigg to Behan. 7 January 1925. RTF 2500.
17. Report of 8 July 1925. RTA/9. pp. 14–16.
18. Memo of 4 June 1926. RTF 1296.
19. Report for 1925–6. RTF 1296.
20. 5 November 1925. PPT 344.
21. Escott Reid. *Radical Mandarin.* Toronto, 1989. p. 49.
22. John Crowe Ransom, *Selected Letters.* p. 45.
23. Wylie to Parkin. 9 May 1905. RTF 2044(2).
24. RTF 2504.
25. 29 June 1929. RTF 2343.
26. *American Oxonian.* 2 (1953) p. 65.
27. Report for 1928–9. RTF 1296.
28. Aydelotte to Kerr. 3 July 1928. RTF 2809(A).

29. Massey to Kerr. 15 January 1930; Peacock to Kerr. 15 February 1930. RTF 2793.
30. Fisher to Lothian. 17 February 1930; Lothian to Smith. 28 May 1930. RTF 2793.
31. *American Oxonian*. 1 (1959). pp. 70–2.
32. Dorothy Allen. *Sunlight and Shadow*. Oxford, 1960. pp. 45–6, 52, 101.
33. Allen to Lothian. 3 December 1935. RTF 3517; Allen to Aydelotte. 3 March 1938. RTF 3266.
34. *The History of the University of Oxford*. Vol. 8. ed. Brian Harrison. Oxford, 1994. pp. 615–16.
35. RTF 1296.
36. Aydelotte to Wylie. 21 December 1922. RTA 5.
37. Forsey. *A Life on the Fringe*. p. 48.
38. Peter Stursberg. *Roland Michener: The Last Viceroy*. Toronto, 1989. p. 1.
39. *American Oxonian*. 3 (1922). p. 122.

Chapter 17: Rhodes House

1. 26 June 1924. RTF 3676.
2. Jennifer Sherwood and Nikolaus Pevsner. *Oxfordshire*. London, 1974. pp. 275–6.
3. PPT Minutes. 15 May 1929.
4. *American Oxonian*. 4 (1929). p. 165
5. Geoffrey Wheatcroft. *The Randlords*. London, 1993. p. 265.
6. *American Oxonian*. 4 (1926). pp. 135–6.
7. Memo by Kerr. 30 April 1926. RTF 2709(1).
8. Fisher to Lothian. 21 May 1931. RTF 2809(A).
9. 31 January 1937. RTF 2326(A).
10. Kerr to Fisher. 14 February 1930; Kerr to Smuts. 13 February 1930; Record of conversation between Fisher and Dr Gunn of the Rockefeller Trust; Dr Gunn to Fisher. 8 May 1931. RTF 2792(1) and (2).
11. Coupland to Curtis. 6 April 1929; Memo by Kerr of 19 April 1929. RTF 2792(1).
12. 19 April 1934. RTF 2637.
13. James Bertram. *Capes of China Slide Away*. Auckland, 1993. p. 64.
14. Kerr to Bordern. 15 February 1927. RTF 2694.
15. Fisher to Kerr. 21 June 1926. RTF 2694.
16. Report for 1930–1. RTF 1296.
17. Allen to Lothian. 9 June 1933. RTF 2694.
18. Elton to Amery. 2 January 1940. RTF 2694.

19. Dawson to Walford Selby. 31 January 1940. RTF 2694.
20. Elton to Williams. 31 December 1954. RTF 2694.
21. A. Cowley to Kerr. 12 July 1928. H. A. L. Fisher Papers. 81. f. 47.
22. 15 October 1928. H. A. L. Fisher Papers. 81. f. 57.
23. 16 October 1928. H. A. L. Fisher Papers. 81. f. 52.

Chapter 18: Money and Empire

1. Kenny. *Rhodes Trust*. pp. 26–7.
2. 8 October 1926. RTF 2709(2).
3. RTM 4236 of 3 May 1932.
4. Memo of 17 November 1933. RTF 2709(3).
5. *The Times*. 17 June 1934; Allen to Millar. 20 June 1934. RTF 1191.
6. Behan to Lothian. 1 July 1930. RTF 2811(1).
7. Ruby Fairbridge. *Pinjarra: The Building of a Farm School*. Oxford, 1937. p. 23.
8. 14 November 1906. RTF 2285.
9. Duthie to Boyd. 2 March 1908. RTF 2285.
10. *The Autobiography of Kingsley Fairbridge*. Oxford, 1927. p. 127.
11. Report for 1908. RTF 1617.
12. Kenny. *Rhodes Trust*. p. 22.
13. Memo by Kerr. 29 September 1925. RTF 2818.
14. Memo by Lothian. 28 July 1930. RTF 2818.
15. 5 May 1939. RTF 2981.
16. James McNeish. *Dance of the Peacocks*. Auckland, 2003. p. 80.
17. *The History of the Times*. Vol. 4. Part II. London, 1952. p. 749.
18. Memo by Lothian. 13 November 1936. RTF 2935.
19. PPT Minute 1436 of 21 October 1937.
20. 30 January 1935. RTF 3675.
21. Hugh Collis Barry. *A Modest Man*. Privately printed, 2004. p. 36.
22. Minute 3292 of 7 June 1921.
23. Butler. *Lothian*. pp. 135–6.
24. 30 October 1935. RTF 2637.
25. Wylie to Dawson. 13 May 1920. RTF 1296.
26. Lothian to Butler. 28 June 1933. RTF 2361.
27. Lothian to Wrench. 26 March 1930. RTF 2208.

Chapter 19: Politics and the Scholars

1. Kerr to Professor F. Clarke. 30 August 1928. RTF 2009.
2. Interview with Philip Kaiser.
3. Howard Smith. *Events Leading Up To My Death.* New York, 1996. p. 59.
4. '*Bridging Two Worlds'. Letters and articles by E. Wilson Lyon.* ed. Elizabeth Webb. Privately published.
5. *American Oxonian.* 3 (1979). pp. 192–203; Arnold Heeney. *The Things That Are Caesar's.* Toronto, 1972. p. 22.
6. *American Oxonian.* 3 (1979). pp. 192–203.
7. Granatstein. *A Man of Influence.* p. 18.
8. *American Oxonian.* 3 (1979). pp. 7–15.
9. Schaeper and Schaeper. *Cowboys into Gentlemen.* p. 125.
10. Alexander. Kenny. *Rhodes Trust.* p. 181; *American Oxonian.* 1 (1924). pp. 182–3.
11. Report for 1923–4. RTF 1296.
12. Reid. *Radical Mandarin.* p. 58.
13. Lewis. *Good Fight.* p. 76; Allen to Lothian. 21 April 1937. RLF 1296.
14. Allen to Aydelotte. 11 August 1938. RTF 2756(A).
15. RTF 1296.
16. Amery. *Political Life.* Vol. 1. p. 330; Report by Wylie on visit to Australia. p. 22. RTF 2044(1).
17. Schaeper. *Cowboys into Gentlemen.* p. 95; Wylie to Aydelotte. 26 October 1936. RTF 1233(A).
18. Lewis. *Good Fight.* pp. 32–4.
19. Allen to Millar. 24 October 1934. RTF 2153.
20. Interview with Bob Rae.
21. Craig Munro. *Inky Stephensen. Wild Man of Letters.* Melbourne, 1984. pp. 18–44.
22. 28 June 1926. RTF 1296.
23. Allen to Aydelotte. 7 May 1940. RTF 1233(A).
24. 30 May 1936. RTF 2790.

Chapter 20: New Rules for the New World

1. Parkin to Gilmour. 26 March 1918. RTF 1296.
2. Aydelotte to Grigg. 12 March 1920 and 21 December 1920. RTF 1296.
3. Frank Aydelotte. *The American Rhodes Scholarships: A Review of the First Forty Years.* Princeton, 1946. p. 30.
4. James Winston to Wylie. 16 February 1928. RTF 1296.

5. PPT Minute 781 of 23 July 1929.
6. Aydelotte to Lothian. 15 December 1930. RTF 1296.
7. *American Oxonian.* 4 (1938). pp. 92–3.
8. Report on visit to United States. p. 3. RTF 2044(1).
9. *American Oxonian.* 2 (1933). pp. 92–3.
10. *American Oxonian.* 3 (1934). p. 161.
11. Dean Rusk. *As I Saw It.* London, 1991. p. 65.
12. Randall Bennett Woods. *Fulbright: A Biography.* New York, 1995. p. 31.
13. *American Oxonian.* 3 (1978). pp. 120–8.
14. Report on visit to USA. September–October 1927. RTF 3675.
15. *American Oxonian.* 4 (1935). pp. 204–5.
16. *American Oxonian.* 4 (1939). pp. 355–6.

Chapter 21: The Other Main Constituencies, 1919–1939

1. Aydelotte to Wylie. 1 August 1921. RTA 5.
2. Memo by Grigg. July 1923. RTF 1296.
3. RST 251 of 16 October 1923.
4. Grigg to Macdonnell. 9 December 1925. RTF 1247(3).
5. Report by Kerr on visit to Canada. September 1925. RTF 3675.
6. Allen to Peacock. 1 November 1935. RTF 2555(1).
7. Nuttall. Kenny. *Rhodes Trust.* p. 263.
8. Report on visit. July–August 1933. RTF 3675.
9. Allen to Lothian. 3 April 1934. RTF 2009.
10. Lothian to Wylie. 15 October 1931. RTF 1296.
11. Wylie to Kerr. 23 April 1925. RTF 1296; Nuttall. Kenny. *Rhodes Trust.* p. 267.
12. Report by Allen for 1936–7. RTF 1296.
13. SF 1052 of 19 July 1932.
14. 24 March 1920. RTF 2500.
15. M. J. Rendall's report. p. 19. RTA/9.
16. Poynter. Kenny. *Rhodes Trust.* p. 331.
17. Newdegate to Dawson. 8 November 1921. RTF 2554.
18. Grigg to Behan. 24 January 1923. RTF 2500(A).
19. Uncut version of John Poynter's chapter for Kenny. *Rhodes Trust.* p. 41.
20. M. J. Rendall's report. p. 12. *Rhodes Trust.* RTA/9.
21. Allen to Elton. 17 February 1941. RTF 1155.
22. Allen to Behan. 6 November 1934 and 3 November 1936. RTF 2500(A).

23. Report by Lothian on visit to Australia. November 1938. RTF 2500(3).
24. Report by Wylie on visit to New Zealand. May 1932. RTF 2044(1).
25. Interview with Sir Geoffrey Cox.
26. Kerr to Wylie. 15 March 1925. RTF 3676.
27. McNeish. *Dance of the Peacocks*. p. 19.
28. Allen to Lothian. 31 January 1934. RTF 1262(3).
29. McNeish. *Dance of the Peacocks*. p. 36.
30. Lothian to Wylie. 15 October 1931. RTF 1262(2).

Chapter 22: Small Fry and Associations

1. Dawson to Edward Ward. 24 November 1921. RTF 2364.
2. Grey to Wylie. 3 October 1927; Wylie to Kerr. 4 July 1927. RTF 1546.
3. Ernest Escott to Wylie. 17 August 1928. RTF 1296.
4. Colonial Secretary, Bermuda, to Kerr. 10 December 1926. RTF 2524(3).
5. Fisher to Kerr. 1 April 1929. RTF 2524(3).
6. RTF 1296.
7. Allen to Lothian. 12 August 1937; Sir Edward Denham to Lothian. 22 January 1938. RTF 1296.
8. Allen to Millar. 19 April 1938. RTF 1986.
9. Allen to Lothian. 19 October 1937. RTF 1986.
10. Allen to Lothian. 8 November 1937. RTF 1986.
11. Challis. *Vicarious Rhodesians*. p. 15.
12. 2 August 1934. RTF 1219.
13. Allen to Millar. 22 January 1936. RTF 1219.
14. Allen to Lothian. 13 January 1939 and 23 May 1939. RTF 1219.
15. Wylie's report of 6 July 1923. RTF 1296.
16. Memo by Kerr of 4 October 1929. RTF 1296.
17. 6 October 1933. RTF 2044(1).
18. 15 May 1933. RTF 2811(1).
19. Lothian to McKenzie. 14 October 1938; Focken to Lothian. 2 December 1938. RTF 1628(3).
20. Wylie's report on visit to Australia. February–March 1932. RTF 3675.
21. Allen's report on visit to Canada. April 1935. RTF 3675.
22. Macdonnell to Lothian. 4 October 1932. RTF 1247(2).

23. Lothian's report on visit to Canada. November 1934. RTF 1296.
24. Wylie's report on visit to South Africa. November–December 1931. RTF 2044.

Chapter 23: Selection, 1919–1939

1. Wylie's report on visit to America. May–August 1919. RTF 3675.
2. Aydelotte to Wylie. 20 December 1921. RTA 5.
3. Report for 1920–1. RTF 1296.
4. Wylie's report on visit to Canada. July 1932. RTF 1296.
5. Boyd-Wilton to Jellicoe. 3 July 1923; Jellicoe to Boyd-Wilson. 13 July 1923. RTF 1628(2).
6. Kerr to Norris. 28 February 1930. RTF 1628(2).
7. Memo by Grigg of 3 June 1921. RTF 2524(1).
8. Kerr to Sydney Braithwaite. 17 February 1928. RTF 2524(1).
9. Grigg to Wylie. 1 April 1921; Wylie to Grigg. 4 April 1921. RTF 2009.
10. Draft by Kerr for meeting of 17 June 1927. RTF 1296.
11. Memo of 4 June 1926. RTF 1296.
12. Grigg to Lothian. 16 May 1934. RTF 2790.
13. Allen to Millar. 1 February 1938. RTF 2962.
14. Report on visit to America. March–April 1935. RTF 3675.
15. *The Times*. 19 June 1933; Memos by Allen and Lothian. RTF 1296.
16. Schaeper. *Cowboys into Gentlemen*. p. 153.
17. Philip M. Kaiser. *Journeying Far and Wide*. New York, 1992. p. 41.
18. Behan to Allen. 28 May 1940. John Poynter's uncut version of his chapter for Kenny. *Rhodes Trust*.
19. Poynter. Kenny. *Rhodes Trust*. p. 338.
20. Bertram. *Capes of China Slide Away*. pp. 41–2.

Chapter 24: Success?

1. 26 November 1920. RTF 3676.
2. Memo by Grigg of 3 June 1921; Lovat to Grigg. 6 June 1921. RTF 2524(1).
3. Memo by Behan of 24 March 1932. RTF 1460(A).
4. Memo to selection committees. 15 July 1932. RTF 1296.

5. Allen to Behan. 16 December 1932. RTF 2500(A).
6. Sarah Gertrude Millin. *Rhodes*. London, 1933. p. 332.
7. *American Oxonian*. 2 (1935). pp. 79–80.
8. Lothian to Master of University College. 13 December 1932. RTF 1233(A).
9. *American Oxonian*. 1 (1921). pp. 1–36.
10. *American Oxonian*. 2 (1927). pp. 29–36.
11. David Halberstam. *The Best and the Brightest*. London, 1972. p. 316.
12. Report on visit to Canada. August–September 1937. RTF 2809.
13. Grigg to Milner. 7 October 1920. RTF 2500.
14. G. V. Portus. *Australian Rhodes Review*. March 1934.
15. John Poynter's uncut version of his chapter for Kenny. *Rhodes Trust*. p. 66.
16. Ibid. p. 83
17. Report by Wylie on visit to Australia. February–March 1932. RTF 3675.
18. Gwyn Macfarlane. *Howard Florey*. Oxford, 1979. p. 68.
19. Report by Wylie on visit to South Africa. November–December 1931. RTF 2044(2).
20. J. F. Hofmeyr to Professor F. Clarke. 17 June 1928. RTF 2009.

Chapter 25: Germany

1. 7 September 1922. RTF 1682.
2. Sheppard. Kenny. *Rhodes Trust*. p. 372.
3. 18 December 1928. RTF 1682.
4. Bihl to Wylie. 24 June 1930; Lothian to Bihl. 8 July 1930. RTF 1682.
5. Adenauer to Lindsay. April 1933; Allen to Lindsay. 28 April 1933; Mendelssohn-Bartholdy to Lindsay. 9 June 1933. RTF 1682.
6. Waley-Cohen to Amery. 1 June 1933; Lothian to Amery. RTF 1296.
7. Report for 1935–6. RTF 1296.
8. Unpublished thesis. Thomas Weber. Oxford, 1998. RT Box 231. p. 42.
9. Record of conversation between Lothian and Bernstorff. 1 August 1933. RTF 1296.
10. Bernstorff to Lothian. 4 October 1934; Lothian's covering memo to Trustees. RTF 1296.
11. 13 August 1936. RTF 1682.
12. Giles MacDonogh. *A Good German. Adam von Trott zu Solz*. London, 1989. p. 77.
13. Butler. *Lothian*. pp. 202–3.

14. 1 December 1937. RTF 1296.
15. McNeish. *Dance of the Peacocks*. p. 64.
16. *The Times*. 6 March 1940.
17. Allen to Lothian. 19 May 1934. RTF 1682.
18. Allen to Lothian. 30 January 1934. RTF 1682.
19. Allen to Lothian. 26 June 1934. RTF 1682.
20. Memo by Lothian of 13 July 1934. RTF 1296.
21. Peacock to Millar. 8 February 1932. RTF 1682.
22. Barbara Wood. *Alias Papa: A Life of Fritz Schumacher*. London, 1982. p. 37.
23. Lothian to Allen. 11 December 1936. RTF 1682.

Chapter 26: The Second World War

1. 28 November 1939. RTF 2985.
2. Allen. *Sunlight and Shadow*. p. 112.
3. Allen to Aydelotte. 8 October 1939. RTF 1233(A).
4. Aydelotte to Elton. 26 September 1939. RTF 2985.
5. *American Oxonian*. 3 (1940). p. 201.
6. 14 September 1939. RTF 2500(A).
7. Elton to J. G. Higgins. 4 October 1939. RTF 2985.
8. Allen to Lothian. 12 December 1939. RTF 2985.
9. Memo for meeting of 27 October 1939. RTF 1296.
10. Elton to Cox. 28 October 1942. RTF 2461.
11. 19 and 20 June 1944. RTF 1546.
12. Allen to Elton. 23 June 1941; Elton to Tyler. 26 June 1941. RTF 2985.
13. Memo of 4 December 1945. RTF 2709.
14. 7 June 1943. RTF 1233(A).
15. Allen to Elton. 31 August 1945. RTF 2504.
16. Allen to Elton. 16 May 1951. RTF 2504.
17. Allen. *Sunlight and Shadow*. p. 118.
18. 10 October 1941. Cyclostyled copy on RTF 1432.
19. Allen. *Sunlight and Shadow*. p. 113.
20. 28 February 1945. RTF 1233(A).
21. Memo by Elton for meeting of 29 July 1941. RTF 1296.
22. Lothian to Elton. 7 March 1940. RTF 2361.
23. Report for 1939–40. RTF 1296.
24. *Toronto Globe and Mail*. 22 November 1944; Peacock to Elton. 17 March 1943. RTF 1460.
25. Munro. *Inky Stephensen*. pp. 204–5, 233.
26. Richard Davis. *Open to Talent*. Hobart, 1990.

27. Malan to Allen. 29 May 1940; Allen to Elton. 5 June 1940. RTF 1296.
28. Memo by Elton for meeting of 24 September 1940. RTF 1296.
29. *Chicago Daily Tribune.* 26 August 1943; 20 September 1943; 27 September 1943.
30. Report for 1942–3. RTF 1296; *American Oxonian.* 4 (1943). pp. 190–4.
31. Woods. *Fulbright.* pp. 65 and 83.
32. 15 March 1941. RTF 1233(A).
33. *American Oxonian.* 2 (1940). p. 112; 3 (1940). pp. 168–70.
34. Report for 1942–3. RTF 1296.
35. Nicholas Cull. *Selling War.* Oxford, 1995. pp. 74 and 177.
36. Sheppard. Kenny. *Rhodes Trust.* p. 401.
37. Conclusion 1844 of 13 December 1939.
38. Hugh Trevor-Roper. *The Last Days of Hitler.* Seventh edition. London, 1995. pp. 105–9.
39. Memo of 30 July 1948. RTF 1296.
40. Schumacher's interview with James Fox. Copy on RTF 1682(C).
41. Memo of 4 April 1945. RTF 1296.
42. Memo by Elton for meeting of 7 October 1944. RTF 1296.

Chapter 27: Play Resumed Again

1. Memo by Allen. 18 September 1945. RTF 1296.
2. Interview with Zelman Cowen.
3. *First Fifty Years.* p. 176.
4. Copy in *American Oxonian.* 2 (1946). pp. 106–8.
5. Allen. *Sunlight and Shadow.* p. 144; *American Oxonian.* 3 (1947). p. 165.
6. 25 October 1948. RTF 1432; Allen to Elton. 14 September 1949. RTF 1432.
7. Memo for meeting of 26 July 1947. RTF 1296.
8. Aydelotte to Allen. 8 January 1948. RTF 1233(A); Allen to Aydelotte. 3 February 1948. RTF 1233(A).
9. Williams to H. M. Finucan. April 1954. John Poynter's uncut version of his chapter for Kenny. *Rhodes Trust.* p. 66.
10. Elton to Michener. 11 November 1952. RTF 1247(6).
11. Elton to Michener. 15 June 1952. RTF 1247(6).
12. Elton to Michener. 16 March 1955. RTF 1247(6).
13. *American Oxonian.* 2 (1999). pp. 146–52.
14. Bryan Gould. *Goodbye to All That.* London, 1995. p. 32.

15. 18 December 1947. RTF 1233(A); Interview with Willem Hefer.
16. *First Fifty Years.* p. 34.
17. Correspondence between 31 May 1948 and 1 December 1950. RTF 2286(2).
18. Memo of 23 February 1950. RTF 1296.
19. Lowe to Williams. 19 January 1948. RTF 2326(A).
20. Williams to Welsh. 4 March 1970. RTF 2009.
21. Elton to McKenzie. 6 May 1947. RTF 1628.
22. Allen to Gie. 19 May 1947. RTF 2009.
23. Memo for meeting of 16 February 1954. RT Secretaries' Reports.
24. Elton to Havens. 3 May 1950; E. F. D'Arms, Rockefeller Foundation, to Elton. 9 November 1951; Carl Spaeth, Ford Foundation, to Elton. 3 October 1952; Elton to Spaeth. 7 October 1952; Elton to Rusk. 16 July 1956. RTF 2095.

Chapter 28: End of Empire

1. 9 February 1942. RTF 3000.
2. 30 March 1943. RTF 3012.
3. *First Fifty Years.* p. 47.
4. Gie to Elton. 26 October 1957. RTF 3143.
5. Kenny. *Rhodes Trust.* p. 460.
6. Ibid. p. 71.
7. RTF 3147.
8. Memos for meeting of 23 July 1955 and 26 October 1955. RT Secretaries' Reports.
9. Memo for meetings of 13 June 1981. RT Secretaries' Reports.

Chapter 29: South African Twilight

1. *Cape Times.* 21 September 1946.
2. Report by Gie of 9 January 1960. RTF 2009.
3. Bamford. *Substance.* p. 44.
4. Gie to Elton. 13 January 1947; Allen to Elton. 14 February 1947. RTF 2009.
5. Report on visit to South Africa. February–March 1948. RT Secretaries' Reports.
6. RTF 3076.
7. Gie to Elton. 7 May 1953. RTF 3088.
8. Bean to Allen. September 1949; Allen to Elton. 1 February 1950; Elton to Allen. 2 February 1950; Elton to Bean. 2 February 1950. RTF 2153.
9. Welfare Trust to Elton. 14 July 1947; Elton to Trust. 25 August 1947. RTF 2790.

10. Report by Gie of 22 February 1966; Williams to Gie. 16 March 1966. RTF 2009.
11. Memo for meeting of 16 March 1967. RT Secretaries' Reports.
12. Memo by John Rowett for meeting of 7 June 2002. RT Secretaries' Reports.

Chapter 30: The Williams Years

1. *American Oxonian.* 1 (1956). p. 29.
2. Christmas Letter for 1965.
3. Willie Morris. *New York Days.* Boston, 1993. p. 44.
4. Interview with Julian Ogilvie Thompson.
5. Interview with James Gobbo.
6. Interview with Peter Conrad.
7. *Los Angeles Times.* 13 September 1968.
8. Interviews with Doug McCalla and Arthur Scace.
9. Kenny. *Rhodes Trust.* p. 50.
10. Allen to Williams. 2 October 1961. RTF 3176.
11. Williams to Franks. 16 February 1961; Elton to Williams 2 October 1961. RTF 3176.
12. 2 December 1961. RTF 3176.
13. Memos for meetings of 13 June 1963 and 23 January 1964. RT Secretaries' Reports.
14. Williams to Peacock. 4 July 1962. RTF 2699.
15. Abell to Williams. 21 June 1974. RTF 3507.
16. Wheare to Boyle. 12 March 1969. RTF 3208; Williams to Price. 26 March 1969. RTF 3218(1).
17. 24 October 1968. RTF 3218(1).
18. Williams to Amory. 3 July 1964. RTF 3189.
19. Memo by Williams for meeting of 6 October 1977. RT Secretaries' Reports.

Chapter 31: Why No President?

1. *Spy.* October 1988. pp. 108–9.
2. *American Oxonian.* 3 (1948). p. 173.
3. Calvin Trilling. *Remembering Denny.* New York, 1993. pp. 100–1.
4. *American Oxonian.* 1 (1938). pp. 15–16.
5. *American Oxonian.* 4 (1962). p. 292.
6. *Chicago Tribune.* 15–31 July 1951; Memo by Elton for meeting of 9 October 1951. RTF 1296.
7. Courtney Smith to Elton. 26 February 1953; Allen to Williams. 5 March 1953. RTF 1233(A).

8. Alexander. Kenny. *Rhodes Trust.* pp. 185–7.
9. David Maraniss. *First in his Class: The Biography of Bill Clinton.* New York, 1995. pp. 151–3; Williams to Abell. 8 September 1969. RTF 3262.
10. Bill Bradley. *Time Present, Time Past.* New York, 1996. p. 126.
11. Schaeper and Schaeper. *Cowboys into Gentlemen.* p. 201.
12. *Los Angeles Times.* 13 September 1968.
13. *American Oxonian.* 3 (1967). p. 117.
14. Schaeper and Schaeper. *Cowboys into Gentlemen.* pp. 177 and 189.
15. Memo for meeting of 26 July 1947. RTF 1296.
16. Hailey to Elton. 16 May 1952. RTF 3074.
17. RTA 30.
18. *American Oxonian.* 4 (1979). pp. 249–58.
19. Interview with George Keys.
20. 1 February 1972. RTF 3262.
21. Memo for meeting of 16 October 1969. RT Secretaries' Reports.
22. Interview with William Barber.
23. Williams to Hailey. 10 February 1961. RTF 3074.
24. *American Oxonian.* 4 (1962). p. 279.
25. Schaeper and Schaeper. *Cowboys into Gentlemen.* pp. 326–7.
26. Halberstam. *The Best and the Brightest.* p. 41.

Chapter 32: The Germans Again

1. Memo of 11 March 1948. RTF 1296.
2. Memo for meeting of 23 October 1952. RTF 1296.
3. Interview with Thomas Böcking.
4. Williams to Abell. 28 January 1960. RTF 3262.
5. Nye to Williams. 12 November 1960. RTF 3150.
6. Heath to Franks. 11 July 1963. RTF 1682; Williams to Amory. 26 June 1964. RTF 3189.
7. *Frankfurter Allgemeine Zeitung.* 11 October 1963.
8. *American Oxonian.* 2 (1979). p. 99.
9. Allen to Elton. 4 April 1949. RTF 1682.
10. Mandt to Williams. 28 April 1969. RTF 1682.
11. Interview with Fritz Caspari.
12. Sheppard. Kenny. *Rhodes Trust.* p. 408.
13. Böcking to Kenny. 13 February 1995. RTF 1682A.

14. Alexander Böker to Fletcher. 20 February 1985. RTF 1682.
15. Fletcher to Böker. 27 February 1985. RTF 1682.
16. Fletcher to Blake. 15 May 1985. RTF 3640.
17. Interview with Thomas Böcking.

Chapter 33: Women at Last

1. 24 September 1952. RTF 2985.
2. Williams to E. C. R. Spooner. 19 August 1953. RTF 1432.
3. 12 December 1957. RTF 1432.
4. Memo for meeting of 5 February 1959. RT Secretaries' Reports.
5. Memo for meeting of 28 March 1963. RTF 1432.
6. Williams to Nye. 26 May 1964; Nye to Williams. 29 May 1964. RTF 3150.
7. Memo for meeting of 9 June 1973. RT Secretaries' Reports.
8. Alexander. Kenny. *Rhodes Trust.* p. 151.
9. Kenny. *Rhodes Trust.* p. 66; Williams to Smith. 2 December 1968. RTF 1362.
10. Memo by Williams for meeting of 14 March 1974. RT Secretaries' Reports.
11. *American Oxonian.* 4 (1972). pp. 293–5.
12. Memo for meeting of 13 December 1973. RT Secretaries' Reports.
13. Moors to Williams. 22 November 1972. RT Secretaries' Reports.
14. Memo for meeting of 9 October 1975. RT Secretaries' Reports.
15. *American Oxonian.* 2 (2000). p. 145.
16. Williams to Bhatia. 28 March 1977. RTF 3022(2).
17. *American Oxonian.* 2 (1999). pp. 167–9; Interview with Alison Muscatine.
18. Memo for meeting of 19 November 1982. RT Secretaries' Reports.
19. RT SF 4123 of 6 March 1992.
20. RT SF 4182 of 3 March 1995.
21. Moore to Kenny. 24 November 1994. RTF 3612.

Chapter 34: The Brotherhood

1. *First Fifty Years.* pp. 46–7.
2. Memo for meeting of 11 February 1960. RT Secretaries' Reports.
3. Minute 2930 of 23 February 1956. RTF 3128.
4. Elton to Williams. 10 April 1956. RTF 3128.
5. Elton to Gie. 13 July 1959. RTF 3088.
6. *American Oxonian.* 2 (1956). pp. 85–6.

7. Interviews with Jonathan Ross, Andrew Moore and Ian Pollard.
8. 6 June 1963. RTF 3148.
9. Interview with Ted Youn and Karen Arnold.
10. Memo for meeting of 26 July 1947. RTF 1296.
11. Michener to Elton. 14 July 1949. RTF 1247(5).
12. Memo for meeting of 23 July 1955. RT Secretaries' Reports.
13. Memo for meeting of 17 May 1958. RT Secretaries' Reports.
14. Hugh Templeton to Kenny. 16 April 1991. RTF 1628(7).
15. Nuttall. Kenny. *Rhodes Trust.* p. 272.
16. Gie to Elton. 7 May 1953; Elton to Gie. 15 June 1953. RTF 3088.
17. Gie to Hatherley. 14 June 1957. RTF 3088.
18. Griffith to Elton. 10 July 1959. RTF 3088.
19. Report by Gie of 3 January 1963. RTF 2009.

Chapter 35: Priorities

1. Memo for meeting of 24 November 1966. RT Secretaries' Reports.
2. 31 May 1961. RTF 3071.
3. Memo for meeting of 19 March 1964. RT Secretaries' Reports.
4. Wheare to Elton. 7 January 1959; Peacock to Elton. 14 January 1959. RTF 3158.
5. 12 March 1970. RTF 3217(1).
6. Blake to Williams. 19 May 1975. RTF 3290.
7. Nye to Elton. 21 July 1958; Elton to Nye. 23 July 1958. RTF 3150.
8. Price to Williams. 4 March 1970; Williams to Price. 10 March 1970. RTF 3218(1).
9. Fletcher to Paton. 26 March 1987. RTF 3217(1).
10. Letter approved by Trustees at meeting of 3 June 1988. RT Secretaries' Reports.
11. RT PPF 1984 of 2 June 1995.
12. RT PPF 1938 and 1948 of 5 November 1993.
13. Allen to Aydelotte. 20 August 1947. RTF 1233A.
14. Memo for meeting of 2 November 2000. RT Secretaries' Reports.

Chapter 36: Whom is the Fight Against?

1. Elton to Kedgley. 19 December 1956. RTF 1628(5).
2. Kenny. *Rhodes Trust.* p. 59.

3. Memo for meeting of 17 October 1968. RT Secretaries' Reports.
4. Williams to Welsh. 12 September 1969. RTF 2009.
5. Mackenzie to Elton. 15 January 1946; Allen to Elton. 31 December 1945. RTF 1628(4).
6. RTF 3037.
7. Memo of 5 February 1947. RTF 1296.
8. Kenny. *Rhodes Trust*. p. 62.
9. Elton to Mehta. 18 July 1955. RTF 2361.
10. RTM. 5 June 1992.
11. 1 March 1961. RTF 1628(6).
12. 27 April 1967. RTF 1628(6).
13. RTF 3624(1).
14. Williams to Haslam. 14 December 1962. RTF 1228.
15. Schaeper and Schaeper. *Cowboys into Gentlemen*. p. 153; *American Oxonian*. 1 (1970). p. 71.
16. RTA 96.
17. Interview with Ted Youn.
18. Interview with Charles Carter.
19. Interview with David Natusch.
20. Report on visit to the USA. 3–7 July 1991. RT 3675(c).
21. Memo for meeting of 9 June 2000. RT Secretaries' Reports.

Chapter 37: Life after Williams

1. Williams to Lawrence Jackson. 22 May 1970. RTF 3654.
2. Interviews with Marmaduke Hussey and Robin Fletcher.
3. Reports for meetings of 20 March 1981 and 11 June 1983. RT Secretaries' Reports.
4. Harcourt to Williams. 19 September 1978. RTF 3510.
5. RT Minutes of meeting of 13 January 1984.
6. Interview with Mary Moore.
7. RT Minute of 12 June 1965. SF 3408.
8. 12 January 1988. RT Secretaries' Reports for meeting of 4 March 1988.
9. Memo for meeting of 18 March 1983. RT Secretaries' Reports; Minutes of meeting of 18 March 1983.
10. R. W. Johnson to Fletcher. 1 December 1984. RTF 2326.
11. *American Oxonian*. 1 (1985). pp. 14–17.
12. Stewart to Fletcher. 19 December 1988; Kenny to Stewart. 21 December 1988. RTF 3628A.
13. Kenny to Ackermann. 31 July and 25 September 1996. RTF 2556.

14. Anthony Kenny. *A Life in Oxford*. London, 1997. pp. 232–3.
15. Kenny. *Rhodes Trust*. p. 99; *American Oxonian*. 4 (1990). pp. 295–6.

Chapter 38: The South African War

1. Memo for meeting of 25 March 1971. RT Secretaries' Reports.
2. *American Oxonian*. 4 (1987). p. 168; Interview with George Keys.
3. Memo for meeting of 25 March 1971. RT Secretaries' Reports.
4. Memo for meeting of 5 June 1971. RT Secretaries' Reports.
5. Kenny. *Rhodes Trust*. p. 113.
6. Blake to Williams. 13 September 1973. RTF 3640.
7. Memo for meeting of 25 March 1971. RT Secretaries' Reports.
8. Nuttall. Kenny. *Rhodes Trust*. p. 286.
9. Interview with Loyiso Nongxa.
10. Conclusion SF 4058. Meeting of 6 March 1987.
11. Nuttall. Kenny. *Rhodes Trust*. p. 296.
12. Memos for meetings of 9 June and 16 November 1984. RT Secretaries' Reports.
13. Memo for meeting 8 June 1985. RT Secretaries' Reports.
14. *American Oxonian*. 1 (1985). pp. 7–13.
15. Lugar to Blake. 26 February 1985; Blake to Lugar. 1 May 1985; Memo for meeting of 8 June 1985. RT Secretaries' Reports.
16. Memos for meetings of 7 June and 18 July 1986. RT Secretaries' Reports.
17. Memo for meeting of 18 July 1986. RT Secretaries' Reports.
18. Alexander. Kenny. *Rhodes Trust*. p. 177.
19. RT Minutes of meeting of 1 March 1991.
20. Minutes of South-Africa-at-Large selection committee. 11 June 1988. RTF 2009.
21. Fletcher to Paton. 11 January 1984. RTF 3217(1).

Chapter 39: A Passage from India

1. Memo by Elton of 31 October 1957. RT Secretaries' Reports.
2. 16 December 1946. RTF 2361.
3. Gwyer to Elton. 2 August 1947. RTF 2361.
4. Allen to Elton. 14 August and 10 November 1947. RTF 2361.
5. 21 January 1948. RTF 2361.
6. K. N. Johry to Williams. 4 November 1966; Williams to Johry. 8 November 1966. RTF 3022(2).

7. Gwyer to Elton. 12 December 1947. RTF 2361.
8. Memo of 18 September 1953. RTF 2361.
9. Nye to Williams. 18 October 1961. RTF 2361.
10. Interview with Anita Mehta.
11. Record of visit to India of December 1994. RTF 3675C.
12. Interviews with Virander Chauhan and Virenda Dayal.
13. Bhatia to Williams. 20 April 1980. RTF 3022(2).
14. Bhatia to Fletcher. 16 January 1981; Fletcher to Bhatia. 30 March 1981. RTF 3022(2).
15. Memo by Bhatia. Undated, 1990. RTF 2361.
16. Memo for meeting of 6 November 1998. RT Secretaries' Reports; Interview with John Rowett.
17. Memo for meeting of 15 December 1950. RTF 1296.
18. Elton to Michener. 26 April 1954. RTF 1247(6).
19. Bishop of Lahore to Elton. 16 January 1949. RTF 2361.
20. Memo for meeting of 14 October 1971. RT Secretaries' Reports.
21. Hailey to Williams. 27 February 1960; Williams to Hailey 9 March 1960. RTF 3074.
22. Memo for meeting of 6 November 1998. RT Secretaries' Reports.

Chapter 40: The Developing World

1. *Daily Telegraph.* 23 December 1958.
2. 21 January 1959. RTF 3153.
3. Memo of 13 March 1959. RTF 3153.
4. Williams to F. H. Cawson. 17 May 1962. RTF 3153.
5. O'Brien to Williams. 28 October and 19 December 1963; Williams to O'Brien. 9 November 1963. RTF 3153.
6. J. B. Eagle to Williams. 19 September 1963. RTF 3153.
7. Report of 24 November 1966. RTF 3153.
8. Hesse to Williams. 9 August 1971. RTF 3153.
9. Fletcher to Arbuthnott. 11 May 1988. RTF 2361.
10. Memo for meeting of 6 March 1975. RT Secretaries' Reports.
11. Report on visit to Nigeria. September 1991. RTF 3675(C).
12. Memo for meeting of 6 March 1993. RT Secretaries' Reports.
13. Silvester to Kenny. 2 October 1984; Kenny to Silvester. 10 October 1984. RTF 3620.
14. Kenny to Silvester. 24 January 1990; Kenny to Ashburton. March 1997. RTF 3620.
15. Kenny. *Rhodes Trust.* p. 72
16. Memos for meetings of 9 June 1984 and 6 November 1998. RT Secretaries' Reports.
17. Letters of 22 May 1996 and 22 June 1996. RTF 3601.
18. Memo for meeting of 19 November 1982. RT Secretaries' Reports.
19. Memo for meeting of 9 June 1984. RT Secretaries' Reports.
20. Memo for meeting of 6 February 1969. RT Secretaries' Reports.
21. Memo for meeting of 14 March 1950. RT Secretaries' Reports.
22. Memo for meeting of 5 October 1979. RT Secretaries' Reports.
23. Memo for meeting of 17 May 1947. RTF 1296.
24. 11 May 1964. RTF 1546.
25. Interview with Arthur Hodgson.
26. Kenny to Collis. 31 January 1992; Report to Trustees on visit to Bermuda. December 1993. RTF 1546.
27. Interviews with Eleanor Brown and Peter Goldson.
28. Allen to Elton. 26 February 1946. RTF 1986(A).
29. Williams to Peacock. 14 October 1961. RTF 2699.
30. Memo for meeting of 2 November 2000. RT Secretaries' Reports.
31. Memo for meeting of 11 November 1996 and 6 November 1998. RT Secretaries' Reports.
32. Interview with Tan Eng-Liang.
33. Fletcher to W. G. Barr. 15 July 1983. RTF 3606.
34. Report by Barr for meeting of 22 March 1985. RT Secretaries' Reports.
35. 19 June 1981. RTF 2326.
36. Memo for meeting of 6 November 1998. RT Secretaries' Reports.
37. RT SF 4275.

Chapter 41: Clinton and After

1. Memo for meeting of 6 March 1987. RT Secretaries' Reports.
2. Memo for meeting of 22 March 1985. RT Secretaries' Reports.

3. Memo for meeting of 2 June 1995. RT Secretaries' Reports.
4. Kenny. *Rhodes Trust*. p. 93.
5. Bradley. *Time Present, Time Past*. pp. 113–14.
6. *New York Times*. 13 December 1992.
7. *American Oxonian*. 1 (1993). p. 83.
8. *American Oxonian*. 1 (1989). p. 64.
9. Schaeper and Schaeper. *Cowboys into Gentlemen*. pp. 334–5.
10. *Washington DC Dossier*. May 1990.
11. Schaeper and Schaeper. *Cowboys into Gentlemen*. pp. 328–9; *Washington Post*. 7 January 1993.
12. *New American*. Vol. 11. No. 4. 20 February 1995.
13. Memo for meeting of 23 March 2000. RT Secretaries' Reports.
14. *New York Times*. 12 January 2003.
15. Memo for meeting of 4 June 1999. RT Secretaries' Reports.
16. Interview with Ted Youn.
17. *American Oxonian*. 2 (1993). p. 238; Schaeper and Schaeper. *Cowboys into Gentlemen*. p. 323.
18. *Sunday Times* (of London). 13 March 1994.
19. Tom Wolfe. *I Am Charlotte Simmons*. London, 2006. pp. 255–61.
20. Report on visit to US. December 1991. RTF 3675(c).
21. Report on visit to US. March 2000. RT Secretaries' Reports.
22. Memo for meeting of 3 May 1995. RT Secretaries' Reports.
23. Rosa Ehrenreich. *A Garden of Paper Flowers*. London, 1994; Memo for meeting of 3 May 1995. RT Secretaries' Reports.
24. Edge to Kenny. 6 January 1997. Circulated for meeting of 7 March 1997. RT Secretaries' Reports.
25. *American Oxonian*. 1 (1993). pp. 133–8.
26. Christopher Hitchens. *Blood, Class and Nostalgia*. London, 1990. p. 301.
27. September 1996. RTF 3675(c).
28. Interview with Elliot Gerson.
29. Memo for meeting of 9 June 2000. RT Secretaries' Reports.
30. Alec Broers to Rowett. 17 May 2000. Circulated for meeting of 7 June 2000. RT Secretaries' Reports.
31. Alexander to Gerson. 21 December 2001. Circulated for meeting of 7 June 2000. RT Secretaries' Reports.
32. Memo of 18 September 1946. RTF 1296.

Chapter 42: The Old Commonwealth

1. Memo for meeting of 14 October 1948. RTF 1296.
2. Memo for meeting of 21 July 1951. RT Secretaries' Reports.
3. McCalla. Kenny. *Rhodes Trust*. p. 240.
4. E. Michael Howarth. Unpublished.
5. Interviews with Doug McCalla and Arthur Kroeger.
6. Scace to Williams. 4 April 1975. RTF 2555.
7. Mordecai Richler. *Barney's Vision*. Vintage edition. London, 1998. p. 66.
8. Interviews with Yves Fortier and Gerard Coulombe.
9. Interview with Arthur Kroeger.
10. Memo for meeting of 6 November 1998. RT Secretaries' Reports.
11. Memo for meeting of 14 December 1949. RTF 1296.
12. 11 May 1952. RTF 3076.
13. Elton to Behan. 15 March 1945; Behan to Elton. 18 May 1945. RTF 2500.
14. Elton to Paton. 22 February 1955; Paton to Elton. 3 March 1955. RTF 2500.
15. Interview with Bob Hawke.
16. Poynter. Kenny. *Rhodes Trust*. p. 352.
17. Interview with John Poynter.
18. *Australia: Whither Next?* Papers presented at the 1988 Reunion of Rhodes Scholars.
19. Poynter to Welsh. 1 May 1979. RTF 2009.
20. Interview with Bob Hawke.
21. Cobham to Elton. 2 May 1958; Williams to Elton. 13 May 1958. RTF 1628(5).
22. Gould. *Goodbye to All That*. p. 25; Interview with David Williams.
23. *American Oxonian*. 4 (1953). p. 201.
24. Interview with David Williams.
25. MS notes on visit to New Zealand 1979–80. RTF 3654(A).

Chapter 43: South Africa Comes in from the Cold

1. Interview with Grant Nupen and Mike King.
2. Ackermann to Kenny. 24 July 1996. RTF 2556.
3. Memo for meeting of 5 June 1992. RT Secretaries' Reports.
4. Interview with Jock de Jager and Derek Swart.
5. Report on tour of Southern Africa of February 1999. RTF 3675(C).

6. Interview with Jock de Jager and Derek Swart.
7. Interview with Edwin Cameron.
8. Interview with Fanie du Toit.
9. Interviews with Michelle Norton, Loyiso Nongxa and Shaun Johnson.
10. Ackermann to Kenny. 31 May 1995. RTF 2556.
11. Kenny. *Rhodes Trust.* p. 97.
12. Kenny's Christmas Letter for 1996.
13. 7 March 1994. RTF 1985.
14. Elton to L. R. Morgan. 29 April 1949. RTF 1219.
15. Tredgold to Elton. 24 December 1953. RTF 1219.
16. Williams to Lewis. 6 February 1967. RTF 1219.
17. Cranborne to Williams. 16 December 1970. RTF 3262.
18. Report on visit to Zimbabwe. RT Secretaries' Reports.
19. Maylam. *Cult of Rhodes.* pp. 39–40.
20. Memo for meeting of 6 November 1998. RT Secretaries' Reports.

Chapter 44: The European Experiment

1. RTF 2482.
2. Elton to Grigg. 29 October 1947. RTF 2367.
3. Memo for meeting of 10 November 1989. RT Secretaries' Reports.
4. Memo for meeting of 6 March 1992. RT Secretaries' Reports.
5. Memo for meeting of 5 June 1992. RT Secretaries' Reports.
6. 7 February 1995. RTF 3653.
7. Memo for meeting of 4 November 1994. RT Secretaries' Reports.
8. Waldegrave to Kenny. 5 July 1996; Moore to Kenny. 12 July 1996; Kenny to Ashburton. 3 October 1996. RTF 3601.
9. Minutes of meeting of 7 June 1996.
10. 12 May 1995. RTF 3653.
11. Tsingarida to Kenny. 25 April 1994. RTF 3653.

Chapter 45: Careers

1. Wolfe. *I Am Charlotte Simmons.* pp. 255–61.
2. *American Oxonian.* 1 (2002). p. 143.
3. Interview with Ross Garland.
4. Interview with Susan Dando.
5. Interview with John MacBain.

6. Interview with Delroy Chuck.
7. Rhodes Scholar Newsletter of 1959. p. 3. Copy on RTF 3128.
8. Schaeper and Schaeper. *Cowboys into Gentlemen.* p. 290.
9. *American Oxonian.* 2 (1999). p. 232.
10. 'Generating Leaders in the Age of Diversity. Fifty Years of the American Rhodes Scholars'. Karen D. Arnold and Ted I. K. Youn. Boston College, June 2003. Working Paper No. 1. p. 28.
11. *American Oxonian.* 4 (1991). pp. 284–90.

Chapter 46: New Worlds

1. Report of 22 February 1999. RTF 3601.
2. Interview with Juliana Snelling.
3. Interview with Prosser Gifford.
4. Interview with Sarah Kelly.
5. *Sunday Tasmanian.* 22 September 1985.
6. *American Oxonian.* 1 (1988). p. 33; 2 (1988). p. 125.
7. Memo for meeting of 6 March 1998. RT Secretaries' Reports.
8. RTM. 1 June 1990.
9. *American Oxonian.* 4 (1995). p. 249.
10. Memo for meeting of 1 June 2001. RT Secretaries' Reports.
11. Memo for meeting of 3 March 1989. RT Secretaries' Reports.
12. *American Oxonian.* 1 (1992). p. 43.
13. Memo for meeting of 13 June 1981. RT Secretaries' Reports.
14. O'Neill to Southwood. 21 August 2001. RT Secretaries' Reports.
15. *American Oxonian.* 4 (1984). p. 191.
16. *American Oxonian.* 1 (1984). p. 67.

Chapter 47: Mandela–Rhodes

1. Memo for meeting of 6 June 1997. RT Secretaries' Reports.
2. Memo for meeting of 1 June 2001. RT Secretaries' Reports.
3. Memo for meeting of 5 June 1998. RT Secretaries' Reports.
4. RT minutes of meeting of 22 March 2000.
5. *Daily Telegraph.* 15 May 2002; Maylam. *Cult of Rhodes.* p. 136.
6. Memo for meeting of 1 June 2001. RT Secretaries' Reports.
7. Memo for meeting of Trustees of Mandela–Rhodes Foundation. 13 July 2004.
8. RT minutes of 18 September 2001.

Epilogue

1. Memo for meeting of 26 July 1947. RTF 1296.
2. RTF 3654.
3. RTF 3076.
4. *Parade Magazine.* 18 August 1985.
5. Annual Newsletter for 1957. RTF 3128.
6. Paton to Margaret Thatcher. 15 May 1981. RTF 3217(1).
7. Interview with Joseph Nye.
8. *New American.* Vol. 2. No. 4. 20 February 1995.
9. Interviews with Jeremy Kirk and Delia Marshall.
10. Interview with Ranjit Chaudhury.
11. *American Oxonian.* 4 (1985). p. 240.

BIBLIOGRAPHICAL NOTE

Manuscript Sources

The Rhodes Trust Archives, in Rhodes House, Oxford, present an astonishingly full picture of the Trust and the Scholarships. Apart from the files on individual Scholars, the main business of the Trust is covered in the Rhodes Trust Files, of which there were 3,700 when the task of cataloguing the collection was completed in 2000. There are also substantial quantities of papers at one time or another brought back from the United States, Canada and (in microfilm) Australia.

Among other manuscripts, the Milner Papers in the Bodleian are of particular importance. Other collections in which I have done more than dip casually are the Rosebery Papers in the National Library of Scotland (copies of some of which are available in Rhodes House), and the H. A. L. Fisher Papers in the Bodleian.

Books about Cecil Rhodes

Much the most comprehensive and authoritative of these is Robert Rotberg's *The Founder* (revised edition, Johannesburg, 2002). Among the earlier biographies, the best is that by J. G. Lockhart and C. M. Woodhouse (London, 1963). Other books on the subject which add something of interest from the point of view of the Trust include:

Baker, Herbert.   *Cecil Rhodes by his Architect*. London, 1934.
Flint, John.   *Cecil Rhodes*. London, 1976.
Maylam, Paul.   *The Cult of Rhodes*. Claremont, South Africa, 2005.
Michell, Lewis.   *The Life of the Rt Hon. Cecil Rhodes*. 2 vols. London, 1910.
Millin, Sarah Gertrude.   *Rhodes*. London, 1933.

Plomer, William.	*Cecil Rhodes.* Edinburgh, 1933.
Williams, Basil.	*Cecil Rhodes.* London, 1938.

Books about the Trust and Scholarships

For the centenary, Sir Anthony Kenny edited a collection of essays published under the title *The History of the Rhodes Trust* (Oxford, 2001). He himself contributed a masterly piece on the 'Trust and its Administration' and an essay on the 'Smaller Constituencies'. National chapters were written by David Alexander (the United States), Douglas McCalla (Canada), Tim Nuttall (South Africa), John Poynter (Australia), Richard Sheppard (Germany) and David Morgan (Zimbabwe). John Darwin added a brilliantly perceptive section on 'The Rhodes Trust in the Age of Empire', while Caroline Brown described the Archives.

Other books of some interest include:

Allen, Carleton Kemp.	*Forty Years of the Rhodes Scholarships.* Oxford, 1944.
Allen, Dorothy.	*Sunlight and Shadow.* Oxford, 1960.
Aydelotte, Frank.	*The Vision of Cecil Rhodes.* Oxford, 1946.
Elton, Lord (ed.).	*The First Fifty Years of the Rhodes Trust and the Rhodes Scholarships.* Oxford, 1955.
Parkin, George R.	*The Rhodes Scholarships.* London, 1913.
Scholz, R. F. and Hornbeck, S. K.	*Oxford and the Rhodes Scholarships.* Oxford, 1907.
Stead, W. T. (ed.).	*The Last Will and Testament of Cecil John Rhodes.* London, 1902.

The American Scholarships have received more attention than those of any other nation. In particular, Thomas and Kathleen Schaeper's *Cowboys into Gentlemen* (New York, 1998) is far better researched and more serious than its slightly catch-penny title suggests (a view evidently shared by the authors since the book reappeared in 2004 unaltered except in its title, which is now *Rhodes Scholars, Oxford and the Creation of an American Elite).* The Schaepers' work is complemented by the series of papers produced for the Spencer Foundation by Ted Youn, Karen Arnold and others of Boston College on the general theme of 'Generating Leaders in the Age of Diversity: Fifty Years of American Rhodes Scholars'.

The *American Oxonian* and its predecessor the *Alumni Magazine of the Alumni Association of American Rhodes Scholars* provide much valuable information, not only about the American Scholarships. The *Australian Rhodes*

Review, though erratic in its appearance, when it exists also contains material of interest. Other national Associations have produced lists of Scholars and ephemeral news-letters, but nothing of great moment.

General Studies

Books which I found of particular background interest, mainly though not exclusively concerned with imperial issues, are:

Gilmour, David.	*The Long Recessional*. London, 2002.
Harrison, Brian (ed.).	*The History of the University of Oxford*. Vol. 8. Oxford, 1994.
Hitchens, Christopher.	*Blood, Class and Nostalgia*. London, 1990.
Lavin, Deborah.	*From Empire to International Commonwealth*. Oxford, 1995.
Madden, Frederick and Fieldhouse, D. K. (eds).	*Oxford and the Idea of Commonwealth*. London, 1982.
Quigley, Carroll.	*Tragedy and Hope*. New York, 1966.
Symonds, Richard.	*Oxford and Empire*. London, 1986.

I find I have consulted more than 150 biographies, autobiographies, diaries or collections of letters dealing with Trustees, officials of the Trust or Scholars. At first I thought I should list those which had been of the greatest use, but I decided that this would be both invidious and superfluous. Details of those I cite will be found in the Notes; to the authors and editors of the rest and the two hundred or so men and women who were kind enough to spare the time for an interview, I offer my most grateful thanks.

INDEX